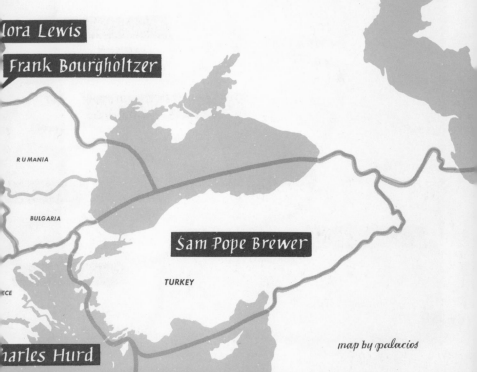

EUROPE

AND

RUSSIA

(U.S.S.R.)

Irving R. Levine

lora Lewis

Frank Bourgholtzer

RUMANIA

BULGARIA

Sam Pope Brewer

TURKEY

ECE

harles Hurd

map by palacios

CAVALCADE OF EUROPE

CAVALCADE OF EUROPE

A Handbook of Information
on 22 Countries
By 14 Noted Overseas
Correspondents

*Edited by Lowell Thomas
and Charles Hurd*

DOUBLEDAY & COMPANY, INC.
GARDEN CITY, NEW YORK
1960

PREFACE

Early in 1958, the Overseas Press Club of America, Inc., and the publisher recognized the need for a comprehensive book wherein seasoned reporters of news in Europe could be enlisted to give the contemporary picture of Europe. During months of planning it became evident that the need was primarily for a "mental guide" rather than for another standard travel book—a single volume in which the traveler could find stimulating background, but even more so the follower of today's news could find at a glance the reports upon which to evaluate events affecting his welfare or arousing his interest.

Out of this planning came *Cavalcade of Europe*. Its chapters share a similarity in general plan but are not uniform; each one reflects the personal experiences and style of its writer. Virtually all of the "authors" are nationally known to newspaper readers. All share a long experience as overseas reporters, averaging twenty-five years or more. The integrity and viewpoint of each have stood a long test of editing and readership. Most also are authors of books and perceptive articles, in addition to their news reporting.

Thanks are particularly due to Lowell Thomas, a former president of OPC, for his editorship and sponsorship of this work, as well as to its contributors, whose chapters were written during a particularly hectic "news period" in the world.

In addition, the publishers are indebted to a special committee of the OPC, under the chairmanship of Will Yolen, that gave much time and study to the planning and production.

This committee consisted of the following editors and writers:

Theodore C. Amussen
Simon Michael Bessie
William Doerflinger
K. S. Giniger
Beulah Phelps Harris
Dickson Hartwell
Charles Hurd
Kenneth McCormick
James Parton

John Lowell Pratt
Eleanor S. Rawson
Quentin Reynolds
M. Lincoln Schuster
J. Wendell Sether
Roger W. Straus, Jr.
Donald Wayne
Victor Weybright

CONTENTS

INTRODUCTION

In today's fast-moving world of ideas, the continents of the earth can no longer be categorized under flat headings of persons, places, or things as seen through the single-minded observation of an ethnologist, a geographer, or a historian. We live in such an age of movement that every American who tries to keep even superficially informed turns automatically to the news reports of the day, printed and broadcast, to bring his knowledge of any continental, regional, or local subject up to date.

The unseen content of these news dispatches is the penetrating and critical analysis of background that every trained journalist uses as the basis for writing the story of the moment. Whether today's news be an election, a revolution, transfer of authority within a great religious movement, or the development of new weapons —always the correspondent writes his dispatch as the last chapter in a continuing story that never will be finished, and one whose beginnings often come from the roots of a forgotten time.

The newsman to whom such responsibility is given—and who must meet the daily criticism of his own editors and a host of informed readers—is unique among writers. It has been said that news correspondents write the reports upon which history is based. But often these reporters establish the observation from which present history will later be interpreted. Furthermore, in every major news dispatch they are rewriting older impressions of the history of the past.

Above all things, these correspondents must try to be objective. Every day's news thus becomes an unfolding, not of things as we would like to have them be, but of things as they are—often due to twists of background out of the past that force events presently to the surface for reasons long since forgotten.

It is this perspective, lying outside the experience or knowledge of the busy reader, which subconsciously must mark the continuing reports of the news correspondent. Particularly is this true of Europe—mainspring and source of so many developments bearing upon our daily lives.

Aside from our own continent, no other people and land mass have been more important to American life than those of Europe. No other continent attracts a fraction as much interest from American traveler, student, or businessman as Europe.

From Europe came the radical revolution that we call communism, with its strange argument that by tearing down the political and religious organizations of the past, something better could be erected for the underprivileged man. From it came, too, fascism and nazism, springing out of the ancient robber-baron theory that the strong man may grab what he likes from the weaker.

But from Europe also came the bases of freedom and dignity of the individual hammered out in a thousand years of English development, the poetry and music and song of half a dozen languages, and a culture built directly on ancient Greek foundations.

To Americans who think—and in our climate the number of these individuals has grown from handfuls to millions—the conclusion is inescapable that Western life is, and must continue for a long time to be, a blending of the best of European thought with our own. And most of it is present, sometimes frightening, reality.

Thus the *Cavalcade of Europe* is literally the story of the background of what we enjoy as the American environment.

We travel to Europe by the millions annually to see the evidences of that background and to feel through our pores the lore of a common past, built upon another ancient cavalcade of often nameless peoples.

Probing a little deeper, and realizing how little time there was to learn in the school years, travelers, as well as those who must limit their travel to study, reach out for further helps in appreciat-

ing the meaning of these things in life today—what the past indicates for the immediate future in which many of us shall live.

Now, for the first time, the viewpoint on these questions as developed by the more responsible writers of present developments
has been turned toward setting down the highlights of the European cavalcade.

Dealing as they do with the broad sweep of living background
that has developed into the conglomerate of Europe, news correspondents see their fields of interest neither in the light of ancient history nor as limited to present activities and personalities.
They see neither a rigid past nor a set present. Policies and the
men who make and administer them often pass quickly from the
scene, but in passing frequently change the perspective of the
whole past.

Yet underlying all the transitions that make up the news of the
day are forces, tastes, and environments that change slowly, if at
all, and that mold even the most radical changes into patterns
set by nature.

In this collaboration on the *Cavalcade of Europe* the high point
of interest naturally is the story of peoples, but the story of peoples
rests upon many foundations, from land to religion, climate to politics, and social development to the always resurging demands for
betterment of environment.

In tracing the many paths which led the countries of Europe
to the point where they now are, the trained news correspondent
necessarily gives clues to the future. The more dramatic evidences
of the past may be seen with the eye, but this work is designed
to give some help in the more satisfying experience of seeing with
the mind, insofar as possible, without prejudice, lecturing, or passing of judgment—as the best news dispatches are written.

The cavalcade of Europe probably begins in a literal sense with
the story of Greece, from whose mountains came our first "Western" art, culture, engineering, and sense of ethics, upon which
have been built modern structures ranging from architecture to
political democracy. Thereafter the cavalcade becomes an inter-
locking romance in which the same factors work through man's
needs and imagination to bring into being the great contrasts of

European nations, which are so often built on great similarities.

One of the most fascinating and puzzling things about Europe, even to the initiated, is the great differences between Europeans themselves—the habits and even the processes of reasoning that separate a Frenchman from a German, or a Spaniard from an Italian, or a Pole from a Russian even though they once lived under the same rulers. Do these peoples simply respond to environment or are there deeper forces within them that have made their environments what they are?

When Caesar marched through France and into lower Germany he found a single type of savage, harsh, and brave men, whom he designated as "Gauls" in tribute to their ferocity. In England his legions encountered an equally brave but different people. In the following centuries, the Britons of Caesar's day were wiped out by invasions from the European continent, but today in differing forms there is still what sometimes seems an impassable gulf of tradition and form separating the continental Europeans and the British.

In this cavalcade peoples move, yet nature imposes rules of change and rules of similarity that seem to be implacable. In England itself today there is a noticeable physical difference between the Welsh, the Saxon English, and the descendants of the Norman French—a physical difference, we repeat, although all Britons have demonstrated twice in this century how tenaciously they unite to defend their institutions against outside attack. The physical differences are an intriguing example, because long ago Dr. John Finley, the noted educator and former editor of the New York *Times*, remarked that any individual today who might proudly proclaim his descent from William the Conqueror would have barely one-millionth part of that old Norman's blood in his veins.

The pattern of Europe, like that of all continents, has followed the classic tradition whereby conquerors first invaded new areas to find wealth to take home and thereafter became settlers in the conquered lands. When the settlers established homes and intermarried, there began to be developed a new race of persons that became established until the next conquest again started a new amalgamation of races.

Holding this work within the practical limits of normal interest, no attempt is made to go back to true beginnings. The archaeologist has a fascinating story to tell, but our story of Europe is confined to the forces and movements of sufficiently recent periods to have had some reasonable connection with the development of Europe as it is today.

Thus we begin with the fairly recent past, while sketching the relative antiquity of Greece and the Italian peninsula as superimposed upon the culture of the eastern and southern Mediterranean shores.

In this broad foundation there existed the highly developed civilizations of Athens and Rome, soon to reflect the irresistible force of a new faith compounded of the ancient Israelite and the newer Christian movements. Spain dangled at the southwestern extremity of Europe with an individual culture that had come up the western trade routes over the Mediterranean Sea from Africa, flowering in the tropical climate of its fertile valleys and cultivated hillsides. In western Europe were the still savage Franks, and to the north of them the even more savage Germanic tribes, who trailed off into the northern capes and the hardy Norsemen. Middle Europe, with its mixture of Slavs and Croats, periodically overrun by the Huns from western Asia, was totally unknown to Western thought less than two thousand years ago. Yet here lay much of the natural wealth that was to mark later European development—the great plains of Hungary, the rivers such as the Danube, the Rhine, and the Vistula, and the enclaves of husbandry lying within the valleys surrounded by the towering Alps.

The future of Europe already had been defined by nature in strata of climate, transportation, and resources. The cavalcade began when restless men began to muster the resources, and bold adventurers to attempt to mold the whole into a single unit of geography if not of thought.

To do it, in their several ways they used weapons of war, ever more complicated and refined; they used the arts of husbandry; they built up trade that made heretofore separate peoples more and more interdependent; and ultimately they used the power of thought as expressed alike in political philosophies and in religious missionary work. Often the various factors were so blended as to make separation almost indistinguishable, with the whole buried under one rabble-rousing slogan.

The Romans, going first as conquerors and then as settlers, swarmed through France and Spain and Italy, while holding southern England as an outpost. Their era seems not too long gone when one views the aqueducts they built in Spain or touches portions of the Roman wall that still stand in London. When the Huns came out of the east and north to threaten Rome itself, after centuries of dominance, the legions left western Europe, but the culture and the bloodlines remained, buttressed by something even more enduring—the continuity of a new faith called Christianity, which erected another common bond through the Latin language.

The Roman language and religion gradually worked northward through the Germanies, at the same time that another concept of Roman civilization—the Byzantine Christian—was emerging out of Constantinople.

In centuries to come, after the Huns finally were stopped in their invasions of Europe, the Latin cross and the Byzantine dome were to meet in middle Europe as the twin symbols of a basic European culture. Right down to the present time, there would be divisions of views and vicious wars fought mainly between the Europe of the East and the Europe of the West. But despite these conflicts, Europe was to be molded into a homogeneity more compact than that of any of the other older continents. Even the onslaught of the Saracens into Spain could not destroy this unity; rather, it drew the culture closer together despite continued wars and pestilence and revolutions.

Yet in its development as a recognizable organization of countries, Europe has continued to develop new sprouts that have enriched its history, even while some retarded its growth.

The small race of people we call the Vikings, those Scandinavians known in earlier days as the Norsemen, repeatedly raided England and by their threats helped to force the English to become a single country instead of a collection of tribal divisions. The Norsemen, in turn, changed from raiding nomads into settlers when they established fortified towns on the coasts of France, and their descendants, in turn, became the Normans, who conquered

England and defied the French kings even while living as part of France.

Every country in Europe bears the marks of the Dark Ages, when individualism separating the warring dynasties of countries —already roughly outlined in modern form—reached its height. By the same token, every European country bears in its churches and public buildings mementos of the Renaissance, which, although rooted in Italy and most often noted in the development of painting, shows in the spires of every great cathedral—in architecture in Paris and London as well as Florence and Rome—and which inspired the new ideas of the sixteenth and seventeenth centuries that reshaped the Western world.

Prior to the awakening that ended the Dark Ages, European rule in all nations followed essentially the pattern of the barbarians—control over groups of persons by rulers physically powerful enough to use them as servants and to maintain their positions in the competition of force with other rulers.

During this period, the world of ideas that had flowered in the ancient city-states slumbered, but the knowledge gathered in the past survived, because the rulers needed clerks, business managers, and diplomats—and for all of these they had to turn to the only survivors of the ancient age of knowledge and perforce keep them alive and well fed. The priesthood that served its masters thus survived in a world of force that despised and mistrusted its education.

From the time of the Renaissance, the cavalcade of Europe is a drama told in terms of individual peoples or countries as they have attempted to turn from rule by persons to rule by ideas—however different may be the scope of the ideas thrown up by individual groups.

With the Renaissance, the men of knowledge suddenly discovered that in some respects they were stronger than their masters: that their painting, their architecture, their culture, and, above all, their thinking was so greatly needed that they were stronger than the barons and the kings who patronized them.

This flowering of thought knew no national boundaries. Some phases started here and others there, but all were shared throughout the continent. For a little while the unfolding promised to create a unity within Europe that rule by force had failed to achieve.

The concept of a Holy Empire, a league of countries all of whose royal houses were bound by common allegiance to the world of ideas typified by the Church, had hardly been given a fair trial before the quest for new ideas tore apart the unity of the realm of ideas.

The German states and England entertained new thoughts at variance with the established church, and continental revolutions over ideas became more bitter than had been the wars over national boundaries or trade.

This warfare is still raging, and in doing so is creating new concepts of thought, at least temporarily changed political boundaries, and—most important of all—new challenges of development.

In this work the individual chapters necessarily dovetail and overlap in the unfolding of the story, and sometimes there is a tragic picture of retrogression. Time and again, one country has grown out of or because of the revolutionary throes of another, only in its turn to become tributary to another. This is the law of political change that man has not yet been able to nullify.

Nevertheless, this is no story of a shifting anthill; it is in its essence the story of ideas struggling within men's minds, of men wrestling in turn with the ideas, of great victories and great defeats by peoples struggling to reach ever higher plateaus.

Each chapter is individual, the story of a nation or a region falling into a present pattern of similarity as seen by its author. However, for purposes of cross-checking by the reader, each is arranged roughly in an order of treatment corresponding to the other. Stripped of transient personalities and movements—those matters treated constantly in news dispatches and magazine reviews—this is the cavalcade of Europe in the background that, with peace, may well continue for a decade or a generation, or—should conflict burst into war—give every thoughtful American, whether his studies be by personal travel or in the thoughtful quiet of his reading, fundamental clues to reasons.

THE EDITORS

THE BRITISH ISLES

Drew Middleton

Drew Middleton became a foreign correspondent for the Associated Press in London in the last year of peace before World War II. From September 1939 to May 1945 he served as a war correspondent with American and British forces in France and Belgium, Algeria and Tunisia, Sicily, Iceland, and, during the Battle of Britain, the United Kingdom. He joined the staff of the New York Times *in 1942.*

Since 1945 Mr. Middleton has been Chief Correspondent of the Times *in the Soviet Union, Germany, and Britain.*

In addition to his work for the Times*, Mr. Middleton has written four books and numerous magazine articles. After twenty years and no one knows how many thousand words as a foreign correspondent, he still considers it the best job in the world. In 1943 he married Stevie Mansel-Edwards and, to steal a phrase from Churchill, lived happily ever after.*

THE BRITISH ISLES

At the high noon of the Third Reich, Berlin's radio commentators were accustomed to dwell on the day of victory when the British Isles would be merely an archipelago in the North Sea off the coast of Europe. This is a fantasy that has comforted other would-be conquerors since the time of Philip II. The British, however, have a genius for survival.

Compared with such colossi as the United States, the Soviet Union, and China there are not a great many of them. The population of the United Kingdom, which includes England, Wales, Scotland, and Northern Ireland, is approximately 51,500,000. The population of Eire, the Republic of Ireland, is just under 3,000,000.

Numerical inferiority in the presence of the titans of East and West troubles the British very little. Save for what is to them a relatively brief period in their history, from 1815 to 1914, the British have always been inferior in population and material wealth to the great powers with whom they have contested. Britain is like a fighter who, consistently overmatched, nevertheless continues to win.

The logical conclusion to be drawn from this historical survival is that the British must be a very special people; a conclusion with which few Britons will quarrel. Moreover, they will discourse at great length—for they are fond of emphasizing quantitative inferiority—on the comparative poverty of the home islands.

By comparison with the natural resources of the colossi Britain is a poor power. But the ingenuity, industry, and aggressiveness of its workers and sellers has since 1945 built prosperity on a small foundation. The basis of Britain's prosperity in the nineteenth century was coal. Today, although coal remains the primary source of power, oil—most of it from the Middle East—is the secondary source of industrial energy.

But prosperity has developed in the last ten years not on the basis of coal, which is increasingly expensive and difficult to mine, or on oil, always subject to the vagaries of international crises, but upon the nation's ability to adapt its industrial economy to the requirements of a changing Britain and a changing world. The bases of British economy today are the industries that turn out engineering and electronic products, ships, metal goods, chemicals. Textiles, long a staple of British industry, have lost in importance.

By venturing into new fields such as plastics and electronics the British have been able to regain a place close to the top of the list among the world's trading nations. They are back where they have been for roughly five hundred years, or since the Tudor dynasty ushered in the first great age of British commercialism.

The British have been manufacturers and traders on a large scale longer than any other power. Trading goods have changed from wool to radar, but these still have to be transported, and today, as in the Middle Ages, the British are shipbuilders and sailors. Their ability to carry goods to foreign markets is in some cases as important as their ability to make goods that foreign markets will buy. Moreover, the sea has had a profound effect upon the culture and history of these islanders.

Britain is the oldest democracy among the great powers. It is also the oldest monarchy among the great states of Europe. For Elizabeth II is a "descendant" of that Egbert, King of Wessex and All England, who ruled from 829 to 839.

Parliamentary democracy, as we know it, first developed in England. It is over seven hundred years since Magna Charta first restrained a king. But even before the barons brought King John to heel, English history had known assemblies in tribes and small kingdoms. The despot, the tyrant, was not an English invention, although plenty of English kings acted as though it were.

Today Parliament is a house of 625 elected members, each representing a constituency in Britain or Northern Ireland. Since 1945 two great parties, the Conservatives, or Tories, and Labour, or Socialists, have contended for power. The Liberals represent a minor party capable at times of influencing constituency elections, and even winning them, but without powerful national support. The Communists politically are a discredited minority without a single representative in the House of Commons.

The House of Commons is the core of British government. In it are vested the chief powers of government. In it sit most, but not all, of the members of the government. It is a continual inquest into the national life, a debating society with interests as wide as the world, an imposer of taxes and a source of handouts. By turns dull and exciting, wise and foolish, melodramatic and stable, the House of Commons quite literally is the basis of British democracy. For nearly four hundred years it has been the chosen forum for some of the greatest orators of history and the workroom for politicians.

The British democracy and the House of Commons have had their failures. British rule in Ireland was one of them. The Republic of Ireland, understandably anxious to rid itself of the trappings of British rule, calls its Parliament the Oireachtas and divides it into two houses, of which the Dail Eireann, or House of Representatives, is far more important than the Senate.

Politically, Eire is a sovereign, independent, democratic state. Economically, she is on the doorstep of British industrial power and dominated by that power. Demographically, Eire is losing large numbers of her most ambitious and industrious workers to the booming British economy.

This migration, reliably estimated at the rate of 40,000 young Irishmen and Irishwomen a year, is one of the two influxes that marginally, at least, have made some alterations in British life since World War II. The other is the migration of Negroes from the West Indies. Like the Irish, they seek work in an expanding economy.

These invasions have not yet altered the character of the peoples who inhabit the British Isles. They are descended from the peoples who inhabited the islands nine centuries ago. Britain owes much of the continuity and stability of her political institutions, from the Crown to the village council, to this freedom from large-scale immigration.

But although the generic term "British" will cover all the people in the main island and Northern Ireland, it does little justice to the variety of peoples. This small country contains stoutly individualistic nationalities like the Scots and the Welsh and, in olden times, the Cornish. There are also the English, who provide most of the population, the gags for music-hall comedians, and the targets for cartoonists. They are the despair of tyrants, foreign and domestic, and, once roused, a fierce and implacable enemy.

All these racial strains may be traced back to the pre-Celts, the Celts, the Romans, the Anglo-Saxons (Saxons and Angles), the Danes, and finally, the last invaders, the Normans—Scandinavian Vikings who had settled in northern France and intermarried. The Scots, Welsh, Irish, and English are all descended from these distant peoples; the Celtic strain is strongest in Scotland, Wales, and Ireland, the Saxon and Norman in England.

This intermingling of races gave Britain one priceless gift. Out of the marriage of Anglo-Saxon and Norman French was born that supple, graceful, forceful tongue the world calls English.

The British are a complex and contradictory people. England was the birthplace of the Industrial Revolution. By far the larger part of its population lives in cities and towns. Most of the people of Scotland and Wales are concentrated in the industrial belt that runs from Glasgow to Edinburgh and in the mining and steel-making towns of South Wales.

This urban Britain is the Britain that counts. It was these smoky infernos of the Midlands, the clanging cotton towns of the North, and the narrow, mist-hung valleys of the Rhondda in Wales that sent British machinery and British products and with them British engineers and tradesmen (the soldiers and administrators came later) all over the world of the nineteenth century. This is the Britain that turns out Comets and turbines, nuclear-energy plants and electronic equipment today. The fox hunters in the shires, the millionaire publisher toasting his hide at Montego Bay, the ballerina from Covent Garden, all owe their existence to this other Britain.

Yet although the Industrial Revolution is close to two hundred years old in Britain, the people are oddly unaccustomed to city life.

By one means or another they seek to establish connections with the countryside and the vanished past, with a greener, sweeter England. This is pre-eminently the country of the private home, no matter how small. An Englishman's home and its tiny plot of garden may not be a castle, but it is his tie with the earth. There is, as Ernest Bevin once remarked, a "stubborn peasant streak" in the English. No Frenchman or Italian loves his garden more than the Englishman or lavishes more care upon it.

This longing for the rural past touches other aspects of life. Cricket is no longer the national sport in terms of either players or attendance. That honor belongs to soccer. But cricket survives and will survive because of its green lawns, its white-clad players, its friendly team play, its acceptance of the rules whereby cricket speaks to Englishmen of the unknown but fragrant England of the past.

The cult of the horse has lasted longer in Britain than in any other highly industrialized Western nation. Here again one encounters the connection with another England, the rural England of opulent farms and beery farmers in gaiters, of coaching inns and quiet copses through which horsemen gallop. There is a good deal of snobbism in English horse worship. But there is a good deal of honest yearning for a vanished society in it as well.

This habit of living with the past through its mementos is not exclusively English. The Scots yearn for the brave days of the past, attire themselves in kilts and plaid, and, in the intervals of making money out of the English, recall Scotland's dashing past and vanished glories.

"'Twas only a mile or so down the glen where they tore the throat out of an English soldier," I was told in a Scots hotel one night. The speaker, a MacCracken, was referring to some incident of "the '45," which had occurred just 210 years before.

The Welsh jealously guard the culture of their principality.

Welsh is still a live language on the northern and western edges of Wales. The deeds of Owen Glendower are still alive to Welsh children, and the visitor will be told that "the English needed the Tudors," a Welsh dynasty, to teach them to be a great power.

This continual harking toward a more spacious past, accompanied in many cases by a happy obliviousness to the inequalities, cruelties, and poverty of that past, may be due in some measure to the sordid dreariness of Britain's urban civilization.

Since 1945 a start has been made in tearing down the ruins of Victorian industrial Britain—ruins in which families lived and for which, we should not forget, men died—and building modern housing.

The old was inexpressibly dreary and sordid. The long rows of two-story houses stretching for miles through the back streets of industrial cities. The phalanxes of "semidetached" suburban villas named "Wee Holme" and "Balmoral." The dark and noisome slums noisy with the roar of engines and the clamor of trams. The garish movie "palaces." The pubs rank with the smell of stale beer, each boasting its quota of drunks. This for many millions was "England, their England," and it is no wonder that so many tried to get away from it.

The promised land has always lain just at the end of the pavement. There stretched the green, lush countryside, as attractive a rural countryside as there has ever been. This England of the squires and the yeomen, with its great trees, its secluded villages, its curling wood smoke in a winter's sunset, has slowly been invaded by the voracious settlers from the dark streets.

Sentimentalists protest. But the New Towns—not, in fact, so new, for the idea first germinated in the last century—the square mile after square mile of neat little houses in Kent and Surrey and Cheshire and Hertfordshire, are a tremendous improvement on the urban slums of the first forty years of the century.

Since the war the city has spilled out into the country. Often the result has been hideous; even to the sternest social moralist it has been a desecration. But it is going on, and most thoughtful men agree that the only course is to plan and guide this spread of population to preserve some of the amenities of the countryside.

Britain at the moment is in the throes of a tremendous change in living habits. Consider this change in only one aspect, that of food.

The country that went to war in 1939 still ate and drank habitually as its fathers and grandfathers had done. "Beef and beer," said George IV and a century and more later, "beef and beer" with a reasonable admixture of potatoes, pastry, and sweets satisfied the subjects of George VI.

Since the war, and to a large extent because of the rationing of the war and the immediate postwar years, the British have moved toward a more varied diet. Orange juice and ice cream, salads and fresh vegetables to replace the eternal Brussels sprouts and "spring greens."

Refrigerators were almost unknown in working-class or lower-middle-class homes twenty years ago. They are commonplace today. So are prepared mixes for cakes and frozen foods. Fruits, such as grapefruit, once viewed with unreasonable suspicion are appearing on working-class tables. To be sure, the recruit from Lancashire will probably ask for "steak, eggs, and chips" (French fried potatoes) at his first meal in the army canteen. But he is changing. So are his sister and his mother.

Accompanying this is the rapid introduction of household appliances which Americans have known for a quarter of a century. Vacuum cleaners, electric washing machines and dishwashers, and a dozen other mechanical helps to housewifery are easing the lot of the working-class woman. This is a new market, eager, indiscriminate, but determined. The women are changing British life. They are giving it more leisure, more comfort, and more utilitarian attractiveness.

There is in Britain a startling contrast between what is superficially a deeply materialistic society and the mass of cultural interests. On one hand, there are the millions who read cheap, irresponsible "popular" newspapers. On the other, there are earnest societies devoted to the study of Milton. Here is a nation spotted with dance halls devoted to rock 'n' roll or whatever is the craze of the day. But there is Wales with its golden-voiced choirs and here are the morris dancers in the village hall. In the grimy back streets of Glasgow a boy recites in Gaelic his story of his adventures abroad.

The British are popularly supposed to be interested solely in red-nosed music-hall comedians, recherché drawing-room comedies, and the pneumatic charms of Miss Marilyn Monroe and her imitators. It came as a surprise to many hardened Fleet Street editors when the prima ballerina of the Covent Garden company, the exquisitely fragile Dame Margot Fonteyn, became involved in a Central American dust-up and evoked a spate of protesting telephone calls and letters. Long-haired artists and sober civil servants took to the pen to warn Panama to be careful of Margot.

All of which indicated to the editors, notoriously behind in catching popular trends, that the ballet had entrenched itself deeply in British society.

Dancing is a major pastime and a major industry. There are probably more dance clubs devoted to learning and exhibiting formation dancing and special numbers in Britain than anywhere else in the world. The boy from the garage and the waitress from the teashop appear in tails and ball dress at the local "Palais de Dance" once or twice a week to re-create for themselves that shining world glimpsed upon the screen.

Organized sport, as the world knows it, originated in nineteenth-century Britain. No one can really know modern Britain who overlooks its games, their players, and the spectators.

Britain's present position and her place in the world cannot be understood without recognition of Britain as a class society of great mobility. The differences between the food, clothing, amusement, and thought patterns of a member of the lower middle class and a member of the upper class are enormous. Nor do they rest upon money alone. What saves Britain from stagnation is that the classes are and have been for centuries constantly in flux, with the upper classes increasingly easy of access.

To take only a few examples. Tudor times brought a new aristocracy to supplant the leaders of the Middle Ages. In the seventeenth, eighteenth, and nineteenth centuries a powerful class of merchants and industrialists rose to power at the expense of the

landowning aristocracy. The most striking change since the end
of World War II has been the eclipse of the old upper middle
class, drawn largely from the professions, the civil service, and
banking and international trade, by the new upper middle class,
whose status rests on the expanding new industries—electronics,
plastics, communications, and the wide application of science in
industry.

"The British are class-conscious." This is both a fact and, to
many, an indictment. But in assessing the characteristics of the
British, I do not believe that *they* consider class-consciousness as
particularly prominent. Obviously there are fervent critics of the
whole class structure. They get a hearing. But it is not a subject
that seems to impinge greatly into the daily life of Britain. Classes
are there. They change. But "shirt sleeves to shirt sleeves in three
generations" is not purely an American saying.

Individual characteristics are as varied as the nation. But to
generalize, it would appear that tolerance, sentimentality—but not
emotion—and a certain furious ruthlessness, usually kept well in
check, are among the characteristics of the British that are worth
noting.

Americans look upon the British as a particularly law-abiding
people. The British have an admirable legal and judicial system,
and the police, although not above reproach, on the whole are
industrious and brave. These are not, however, the result of a general respect for law and order long ingrained in the people. On
the contrary, they seem to me to be necessities imposed by the
turbulent and unruly nature of the British. British history in the
field of municipal government until the first quarter of the nineteenth century is one long, dark record of riots, arson, corruption,
and intimidation of police and law officers. There *had* to be a
Scotland Yard, an unbribable judiciary, and swift action if Britain
was to evolve into a modern society.

Tolerance is a British characteristic with a wide application. It
is one reason why the political system performs adequately and
why it has withstood in the last century the terrific psychological
pressure arising out of a transfer of national power westward to

the United States and a succession of drastic changes of political power from class to class within British society.

The British are a political people. This means, among other things, that they are skillful in the arts of compromise, that they work well together in committees, and that they avoid extremes. Extremism in British politics of the type personified in the United States by Senator McCarthy went out with the end of religious animosity in the early eighteenth century. This, too, can be traced to British tolerance.

Tolerance can ask too high a price. As a national characteristic, it played its part in the national mood that led to Munich. Appeasement, no matter what is said about it now, was not an unpopular policy. There were many British fifteen years after World War I who wished the Germans well; there are, incidentally, far fewer today, fourteen years after the second war.

The British, because of their essential characteristics and because of the terrible vulnerability of their island economy, will go to great lengths to avoid a war. Then war comes and with it a transformation. The smug, peaceful shopkeepers and the nonchalant, "couldn't care less" young men suddenly become incomparable infantry and dashing pilots. But this is not all. In war the British give full rein to that streak of ruthlessness that lies just below the surface and that is curbed ordinarily by the bobby on the beat and the white-wigged figures of the judges at the law courts.

Another misconception about British character is that the British, or at least the English, are a quiet, somewhat dull people. This arises, I feel sure, from the common mistake of accepting the outward aspect of one class—in this case, the traveling upper middle class of fifty years ago—for the whole people. The British, far from being dull and routine, have as a nation produced a greater crop of eccentrics than any other.

It can be argued, of course, that T. E. Lawrence and Orde Wingate, to name only two, were eccentrics because their eccentricity was forced upon them by the dull routine of middle-class life. Yet anyone who knows an English village knows it is bound to contain two or three eccentrics who, in a smaller compass, are, in the kindly words of their friends, "mad as hatters."

There is always the retired major who is convinced the English are descended from the lost tribes of Israel. No village is so small that it does not house at least one fervent food faddist.

But beyond the known eccentrics the British are a talkative, opinionated, and gregarious people. For every upper-class traveler who will sit silent in a railroad carriage from London to Edinburgh there are fifty of all classes who will talk, argue, and, if the mood is on them and the beer good, sing. In the last war it was not those merry Latin races the Italians and the French whose troops were known for their singing, but the stolid Germans and dull English.

One final point. The British like the popular picture of themselves as a silent, withdrawn race, keeping, as they say, themselves to themselves.

The outsider is prone to identify as British characteristics those displayed by the English. There is a tendency to label the other peoples of the British Isles: that is, the Scots are tightfisted and proud, the Irish are merry and rebellious, the Welsh melodic and sly. There are, as anyone knows, generous Scotsmen and straightforward Welshmen. On the whole, however, the Irish come off worst in the business.

Most Americans think of the Irish in terms of Irish Americans. On home grounds the Irish are a much different race. Far from being a nation of merry-andrews, they are in fact a serious, almost mordant people. They lack the sentiment of the English, but they are far more emotional. The tradition of Irish rebelliousness arises from their long and ultimately successful struggle against English rule. Now that the struggle has been won and the gains consolidated, they appear less unruly than the English, Scots, or Welsh. It is a sad state of affairs, but there is far less fire in Irish politics than in British politics and the authority of the Church and of the government is seldom challenged. Even Eamon de Valera nowadays is slightly critical of the doings of the I.R.A., and although he acknowledges the pull of "the old cause" of a united Ireland, De Valera is now as stanch an upholder of law and order as any English minister.

It is a mistake to consider these national groups as penned in their respective countries. The bad times of the thirties, when the mines and mills of Wales were closed, spread Welshmen all over England looking for work. Generally these immigrants from the principality were socialists of the most extreme kind. Aneurin Bevan, for instance, was a transplanted Welshman from Ebbw Vale who farmed in Buckinghamshire and politicked in Westminster.

During political campaigns a visitor to the North of England or to the Midlands will often find that the leader of the local Labour party is an émigré Welshman. Their bitter personal memories of the bad times, which they are convinced were worse in Wales than anywhere else, have made them violent opponents of the Tories and have exacerbated local politics.

The Scots migration into England has been going on for three and a half centuries. The British engineering industry, the civil service, and, of course, the big banks are heavily infiltrated with Scotsmen. They are prone to yearn sadly for life north of the river Tweed and to talk at length of Scotland's glories. But most of them are content to remain in England, where they maintain an amused detachment. "I've lived among the English for thirty years," a Scotsman said once, "but I really know no more about them today than I did on the day I left Aberdeen." No more do the Irish, who come to England yearly in their tens of thousands for steady jobs and ready money, or the Welsh.

For the English, with their varied character, are the enigma of the islands. Sentimental but not emotional, peace-loving but most ruthless fighters in war, homogeneous despite a great variety of local customs, accents, and prejudices, highly imaginative and inventive in politics yet bound by the traditions of a thousand-year-old monarchy, they are as difficult to grasp as a handful of mercury. They have, above all, a supple strength, a group intelligence, and, basically, a deep sense of national importance. The British have been all over the world and they interest themselves in the causes of far-off peoples. But they never forget they are a nation.

The British have been a nation for so long that we tend to forget the centuries of strife that preceded the emergence of the British nation. No one has invaded England since 1066, although all the more enterprising European conquerors have thought about it. But up to 1066 Britain had been a playground for invaders and adventurers: Romans and Saxons, Danes, and, ultimately, the Normans. The land itself contributed much to this situation.

For the England of Roman times and of the Dark Ages was a land of broad, deep rivers, up which the invaders sailed their galleys and long boats; an invitation to invasion. There were no mountain ranges along the coast to bar the legions' progress or to impede the bands of Saxons and Norsemen who left their long boats at the river's edge and swept ravaging and burning across the country.

It is difficult to envisage the neat, manicured English countryside and the teeming cities of today as the product of a pioneering movement, but, of course, that is what it is. The Saxon farmers plunged into the great masses of forest after their initial raids to carve homes out of the wilderness very much as the first American settlers pushed westward from the seacoast to hack their farms out of the inland forests.

Then as now, southern England was an immensely fertile country. By the Middle Ages the standard of life of the English yeoman was the envy of travelers from abroad, and knowledge of the richness of the land and the wealth of the countryside lured further waves of invaders. The Danes and the other Norsemen were fierce and implacable foes. But like the Saxons before them, they were also farmers.

The waves of invasion gradually pushed the Celts, the British of Caesar's day, westward into the mountains of Wales and north into the hills of Cumberland and Westmorland. The Scots remained unsubdued in the Highlands, and what is now called the Celtic fringe was established. The Norsemen, of whom the Danes were the most numerous, drove many of the Saxons westward into Wessex and settled largely in eastern England. The Normans, the last of the conquerors, took all England and settled down to rule a population predominantly Saxon but with strong infusions of Danish and Norwegian blood. The Normans themselves were Norsemen who had settled in northern France.

The institutions of government in the Middle Ages were Norman. But in the countryside the old Saxon forms persisted. Gradually the two blended together, so that Parliament, which owes its name to Norman French, took on some of the attributes of the Saxon tribal meetings. Similarly, the language that developed was a mixture of Norman French and Saxon English. The first, the language of the court and government, began to assimilate Saxon words while the latter, much more slowly, began to use some words from the French.

Britain is too small a country for migrations. But two processes occurred that had a tremendous effect upon her history. The islanders, initially, were a largely agricultural race. They were forced to the sea to defend themselves; the first great development of English sea power came in the reign of Alfred the Great, when a navy was built to check the invading Danes. In time the English became most bold and skillful mariners, part traders, part pirates.

As trade developed, London expanded. The Romans had made Londinium on the Thames a thriving center for trade. But when the legions departed and the long night of the Dark Ages descended upon England, the city's importance diminished. The population dwindled and the Saxons, living in their farming communities at places like Twickenham, regarded the cluster of stone buildings built by the Romans with superstitious awe.

But with the expansion of trade in the reigns of the late Saxon kings, London once more became the commercial center of England and a leading trading center of the Western world. Its merchants began to exert influence upon governments, as they do today. Its common people became independent and highly developed politically, just as they are today. The City of London became a center of political activity often at odds with the authority of the Crown and government further along the river at Westminster. As the Norman kings brought a more centralized and firmer government to England, this tendency increased.

The last Saxon kings had done much to unite the country and dispose of the independent kinglets who had risen to local power as the country emerged from the Dark Ages. The Normans, with their disciplined, harsh minds, completed the job. The Conqueror's nobles took over great tracts of land, ruling in the King's name, and the idea of monarchic government became established. Angevin kings introduced techniques of government that increased the royal power.

But the Normans and their descendants were affected by the rebellious instincts of the people they ruled. Saxon defiance of the Normans lasted for centuries. The Norman nobles themselves took issue with the King's power and forced John to sign Magna Charta, the beginning of written English liberties. Parliament, at first a group called to discuss the affairs of the kingdom, slowly began to reach for power. As the Middle Ages drew to a close, Parliament's power waxed. By Stuart times it was powerful enough to lead a rebellion against the monarchy, to oust Charles I, and finally to behead him.

Parliament's power was not invariably at odds with that of the sovereign. Elizabeth I, who must be accounted the ablest woman ever to rule in Britain, got along well with Parliament. Between them, the Queen and Parliament co-operated to stabilize England's tottering finances, halt the religious strife that had tormented the country since Henry VIII's time, and, in the greatest foreign test faced by England since the Norman invasion, humble the Spain of Philip II by routing the Armada.

Parliament's victory in the Civil War and the establishment of Oliver Cromwell as Lord Protector was followed by the restoration of the monarchy under Charles II. There followed a period of political unrest and uncertainty in which the revived religious issues of the last century, and the desire for revenge of the Cavaliers beaten and stripped by Cromwell and Parliament, all played a part. Then, suddenly, when England appeared to be sinking into anarchy, William and Mary appeared on the scene, Parliament continued, and government moved gropingly into a new period.

The eighteenth century, which opened with the reign of Queen Anne and ended with the rise of a constellation including Pitt, Wellington, and Castlereagh, was a formative period of British government. The Hanoverian kings' ignorance of both the government and language of their new domain fostered the rise of cabinet government. The House of Lords attained a new ascendancy in Parliament, but the emergence of the two William Pitts, Charles James Fox, and other luminaries restored the balance. British government in this period suffered one of its greatest defeats, the loss of the American colonies. But the century also saw the conquest of Canada at Quebec and the conquest of India at Plassey. By the century's end the British Parliament had begun the long, expensive, and difficult struggle with Bonaparte's France. Parliament won.

British democracy as we know it today took shape in the century that followed the victories of Trafalgar and Waterloo.

The years between 1815 and 1914 saw the expansion of the people's political power at the expense of the entrenched aristocracy in the House of Lords and of the Crown. The Reform Bills and the extension of the franchise took place during a period of great imperial expansion. By 1900 Britain appeared to be a great imperial power whose government was in the hands of a trained, skillful, and purposeful civil service supporting a relatively small ruling class of great experience and prestige. Undoubtedly this was the superficial picture. Actually the conditions had been created for the emergence of the industrial democracy we know today. That democracy has been more sorely tried in two world wars than any other in the English-speaking world. Yet Parliament and the British political system have survived.

A word about the Crown. The nineteenth century saw the gradual whittling away of the powers of the sovereign, and this process continued through the first half of the twentieth century. When Elizabeth II was crowned in 1953, the powers of the Crown had been limited to consultation, advice, and warning. Nonetheless, the Crown's influence in many fields was far greater than the outsider was led to believe. The emergence of Prince Philip, an intelligent and gifted man, as consort to the Queen raised the question of what position he would attain after, say, thirty years at the center of things.

The British government, always changing but basically changeless, had by the middle of the century survived not only the two wars with Germany but the social revolution that followed the landslide victory of the Labour party in the elections of 1945. Parliament and government, as always, were the focus of trenchant attacks. To many, the very virulence of these attacks, and the stoutness of the defense, reflected the health of British government institutions. Parliament has prospered in the last two hundred years because it has been subjected to searching, intimate criticism.

When in the winter of 1958–59 parliamentary government was analyzed and criticized in a series of articles in a Sunday newspaper, students found comfort in the fact that almost the same arguments had been made against Parliament frequently over the last century. This was a very British reaction. A thousand years of continuous political and social history have made the British acutely sensitive to the past and their heritage from it.

This is probably more true of the country's literary and cultural heritage than it is of the physical reminders of the past.

There are, however, many of these, and despite the pace of modern construction new reminders of Britain's history reappear daily. Not long ago a construction gang in the City of London uncovered the ruins of a Roman temple to Mithras. Only last year the Jewel Tower of Westminster, built six hundred years ago, was restored and opened to the public. From the frowning stones of Stonehenge to the ruined castles that dot the countryside, the past is omnipresent.

The great period of public-works construction in Britain came in the nineteenth century. Since the end of World War II the nation has embarked on vast new public-works projects, but the seeker for monuments of the past must go further into history.

One testimony to the British past exploited in recent years is the stately homes of England. The houses of noblemen, dating back to the time of the first Elizabeth, have been thrown open to the public by their owners, whose ability to maintain the homes has been reduced by punitive taxation and death duties.

Through the ornately decorated rooms, across the velvet turf, and through the long echoing galleries, in jeans and sandals or the honest blue serge of the holidaying industrial worker, march the people of modern England. What they think of it all, the Van

Dycks and the Inigo Joneses, the armorial bearings and the empty
stables, God knows. They are not an articulate people in the
presence of their past. But they are not insensitive to it, and it
would be strange if they do not return from these visits to a more
spacious past with some sense of identity with their history.

But if, physically, Britain has nothing to offer to compare with
the Champs Elysées or the Escorial, London has an attraction all
its own. Individually many of the buildings are hideous. Taken
together in the harmonious whole of solid London, the Houses of
Parliament, the government buildings in Whitehall, Westminster
Abbey, Buckingham Palace, convey a sense of stability and dignity
seldom found in other capitals.

There is another past ceaselessly exploited. This is Olde England, the England that began to die with the start of the Industrial
Revolution and that has now almost gone save for carefully preserved tourist centers like Stratford on Avon. But the wanderer
through the countryside will encounter, if he is lucky and persist-
ent, unspoiled country villages that mirror the true charm of England's past. But there are not many of them and the traveler must
hurry.

The literary and cultural heritage of Britain centers around
English literature. As painters, sculptors, and composers, the
British are not distinguished. But they can write their blunt Saxon
tongue, and it is in the writings of the British from Chaucer to
the present that the national culture finds its stronghold.

Since the theater has been the vehicle for many of the greatest
of English writers, this part of the cultural heritage exists to be
seen and be enjoyed in England. There is, and the stage laments it,
no national theater. But there is the Old Vic in London and the
Memorial Theater in Stratford. And on these and on dozens of
other stages the British heritage comes to life.

There has been for the past decade an evident compulsion on
the part of the British to remember and to rejoice in their past.
When this is exploited by jingo newspapers trying to convince
their readers that nothing has really changed since 1900, the sentiment is debased. When it serves to remind the people that grave
though their difficulties and dangers may be today they are no

worse than those they have faced in the past, the movement to renew ties with the past serves a useful national purpose.

One reason why so many people continually hark back to the past is to be found in the tremendous change that has taken place in the life of Britain in the last quarter of a century. American visitors often are surprised at the way the British "carry on" about the Second World War. The answer is that not only was the war itself a tremendous emotional experience that touched everyone in Britain, but the decade that followed the end of the war in 1945 was a period of social revolution that altered British society.

This revolution was prepared by the sacrifices necessitated by the war. The struggle with Hitler cost Britain her overseas investments, the source of thousands of incomes, and, briefly, most of her overseas markets. When the guns fell silent in 1945, Britain was a victorious power. She was also broke. After the initial thanksgiving and merrymaking there came a long period of austerity, which marked British life almost as much as the war itself.

During the war the national spirit, brought to flaming life by the disasters and glories of 1940, never wavered. Morale withstood prolonged bombing by the Luftwaffe and by V-1 and V-2 weapons, the shattering defeats in the Far East in 1941 and 1942, and the slow attrition of physical health due to unremitting toil, poor food, and sleepless nights. But morale did alter under the impact of the austerity imposed by Britain's economic condition.

The revolution of the late 1940s took place on two levels.

On the economic level, the legislation introduced by the Labour government nationalized a wide area of Britain's economy. This was the most spectacular of the changes of the postwar years, but since it fulfilled long-standing pledges by the Socialists, it was not a direct result of the war. The social revolution that took place, on the other hand, grew directly from the changes in British life that took place from 1939 to 1945. Some of these had been discernible before the outbreak of war and were exacerbated by the upheaval. Others started during the war as direct consequences of it.

The change affected the old middle class more than any other. This was the class that had attained affluence and influence in the Victorian era. By the 1930s it provided most of Britain's civil servants, the majority of the officers in the fighting services, the officials of the banks and great commercial corporations, and most of Britain's lawyers, doctors, and Church of England clergymen.

Most of its members lived on fixed income. The rising wartime taxation hit them hard. They sent their children to the public schools (that is, private schools), and with the rise in tuition costs this became more and more difficult. Fathers stopped smoking and mothers wore last year's dress with the bow on the other side to make sure that young Miles followed his father to the old school.

The voracious demand of the war effort had brought more and more women into industry and business. They found they liked the freedom and the pounds, and when the war ended they stayed on the job. The old middle class found itself without servants to run the big, rambling country houses with their coal grates or the roomy, old-fashioned apartments in the cities. The laborsaving devices so dear to the American housewife had not appeared in Britain in any number at the start of the war, and during the conflict there was no time for that sort of production. Consequently, the housewife of the late 1940s found herself doing the housework formerly done by two or even three maids and standing for hours in line to buy food. Many items of food remained rationed until the first years of this decade.

The social upheaval of the postwar years was accompanied by the gradual emergence of a new middle class and by the rapid improvement in the economic status of the industrial working class.

The new middle class was chiefly concerned with the new industries that developed in Britain after the war and with some old industries which assumed new importance in the changed pattern of British life.

First there were the scientists, highly skilled technicians, industrial managers, and international-market experts associated with electronics, jet aircraft, plastics, and machine tools, all of which have become important as exports and consequently vital to Britain's life. Then there were the communications experts, men steeped in the lore of advertising, newspapers, television, and the theater, whose importance increased as Britain's industrial millions,

with more money than ever before, began to spend it. There arose
a corps of designers to meet the demands of the new middle class,
who sought gayer colors and more modern design and rejected the
chintzes and heavy furniture that had satisfied the old middle
class.

There were certain well-defined differences between the new
middle class and the old. Although many members of the former
had a "public"—that is, private—school education, they do not
venerate the old school and its associations as did the old middle
class. They are on the whole less interested in government and
the Commonwealth, slightly further to the left politically, and less
immersed in the established pastimes: shooting, cricket, rugby
football, tennis, and golf. The old middle class generally was a
reading class, omnivorous and undiscriminating. The new middle
class is not, although it reads the newspapers, particularly the
popular press. The old middle class doesn't think much of television, and this is not merely a question of economics. The new
middle class loves it. To some degree the television industry is
its product, for it arranges the programs, runs the systems, and
designs and produces the sets.

The industrial working class in Britain is certainly the oldest
and may be the most advanced politically of any in the world. Its
political progress that produced the Labour party is partially a
consequence of the appalling conditions of Britain's mines, shops,
and factories in the early years of the Industrial Revolution; the
left in Britain is very susceptible to ancestral voices murmuring of
"dark, satanic mills" or of the unemployment and the dole of
thirty years ago. Indeed, the Labour party often gives the impression of living in the past to a much greater extent than its supporters in the industrial working class.

Nowhere is there a greater transformation in British life.
Twenty years of relatively high employment and rising wages
have provided the financial improvement. A secondary factor is
an increase in the number of women working. Families living in
subsidized housing, with father, mother, two sons, and a daughter
all working, are extremely well off by any standards.

By British standards, wages and the cost of living are both high.

But to an American, the difference between the total income of a working-class family and its total expenditure also seems great. This is because British buying habits have not changed as rapidly as the market researchers and the manufacturers would like. The industrial working class is being taught, principally in the new housing developments and in the New Towns, to want and to buy new products. But sales resistance continues to be formidable in an inherently conservative working class.

For example, a Londoner told me recently that although he had bought a washing machine on the "never-never" (installment plan), neither his wife nor his mother-in-law took to the idea of letting a machine do what they had done during all their adult lives. They preferred, he said, to save the money and do the work themselves. This example could be contrasted with the young working-class wives, who immediately accept and use any kind of laborsaving device.

Prosperity has opened new horizons to the workers. Perhaps the most significant remark I have heard in Britain in the last three years was that of a Labour party politico about the timing of the next general election.

"Of course, the months of July and August are out," he said. "Too many of *our* people will be abroad then."

He meant that a considerable number of British working families are going off to the Continent on two-week holidays either by bus on carefully arranged, inexpensive tours, or independently. I know one young man, who works in a street market, who last summer took his wife on a two-week trip through Italy on a motorcycle. They liked it fine.

Twenty years ago a motorcycle was the goal of the young working-class man. Today it is the automobile. The great expansion of automobile sales which the United States knew thirty years ago has struck Britain in the last five years. Why the delay? The answer is simple: the war. Six years of war retarded British development in this and many other spheres.

Here it might be advisable to warn those visitors to Britain, especially to London, who are struck by British "imitation" of the United States. These superficial aspects of British life—soda fountains, for instance, which the British call "milk bars," or mass-produced women's clothing—all were germinating in Britain in 1939. Like much else, they were postponed by the war and postwar austerity. The British are not imitating so much as finally adopting products, social trends, and living habits natural to an advanced industrial society.

The working class has bought largely of some types of the new consumer goods that have flooded the markets since 1953, the end of austerity. The women of this class are the great purchasers of mass-produced women's clothing, often sold as "Hollywood" or "New York" styles. The men buy clothes similarly produced, aping American fashion. The time is fast approaching in Britain when it will be impossible to tell a countess from a shopgirl by their clothes. But it will be some time before the industrial workers adopt the habiliments of the Londoner, dark suit, black shoes, white starched collar, derby, and striped tie. The worker is turning to lighter, gayer fabrics. And he'd sooner be found dead than in a derby or "bowler 'at."

It is the working class, too, that is chiefly responsible for the enormous boom in television. Commercial television, which the British, for reasons best known to themselves, tend to dignify as "Independent" television, is the biggest money-maker that has hit these islands in this century. It owes its expansion chiefly to the industrial working class, and even the casual viewer will be impressed by the manner in which the tastes and pocketbook of that class is catered to by the producers.

Advertising on commercial television concentrates on the "pocket money" products that the industrial working class buys. The soap that makes the shopgirl lovelier. The hair cream that insures success for the young man. Cigarettes, chocolate, and beer.

But there has been a recent increase in the frequency of gasoline advertisements, too. Again, thirty years ago the virtues of specific gasolines, motor oils, or tires would have interested an infinitesimal section of the British public. Today, with 40,000 cars being sold each month, they are of general interest.

I have discussed these changes in the context of British life. The reader should be warned that these alterations in the living conditions of the industrial working class, the rise of the new middle class, and the pressures exerted on the old middle class do not apply to the same extent in Ireland, either north or south. Both Northern Ireland, which is loyal to the British Crown, and the Republic in the south are going through a testing period. The difference is that the trials in the North are the result of modern industrial strains while those in the South arise from fundamental weaknesses in Irish society.

Most Americans of Irish descent tend to accept the romanticized, fictional idea of Irish life. They would serve Ireland better if they recognized the difficult, almost desperate situation facing the Republic. A gift of fifty dollars to a fast-talking representative of the I.R.A. is all very well. But Ireland's real needs now are more important. For Ireland, that part of it, at least, within the boundaries of the Republic, is a sick country.

The population has been falling steadily since the end of World War I. The Irish marry late. Since primogeniture is not the rule, as it is in England, the farms, often pitifully small to begin with, are divided by the father among three or four sons. The income from such farms is small. The heirs, who may be men in their forties or fifties when they inherit, are slow to marry because of economic necessity. Consequently, they marry late and their families are small.

The proximity of England, where the economy has been booming for a decade and where there are, moreover, the inducements of the modern welfare state, complicates the situation. Each year sees the migration of thousands of young Irish people to Britain. There they take on the manual tasks connected with the building and construction trades at salaries that are munificent by Irish standards. In some years the migration amounts to about 40,000 people a year.

The visitor will see the result if he travels through the villages and towns of rural Ireland. Sometimes he will encounter whole streets in which every house is vacant. In Dublin not long ago, construction workers struck. By the time the strike was over, 60 per cent of the strikers had left for England and better-paying jobs.

This is a problem far more important to Irishmen and people of Irish descent than the pathetic vainglory of the I.R.A. It comes down to the question: Is Ireland with its great past, the Irish race with its great gifts, to degenerate into a forgotten people living in an underpopulated island off the English coast?

The writer has emphasized the changes in British society since the war, and the changes that periodically have swept British society since Tudor times, for what seems to him to be an important reason. It is that these changes, reflecting as they do the inherent mobility in British society, are by far the best guarantee that Britain will remain one of the great powers for many years to come.

Again, it is necessary to reiterate a contemporary historical situation that is of the greatest importance to any assessment of Britain today. This is that at present the British are living in the sort of world situation that in the past has invariably stirred them to their greatest efforts. They are a comparatively small people, of roughly 51,500,000, forced to earn their living through the sale overseas of their products and asked to compete politically with the Russian, American, and Chinese colossi. To repeat, this is nothing new to the British.

Once again, as so often before in their history, the British face a multiplicity of challenges at home and abroad.

The basis of their ability to meet the challenge lies in the national character. In the past it has not failed them, and although the prophets take each passing craze, of which rock 'n' roll is the latest, as an indication that the country has gone to the dogs, there is no reason to believe it will fail them again. The British have many faults. But they are essentially a tough people prepared to alter the habits of their lives as long as the beloved façade remains unchanged. Moreover, despite the presence of Welsh, Scots, and Irish peoples in England, they are a homogeneous people, able, under stress, to forget differences and work together.

British politics are no less fierce than American. But in times of national crisis, the British are less likely to stress political differences than we are. During World War II, for instance, Winston

Churchill, not at the outset of his premiership a man universally loved and trusted by his fellow countrymen, was never subjected to the fierce and unremitting criticism directed at Franklin D. Roosevelt. One reason for this may be the presence of a higher symbol of allegiance, the Crown, outside politics. Another, simpler explanation may be plain good sense.

The British, historically aware of their exposed position, know that their great disasters in the past have always fallen upon them when they did not have sense enough to unite in the face of peril. Another point: there is plenty of extremism in British society, but aside from a handful of fascists and communists it does not affect politics. Political convictions are deeply held and fiercely debated. But the British learned long ago that religious and racial extremism erode the basis of the political structure. No single event in British social relations since the war has aroused so much concern as the race riots in the Notting Hill district of London in September 1958.

There were many causes. The reappearance on the scene of Sir Oswald Mosley's fascists worried many. Others were concerned at the sordid interracial relationships in the district described by the newspapers. But the fundamental irritant was the appearance in Britain of racial intolerance, something which the majority had thought impossible in a traditionally homogeneous community.

The writer has advanced several aspects of British character and of British society as reasons for believing the nation will be able to meet the challenge of the times. But the skeptic can reasonably inquire if these reasons, based on an assessment of the intangibles of national character and the British society, outweigh the very serious economic difficulties which face the country now and will face it in the future.

Are British energies and ingenuity enough, the skeptic may ask, to compensate the country for the loss of its overseas investments and the gradual deterioration of the coal supply, industrial Britain's chief raw material? Can a homogeneous society, no matter how patriotic, avail in the competition against German enterprise and Japanese low costs in the fight for world markets?

Finally, aren't homogeneity and patriotism canceled by the divisive influences in British society starting with the trade-unions?

Let us begin by examining the bases for Britain's ability to meet the challenge.

We start with a nation whose industrial labor force contains a very high percentage of trained and experienced technical workers and whose theoretical science maintained itself in the vanguard of Western scientific thought a decade ago even though the country as a whole was broke.

This is a country that traditionally has earned its living by exporting or re-exporting manufactured products. In the United States we are prone to consider the Rolls-Royce or the cashmere sweater or the Wedgwood tea service as British exports. But in South America or in India people are likely to think of marine engines, tractors, railroad signal systems, or locomotives as typical, and necessary, British exports.

Indeed, the main emphasis on exports in Britain is on this type of product. Cars for the United States, Africa, Australia, and the Continent. Electronics for Turkey. Plastics for Africa. In the long run these are the exports that count.

A political issue intervenes. The British, with their strongly developed commercial sense, have always traded with hostile powers. In the present world situation they are doing their utmost to increase trade in non-strategic goods with the Soviet Union, Communist China, and Communist satellites east and west. For Americans, secure in a continental economy, there is something disturbing, almost treasonable in such trade. To the British, always conscious of their need to trade or die, this commerce is entirely natural.

For only by such trade can Britain purchase abroad the raw materials that are necessary to maintain the industrial economy. Coal was almost the only raw material the British had when the Industrial Revolution began and they have made it go a long, long way. But today they must buy oil, copper, tin, bauxite, iron ores, timber, and dozens of other basic materials to feed their industrial machine. When international trade prices favor them—that is, when the prices of these imports are low—the British can indulge themselves, as they have in the last six years, in meeting the demands of the home market. But when prices abroad rise, then any British government, Conservative or Labour, must find means of restricting spending at home.

In an economy so delicately balanced, production costs are vital. There is very little fat on the British economic structure. The dwindling of the island's coal resources has increased British dependence on oil supplies, most of them from the Middle East. These supplies are increasingly expensive and increasingly vulnerable to pressure from the representatives of the new Arab nationalism.

Since 1955 the British have attempted to meet this situation by launching the world's most ambitious program for the production of industrial power from nuclear power plants. The program envisages the construction of a series of power plants feeding electrical energy to industry and to private homes. As it stands now, the plan will just compensate Britain for its losses in coal production by the mid-1960s. But scientists believe that improved utilization of nuclear power, short cuts in its production, and the expansion of the national program will push the plan beyond this frontier. Britain, of course, is concentrating on nuclear power for civilian use because it has to do so.

The program for nuclear power stations and the involvement of much of British heavy industry in the program has enabled exporters to venture into a new export field. Isotopes and nuclear reactors are now on the national selling list. Technicians and scientists trained in Britain are going overseas to teach and to build.

The expansion of the steel industry is another project on which both Conservatives and Labour are betting heavily as a means of helping the country meet foreign competition. This expansion has been planned to help meet the development of new industrial areas as well as the increased activity in recognized locations like the Birmingham area and South Wales. The steel industry, too, is paying more attention to the needs of the new engineering industries turning out machine tools for South Africa and electronic calculators for Europe.

In assessing Britain's capacity to compete and endure in the
modern world, the visitor must also recognize the country's invisible assets. These include the surprising amount of world trade
carried out through the City of London, the ubiquity of the
British Merchant Marine flying "the old Red Duster" on the seas,
and the remarkable extension both of the country's overseas airlines, British Overseas Aircraft Corporation and British European
Airways, and of the overseas sales of British aircraft like the
Viscount and the Britannia.

In 1956 I was flying to Chicago from New York listening to
the argument of three Middle Westerners in the nearby seats.

"Well, dammit, if the British are in such bad shape why in
hell are we flying to Chicago in a Viscount?"

Those Americans who were born before the dissolution of the
British Empire are too ready to equate the decline of Britain's
fortunes with the decline of the Empire. It is, of course, quite
correct that the loss of various parts of the Empire and their reappearance as sovereign nations within or outside the British
Commonwealth has reduced the position of Britain as a decisive
imperial influence upon world affairs. But the British, a hardheaded people, have never spent much time bewailing this
change. Increasingly they have sought to replace the political ties
with economic links. In India, Ghana, Nigeria, and Burma, British
business is on the march, exploiting the old, and despite the
communists, not unrespected connection between the mother
country and the peoples across the seas.

The work has been handicapped in the immediate postwar
years by the reduced scale of British investment. This investment
has increased in the last decade, and the tendency of Commonwealth nations to look to London for both financial and technical
assistance is greater now than it was in the years of austerity.
The ties that bind the older Commonwealth nations, such as
Australia and New Zealand, to the United Kingdom are often
difficult for Americans to assess. They begin with that semi-mysti-
cal connection with the Crown and they end with the sharp reminder that New Zealanders and Australians, no matter how
much they seem to resent British manners and customs, usually

have more in common with the British than they do with Americans.

In the course of this chapter I have stressed the external challenges that face Britain: the political and military power of the United States and the Soviet Union, the economic competition with West Germany, the United States, and, ultimately, the Soviet Union, and the narrow margin whereon the British economy must operate to meet this competition and remain solvent.

It is my conviction that Britain can meet these challenges.

By making and exploding nuclear weapons and by equipping a small but highly efficient V force of high-performance bombers, Britain has entered the nuclear age. The entry came late in view of the sizable British contribution to the making of the first atomic bomb; a contribution whose fruits were largely denied Britain by the passage of the McMahon Act. At any rate, Britain is now a nuclear power equipped not only with the V-force bombers but with intermediate-range ballistic missiles as well.

The government of the United Kingdom is thus installed in the seats of the mighty, for it is a peculiarity of nuclear armament that it is the great equalizer. Once a nation has the hydrogen bomb and the means of delivering it, other nations must reckon with it as a destructive power whose capacities, if less great than their own, are still important and might, in some circumstances, be decisive. This is not a situation that endears itself to a large number of Britons. But it is the way things happen to be.

Granted this nuclear potential, the British government has an important role in the affairs of the Western alliance. But since the government of Sir Winston Churchill, successive governments have scaled down the manner in which that voice should be employed.

The British now advise, reason, and argue; they do not command. But since they have at their disposal centuries of experience and a diligent and informed civil service that attains its best expression in the Foreign Office, their voice is often disproportionate to their actual physical strength.

This condition will endure only if the British continue to master the economic difficulties that face them. I have pointed out how the advent of nuclear power, the expansion of new industries, and the intensification of the British trade drive overseas are helping now to meet these problems. Frankness demands, however, that we take into account the internal political and social reasons that might reduce Britain's capacity in the economic field.

Important among these reasons is the seeming inability of the great trade-unions to accustom themselves to changes in British society.

Throughout the business world there has been and is a reluctance to accommodate profits and practices to the exigencies of the nation's present economic condition. There is also among some of the labor unions an almost frivolous attitude toward the immense importance of maintaining exports. The strike weapon has been and is used immoderately in industries on whose prosperity the very future of the nation depends.

To say, as many do, that this is the result of communist influence in the unions is to beg the real question. Admittedly, communists do wield important influence in many key unions. But the basic trouble, in my opinion, is the failure of the union leaders, a failure they share with some groups in the Labour party, to realize that the social and economic revolution is over in Britain.

Let us take one instance. On the whole, the unions have varied from hostile to lukewarm in their reactions to schemes for extending industrial ownership to the workers, a process well established in the United States. The Trades Union Congress, a confederation that controls most of the country's 9,000,000 trade-unionists, has been slow to control the wildcat strikes, often inspired by communists, that have crippled key industries. The distinction between industrial democracy and industrial anarchy must be redrawn.

This is a difficult problem to solve in times of comparative prosperity. And Britain since 1953 has been a prosperous nation. The principal reason for believing the problem will be solved is the underlying homogeneity of the British nation. Once the issue is presented to the British in all its stark reality and with all the dire consequences to the nation's future presented in detail, the balance between the just demands of the workers and the national need for expanding industry and export will be found.

The employers, to be sure, are far from blameless. Industrial expansion has not progressed at a proper rate in Britain for many reasons, among them the reluctance of the leaders of finance capital to leave the shelter of steady and sure profits for the uncharted seas of industrial expansion. Given the innate conservatism of the business community, it is surprising how much has been done. Both the great partners in the British economy, the employers and the employed, are by nature conservative. But they are also hardheaded folk with a well-developed sense of self-criticism.

No one abroad should expect that the British in contemporary circumstances will be able to recapture the political power and influence or the economic affluence that carried them through the long, happy weekend between Waterloo and the Marne. What Americans must realize is that despite economic, physical, and political losses, the British still have a role to play in the world and are intent on playing it to the hilt.

One word about the alliance between the United States and the United Kingdom, which, although unwritten, is so much stronger than many written alliances. The British are never going to be easy allies. They are not sycophants. Despite all the bickering and debate of national politics in Britain, they preserve in their relations with other powers a confidence in the wisdom of their own policies that is always irritating and occasionally maddeningly so. The British consider themselves allies, not satellites.

Because of their exposed geographic, economic, and military position, the British invariably will be more anxious to seek accommodation with hostile powers than American governments will be. On the other hand, the history of this strident century indicates that on matters of principle the British are much more likely to fight—bewailing loudly that the whole thing is unnecessary—than any other of our allies.

They are a people and a country difficult to understand. They are hard to classify. What more can one say? Only that they are tough, intelligent, and wedded to those same great principles of human behavior to which we Americans owe allegiance. When the chips are down—and these days no one really knows when they will go down—the British are good people to have on our side.

When, early in 1959, Prime Minister Harold Macmillan went to Moscow there was a great furor about "appeasement" and "softness" in Washington, Bonn, and Paris. To those who know what happened, a group that includes the President of the United States, this is ridiculous.

For one winter's afternoon in the Kremlin, Nikita Khrushchev, irked at Mr. Macmillan's repeated assertions that if anything serious happened over Berlin it would be the fault of the Soviet Union, told the Prime Minister that he might push his demands to the ultimate. His guest looked out on the driving snow and drummed his fingers on the table.

Well, he said, that would be a pity. He was sorry the Premier felt that way. But the British were not giving in. If this was the case, then he (Macmillan) had a lot to do. He must arrange for the evacuation from the British Isles of some 20,000,000 women and children. He must arrange to increase the strength of the V-bomber force. He should bring back some of the British troops now stationed overseas. But he was not going to give in. After that Mr. Khrushchev became more amenable.

In his way Macmillan is a good symbol of Britain today. Elderly but enterprising; aristocratic in exterior manners but solidly based in the tradition of personal advancement and class mobility that can bring a poor crofter's great-grandson to Downing Street in three generations; casual and almost dilettantish in manner; tough and unyielding underneath.

FRANCE

David Schoenbrun

As a veteran of the relatively new medium of television news reporting, David Franz Schoenbrun has become almost as familiar to Americans as the people he interviews. Schoenbrun has been since 1947 Chief of the Paris Bureau of the Columbia Broadcasting System and is one of the best-known reporters of the intricacies of the French political scene.

His Paris residence and specialization in the story of France actually began in 1945, when he became Paris Bureau Chief for the Overseas News Agency.

Born in 1915 and graduated from the College of the City of New York in 1934, he was a teacher of French and Spanish in New York City high schools for two years before he reached the age of twenty-one. A brief stint as trade-union negotiator and labor-news writer led to a newspaper career and to the desk of Chief of European Propaganda for the OWI in 1942 and 1943, intelligence liaison officer with the French Army in 1944–45, and subsequently combat correspondent with the U. S. Seventh Army.

Schoenbrun has contributed to most of the major magazines and is the author of the book As France Goes.

FRANCE

When Charles de Gaulle put down the sword of Lorraine and picked up the pen of a historian, the very first thing he did was to profess his love for France. All his life, he wrote, he had had a certain vision of France. He saw her as the "princess in the fairy tale, or the Madonna of the frescoes."

The essence of De Gaulle and of the country he loves and rules, or, as he would put it, guides and protects, is contained in that portrait of a stern, dour soldier, sitting at a desk, composing a literary masterpiece, dreaming of his country as a boy would dream of a girl he loves and has always loved long before destiny made him her lover. Nothing could be more French than Charles de Gaulle and his vision of a fairy-tale Madonna.

The contrast between De Gaulle's stern exterior—his icy, haughty, austere appearance—and his passionate, romantic inner nature is a key to France and to the French, the best-known, least-understood nation and people in the world today. More has been written about France and the French than about any other country and its citizens, yet no country, not even Russia, that mystery enveloped in an enigma, nor the traditionally "inscrutable" Chinese, is as little understood or as unpredictable as France, the country of idealistic cynics and romantic rationalists.

France is a paradise of paradox. It is a paradise because of its fertile fields, flowered valleys, swift yet graceful rivers, and the treasure house of minerals, from coal and iron to natural gas and uranium, contained within its compact territory. It is a paradox because this potential paradise has been for many centuries a political purgatory, perpetually suspended between the hell of war's destruction and the heaven of peaceful creation. Other peoples have had a martial history. Other peoples have ardently desired to live in peace. But no people has so ardently desired peace and so frequently waged war as the French.

As the world entered the seventh decade of the twentieth century France alone, among the great powers, was still at war and had been at war virtually nonstop for the past twenty years. From 1939 through 1959 the French had fought on three continents, against Germany in Europe, Indochina in Asia, and Algeria in Africa. France was rapidly and ignominiously defeated by the Germans, slowly but perhaps even more ignominiously defeated by the Vietnamese. In the case of Algeria, the best the French can hope is for a peace with honor but without victory. France can lose but cannot win the Algerian war. Yet, despite this inglorious record, so vividly contrasting with the glory and the grandeur that was France in the past, the government of President of the Republic Charles de Gaulle and of Prime Minister Michel Debré acts and speaks as though France still is one of the first-rank powers of the world. Never has France been so weak, so isolated, so criticized by friend and foe alike, yet, despite this, or perhaps because of it, rarely have the French talked more of their grandeur and the role they play in the world.

The French have long been masters of the art of self-deception and have succeeded in fooling both the world and themselves for countless generations. The writing of national history is, in all countries, an art rather than a science, but in France it is more poetry and fiction than the art of history. If Charles de Gaulle sees France as the princess in the fairy tale it is because his father was a professor of history, and French history is one long fairy tale, one of the most enthralling but mythical collections of alleged facts ever preserved in human annals.

The myth begins in all French primers with the phrase "Our ancestors, the Gauls."

The ancient Gauls, as the Romans named them, or the Celts, as they called themselves in their own language, were heterogeneous groups of tribes, without central government, without common origins. They were the descendants of countless waves of migrations into the peninsula of Europe for thousands of years. After the glaciers retreated, and the original "Frenchman," the Magdalenian man, had followed the reindeer and the bison north, there came a continuous flow of men from beyond the Danube and the Baltic, seeking new lands in the West. Slavs and Huns, followed later by Phoenicians and Greeks, by Iberians and Goths, migrated west until they could go west no longer, brought to a halt by the vast Atlantic sea.

These migrating peoples were longheads and shortheads, blonds and brunets, stocky and slender, tall and squat. Some were Gauls and some were not. Some looked, perhaps, like Charles de Gaulle, some like Brigitte Bardot, but who would say that they, like the General and the Vamp, were members of the same "national family" or that De Gaulle and Bardot descend from the Gauls?

There is, of course, no such thing as a national family, no race of Frenchmen or of Frenchwomen, just as there is no American race, nor any other truly distinct national species of man. Yet the supposedly logical French persist in the notion that they descend from the Gauls and that many of their national traits and characteristics are of Gallic ancestry.

The Gauls were a fiercely individualistic people. So are the French. Ergo, it is an inherited characteristic. The family unit was the basic unit of otherwise chaotic Gallic "society." The French family is also the basic unit of modern France. The Gauls were creative artisans, particularly gifted in working gold, silver, pottery, and glass. They invented the trouser, the wine cask, the mattress, or so French historians claim, seeing here early evidence of French pre-eminence in the graceful arts of fashion, food, drink, and decoration. If this is true, if the link to the Gauls is an unbroken line of history, then the French, as they do, may count their age in thousands of years, making theirs one of the oldest societies of mankind.

This sense of age, of historical continuity, is deeply rooted in the French mind and plays an important part in influencing

French attitudes today. It is both a good and a bad influence, as
is the case with most French myths. A sense of age and continuity
gives a sense of proportion. To an ancient people no disaster is
final, no cataclysm as terrible as it seems, for men of great age
have seen and survived many disasters. Invaders come and go
but France remains. France is frequently defeated but just as
frequently rises like a phoenix from the ashes to fly free again. The
danger of this sense of history, however, is the danger of old age
itself, its stiffness and inflexibility, its unwillingness to adjust and
adapt to a changed world. And this has been the most powerful
psychological neurosis of twentieth-century France, this refusal
to adjust to a fundamental change in the world power equation.

The French refuse to be impressed by the change, for, in the
course of their long history, they have seen many a shift in power.
They have seen the rise and fall of the Roman Empire, which, in
its declining years, was absorbed by their own dynamic growth
to become the Gallo-Roman Empire. They have fought off the
invasions of Attila the Hun, and the Saracens, the mighty Arab
warriors. They have had parts of their territory occupied by the
fierce red-headed Vikings, by the Goths and the Franks, finally
to absorb those whom they could not repel and to make of them
all something new that evolved, the Frenchman.

Because of his history the Frenchman is above all else a resistant. From the dawn of his existence he has had to resist invasion.
The very first French hero was Vercingetorix, the leader of the
Gallic tribe the Arverni, who resisted the legions of Caesar and
fought off superior Roman forces for seven years. Vercingetorix,
the Gaul, is more than just a historic hero; he set the pattern
of the hero-type of France, the "Resistant." The Resistant is a
popular French figure, more deeply rooted than the legendary
figure of the pioneer in American folklore.

French history is rich in reincarnations of Vercingetorix. St.
Genevieve, patron saint of Paris, who led the people to resist the
ferocious horsemen of Attila; St. Joan of Arc, who resisted the
British and who was brought into the court of King Charles to
give him courage by a nobleman named Sir Charles de Gaulle;
and the present-day Charles de Gaulle, greatest resistant of them

all, for he fought simultaneously, militarily or politically, the
Germans, the Russians, the British, and the Americans—all these
are one and the same person. They are all Christian knights of
France, defending the princess of the fairy tale against the ogres
of the world, who lust for the beautiful Madonna and the treasures of her realm.

The myth of foreign ogres and the French fairy princess persists mainly because, like all successful myths, it is based upon a
very large measure of truth. Among the major nations of the
world none has suffered so many foreign invasions, from the migrations of prehistory to the aggressions of the twentieth century,
as has France. The French, like the Chinese, have good reason
to believe in foreign devils, in modern as well as historical times.
Three times in sixty-nine years, from 1870 through 1939, an average of once every twenty-three years, the Germans invaded
France. Whatever the culpability of the French in warring on
the reigning houses of Europe in the past, the experience of recent
years far surpasses it, and the French can hardly be blamed, or at
least might be understood, if they feel more sinned against than
sinning.

The French resentment of foreign aggressors, lusting after
French treasures and seeking to replace French influence in the
world, embraces France's closest friends as well as her traditional
enemies. The French resented the Americans and the British in
the Second World War more than they resented the Germans.
They expected the Germans to behave the way they did. It was a
familiar enmity, heightened but not changed by the horrors of
nazism. Roosevelt's attitude, however, was unfamiliar and particularly painful. He was a dangerous if not a treacherous friend,
in the French view—that is, the view of De Gaulle and his Free
French movement—because Roosevelt threatened to wreck the
French empire and destroy forever France's position as a major
world power. De Gaulle never feared Hitler, for he was certain
that Hitler would be defeated by the Allies, but he did fear and
resent the powerful Allies themselves. British imperialism, Soviet
communism, American leadership ambitions, these were grave

perils in De Gaulle's eyes, as grave as any threat faced by St. Genevieve or St. Joan.

In all the troubled history of the French there has been no more dangerous period, no greater threat to French pre-eminence, than that of the twentieth century. Verdun was France's finest and almost last hour of glory. The French have never completely recovered from that terrible bloodletting. The French have never completely replaced the best sons and future fathers who died at Verdun. Added to the physical loss is the psychological frustration of adjusting to the fact that Verdun was the last battle in which the French would lead a great coalition of nations. The leadership of the world has passed into other hands. This fact of life will be accepted by future generations of Frenchmen. It is recognized but not accepted by the present ruling generation, for they are men who once led the world and who cannot bring themselves to admit their decline.

If this psychological disturbance of the French is not understood by travelers to that country, or, if understood, not sympathized with, then it would be far better not to travel through France. Italy would be a wise substitute. The Italians are less sensitive and have long accepted their decline. The French are hypersensitive and have not accepted their decline and are not likely to do so in the foreseeable future, or, more accurately perhaps, if they do accept it they are certainly not going to admit it to foreigners, particularly not to the very Americans who have replaced them as the leaders of the Western world. For this reason, among others, tourism in contemporary France is a delicate and difficult adventure for all but the most sensitive and thoughtful traveler.

For the thoughtful traveler, France remains one of the most rewarding countries to explore.

There are countries, like America, which have more diversity of landscape than France. There are countries, like Switzerland, that have more mountain peaks and lakes, for those who like mountains and lakes and efficient hotels and smiling service. There are countries, like Denmark, where the people actually like Americans and where Americans can find the sweet cream they must have with their coffee and a variety of sandwiches which puts to shame the most imaginative American roadhouse drive-ins. The Italians are gayer, the Spanish more suffering and miserably noble, the Germans more familiar, the Austrians more *gemütlich*, the Russians obviously more exciting. But none of these countries and peoples can offer as complete an assortment of excitement, *Gemütlichkeit*, familiarity, suffering nobility, gaiety, delicious sandwiches, luxurious hotels, sparkling lakes and snow-capped mountain peaks—practically everything in the world except possibly sweet cream and smiling service—as can France and the French.

The French do not like sweet cream and see no reason to make it simply because some American tourists think it a necessary accompaniment to coffee. The French brew delicious coffee, strong and black, as an after-dinner drink. Breakfast coffee they regard as something to help one wake up, and anyone who can bring himself to swallow the stale, overboiled, gritty liquid mixture of coffee grounds and skinlike milk that the French call *café au lait* is a man who wakes up quickly. One does not linger over French morning breakfast. It prepares one swiftly for facing a hostile world on a particularly bad day. It has, however, one advantage, and this is the genius of the French, for, after downing a bowl of morning *café au lait,* anything one meets later in the day seems better in comparison.

The French do not believe in smiling service either. In this respect they are closer to the Americans, another nation which is founded on the principle that all men are born equal, a notion that does not make for pleasant servants. The difference between the American Declaration of Independence and Bill of Rights and the French Déclaration des Droits de l'Homme is that we hold that all men are born equal and the French argue that all men are born *and remain* equal in their rights before the law. There is one class of men who have never quite accepted this egalitarian principle. They are the waiters. They feel superior. The only way to treat them is to accept the fact of their superiority and ask their advice or petition for their help. You will then do much better than you could on your own.

This rule applies to all who are in service but particularly to French cab drivers. There may be no such thing as a French national race, but there certainly is a special race of taxicab drivers, a race apart. It is not that they regard themselves as superior to all other men; it is that they are not members of the human race, or at least do not subscribe to normal rules of human behavior.

Cab drivers cannot be argued with, nor can one appeal to their better feelings or human emotions, for they have none. There is only one attitude to adopt, the same attitude in fact to adopt when dealing in general with Frenchmen: regard them as fascinating people, be interested in what they have to say, read them as one would read a psychological thriller, and, if an appeal has to be made, then appeal to the mind, not to the heart. They have magnificent minds. They can be maddening but never boring.

Recently, in Paris, I was riding home in a cab that was speeding at a frightening pace through a crowded street. Despite the many years I have lived in Paris, I failed to take my own advice and I appealed to the driver to go more slowly. He promptly increased his speed, muttering oaths under his breath. Making the mistake of getting angry myself, I shouted at him to slow down. He shouted back, and increased the peril by turning around to glare at me and to tell me that he was a working man, that he had a family to support, that taxes were too high, that prices were rising, that he had to go fast in order to earn a living and could not afford to dawdle along simply to please a rich bourgeois who did not have to hurry.

I decided to try the shock treatment and to direct myself to his mind. I shouted, as peremptorily as I could in my terror: "I *order* you to slow down!" And that did it, as I knew it would.

The brakes screamed and I was tossed forward against the partition as he pulled the cab sharply over the curb.

"Did I hear you say 'I order you'?" the driver asked in a strangled voice.

"Yes, that's what I said. And before you say another word, just hear me out," I said in as calm a voice as possible. "You think you own this cab and can conduct it as you see fit within the law, or outside the law if you can get away with it. Well, you are certainly free to do so when you are alone in it, but not with a fare. Do you not realize that at this moment I am in effect the owner of this cab?"

The driver looked at me in complete astonishment, not sure if I were mad but beginning to be interested in what I was saying. "So you own the cab, do you? And just how do you arrive at that conclusion?" he asked.

"Well," I replied, "I am not exactly the owner. You are. But I am, if you like, the tenant. I have leased the taxi from you and have contracted for your services to deliver me to a given address. By accepting my contract you also accept its terms."

"Ah," he said, pouncing on an opening, and now thoroughly enjoying the debate, "but what are those terms? They are only to deliver you to an address, but I know of no contract specifying the speed of delivery. What about that, eh?" said he triumphantly.

"You have an excellent point," I admitted shamelessly, knowing that I now had made progress by letting him outargue me. "However," I added, "I am legally in possession of this cab until I choose to let you go. Since you have a certain rate for waiting time, I could, if I chose to do so, keep you waiting at the address on arrival and make you lose a good deal more time than you would lose if you drove me more slowly. I regard this as a kind of stalemate. You can drive me rapidly, but I can make you wait. Can we compromise? Drive me slowly and I will release you rapidly? It is an equal bargain."

He looked at me stony-faced for a long moment, but there was a bright gleam in his eyes as he finally said: "At what speed would Monsieur my tenant like to be conducted before the imminent expiration of the lease?"

I suggested that fifty kilometers an hour would be reasonable and, with a clash of gears, we were off again, at exactly fifty kilometers an hour, which was not exactly reasonable but was, I thought, the minimum he would accept as consistent with his dignity.

A dignified appeal to the intellect, an invitation to a debate, intrigues Frenchmen at every level of society, from cab driver to cabinet minister. Even the President of the Republic, the one man in France with whom one does not argue, is susceptible to argument if it is properly presented.

Like every reporter in Paris, I tried by every means, through every influence and contact I had, to get an audience with Charles de Gaulle, after May 13, 1958. Try as I would, I had no success. De Gaulle would not see a foreign journalist. He saw very few French journalists, perhaps five or six at the most, including owners of big papers. As for an interview, it was absolutely out of the question. De Gaulle had never granted an interview for publication. After he became President of the Republic, all hope of an interview vanished, because the chief of state does not give interviews in France. It is similar to the tradition in Britain and America.

I was still determined to get to see Charles de Gaulle and, if possible, to interview him. I waited for an opportunity to renew my request in a manner that would appeal to his logical mind and his Frenchman's love of a clever argument, even if he has to lose it.

The opportunity came in the spring of 1959, almost a year after his return to office. He had still not seen a foreign journalist, with one exception, and that was Walter Lippmann. As one of De Gaulle's aides said, with frosty French hauteur: "Mr. Lippmann was not received as a journalist. He was granted an audience as a distinguished historian of contemporary world affairs."

That gave me the opening I had been looking for.

I sent a letter to the Presidential Palace explaining that I had been commissioned by the *Saturday Review* to write a review of the memoirs of Charles de Gaulle. I said that it would be very useful for me to see the author and discuss the memoirs with him, to permit me to do a more useful and accurate analysis of his works. I added that I was doing this not as a reporter but as a writer myself, author of *As France Goes*, a contemporary history of France. I did not want to see the President of the Republic of France, I pointed out. I desired only to see an author, a French historian, whose name was Charles de Gaulle. I offered to limit my conversation to the memoirs and to past history, in a purely literary conversation "between authors" and not between a reporter and a President.

Three days later my phone rang, and a presidential aide, whom I knew well and who had many times explained to me why I could not see De Gaulle, wished me good morning and dryly added: "If the author of *As France Goes* is free on Friday morning, the author of *De Gaulle's memoirs* would be delighted to receive him." I saw Charles de Gaulle that Friday and we talked for an hour of many things. I was authorized to write my review and to quote De Gaulle, thus breaking his rule against interviews, except that technically speaking the rule was not broken, for the authorization empowered me not to write an interview but "to recount a literary conversation." This is French wit at its driest. The French love a good joke but it must be subtle and intellectual. They have a fine sense of humor but not of comedy and rarely if ever of farce. There is no word in French for "belly laugh."

The nearest French equivalent to the Anglo-Saxon term "belly laugh" is *le fou-rire*, "mad laughter." It is significant of French attitudes that hearty laughter is considered to verge on lunacy. The French are not given to hearty laughter nor to the Anglo-Saxon tradition of "telling jokes." They do not tell jokes in French; they deliver themselves of *boutades*, which means witty sallies or, as Americans put it, repartee. Anglo-Saxon humor is more genial than the caustic wit of the French. The Americans tend toward the pornographic in their "jokes," and the British to the scatological, two areas of low comedy which the French abhor. "Dirty jokes" are virtually unknown in French society, but the French will use language to describe someone who is stupid which could never possibly be used in the English language in mixed society.

A number of basic attitudes may be illustrated by semantics. An American mother, for example, giving advice to a daughter or son going out for the evening, or leaving on holiday, would almost certainly end by saying: "Be good." A French mother, with the wisdom of a long history behind her, and few illusions about the human race, would just as certainly conclude her counsel with the admonition: *"Sois sage"*—"Be wise."

The Anglo-Saxon phrase "fair play," containing a basic concept of correct social behavior, does not exist in the French language and cannot be translated. Similarly, one cannot translate into French the expression, or the idea, "gentleman's agreement." Not that the French do not play fair or are not gentlemen. It is just that the French have a Roman concept of statute law as against the Saxon concept of common law or customs. As for "playing fair," this is a strange foreign concept, vague, sentimental, and impossible to apply logically. One can know with a measure of certainty or exactness what is correct or incorrect, what is legal or illegal, but who can truly define what is fair and unfair? This is a concept rejected by the Cartesian mind, of which the French are so proud.

Their pride in being Cartesian is one of the many paradoxes and deceptions of French society. Despite their conscious effort to be logical and to follow the dictate of Descartes, the French are, underneath their logical, cynical masks, a very sentimental and illogical people, easily swayed by emotions. They may proclaim, "I think, therefore I am," but inside every Frenchman there is a secret disciple of the Christian philosopher Pascal, whispering the counterpoint of rationalism: "The heart has reasons that reason does not know."

A logical, pragmatic people would not have so long suffered through wars—international, colonial, and civil—as often and as long as the French. The Americans, supposedly so sentimental and swayed by emotions, are far more practical than the French. We are a nation that hates war. We have always been slow getting into world wars and fast getting out of them. After the First and Second World Wars we demobilized as fast as we possibly could, wrecking almost overnight one of the greatest armies the world had ever known. We accepted the galling fact of stalemate and ended the Korean War, although it stung our national pride to quit without a victory. The French, however, fought on in Indochina for seven long, exhausting years and then followed up with another struggle in Algeria, which is in its sixth year as these lines are being written, in the closing weeks of 1959. The French are a stubborn rather than a logical people.

It is not logical for the French to divert money, skills, and energies, badly needed elsewhere, on their single-minded drive to have a few atomic bombs, just at a moment when the atomic powers are discussing a cessation of atomic testing. The French know perfectly well, and will admit it if pressed hard enough, that they can never hope to have a big atomic military stock. But they want what they consider to be the prestige of being an atomic power. Yet if you ask a Frenchman to name the great powers of the world, he will unhesitatingly reply, "America and Russia," without naming Great Britain, despite the fact that Britain does have a stock of atomic weapons. If Frenchmen do not recognize Britain as a great power because of its atom bombs, then why should France spend so much national strength on getting to where Britain is, if Britain is not great?

I have asked this question of dozens of French friends, including cabinet ministers, who espouse the atomic military program. When I point out the illogicality of their policy, and point up the case of atomic but not powerful Britain, my French friends always look surprised, as though the idea had never occurred to them. They even admire the logic of my argument and frequently say it is a very powerful contradiction of their position; nevertheless, they just as stubbornly insist that they will have their atomic explosion, logical or not.

The same Frenchmen will tell you, with grim and unyielding faces, that Algeria is French and will always be a part of France, when they know very well that this is, at the very best, a policy that cannot be maintained very much longer. Sometimes, at the end of a long evening, when defenses are down, these Frenchmen will admit that it is only a matter of time before Algeria becomes an independent nation. Some optimists put it at twenty years, some at ten, but all admit that sooner or later there must be a change in Algeria. When one suggests that, if this is true, then surely sooner is better than later, in the interests of France and the French, irrespective of Algeria itself, one meets the same illogical attitude that reveals itself in the discussion of atomic weapons: right or wrong, this is the way we are going to do it.

This French fatalism, this acceptance of needless sacrifice, this tendency to prefer the shadow to the substance, was never more poignantly illustrated than by the angry statement once made by the then President of the Republic, Vincent Auriol, who said: "France has a right to retire into her grief!" This is the ultimate rejection of reality, the final retreat from a harsh world of fact into the world of fantasy. It borders dangerously on the pathological. The truth is that France does not have the right to retreat from the world and indulge herself in self-pity and futile tears. No man worthy of leading so great a people as the French has the right to lead them into neurotic demonstrations of pathos. France cannot leave the world, of which she is a most important part, any more than she can lead that world as once she did. Extreme introversion or extroversion is fitting and possible only for very small or very large countries or countries geographically isolated, and France is none of these.

France is a middle-sized, middle-class country whose only extreme is a surfeit of natural blessings prodigally wasted. All of France, north to south, east to west, can be traversed in about two hours by plane. Yet inside that relatively small hexagon is an almost complete variety of everything a country needs for success.

Switzerland may be the country of mountains in Europe, but the tallest, loveliest mountain peak of the continent, Mont Blanc, is on the French side of the Alpine frontier. Lake Leman is a jewel but no lovelier than Lake Annecy on the French side, and on the shores of Lake Annecy there is the genial host, Père Bise, who presides over one of the greatest restaurants in the world. Many a time have I sat in Geneva, at an international conference, thinking that one of the most attractive features of that very lovely Swiss city is the fact that in twenty minutes, in any direction, one can be in France, in even more beautiful surroundings, in far better inns. Any country that can boast of two such heavenly spots so close to each other as the Père Bise inn, at Talloires, and Verdier's inn, La Verniaz, just above Evian, is entitled to call itself a paradise.

Any country that could boast of two or three inns of that quality could claim first rank on the traveler's list of places to visit. But

France can claim a dozen and more jewels in her crown, each of
which is a rare gem. The inn of William the Conqueror, in Dives-
sur-Mer, built on the site from which the Norman Bastard
launched the armada that conquered England in 1066, can well
claim to be one of the most beautiful in the world, with one of
the finest kitchens and superb cellars. Whenever I am in Normandy, driving through the soft green farmlands, speckled with
red poppies and bright yellow mustard, en route to the rustic flowered garden of Guillaume le Conquérant, I think that this surely
must be the loveliest site of all, until I find myself in Savoy, driving through the wooded valleys in the shadow of the snow-capped
Mont Blanc, heading for La Verniaz and Monsieur Verdier's
truite saumonée, served with a chilled Montrachet 1949, from the
vineyard of the Marquis Delaguiche . . . until I find myself twisting through the groves of gnarled brier trees, in the gold-rose twilight of Provence, descending toward the Côtes des Maures, whose
terra-cotta cliffs jut out over the sapphire waters of the Mediterranean . . . until, until—one could add countless untils of one's vision
of beauty and graceful living in that tranquil-tortured bittersweet
land of France.

There is coal in abundance in the North, where the hard-working skilled miners have for more than a decade held the European
record for production per man. There is iron ore in the East, fish
and fruit in the West, wheat in the center, grapes everywhere,
gas and oil in the Southwest, uranium in the hills, and vegetables
in the gardens—all in greater quantity per head of inhabitant and
in proportion to the area than in any other country in Europe
and possibly in the world. The French need export only some
15 per cent of the national product to pay for the imports it needs
from the outside world, whereas less favored nations, such as Denmark, Germany, and Holland, must export up to half their total
resources to buy what they need and do not have within their own
borders. France is literally a Garden of Eden for its own people
as well as a fairyland for foreign visitors. The trouble is that the
greatest crop of all the fertile crops in France for centuries past
has been the apple of discord. The French are their own worst
enemies, and when they are not fighting with their neighbors or

quarreling with their best friends they are fighting among themselves. Only a nation as rich and fertile as France, with so skilled a people, could so brilliantly have survived its own follies.

The question everyone has been asking for many years now is: How long can France survive these follies, or how long will France continue to pursue policies which seem so foolish to her friends and allies?

Many had hoped that the return to power of Charles de Gaulle would restore a stability and a sense of purpose that France so badly lacked during the up-and-down days of the collapsing governments of the Fourth Republic. In America, as in England, Germany, and Italy, De Gaulle's return was cheered by the majority of the people. They knew from past experience that De Gaulle might well be a difficult ally, but they were prepared to deal with a strong man if he could give strength back to one of the key countries in the Western alliance. It may be hard to make a deal with De Gaulle, but he is a man of integrity and once he makes a deal he will keep it. Too many deals had been made with previous French governments, only to collapse as the governments fell.

Charles de Gaulle, as expected, has proved to be a difficult ally. Since his return to power France has been a member of the Atlantic Alliance in name only. De Gaulle has shaken the alliance as it had never been shaken before, except from outside. He has insisted on revising the structure and purpose of the alliance. He finds it too narrowly based on Europe and believes that an alliance must be wider, broader, more intense. He does not think one can be allies in Europe but rivals in Africa and Asia. He does not believe that one can base an alliance on negative opposition to one adversary, without some positive program for extending influence and making friends in noncommitted areas, by waging economic as well as political warfare.

These ideas are not particularly original with De Gaulle. NATO Secretary General, Paul Henri Spaak of Belgium, has long advocated closer political co-ordination on a broader scale. American congressmen in 1958, before De Gaulle, proposed the creation of an International Loan Association, to help underdeveloped countries, and took measures to begin operations in 1959. Former Prime Minister Edgar Faure had proposed a joint development program of the great powers for the less-favored nations as far back as the summit conference of 1955. What made De Gaulle's proposals important rather than original was the power and personality of De Gaulle himself.

Unlike other French Prime Ministers or Presidents, Charles de Gaulle is in a position to commit his country to his own plans. And unlike others, De Gaulle is prepared to back his plans against friend and foe alike. Since neither America nor Britain gave him satisfaction on his request for a broadening of NATO, with a parallel increase of French authority in the alliance, De Gaulle ordered his ambassadors and generals to stop co-operating on NATO programs. He would not integrate France into NATO's air-defense system. He would not permit Americans to stockpile atomic weapons in France, thereby putting out of commission American bombers based in France, for bombers without bombs are not of great value. He announced that in time of war the French Mediterranean Fleet would be withdrawn from the NATO command, for France, he said, had to protect its own interests in Algeria, in view of the allies' failure to give France support there. And his Prime Minister, Michel Debré, told Parliament that French support for NATO in the future would depend on NATO's support for France in Algeria.

All this made 1959 one of the most critical years in the history of the Western alliance. And this happened just at a historic turning point, when for the first time a Russian chief of government, communist or czarist, visited the United States, while an American chief executive was invited to visit the Soviet Union for the first time in peacetime history. Charles de Gaulle could not have chosen a worse moment to shake up NATO, not from NATO's viewpoint necessarily, but from the viewpoint of French interests, for obviously French co-operation is somewhat depreciated in value if one is finding the common adversary more approachable.

The search for a thaw in the cold war with Russia is still very new and the chances of finding a way to live together peacefully still very fragile. New crises may well break out at any time. Berlin and Laos are time bombs that have been ticking away ever since the end of the last war, and the Communists can move the hands to zero hour any time they choose. NATO is still and should remain a fundamental plank in the foreign-policy platforms of all Western nations. It would certainly be flirting with disaster to trust any Soviet shift in policy to the extent of abandoning or weakening one of our main arms of defense. So France is still a most valuable ally. But this cuts both ways, and the alliance is at least as important to the French as the French are to it. To put it realistically, it is more important to the French, for fourteen nations, if they have to, can get along without one, better than that one can get along without the other fourteen.

This is a reality that the present French regime does not like to contemplate. Some French leaders appear to be in an almost suicidal mood. Men like Debré and Jacques Soustelle quite genuinely feel that Algeria is more important to France than NATO. Or, put another way, NATO is too costly an alliance if it means losing Algeria. And they have persuaded themselves that their allies in NATO are at least partially responsible for their troubles in Algeria, by failing to give them the support they need. Some French politicians, the most vocal of course, have actually convinced themselves that their "friends" covet the oil treasures of the Sahara and are trying to get the French out so that they can move in. This has become an obsessive and unreasoning fear with many Frenchmen. The Sahara has become a kind of symbol of a new future, which will permit France to be independent of Middle East oil, and of American dollars, and to maintain a position as a great world power.

There is just enough truth in this obsession to give it durability. The oil of the Sahara is very important. Western countries and Western companies would certainly like to share in its exploitation and would certainly make every effort to implant their influence if French influence were eliminated. But this is very different from imagining, as many French do, that Western countries or companies would actually like to force the French out. This is, in fact, totally absurd.

No one would be happier than the Americans if the French

were to make peace in Algeria and keep Algeria French. Anyone who thinks that America covets French territory or oil is either totally ignorant or willfully seeks to make mischief. The French themselves obviously do not believe their own propaganda, for it was the government of Michel Debré and Jacques Soustelle that went further than any previous government in offering advantages to American engineering and oil companies to help develop the Sahara. If they fear our motives, why do they ask us to come in with them?

The truth is that Americans—and not only Americans, for one can include most of France's neighbors and allies—do not trust French motives in Algeria and have not had confidence in France's ability to hold Algeria. The truth is, too, that Algeria may be vitally important to France, but no more important to the allies than all of the other African territories which have emerged and are emerging as independent nations and peoples and who all look upon Algeria as a true test of the West. If we hold Algeria, with the French, against the Algerians, while the revolt spreads and increases in intensity, then all of Africa may turn against all of NATO. And how long, under those conditions, could Algeria be held? These questions, these other considerations, are quite important to the allies but they are simply dismissed by the French.

Until these questions are satisfactorily answered, it will be impossible to answer the primary question: whither France, whither the alliance? This reporter predicted three years before the coup of May 13, 1958, that Algeria would be the graveyard of the Fourth Republic of France. I was not alone in so predicting. Many Paris-based foreign correspondents saw the end in sight long before it came. Many Frenchmen saw it themselves but seemed helpless to do anything about it. The same may be said today, of the Fifth Republic. Algeria may be the graveyard of De Gaulle's regime, too, if the conflict there continues very much longer.

In the period 1958–59 France became more and more turned in upon herself, more and more isolated from her friends. The initial prestige and rebirth of hope with the return of De Gaulle in 1958 began to decline and give way to disenchantment in 1959. When Eisenhower invited Khrushchev to Washington, all of the Western allies expressed public enthusiasm for the initiative, while some expressed private misgivings. Only the French expressed public misgivings, as Prime Minister Debré, in a political speech, in late August, shortly before Eisenhower's own trip to France, told his people that France must take care not to be crushed between the two great powers. Paris was alive with inspired reports about France taking the lead in creating a European "third force," as though the Germans, Italians, Belgians, Dutch, and others would choose to cut themselves voluntarily off from America, just at a moment when Americans were beginning to wonder whether they needed to continue their expensive alliance with the Europeans. One wonders why the French imagine for a single moment that other Europeans would accept French leadership in place of American leadership, and to what end?

There is a nightmarish quality of utter unreality to this extraordinary development. One keeps thinking that one will wake up any moment. There are so many reasons for France and America to preserve and strengthen their traditional friendship, so many compelling reasons for France to seek to extend her alliances rather than reduce them, that one can hardly believe what is happening.

Certainly the French do have reasons, many reasons, for resenting allied policies. If I were French I would resent America's refusal to help France develop an atomic program. The French made a vital contribution to our own first atom bomb, without which we may not have had it in time for us to use it the way we did and to seize world leadership in the atomic field. The work of Joliot, Halbans, and Kowarski in Paris before the war, in demonstrating the phenomenon of a chain reaction in the splitting of the atom, was itself a vital link in the chain that led to Einstein's bringing this work to the attention of Roosevelt. The French feel that the very least we might do is to help them now by making available our knowledge and experience, since it is certainly no secret to the Russians, who have their own highly ad-

vanced atomic establishment. The French have a justified griev-
ance in this area, and in many other areas.

But justifiable grievances, on both sides—and each has many
justified complaints about the other—cannot be settled by a public
brawl. The crisis of relations among old friends is far too serious
for mutual name calling. The need is not to prove who is right
or wrong but rather to eliminate the wrongs, so that everyone
can be rightly satisfied as far as it is possible to satisfy national
ambitions and interests.

The French and the Germans fought each other for one thousand years until in this mid-century they decided to embark upon
a new course of co-operation in a common market, leading to a
Community of Europe. If the French and Germans can be recon-
ciled, if America can seek conciliation with Russia, then perhaps
someday soon America and France can end their quarrels. It will
probably be more difficult, since America and France have never
made war upon each other, have always been friends.

It is so much more difficult to forgive a friend than an enemy.

SPAIN AND
PORTUGAL

Emmet Crozier

After nearly forty years in American journalism, including service as war correspondent and editorial writer for the New York Herald Tribune, Emmet Crozier retired in 1949 to travel and write books. His travels in 1956 took him to Spain, where an interest originally discovered in the pages of Washington Irving and Prescott was revived and extended. On that first Spanish journey, Crozier followed the tourist trail out of Madrid to El Escorial and Toledo, watched gypsies dance in the caves of Sacro Monte at Granada, saw Holy Week's pageantry in Málaga. Two years later he returned for a longer stay at Torremolinos on the Costa del Sol to work on a book. He has never seen a bullfight.

Crozier began newspaper work on the Kansas City Star *in 1912, coming to New York in 1918 to work on the* Evening Sun *and subsequently on the old* Herald, *the* Evening World, *and the* Globe. *He wrote scenarios at Paramount's Astoria studio in 1925 and 1926, served as director of public relations for the Radio Corporation of America from 1928 to 1931. A founding member of the American Newspaper Guild, he became its first national treasurer, serving in 1933, 1934, and 1935.*

Crozier is the author of Yankee Reporters: 1861–1865, *a study of Civil War journalism, and* American Reporters on the Western Front: 1914–1918, *published in 1956 and 1959, respectively. A billiard enthusiast, he also wrote* Thirty Years of Billiards *with the late Willie Hoppe. He is married and between travels lives in Bethel, Connecticut.*

SPAIN AND PORTUGAL

A mountain range separates Spain and Portugal from the rest of
Europe, and that simple fact of geography, although it did not
balk Napoleon's armies, may account for some of the isolation
and contrariness that distinguish Iberia in the modern world. Below the high Pyrenees, Spain and Portugal exist side by side in a
curious political vacuum. They are on the edge of Europe, like
England and Russia, yet somehow apart from it. In recent times
two great wars roared over the face of Europe, upsetting thrones,
changing governments and boundaries; but they did not change
anything below the Pyrenees. Invisible barriers, more formidable
than the mountain wall, seem to cut the peoples of the peninsula
off from twentieth-century ideas and make them prisoners of
their own history. Once they were great nations, but they are not
great now. Beautiful and melancholy, warmed by a friendly sun,
washed by Atlantic tides and the storied Mediterranean, Spain
and Portugal present a scenic panorama of great beauty for the
tourist, a bargain counter for the thrifty, a tragic enigma for the
student of history.

The Iberian Peninsula would not now seem so drowsy and im-
potent if it had not played such a vital role in shaping the modern
world. In the late fifteenth and early sixteenth centuries, Spain
and Portugal led all Europe in the discovery of new continents
across the Atlantic. Their navigators broke through those formidable ocean barriers which, since prehistoric times, had confined
civilization and men's minds to the Mediterranean basin. Their
explorers were the first to open the Western Hemisphere to coloni-

zation and Christianity. They rounded Africa and circumnavigated the globe. They were the first to see the world whole as we know it, geographically, today. For a brief century or two all the new lands they discovered, including the great quantities of gold which they found in Mexico and Peru, were theirs to exploit.

Not much of those vast colonial empires is left to them. They did not know how to govern or administer and they fought among themselves. Their golden age was soon over. They still have their ancient pride and a certain awareness of their destiny, but both Spain and Portugal have fallen behind in the march of the twentieth century. Neither country wields much power in world affairs. No valid political idea—except the negative concept of anticommunism—has stirred the peninsula in modern times. Their literary heritage is dormant. Their economy is tied to the nineteenth century.

The causes of Iberian backwardness are rooted deep in the past, yet some factors contributing to the plight of these amiable peoples lie close to the surface. Education has been neglected or left to the sectarian interests of the Jesuits. Illiteracy, widespread in Portugal and Andalusia, retards the flow of ideas and narrows the peninsular vision. In all Europe only Bulgaria, Greece, and Albania have so large a proportion of citizens unable to read or write. From this indifference toward education flows a corresponding lag in science, research, and invention.

Spain and Portugal lack essential raw materials (as well as competitive zest) to develop industrially. Their mines yield some copper, zinc, mercury, wolfram, and a little silver; the coal is poor and scarce. If there is any oil under the varied terrain, they have failed to discover it. They are just beginning to harness their water power. Such heavy machinery as the two countries possess is old and outmoded. Industrial methods are antiquated. Even with lower wage scales, they cannot compete with their European neighbors.

Iberians still place their main reliance on agriculture. A majority of the people in both Spain and Portugal live close to the soil. In the temperate climate they grow olives, wheat, grapes, citrus fruits, cork. The main sources of foreign exchange for both countries are the wine, olive oil, and cork products they export to northern countries and the United States. Agricultural methods are primitive. Horses, mules, and donkeys provide most of the farmers' motive power, but the tractor is becoming a more familiar sight on the rural landscape. Efficient use of the land is retarded, particularly in Spain, by absentee-landlordism, ignorance, and tradition.

Where the Iberians really turn their backs on the modern world is in the field of government. Elsewhere in Europe, and in fact throughout most of the world (except in Communist and satellite countries), liberal constitutional government makes hopeful progress, or at least struggles determinedly to survive. Elsewhere men and women vote, laws are passed and amended, politicians debate taxation, the welfare state, free enterprise, and free trade.

But in Spain all authority rests in the dictatorship of the Caudillo, General Francisco Franco, whose totalitarian power is sustained by the Roman Catholic Church and the Army.

In Portugal it is a college professor, Dr. Antonio de Oliveira Salazar, who directs the authoritarian regime and makes the decisions. Dr. Salazar's economic reforms have balanced the Portuguese budget and made the escudo one of the soundest currencies in the world. Nevertheless, despite his amiable temperament and philosophic mind, he is a dictator.

In Spain for the last twenty years, and to a lesser extent in Portugal since 1931, no free elections have been held to give the people a voice in their government, no healthy ferment of political debate has been encouraged. Iberian inertia and political intransigency have created a climate in which individual freedom languishes and the political tyrannosaurus survives.

If Spain and Portugal have failed to match the material progress and political maturity of other Western countries, their very backwardness has made possible the preservation of an old-world atmosphere and a gracious heritage from the past. Nowhere else in Europe does life jog along at such an easy pace. The natural beauty of the land is enhanced by old towers and castles, cathedrals out of the Middle Ages, airy Moorish palaces, Roman ruins. Winding mountain roads, wayside inns, olive groves, and small hill towns are much as they were when Washington Irving set out on horseback from Seville in 1829 to journey to Granada. Women still wash their clothes at roadside streams. The black leather hats of the Guardia Civil are unchanged since the Napoleonic Wars. Bullfights, fiestas, Holy Week processions, costumes, and customs all preserve the charm of a bygone time. Here is the World's Fair of the Past.

The people have a special quality which is not so easy to classify or describe. The struggle to survive has made them tough and resilient, like their Toledo steel, yet they are friendly and hospitable. Many are poor but none is servile. Even those in humble circumstances possess integrity and ancient pride. Each preserves his individuality, each has an inner dignity, a stubbornness, an Iberian ego. Politically and intellectually, each goes his own way. It would be difficult to make them understand what we mean by "inferiority complex" and it is difficult to get them to agree on anything or work together.

Portugal is not quite as large as Indiana. Spain's land area is about two thirds the size of Texas. The entire Iberian Peninsula with its island appendages—the Balearics in the Mediterranean (Majorca, Minorca, and Ibiza) and the Azores and Canaries in the Atlantic—would fit easily inside our second-largest state. (Texas would be confused by their four languages and their politics.)

The land area of some 230,000 square miles has an average altitude of 2000 feet, higher than any country in Europe except Switzerland. Its main feature is a great central plain, or tableland, which in parts of New Castile reminds the visitor of Kansas or Nebraska. In the North, rising in the foothills of the Cantabrians in Old Castile, the river Ebro follows a leisurely course southeastward to the Mediterranean, flowing with the gentle tilt of the plain across a corner of Navarre, through Aragon and Catalonia, and creating a broad estuary as it reaches the sea below Tarragona. Below the southern edge of the central tableland another great river flows westward from the region of La Mancha to empty into the Atlantic just north of Cádiz. This is the Guadalquivir. Navigable inland as far as Seville, it touches historic Cordova, drains and nourishes Andalusia, Spain's southern region of orange and olive groves and sunshine.

Once the peninsula was united politically or at least lived under one central government. But Portugal, although closely knit to Spain by racial origin and history, was restive under Spanish rule and in 1668 won permanent independence. Geographically compact, blessed by scenery and climate, economically self-sufficient, Portugal now turns its back on Spain and looks to the Atlantic—and England.

Spain divides into fourteen political subdivisions or provinces. Galicia is the northwest corner; then, following the coast and the Pyrenees wall along the northern boundary, come Asturias, the Basque Provinces (Biscay, Guipúzcoa, Alava), Navarre, Aragon, and Catalonia. Again, scanning the map from west to east, Portugal lies below Galicia on the west coast; just inland from Asturias is the ancient kingdom of León, which borders Old Castile. Further east and south New Castile completes the great central plain below Aragon, and south of Catalonia, Valencia lies between the central tableland and the sea. Below León, on the west, Extremadura borders central and southern Portugal. Below it Andalusia reaches both Atlantic and Mediterranean at the peninsula's southern tip, and to the eastward along the sunny coast, Granada and Murcia complete the provincial patchwork.

Each of these Spanish states has its own color and character and dialect. The provinces differ from each other as England from Scotland, or as Massachusetts from Louisiana.

Four languages are spoken on the peninsula: Portuguese, Castilian, Catalan, and Basque. Some classify Catalan as a branch of Castilian Spanish, but it has characteristics of its own, stemming from historical association with the French Roussillon and Provençal. The Basque tongue is a philological curiosity handed down from the primitive Celtiberian culture. There are many dialects.

The people who display such talent for linguistic diversity are descended from a very old Mediterranean strain. The Iberians may have crossed over from North Africa in prehistoic times, when, as geographers believe, there was an isthmus, or land bridge, connecting the two continents across the Strait of Gibraltar. Wherever they came from, they displaced another primitive race, the Ligurians, earliest-known inhabitants of the peninsula, who moved on across southern France and finally settled in northern Italy. By the time Greek traders arrived on the peninsula in the eighth or ninth century B.C., the Ligurians were gone. The Greeks gave the name "Iberians" to the dark, longheaded, smallish people they found living in the basin of the Ebro River, whose ancient name was Iberus.

The term "Iberian" came in time to apply to those living all along the Mediterranean coast and, eventually, to all inhabitants of the peninsula as far north and east as the Rhone Valley.

Two or three centuries before the first Greek traders arrived on the eastern (Mediterranean) shore, Phoenician galleys had passed through the Strait and turned north up the Atlantic coast. Finding a good harbor protected by a jutting arm of land, they established the trading post of Gabes, now Cádiz. Historians place the date of this early Phoenician settlement in the eleventh century before the Christian Era. Cádiz is thus much older than Rome or Alexandria; indeed, it may be the oldest city in Europe which has retained its name and continuity of existence from its original beginning.

From the North, Celts pushed through the Pass of Roncesvalles in the Pyrenees in the sixth century B.C., not to trade with the Iberians, but to settle on the land and mingle their blood with the people from the South. This mingling was so extensive in the Northwest as to produce a Celtiberian sub-race, whose descendants survive in Galicia and the Basque Provinces.

Carthaginians arrived in the fourth century B.C., taking over the Phoenician trade and settlements, dislodging the Greeks from Murcia and Alicante, and founding two important settlements along the east coast, Barcelona and Cartagena. The Carthaginian period was relatively short, but it was dynamic. Not content merely to establish seaports and trade along the coast, the Carthaginians pushed inland, investigated the basin of the Ebro and the great central plain. Stimulated by this vigorous example, the

Iberians extended their own settlements. For the first time the peninsula was explored, traveled, and known from the Pyrenees to the Pillars of Hercules. Accepting the domination of Carthage, the Iberians enlisted in Hannibal's armies and joined the fight against Rome.

After the Second Punic War, Carthage was finished and Rome took over. This was the beginning of an important period in the peninsula's development. From 201 to 133 B.C., Rome's efforts were directed largely to subduing Iberian resistance, but after the fall of Numantia, Spain bowed to Roman arms and civilization. Roads, amphitheaters, aqueducts, laws, language and letters —and above all, order—followed the Roman conquest. The Iberians responded energetically to those civilizing influences. By the beginning of the Christian Era writers of Spanish origin—Seneca, Martial, Lucan, Quintilian—dominated Roman letters. Thousands of officers and soldiers, having won meritorious discharge from long service in Roman armies, settled in Spain and furthered the Romanization of the peninsula. Two of the great Antonine emperors—Trajan and Hadrian—were born in Spain.

The collapse of the Roman Empire in 406 A.D. ended five centuries of order and cultural progress. With the coming of the barbarians, a murky twilight descended over the peninsula, as over the rest of Europe. Later, in this same fifth century, Visigoths arrived to drive out the marauding Vandals and Suevi, destroy the Alans, and reinstate some basic institutions of government on the Roman plan. By the beginning of the eighth century the Visigothic kings, although warring among themselves and involved in a continuous struggle for power, had restored a semblance of civilization, defeated Attila the Hun and his hordes at Orléans, embraced Christianity as the official religion, and established a capital at Toledo.

The present-day traveler in Spain is almost certain, at one stage of his journey, to make the two-hour trip from Madrid to Toledo and, from the heights across the river, survey the classic scene which El Greco portrayed in his "View of Toledo." Frequently, the Spanish guide, after pointing out citadel, cathedral, and other distinguishing features of that remarkable hillside, will draw the visitor's attention to a rude heap of stones at the bend in the river Tagus. Those, he will tell you, are the ruins of the Baths of La Cava. It was there, so the legend runs, that the last king of the Visigoths, Roderic, in 710 seduced, or rather took by force, the beautiful Florinda, daughter of Count Julian.

Actually, the ruins have been identified as the debris of an old stone bridge, and the affair of Florinda and King Roderic is so obscured in the mists of time that historians do not take it too seriously. Yet it persists in the poetry of *Romancero* and it has an abiding place in Spanish legend.

Count Julian, probably a Byzantine, had checked the advance of the Moslem general Musa in North Africa and in 710 governed a Visigoth colony there, with his capital at Ceuta. The legend states he sent his daughter Florinda to Toledo to be educated and to take her place in court society. When the news reached him that King Roderic had ravished the young woman in a riverside bath house, the Count determined to revenge himself by betraying the whole peninsula to the Moslems.

Whether his motive concerned his daughter's honor, as the old poets maintain, or grew out of a political wrangle over Roderic's right to the crown, it is a fact of history that Julian advised the Arab chieftain, Musa, how to cross the Straits and gain a foothold on the Iberian Peninsula. Sooner or later the enterprising Moslems probably would have found their way across the Straits, but Count Julian's connivance hastened the project and won him enduring fame as an arch traitor.

A small expedition led by the Berber El Tarif in 710 confirmed Julian's assurances. The landing place, on the southernmost tip of the peninsula, was named Tarifa; as the point at which the caliphs later collected trade duties and fees, it gave the term "tariff" to modern language.

Another Berber chief, El Tarik, led a larger force across the Strait in the year 711, landing at the foot of the great rock which perpetuates his name in Gibraltar. Pushing inland, the Berbers were joined, as Julian had predicted, by political opponents of the Visigothic king. The invaders defeated Roderic's army near the Laguna de la Janda, between Medina Sidonia and Vejer de la Frontera. After this battle, Roderic disappeared and the Visigothic armies disintegrated. The Berber advance to the north and east was not so much a conquest of arms as a procession. The Arab general, Musa, jealous of the spectacular progress of his Berber lieutenant, arrived with his own troops and a force of Syrians to share the easy conquest. Only one town, Mérida (where some Roman tradition survived), offered more than token resistance. The people of the peninsula had neither will nor leadership to oppose the Moslem advance. Accustomed to the ravages of invading hosts, they saw themselves no worse off under the dark-hued horsemen from Barbary than under the fair-haired Visigoths. The newcomers appeared more interested in grain, goods, and women than in converting Iberians to the faith of Islam. So Africa overran Iberia, and the Star and Crescent moved up to the Pyrenees.

The Moors, or Moslems, remained on the Iberian Peninsula 781 years, from 711 to 1492. During that period Europe emerged from the Dark Ages, embarked on the Crusades, erected the Holy Roman Empire, progressed through the feudalism of the Middle Ages to the dawn of the Renaissance. What was happening below the Pyrenees? Historians have tried to evaluate the influence of Islam on Spain against the background of European development. The Moslem occupation certainly isolated the peninsula from the main stream of European history, but whether Iberian civilization gained or lost is still under debate.

Arab culture reached a high level in the tenth century, and Cordova, under the Caliph AL-Hakem, became the intellectual center of the Moslem Empire. During those dark years, when learning in most of Europe had shrunk to pin points of candlelight in a few obscure monasteries, the Arabs kept open avenues of communication with Damascus, Baghdad, and Constantinople. Every ship from the Levant brought, in addition to articles of commerce, a store of manuscripts—translations from the Greek, scientific literature dealing with astronomy and mathematics, works of philosophy and poetry. AL-Hakem's palace, which housed six hundred thousand volumes, became a sort of academy, or university, attracting scholars from many countries. There were eighty free schools in Cordova. It was here that the great Jewish philosopher Maimonides was born and received his early education. Similar centers of learning developed at Seville, Toledo, and Granada. Algebra, Arabic numerals, a greater knowledge of the stars and the solar system, all flowed from that period of Arabian civilization which came to full flower in Spain.

Rivaling in importance those intellectual attainments was the work of Moslem craftsmen, artists, and architects. They were ingenious and imaginative builders. Many monuments survive in Spain to testify to the daring and originality of their plans and the meticulous detail with which they were carried out. Likewise in trade and commerce, manufacture of textiles, craftsmanship in brass and steel, the Arabs made a substantial contribution to the life of the peninsula.

On the other side of the ledger, the harem brought oriental softness, amorous indulgence, and intrigue to the peninsular scene. Not only did the harem absorb much of the Moslems' time and energy; it produced too many prospective heirs to the caliphate. Many of the internecine wars that divided Arabian authority and broke the land into petty kingdoms had their origins in a harem squabble. Where a caliph produced thirty or forty offspring from a dozen wives, there was certain to be a difference of opinion on the legitimate heir to the throne. Often the caliph was inclined to humor his latest favorite in the matter. As a result of these rivalries and small wars, the peninsula had a multitude of rulers.

Whatever else it did or failed to do, the long Moslem occupation greatly complicated the Iberian racial mixture. To the earlier blending of Phoenician, Greek, Celt, Carthaginian, Roman, and Visigoth (not to mention Vandal, Suevian, and Alan), the Moslems now added Arabs, Berbers, Syrians, and Jews. A further infusion arrived in a large mercenary force of Negroes and Christian slaves, largely Slavonians, forwarded to Spain from North Africa and the slave market at Verdun. One of the paradoxes of Spanish history is that such a melting pot of infidel, Semite, Oriental, and pagan should produce, five or six hundred years later, the most fanatically Catholic of all European countries.

For the newcomer, the way to discover Spain is to go at once to Granada. This small city of gardens and hillsides 270 miles south of Madrid is the key that unlocks a great period of Spanish history. As at Toledo a heap of stones beside the river Tagus gives us the year 710 and the beginning of the Arab-Berber inundation, so Granada leads inevitably to 1492 and the solemn figures of Ferdinand and Isabella.

Granada lies at the edge of a fertile farm region, the Vega de Granada. The climate is mild, almost subtropical most of the year, but a few miles to the east the Sierra Nevada rises in a vast snow-capped range to 11,000 feet (highest peak of the peninsula is Mulhacén, 11,421 feet) and skiers are on the slopes all year, except for a few weeks in midsummer.

Never a great capital under the Moslem occupation, Granada nevertheless became an important trading center. The chiefs of the Nasrides dynasty developed a wide variety of commerce, chiefly the silk trade with Italy, and Granada became the wealthiest city in Spain. Under the patronage of the Nasrides, Granada also became an important seat of learning, literature, and art, attracting such scholars as the historian ibn-Khaldun and the geographer ibn-Batuta. It is probable that Arabian civilization reached one of its highest points at Granada early in the fifteenth century. The monument of this flowering of Islamic culture, and the most celebrated of all the structures left by the Moslems in Spain, is the great hillside fortress palace, the Alhambra.

When all the rest of the peninsula had been reconquered from the Moslems, including the last important Mediterranean port at Málaga, Granada still held out. The red-roofed architectural wonder, with its inner courtyards and halls, its fountains, gardens, and towers, became the last outpost of Islam in Europe, the final stronghold of Moorish arms and ideas.

Ferdinand and Isabella arrived with their armies and camped on the Vega before Granada late in April 1491. The present-day visitor can stand on the plain where they pitched their tents and visualize the scene; the walls of the Alhambra rising on the wooded slope appear much as they did when some forty thousand Moors swarmed along the battlements, yelling defiance at the Christian army. The river Genil still winds through the city, and off to the east the high Sierras frame the scene in grandeur.

The defensive forces had been weakened by a palace struggle for power in which Muley Hassan's first wife, Aisha, aroused by the King's marriage to a beautiful Spanish slave, Zorayah, sought the succession for her son Boabdil. Boabdil succeeded in forcing his father's abdication, but the feud left a divided house, and when the Christian siege threatened, the young king had to call his father back to man the defenses.

The Spanish sovereigns were in no hurry to force the issue. As they distributed their forces and settled down to organize the siege, Moslem knights rode out singly or in small bands, challenging the Christians to equal combat.

As Prescott describes it:

> Numerous were the combats which took place between the high-mettled cavaliers on both sides, who met on the level arena as on a tilting ground, where they might display their prowess in the presence of the assembled beauty and chivalry of their respective nations; for the Spanish camp was graced, as usual, by the presence of Queen Isabella and the Infantas, with the courtly train of ladies who had accompanied their mistress from the Alcala la Real.

When summer waned without a decisive encounter, the Christians built a town of stone and stucco a few miles west of the city to house their military establishment. The construction of this town, which they called Santa Fe, indicated the fixed purpose of the Spanish sovereigns and filled the defenders with dismay. In the autumn, the Moors opened negotiations for surrender.

While these carefully guarded negotiations were in progress, the Italian navigator Christopher Columbus appeared at the camp of Ferdinand and Isabella, accompanied by his sponsor, Juan Perez. Together they waited for a propitious time to lay before the Catholic sovereigns the project of a voyage of discovery across the western ocean. Columbus was present when, on January 2, 1492, the Spanish armies with their banners marched into Granada to receive the capitulation of the Moors and plant a large cross of silver on the wall of the Alhambra. The last Moorish stronghold had fallen; the way was open, after long, exhausting campaigns, to bring peace to Spain and unite the country for the first time under the Catholic monarchs. The propitious moment had indeed arrived.

Every schoolboy knows how Isabella offered to pawn her jewels to further Columbus' project, but the historians tell us this was not necessary. The cost was only seventeen thousand florins, and although the royal treasury had been depleted by the costly wars against the Moslems, the receiver Santangel was able to provide the necessary funds out of Aragonese revenues.

It is also well known that Ferdinand was indifferent to the Italian navigator's plan, considering it visionary; but his principal objection was that Columbus demanded too large a share of the rewards, in addition to titles and governing authority over the newly discovered lands, if any. When Columbus refused to accept lesser conditions, Ferdinand rejected the whole project, and the disappointed Italian was starting his return journey to the coast when overtaken by messengers directing him to return and lay his case once more before the Queen.

What is not so well known is that Columbus, in addition to holding out the prospect of a new trade route to Cathay, outlined the project to Isabella in terms of a crusade. He would not only discover new lands, and a shorter route to the Orient; he would also use the discovery, and its money rewards, to attack the infidel from the East and recover the Holy Land. It may have been the bright illusion of this crusade to end all crusades which finally won Her Catholic Majesty. Agreement was reached and the papers signed at Santa Fe on April 17, 1492.

All this comes alive at Granada. It is impossible to visit the place without feeling the heartbeat of Spanish history: Spain unified at last under Ferdinand and Isabella; Spain rid of the Moslem intruder after 781 years of bondage; Spain embarking on unknown seas; Granada the birthplace of modern Spain and the gateway to the new world.

The well-to-do traveler will find the Alhambra Palace, overlooking the grounds of the Alhambra, one of the fine hotels of Europe. Some discerning visitors prefer the more modest Parador San Francisco, operated by the Government Tourist Agency. This inn, once a Franciscan monastery, adjoins the Alhambra, and its terrace affords a view of the Generalife, the summer palace of the Granada caliphs.

The guidebooks suggest, in addition to the traditional tours through the Alhambra and the Generalife, a visit to the Carthusian monastery, or Cartuja, whose *sagrario* offers a superb example of Spanish Baroque art, and at night, a trip to Sacro Monte, where in whitewashed caves hollowed out in the hillside gypsies dance the *zambra*.

For many, the most solemn moment of the Granada adventure is a visit to the Royal Chapel, which adjoins the cathedral. Ferdinand and Isabella are buried here, near the scene of their great triumph. Larger than most cathedral appendages, the Royal Chapel contains a fine plateresque grille, the work of Bartolomé de Jaén, with heraldic scenes and Biblical episodes. The tombs in the center of the chapel are of Carrara marble, carved by Dominico Fancelli in Genoa. In a nearby alcove are some relics of the two monarchs, Isabella's crown and scepter, and a chest and mirror which accompanied her travels; Ferdinand's sword and a parchment containing his plans for the reconquest of Spain. The carved marble tombs, heraldic scenes and devices, the elaborate grille and ornamentation, all seem to deny the royal sovereigns' wish for a simple resting place, without pomp or ostentation. But a visit to the crypt discloses how the royal wish has been observed. A short flight of steps leads to the chamber directly below the marble effigies. Here, in a glare of electric light, behind a glass pane, two lead caskets lie side by side. They are small and plain. There is no wreath, or drapery or inscription. Just the two leaden boxes under the electric bulbs. As the visitors follow each other down the steps of the crypt, an attendant keeps the line moving slowly toward the ascending stairway. There is just time to glance at the stark entombment; small in stature, for the caskets are not six feet long, and one glance takes it all in.

Ferdinand and Isabella, together. Here in Granada, where they shared the triumph over the infidel and started Columbus on his journey.

After Granada, Seville. The Andalusian capital is known the world over for its elaborate and colorful celebration of Holy Week. Other cities in the South of Spain, including Málaga and Granada, observe the religious occasion with processions and ceremonial pomp, but Seville surpasses all others in the beauty and splendor of her Holy Week festival.

Ten days before Easter Sunday, the city begins to fill up with visitors. They come from all parts of Europe, some from overseas, to witness the spectacle and the Andalusian Fair, which follows. Hotel and pension rates are tripled, and the accommodations—especially those with balconies and windows overlooking the procession route—are booked many months in advance.

The organization and direction of the Holy Week pageant is in the hands of Brotherhoods, or Cofradías, semisecret societies representing the city's various churches. Those hooded figures, wearing long robes of various colors, accompany the floats, or *pasos*, as marshals. Suggesting both crusaders and the Ku Klux Klan, they give the affair a medieval atmosphere.

Each year the Brotherhoods invite the wealthy Spanish women of Andalusia to lend their jewels to the Virgin. The response is impressive; diamond necklaces, bracelets, rings, strands of pearls, antique lavalieres, and gold chains pour into the Cofradías' headquarters. These are used to deck the numerous images of the Virgin carried on floats through the city's streets. It is a tradition of Seville that no article of jewelry thus lent to adorn the Virgin has ever been lost, mislaid, or returned to the wrong donor. The drama of the religious pageant is enhanced on Friday night. All lights are extinguished. As the procession moves through the darkened city, lighted only by the candles of the Brotherhood marchers, singers appear on second-story balconies at strategic points. As the float bearing the resplendent image of the Virgin approaches, one voice will sing a *saeta*, or "arrow of song." The notes die away and an answering *saeta* comes from across the street. The verses are brief, the wailing music sad, as if reflecting the anguish of Calvary.

Seville Cathedral is the second-largest church in Christendom, but it can scarcely accommodate all who try to crowd in for the Corpus Christi service; a ceremony in which ten choirboys dance with castanets before the high altar.

Across from the cathedral, whose tower served Stanford White as a model for the original Madison Square Garden, is the Alcazar, a Moorish palace second only to the Alhambra in extent and magnificence. This structure, the great cathedral, the Fine Arts Museum, and the huge tobacco factory vie with the bull ring for the tourists' attention. The Andalusia Palace, formerly the Alfonso XIII, is reputedly the best hotel on the peninsula.

Almost unnoticed among the varied tourist attractions of Seville is a square Greco-Roman building which once housed the mercantile exchange. It is the old Lonja, completed in 1598. The building faces the Plaza del Triunfo, almost in the shadow of the great cathedral, and guides often point it out as they shepherd parties of tourists from the cathedral plaza to the Alcazar.

Inside the old stone building a magnificent brown-and-red marble staircase leads to the second floor. Here is a library of unique interest for Spanish-American scholars—the Archives of the Indies. The thirty thousand volumes, handwritten mostly on parchment or vellum, are the original reports of the Spanish explorers who followed Columbus to the new world in the West. Among them are logs of the voyages, ships' manifests, lists of cargoes, trade accounts, diaries, records of administration, descriptions of the newly discovered land and its inhabitants, tales of treasure. Here, in the handwriting of Cortes, Bernal Díaz, Pizarro, Ponce de León, Narváez, is the new horizon in the Western Hemisphere and the beginning of Spain's golden age. Here Seville takes up the story of Ferdinand and Isabella started at Granada in 1492.

After the navigators and explorers, men of more ordinary occupations crossed to the New World. Carpenters, blacksmiths, and farmers, geologists hunting for gold, botanists, teachers, priests, scholars—they followed their several vocations and applied old skills to new conditions. They wrote letters home. Some of the narratives and reports were published; nearly all were circulated from hand to hand. Many of these are in the archives in the old Lonja.

Something grew out of this that neither Ferdinand and Isabella nor Columbus anticipated. The discoveries in the New World, thus communicated and verified, freed men from the strait jacket of antiquity, disclosed horizons far beyond anything taught by the clergy. For centuries men's minds had been circumscribed by Church authority and preoccupied by the Mediterranean struggle between Islam and Rome. Religious dogma was sacrosanct and the idea which dominated Christendom was a narrow Mediterranean concept—recovery of the Holy Land from the infidel.

Suddenly, in the sixteenth century, all this was changed. A curtain was raised, a fresh wind blew across Europe, a new world perspective broadened the human vision. This was Spain's great contribution, albeit involuntary, to the Renaissance. More important than the gold and the territorial acquisitions, and the new geography which had developed from Columbus' voyages, was the liberation of men's minds. It was individual, self-reliant man who had crossed the ocean. If he could discover a new world, man might also learn to think for himself. Paradoxically, the lesson is better understood elsewhere today than in Spain. Yet if there is any place in Europe where that great liberating stride across the threshold of the New World may be visualized, it is the old Lonja in the Plaza del Triunfo, Seville, where the Archives of the Indies wait at the head of the marble stairs.

Spain's golden age was soon over. Probably the nation came too suddenly to greatness and power and prosperity. Preoccupied with the long struggle against Islam, Spain had no opportunity to develop a code of law, a system of government, a leadership capable of meeting the challenge of the new age. Elsewhere in Europe, despite interminable wars, feudalism had developed slowly into stable and responsible forms of authority. Without any such healthy preparation, Spain suddenly became intoxicated with power and conquest. Great cargoes of gold, wrested from the Aztecs and Incas in Mexico and Peru, came back to fill the royal treasury. The whole peninsula was drained of manpower and deprived of orderly growth as the young gallants hurried overseas or enlisted in the Army for service in the Low Countries and Italy.

At the height of its overseas expansion Spain held the southern half of North America, including what is now California, New Mexico, Arizona, Texas, Louisiana, Mississippi, Alabama, and Florida (which then included the southern portion of present-day Georgia and South Carolina), and Mexico; and all of Central America and South America, except Brazil and Paraguay on the east coast and Patagonia in the South. Its possessions also included Cuba, Puerto Rico, Hispaniola, and the Philippines.

In Europe, at the beginning of the sixteenth century, the Spanish monarchs made a series of brilliant marriages for their children. The Infante Don Juan married Margaret of Austria, daughter of the Emperor Maximilian. The Infanta Juana was married to the Archduke Philip, "the Fair," brother of Margaret and son of the Emperor. This young prince, through his mother, Marguerite of Burgundy, ruled Namur, Brabant, Hainaut, Holland, Zeeland, and Luxembourg—all of Flanders. Finally, completing the royal alliances, Ferdinand married his daughter Catherine of Aragon to the English prince who was soon to become Henry VIII. Spain, in addition to her conquests overseas, was thus allied to England, to the Austrian Hapsburgs, and was involved in the Low Countries and in Naples.

There was more to Spain's golden age than conquest overseas and European domination. It was during this same sixteenth century that Spanish culture flowered in Cervantes' *Don Quixote,* in the construction of some of the country's great cathedrals, in the painting of El Greco, Velásquez, Morales, Zurbarán, Murillo, and Ribera.

In literature, drama, architecture, and art, in the military genius of the Great Captain, Gonzalo de Córdoba, and the intrepid spirit of the Conquistadores, Spain's achievements lifted her for a time to world pre-eminence. If the Hapsburg rulers had brought more common sense and less vanity to the tasks which such greatness imposed upon them, the history of modern Spain might have taken a different course.

From Seville the road leads north across the central plateau to a little hamlet on the edge of the Sierra de Guadarrama thirty-one miles northwest of Madrid. The name of the place is El Escorial, which means slag heap, or what is left of a mine when the ore has been worked out. The little hamlet's name, El Escorial, also applies to an enormous stone building erected here by Philip II. The cornerstone for the monumental edifice was laid in 1563, the year before William Shakespeare was born at Stratford on Avon, and two years before the Spaniards built the first settlement on the North American continent at St. Augustine, Florida.

El Escorial is so huge and so unusual that it has become one of Spain's leading tourist attractions. Construction of the stone walls and roof—the shell of the structure—required twenty-one years. It was, at the time of its completion, the largest building in Christendom, and the Spaniards often refer to it as the Eighth Wonder of the World.

The building combines in one architectural complex a monastery, convent, royal palace, church, college or seminary, library, art gallery, and pantheon for the royal dead. Thus El Escorial exemplifies the continuing interdependence in Spain of government and Church. The royal apartments were so arranged that Philip's bedroom overlooked the sanctuary and the high altar. In his last years, crippled by gout and arthritis, the Hapsburg monarch, propped up by pillows, could attend the ceremony of the Mass, and join in prayers at matins and vespers, without getting out of bed.

Here at El Escorial, Philip tried to carry on the vast affairs of his realm almost singlehanded. He received reports from his ambassadors and spies in all the courts of Europe and from his viceroys overseas. He insisted on reading them all and carried on an extensive correspondence. He worked alone, delegated little or nothing, trusted nobody. Spain was too big to be governed by such petty, one-man rule.

As Ferdinand and Isabella at Granada symbolize the beginning of Spain's great age, so Philip II and El Escorial symbolize its decline and fall. A year after the great structure was completed, Spain was at war with England. Three years later Philip forced the reluctant, inexperienced Duke of Medina Sidonia to lead the Spanish Armada on its ill-starred expedition to the British Isles. That was the most disastrous of a series of misfortunes that included a revolt against Spanish rule in the Netherlands, rebellion in Granada of the Moriscos (descendants of the Arab-Berber invaders), and costly intervention in the French succession.

The next century continued the gradual decline, politically and economically, although the nation continued to shine in art, literature, and science. Portugal fell away from enfeebled Spain in 1640 without a battle, the government being occupied at the time with revolt in Naples and insurrection in Catalonia. When Spain attempted to subdue the seceding state by force twenty-five years later, Portugal won the battle of Montes Claros and a subsequent treaty guaranteed Portuguese independence.

A Bourbon dynasty followed the Hapsburgs on the Spanish throne. With the accession of seventeen-year-old Philip V, grandson of Louis XIV of France and Maria Theresa, Spain's fortunes were linked with her northern neighbor. The youthful monarch tried to strengthen the central government, but the separatist tendencies of the eastern states resisted his reforms and he was compelled to fight a small war to bring Catalonia, Aragon, and Valencia back into his kingdom.

The French Revolution brought another train of disasters to the peninsula. The execution of Louis XVI and Marie Antoinette aroused the Spanish royal house, and they set in motion a military force through the Roussillon. But a French Army drove them back across the Pyrenees and advanced to the Ebro. Powerless to cope with a militant France, devoid of leadership, Spain was forced to make a treaty pledging assistance to the French in their struggle against England.

The Napoleonic era had tragic repercussions in Spain. The

Corsican's early military triumphs coincided with a sorry chapter in Spanish royal affairs. A weakling Bourbon king, Charles IV, had entrusted the government to a controversial figure, Manuel de Godoy, who was both Prime Minister and amorous favorite of the Queen, María Luisa. The heir to the throne, Ferdinand, Prince of Asturias, plotted to seize the throne from his father and rid the government of Godoy. An angry demonstration outside the royal palace in Madrid assisted the young prince's plan. Charles IV was frightened into abdicating and handing over the crown to Ferdinand.

The news of this royal squabble reached Napoleon as he advanced with a French army toward the Spanish border. At Bayonne, he summoned the Spanish royal family to an accounting. Meekly they obeyed the summons—the weakling ex-king, María Luisa and her lover, Godoy, and the youthful Ferdinand VII. Napoleon's staff abused and maltreated the young king, and he was required to hand his crown back to his father. When Charles IV laid the crown at Napoleon's feet, the French emperor declared both Charles and Ferdinand unacceptable and then named his brother, Joseph Bonaparte, King of Spain. Charles and María Luisa were packed off to exile in Rome; Ferdinand placed under guard in a French château. Once proud and mighty, Spain had reached a low point in its history.

The news that Napoleon had put a puppet on the Spanish throne gave impetus in the Americas to the movement for liberation from Spanish rule. Inspired by the Liberator, Simon Bolivar, separatist revolts swept Venezuela, Colombia, Ecuador, Panama, Peru, and Bolivia, and although some of the struggles dragged on for ten years, all won their independence. Argentina broke away from Spain in 1816, Mexico in 1821. Thus the Napoleonic upheaval not only overthrew the Spanish government and precipitated the long chaos of the Peninsular War but promoted the disintegration of Spain's overseas possessions.

By the end of the nineteenth century that disintegration was complete. In the Spanish-American War of 1898, Spain's navy was destroyed; Cuba, Puerto Rico, and the Philippines and the Marianas were liberated from Spanish rule.

Some of this melancholy history emerges at El Escorial. Nearly all the Hapsburg and Bourbon kings are buried there in an octagonal marble crypt under the church. Charles V of the Holy Roman Empire, who passed most of his time in Flanders and could not even speak the Spanish language; Philip II, who built the great pile and launched the Armada; his son, Philip III, and grandson, Philip IV; the first Bourbon, Philip V; and a number of lesser royalty—all the inept and vain rulers whose grandiose schemes and futile wars squandered Spain's inheritance came to serve their lonely term in El Escorial's rotting room and now lie in their marble sarcophagi in the underground chamber.

In recent times another has been added to the aristocratic dead at El Escorial. José Antonio Primo de Rivera had no pretensions to royalty and he does not lie in the octagonal marble crypt beneath the altar. His ashes lie in a place of honor in the floor of the church at the crossing, before the sanctuary. A bronze plaque identifies the young man as the founder of the Falange.

One of the few Spanish monarchs not entombed at El Escorial is Alfonso XIII. The last King of Spain, he died in exile in Rome. His reign, from 1902 to 1931, marks a period of transition from the fading grandeur of the Hapsburg-Bourbon dynasties to the bloody civil war and dictatorship of modern times.

The Royal Palace in Madrid today is much as it was when Alfonso, last of the Bourbons, left it nearly thirty years ago. It is one of the great residences of European royalty. Furniture, paintings, tapestries, crystal chandeliers, embossed-leather volumes on library shelves, all combine to form a museum of nineteenth-century grandeur and futility. Tourists from the Americas—many from Mexico, Venezuela, Peru, and the Argentine—wander in groups through the high-ceilinged rooms listening to the guides' tales. In one of these chambers Charles IV heard the roar of an angry crowd outside the palace windows and handed the crown of Spain to Ferdinand VII. Through these corridors came messengers with the news that Peru, Argentina, Mexico, had broken off from Spanish rule. In this chamber in 1898, the Regent Queen Cristina learned from her ministers that one

Spanish fleet had been sunk off Santiago; another destroyed in Manila Bay; and that Cuba, Puerto Rico, and the Philippines were lost. Here, on an afternoon in April 1931, Alfonso XIII studied the election returns, took one last look around, and, bidding English wife and royal children good-by, climbed into his Hispano-Suiza for the long ride to Cartagena and exile.

The last years of Alfonso's twenty-nine-year reign brought a new pattern—military dictatorship—to the government of Spain. The country had managed to stay out of World War I and had prospered greatly by the sale of food, shipping, and war supplies to the belligerents. But the old regime was unequal to the tasks imposed by the war in Morocco, and a deteriorating political situation enabled the captain general of Catalonia, Don Miguel Primo de Rivera, to seize power in September 1923. This army figure was the father of José Antonio, who was later to play a martyr's role in the Falangist movement. Primo de Rivera's coup won the approval of King Alfonso, and the seven-year dictatorship had the support of Army, Church, and Royal Palace. Beneath a surface calm and order, liberal and radical political movements gathered headway. In a general election of municipal councilors in 1931, candidates pledged to support the monarchy were defeated everywhere except at Cádiz and Bilbao, while those pledged to a republic were elected.

The republic which followed Alfonso's abdication was born in an atmosphere of public rejoicing, but it did not rest on a secure foundation and lasted only four and a half years. Popular enthusiasm was not enough. There was no sound political group which could draw support from Right and Left; no moderate, liberal leadership to win the nation's confidence. The new consitutution struck at the Church, cut off the modest salaries of the priests and outlawed the Jesuits, and took education out of religious hands. Many local priests sympathized with the aspirations of the people and would have worked for the success of the republic, but the harsh measures of the Constituent Assembly drove them into the conservative camp. The reform measures undertaken by the Republican Left, including redistribution of the great landed estates (chiefly in Extremadura and Andalusia), alienated the conservatives without greatly benefiting the lower classes. The new constitution had fatal weaknesses. It provided a unicameral parliament, without a senate, weakened the chief executive by limiting his power to dissolve the parliament, and instituted unduly harsh, vindictive measures against the Church. Two governments of the Left, one of the Right, tried to make the new order work. The greatest element of weakness in the republic from 1931 to 1936, and the factor which encouraged the reactionaries to organize for civil war, was the deep-seated animosities which split the Left into warring camps.

Some historians and a number of journalists have portrayed the Civil War (1936–39) as a preliminary trial of strength between nazi-fascism and communism, in which each tested new weapons and techniques. It is true that the Fascists aided Franco and the Communists rallied to the support of the so-called Loyalists. But primarily the struggle was Spanish in origin, and Spanish in its bitter, bloody execution. No outside power could have inspired it, and the assistance which Russia, Italy, and Germany contributed canceled out. The cost in lives and treasure has never been accurately calculated, but it was enormous, and it settled nothing.

One of the ironies of the Civil War concerns Spanish gold. Early in the struggle, the government, on the authority of the Minister of Finance, Dr. Juan Negrín, shipped a large part of the nation's gold reserve from Cartagena to Odessa, Russia. One version states that the shipment consisted of 7500 boxes of gold weighing 510,079,592 grams. Don Indalecio Prieto, who was Minister of Air and Navy, later wrote that the number of boxes was not 7500 but 13,000, weighing 851½ tons, of which 510 tons went to Odessa, 170 tons to Marseille, and 170 tons to Barcelona.

Four officials of the Bank of Spain accompanied the shipment to Odessa. They were detained for two years on the pretext of counting and testing the gold bars. When finally released, one turned up in Stockholm, another in Buenos Aires, a third in Washington, and the fourth in Mexico. Later a receipt for the gold was sent to General Franco by the heirs of Dr. Negrín. Soviet officials insisted that the amount of the gold shipment had been exaggerated, and all of it, they said, had been applied to purchases of war supplies and equipment by the Spanish government in Russia. None of the gold has been recovered by the Franco government. It is a matter of speculation whether the treasure thus handed over to the Soviets equaled the gold and silver which the Spanish Conquistadores appropriated from Mexico and Peru in the sixteenth century.

The story of Spain since 1939 is the story of the Franco regime. From the conservative viewpoint, this compact, earnest, humorless man has brought order, peace, and stability to his country. His adherents say he was foremost among Western leaders to recognize the sinister threat of communism, the most courageous and clear-eyed in dealing with it. They speak admiringly of his skill in keeping Spain out of World War II, admitting that he favored the Nazi-Fascist dictators and was ready, if his terms were met, to join them.

Furthermore, the conservatives point out, Franco's diplomacy has won a seat in the United Nations and a friendly, close, and profitable relationship with the United States. In the last ten years, largely to further the construction of military air bases and pipelines, the United States has poured approximately $700,000,000 into Spain, and the total program of construction and other forms of economic aid is expected to reach $900,000,000. In addition, we have turned over to the Franco government as a virtual gift about $30,000,000 worth of bulldozers, power shovels, and road-building equipment. This economic assistance has helped Spain bolster its wobbly peseta and maintain a semblance of internal stability. Some of the aid has filtered down to the working class.

The other side of the Franco coin presents the Generalissimo as vain, pompous, harsh, and, like most dictators, unscrupulous in his scheming to retain power.

A critic who may be described as both liberal and moderate charges that Franco has failed completely in the larger tasks which devolved upon his leadership at the end of the Civil War. One of those tasks was practical and economic: to marshal the nation's resources and rebuild the economy. His record here is negative. Except for some hydroelectric development, the only major construction project—aside from airfields and pipelines—is the Generalissimo's mammoth memorial to the war dead—The Valley of the Fallen. Granted that this is an imposing monument, his critics say it is more a reflection of Franco's vanity and preoccupation with death than a national achievement.

More serious than his failure in the field of practical accomplishment, his critics charge, is his failure to "bind up the nation's wounds." Confronted with an occasion calling for compassion, magnanimity, forgiveness, the Generalissimo displayed only vindictiveness toward the Loyalist, or revolutionist, forces defeated in the Civil War. Only recently, in the dedication of The Valley of the Fallen to the war dead of all factions, has he shown any respect or forgiveness for his enemies.

The Fuero de los Españoles, or Charter of Rights, which Franco promulgated in 1945, purported to be a guarantee of freedom and certain basic rights for the individual, but in practice the government has disregarded most of the rights it promised to respect. Censorship, surveillance, ruthless suppression of political opposition—all the tyranny of the police state have been invoked to maintain the Dictator's power.

Between those extreme judgments of Franco a more philosophic viewpoint holds that what he has done reflects Spanish character and tradition. This is a harsh, proud people. It is their nature to seek vengeance rather than compromise. The military figure is patriotic and, within his lights, sincere. But he wants to save Spain in his own way, not through orderly process of law. Franco is a product of Iberian, Visigoth, Roman, Moor, Berber; his code is the simple code of the Conquistadores in the New World: impose your will on those around you.

The tragedy of Spain today is not that it is ruled by a dictator, but that when he steps down no healthy political alternative is available to succeed him. Those who oppose his rule—and they represent a substantial majority—are unable to agree on a liberal constitutional program to take over when he is done. At least no evidence of such a program is apparent.

The political picture in Spain has changed little during the

Franco regime. It still is a sorry patchwork of conflicting interests and wishes.

On the extreme Right are the Carlists, those of the ancient regime who are mainly concerned with theoretical legitimacy in royal succession. There are not many of them, but they would turn the clock back four hundred years.

The Falange, the Statist party organized by José Antonio, seeks to subordinate the individual to the state, invoke discipline, and, under a Führer, move toward state socialism.

The Monarchists are those who sincerely desire a constitutional monarchy such as now combines tradition and enlightened government in England and the Scandinavian countries. They still represent a substantial body of opinion in Spain and look forward to a realization of their aspirations when Franco dies or retires.

The Church, always conservative, but not as powerful politically as some imagine, would remain in the background of any political campaign.

On the other side of the political spectrum, there are some Leftist Republicans who would like to go back to the republic of 1931 and proceed with drastic social and economic reforms.

The Socialists would like to proceed toward socialism by Fabian methods, winning adherents from other sections of the Left.

Another group of moderate Republicans would work for a new constitution, profiting by the mistakes of 1931 and seeking a broader base.

The Communists still have a skeleton organization, but they have not recovered much from the setback of the Civil War and their cause lost additional ground in the ruthless Soviet suppression of the Hungarian Revolt.

There is a small group of Anarchists (Libertarians), who scorn the ballot and would like to do away with practically all government.

In addition to these are two groups of exiles in Paris and Mexico, whose leaders have tried to hold them together for political action but whose strength wanes with the passage of time.

None of those groups can function openly, for the dictatorship has outlawed all political parties except the Falange, now known as the National party. Several would coalesce to get rid of the Dictator, but it is doubtful whether they could work together subsequently in a stable coalition.

Early in 1959 some influential liberals and conservatives opposed to the Franco regime organized a new patriotic society, which they called Unión Española. Its leader and spokesman, Joaquín Satrústegui Fernandez, challenged the legality of the Franco dictatorship and criticized its policies in an address before a Madrid gathering of one hundred persons, which included army officers, bankers, lawyers, and university professors. The government could not ignore the affair, because of the wide publicity. Don Satrústegui was arrested, interrogated, and released on payment of a $1000 fine. This was more face saving for Franco than penalty against the wealthy Basque industrialist. It may be assumed that Unión Española continues to function quietly, waiting an opportune time for political action.

Many Spaniards believe that Franco's days are numbered, but the Dictator will choose the date of his retirement and determine the government that will succeed him. The expectation in informed quarters is that Franco will allow the Monarchists to bring back the twenty-one-year-old Prince Don Carlos, son of the Pretender Don Juan and grandson of Alfonso XIII. This would please most of the groups on the Right and would also be acceptable to some liberals and moderate Republicans, but it would embarrass the Falange, which is on record as opposing the return of the monarchy in any form.

The youthful prince has had a good education and appears normal and healthy. No gossip is circulated about him, and except for a preoccupation with small sports cars, he seems to have no vices. Lacking outstanding qualifications, his assumption of the tasks of government would depend entirely on the men selected to form his Cabinet and the ideas which dominate the royal palace at that time.

Franco's departure almost certainly will bring a better political atmosphere to this long-suffering country, but it will solve nothing. Whether a monarch succeeds him or a new constitutional government emerges, shaped by orderly balloting and a national convention, Spain has a long, hard road to travel to political stability. The country now lacks: (1) an informed middle class; (2) courageous, articulate leaders; (3) an idea.

Without an idea, men and nations perish. Friends of Spain wait hopefully for some idea of freedom, some inspiration, some new national vision which will revitalize the land and make it whole again.

Newcomers to Portugal wonder why that small nation should achieve a separate existence when the map shows it so closely akin to Spain. Why should peoples of the same racial origins and religious beliefs, peoples with a similarity of language who have shared so much history, turn their backs on each other and demand passports and baggage inspection at the frontier? The explanation is complicated by factors of geography, climate, dynastic rivalries, old grievances and alliances.

Portugal first broke off from Spain and established its own rule in the twelfth century, and in the fourteenth appealed to England for help against Castile. This was the beginning of a long and close alliance between Portugal and England, which profoundly affected Portuguese history, found an outlet for its port wine, and virtually underwrote its independence.

Although the original causes of the peninsular dichotomy may be obscure, there is evidence today to justify the separation on grounds of temperament and character. As the Portuguese climate is generally mild and moist, so the people are inclined to be more sunny and amiable than their Spanish neighbors. One aspect of this temperamental contrast emerges in the bull ring. In Spain, the bullfight often results in the disembowelment and death of horses ridden by the picadors, whose function it is to plant barbed darts in the bull's shoulders. Portugal blunts the bull's horns, protecting horse and rider. In Spain the "hour of truth" brings death to the exhausted bull by the matador's sword thrust to the heart, and the carcass is dragged out of the arena by mules. In Portugal the bull is never killed. If he has put on a spirited show, he trots out of the ring to the applause of the crowd, with a wreath of

flowers around his neck. The worst that can happen to him is
that he may be hissed.

As in the bull ring, so in the arena of government. The two
dictators, Franco and Salazar, provide an illuminating example
of the contrasts in national character. The Spanish generalissimo
is harsh, vindictive, humorless, and his power rests almost entirely
on the Army and the Church. Salazar, on the other hand, tilts
at his political opposition with gentle irony, lectures the people
on their responsibilities, demands economy and integrity from his
subordinates. Although political opposition has greater freedom
to coalesce and express itself, no serious threat to Salazar's leadership has materialized and in the last general election he received
more than 70 per cent of the popular vote.

A professor of economics at the University of Coimbra, Antonio
de Oliveira Salazar was induced to become Finance Minister early
in 1928 in the Cabinet of President Carmona as a result of a published thesis on Portuguese currency. His first experience in the
government was distasteful, and he resigned and returned to Coimbra after only a few days in the Finance Ministry. Carmona
persuaded him to return, however, and he re-entered the Cabinet in May 1928. From that time until the present he has been
the strongest force in the Portuguese government, and the dictator of all its major policies. As a result of his fiscal reforms, Portugal
is paying off a heavy burden of external debt, and out of current
surpluses building public works and schools.

Like Spain, Portugal once passed through a golden age and
possessed a vast overseas empire. The little nation's great period
of exploration and expansion was due largely to the national hero,
Henry the Navigator. This young prince, third son of John (João)
I, became interested in exploring the African coast and offshore
islands. To further his purpose, he gathered maps and navigating
instruments in his villa at Sagres, on the south coast, and there
exchanged ideas and discussed exploration projects with the nation's leading seafarers.

With his encouragement and sponsorship, Portuguese ships
sailed down the coast of Africa, passed Cape Verde, and reached
Senegal. After his death in 1460, a Portuguese navigator, Barthol-

omeu Diaz, rounded the Cape of Good Hope, and Vasco da Gama pushed on to the west coast of India. By the middle of the sixteenth century, Portuguese colonies were established at Goa and Malacca, and at Macao on the China coast. Brazil and large sections of equatorial Africa came under Portuguese domination, and Ferdinand Magellan made the first voyage around the world.

Many of these achievements are celebrated in the *Lusiads* of Luiz Vaz de Camões, the epic poet whose rank in Portugal is comparable to that of Dante in Italy, Shakespeare in England, or Cervantes in Spain.

ITALY

Frank Gervasi

Frank Gervasi, born in Baltimore, February 5, 1908, attended Drexel Institute of Technology, where he studied engineering, and the University of Pennsylvania, where he took a liberal arts course. He found that college was interfering with his ambition to become a newspaperman and joined the staff of the Philadelphia Record *in 1930. After two years, Gervasi joined the Associated Press in New York and in 1934 moved over to International News Service to begin his long career as a foreign correspondent. He served an apprenticeship in Madrid and London before becoming Chief of Bureau in Rome in the spring of 1935. At the outbreak of World War II in 1939, he joined the staff of* Collier's *as associate editor, covering European and Mediterranean war fronts, with side trips to Asia and Latin America.*

At war's end Gervasi became Chief of the Collier's *bureau in Washington and remained until 1949, when he took a year's leave of absence to return to daily journalism, traveling in Europe, and writing a syndicated Sunday feature for the Washington* Post. *After two years' service as Chief of Information for the Marshall Plan in Rome, Gervasi returned to journalism, and for three years his column appeared in the New York* Post *and was syndicated by some thirty-five newspapers in the United States, Canada, and the Far East.*

In January 1958, he joined the Eric Johnston organization as Director for the Mediterranean Area of the Motion Picture Export Association of America.

He has written four books, the last of which, Big Government, *was published in 1949.*

Married to Kathryn Elizabeth McGuigan in 1930, he has two sons.

ITALY

Knowledge of the Italian people's origins and history is indispensable to true understanding and appreciation of their faults and virtues. Every year some 15 million tourists, mostly Americans, Britons, Scandinavians, and West Germans, visit this wondrously hospitable and abundantly beautiful land. It is amazing, however, what misconceptions concerning its inhabitants a large percentage of the visitors carry among their mental baggage.

Myths about Italians are as numerous as they are firmly fixed in the Anglo-Saxon and, particularly, the American mind. One of the most widely held is that they have no stomach for combat, the inference being that Italians are, as a people, a cowardly lot. That they shrink from mass violence, as all highly civilized people should, is quite true. But no one who has seen an Italian auto race like the Mille Miglie, or watched a Roman or Neapolitan weave through traffic astride a motor scooter, can honestly question Italian individual courage!

History, certainly, does not support the myth. On the contrary, it amply demonstrates that Italians have acquitted themselves heroically enough whenever they have had anything substantial to fight for, as in the Garibaldi campaigns for their country's unification and her liberation from Church influence, or as in World War II, when circumstances permitted them to reject fascism and its alliance with nazism to join the forces of democracy against the Axis.

The story of Italy from the time of the collapse of the Roman Empire until the emergence of Cavour, Mazzini, and Garibaldi is more the story of a people acted upon than acting, of a people victimized by their own and foreign tyrants. The Italians of today are the product of historical processes in which geography, climate, invasions, wars, revolutions, and other factors exerted definite influences.

Unless those processes and influences are understood, it is difficult or impossible to grasp the significance of day-by-day developments in the political, social, and economic life of this important member of the Western community of nations or fully enjoy a visit to the country which offers an incomparable patrimony of Etruscan, Greek, Roman, and medieval art and architecture.

Geography has been—and remains—an all-important determinant in the development of the Italian society. Napoleon, preparing to invade Italy in 1800, illustrated for his generals the rugged nature of the Italian terrain by crumpling a sheet of parchment. Italy is, indeed, a preponderantly mountainous land, roughly shaped like a fancy flare-topped jack boot. It is about the size of New Mexico, but long and narrow, seldom more than 100 miles wide but extending some 800 miles southeastward from the European mainland into the Mediterranean, midway between that noble sea's western and eastern gateways, Gibraltar and the Dardanelles, a position as strategically important in this Missile Age as it was when Venice and Genoa were the epicenters of world trade.

Italy's fifty million inhabitants differ little in size, shape, or coloring from their French, Austrian, or even Swiss neighbors. They are not, on the whole, a tall people, and they most resemble, physically, the Greeks and Spaniards. They are a dark-haired, dark-eyed race, although the percentage of fair, blue-eyed, and blond men and women among them is astounding, not only in the North but also in the South, including Sicily. For the Italian is, really, a Mediterranean racial cocktail, a mingling of many strains, Latin and Teutonic, Phoenician and Greek, Gallic and Celtic, the product of successive invasions by land from the north and by sea from virtually every other point of the compass.

The Italians, like most people, have self-evident virtues: a keen intelligence, generosity, an infinite capacity for improvisation. But they most certainly also have their faults. Highest on the list thereof this writer would place a tendency to shirk responsibility, at least in small matters, in the common everyday mechanics of plain living.

No Italian will tell you that he does not know the answer to a question, whether it be a request for information as to how to reach a certain restaurant or an inquiry about alcoholism. "Alcoholism," he will reply, "does not exist in Italy. Italians are not drunkards." That is, to a degree, correct; Italians are not, as a people, inebriates. Italy, however, does have alcoholics, but only the most advanced doctors will admit their existence.

By and large, the Italian is less pigheaded (or piratical) than the Frenchman (perhaps Parisian would be fairer) and less punctiliously proud than the Spaniard. He is, on the whole, a warmhearted and rational being capable of and responsive to affection. He also has the gift of forgiveness. The vendetta is more Spanish than Italian. Wrong a Spaniard, however unintentionally, and he is your enemy for life. While this is also true of the Sicilian, the Italian mainlander from Rome and northward is as quick to forgive and forget as he is to resent.

The Italian stems from an ancient civilization, knows it, and is proud of it. He is proud of many things: his ability to make music with his larynx; his antecedents, real or imaginary; his children; his possessions, if any, although he is careful not to flaunt them; his skill in hoodwinking the tax collector; in short, his all-round cleverness. He is inclined to be vain about his looks and, if he can afford it, his clothes.

Perhaps above all else the Italian is proud of his skill with his hands, whether it be in making things grow from the earth, in designing motors and bodies for automobiles, or in making motion pictures, shoes, clothing, or any of the innumerable items of handicraft for which Italy is justly famous and which have contributed enormously to Italian postwar prosperity.

Present-day Italy ranks among the two or three most prosperous nations of Europe, with nearly three billion dollars in gold and dollars on hand, its currency stabilized and interchangeable at parity with all other European monies, and increasingly convertible against the dollar. The lira is as "hard" a currency today as the West German mark and nearly as prized as the Swiss franc.

A republic since 1947, with a President elected every five years, a two-chamber parliament, a Supreme Court, and a constitution which proclaims and defends individual political, social, and religious freedom, today's Italy, in theory and in face, is a modern democracy, a going concern. Although American economic assistance never equaled more than 5 per cent of the national budget in any given year, the citizens of the United States may point with justifiable pride at the contribution they made to Italian recovery. It would behoove them, however, not to stress the amount or importance of that assistance. The recipient is touchy on the subject. He is tired of saying "Thank you, Mr. and Mrs. America," and he is abundantly aware of his own contribution to his country's recovery as measured by his own toil and sweat.

The firm economic foundations laid in the years between 1948 and 1953, the high-water mark of American help—thereafter it became Mutual Assistance for Defense and was overwhelmingly military rather than economic—have enabled the Italians to erect a solidly democratic structure. Since the republic was founded the country has been governed by the Christian Democrats, either by one-party rule or in coalition with other moderate Center groups, such as the Republicans, Social Democrats, and Liberals. The Italian Communist party, second-largest in the country and biggest west of the Iron Curtain, has never proved strong enough, even in its 1946–48 heyday, to upset the democratic balance of power.

The existence of so large a Communist element in an overwhelmingly (97.3 per cent) Catholic country is a common source of amazement to visitors. Italian communism, it should be known, draws its strength less from poverty—still widespread in this however prosperous nation—than from wellsprings of anticlericalism as old as Italy's struggle for unification and for separation of Church and State.

There is more communism in the highly industrialized and agriculturally progressive North, for instance, than in the still backward South. Plainly, the answer to the most important single question of the contemporary Italian political scene—Why are so many Italians members of the Communist or other Left-wing parties?—must lie elsewhere than in economics.

A partial answer is provided, it is true, by economic factors. Italy, notwithstanding the upward movement of virtually all of the classic indexes of prosperity—the graph lines recording sweeping increases in the number of telephones, automobiles, radios, television sets, and washing machines in use; the quantities of electric energy, tobacco, sugar, meat, and other utilities and commodities consumed; and the amounts of money in circulation and/or deposited in banks—is a poor country. Again, geography is the principal culprit. Much of Italy is unfarmable wasteland.

Although in the eyes of the foreigner there exists a people identifiable as Italian, the Italian is more apt to consider himself a Veneziano or a Genovese, a Milanese or a Romano, a Bolognese or a Napoletano, or to protest most vigorously that he is a Siciliano or a Sardo rather than an Italiano. This is because, in spite of Augustus and Julius Caesar, Napoleon and Garibaldi, Mazzini and Mussolini, and a few others, notably Niccolò Machiavelli, the Italians have retained their loyalties to cities and provinces, defying all efforts at unification in the broader, spiritual sense of the word. *Campanilismo*, they call it, an acute version of the kind of loyalty to birthplace typical of our own Texans, Virginians, or Brooklynites. The *campanile* is the town or village bell tower. Italians say that the sound of their own city or village bells is always sweeter than their neighbors'. Knife duels have been fought in Sicily to settle arguments over the civic beauties or virtues of rival towns.

It is a common fallacy that Italy was a well-knit, tightly organized nation under a succession of Caesars. The Roman Empire was never a federal union, but a vast confederation of states which paid tribute to Rome in return for protection. Until 476 A.D., when the German Odoacer became the head of the already crumbling Empire in the West, the story of Italy was the story of Rome. Italy, the Italia of the poets and the dreamers, simply did not exist. What did exist and what followed the fall of Rome was an elaborate, almost gerrymandered patchwork of city-states, petty kingdoms, and puny principalities.

From 800 A.D. onward, popes, Normans, Lombards, Saracens, Greeks, Spaniards, and Austrians threaded through the passes of the Alpine barrier and pushed on down to the Apennine spinal column of Italy from the north or hacked away at the peninsula from the south, to grab what pleased them. It was a time of plot and counterplot, of misrule and mismanagement. Government became, for the people, a mechanism to be defeated and frustrated by every device conceivable. Responsibility dropped out of the public vocabulary and authority became a synonym for tyranny. Italy was being psychologically prepared for revolution, communism, and, eventually, fascism.

Her proud citizens like to think of Italy as "the eldest daughter of civilization." The truth is, however, that it was not until the latter part of the nineteenth century that she became a nation. Throughout the fifteenth and sixteenth centuries, while other countries were achieving political maturity and national unity, Italy failed to produce a single prince powerful enough to resist foreign influence, conquer the entire peninsula, and unify all Italians under one rule. Machiavelli, probably the greatest political philosopher ever produced by Italy, dreamed of a united Italy under a single king and strove toward that end with every argument his fiercely logical mind and ruthless pen could contrive. But the Republics of Venice and Florence and the Kingdom of Naples successfully resisted political and military efforts at absorption.

Intense local patriotism developed, leading to bitter rivalries, intramural quarrels, and frequent bloody wars. National union was regarded as a Machiavellian device for aggrandizement of one state at the expense of the others. For at least two hundred years, the national idea virtually faded from the collective mind of the Italian masses, although here and there in Italian history the idea did have its champions.

None was to be found, certainly, in an element unique in Italian politics and unparalleled in any other land—the papacy. Since Charlemagne's day, the popes had ruled the region which comprised the Papal States—roughly all of central and most of northeastern Italy—and were princes in their own right. They were closely allied against unification, for it would mean the end of the Papal States and the disappearance of their temporal power. Recalling the "Babylonian Captivity" of 1309–77 at Avignon, they were determined not to become "captives" in Italy. History records that they opposed and effectively prevented Italian unification.

Nevertheless, the Italy of the fifteenth and sixteenth centuries achieved unprecedented civilization and prosperity. Venice, Florence, Genoa, and Rome became centers of art, scholarship, and science, citadels of the warming glory of the Italian Renaissance.

But the discovery of America and of the Cape Route to India wrought far-reaching changes in Italian fortunes. The Atlantic, rather than the Mediterranean, became the world's highway of trade. Commerce shifted from southern to northern Europe. Italian prosperity declined, and by the turn of the eighteenth century commercial centers like Florence and Milan and ports like Genoa and Venice were stricken with economic paralysis. Their market places became silent and empty. Their influence in international affairs declined. Their cultures decayed.

Greatness survived only as a nostalgic memory. The people sank slowly into poverty, ignorance, and superstition and were ruled by a host of corrupt and thieving monarchs. The Italy of the eighteenth century fell into a coma-like sleep from which it seemed she would never awaken, when suddenly there came the rousing trumpet call of the French Revolution. Freedom-loving Frenchmen poured over the Alps. Italian princes and princelings fled in terror. Their astonished subjects had always regarded them as monarchs by divine right, perpetual and irremovable symbols of power, tyrants to be borne like death and plague and taxes. They turned eagerly to the newcomers who preached Liberty, Equality, and Fraternity and who set about abolishing the old order.

The Italian states of the North were reorganized as republics under enlightened legal and administrative systems which almost obliterated the remnants of medievalism. Social, political, and economic reforms were introduced. In one decade of French rule the Italians of the northern areas made centuries of progress. Although many Italian intellectuals had dreamed of unity, it took a Frenchman, Napoleon, to lay the foundations of eventual unification.

Napoleon proclaimed himself King of Italy in 1805, but by 1815, after Waterloo, his empire was at the mercy of the reactionary monarchs of Europe. At the Congress of Vienna, Austria, Russia, Prussia, and Britain partitioned the Empire according to dynastic rather than nationalist consideration. "Legitimacy" was the watchword. Prior "rights" of old dynasties to govern former subjects, regardless of whether the latter wished to be governed by such rulers or not, were given exclusive precedence over nationalist considerations.

It is interesting to note in passing that at Vienna, 145 years ago, Russia was "permitted" to keep Finland and Bessarabia as her share of the spoils.

Austria emerged as the fat cat of the Viennese feast. She gobbled up the Illyrian segment of the Adriatic coast and the two richest provinces of all Italy—Lombardy and Veneto. But she swallowed therewith five million fiercely rebellious Italians.

Italy suffered additional setbacks to unity. Exiled rulers were restored in Lucca, San Marino, and Monaco. In the South, the Kingdom of the Two Sicilies was created, including the island itself and most of southern Italy, with Naples as the capital.

The States were restored to the popes, and the duchies of Parma, Modena, and Tuscany re-established. But the Kingdom of Sardinia, comprising the island and Piedmont, was recognized, although stripped of Lombardy and the Veneto.

Cruel, and perhaps unfair, as the treatment accorded to Italy at Vienna might seem, the Congress set in motion forces which ultimately drove the Italians to desperate means to unify their country. Vienna revived old inequalities and intolerances. Freedom of speech and assembly were abolished; only Catholics could enjoy freedom of worship. The Church was restored to all its previous grandeur, temporal and spiritual, and it was this fact, perhaps above all others, which inspired ultimately successful rebellion. "Liberty and Union" became the battle cry of the masses.

From this point onward the political history of Italy paralleled closely that of Germany. The Italians, like the Germans, encountered one main obstacle toward nationhood and freedom—Austria. The Italians, however, had an additional enemy, the papacy, whose power in Italy and influence in the world beyond the Alps mightily operated against unification.

Unable to meet and speak freely, the Italians resorted to conspiracy and violence. In the South, inspired partly by the Spanish revolution of 1820, the Carbonari rose in revolt against King Ferdinand I. He glibly promised a constitution, solemnly swore to install democratic institutions, and promptly enlisted the aid of the Austrians to crush the rebellion. The Austrians ousted the newly established democratic government, reaffirmed Ferdinand as absolute monarch, and thousands were imprisoned, exiled, or executed.

Hardly a year passed before the flag of revolution—green, white, and red—was raised in Piedmont by men who demanded not only a constitution but war against Austria. Unlike Ferdinand, Piedmontese King Victor Emmanuel I of Sardinia was unwilling to use foreign troops to keep his throne and abdicated in favor of his brother Charles, who was opposed to constitutional government and had no scruples about asking Austria and Russia to suppress the uprising. The Austrians also helped to crush revolutions in Modena, Parma, and the Papal States. Italian hatred of Austria rose to a white fury.

There was just enough gangsterism in the Carbonari movement to discredit it with the Italian masses, and not until Giuseppe Mazzini emerged did the dream of an Italian fatherland find a literate, articulate, albeit often inept, champion. Mazzini and the poet Dante may be called, nevertheless, the true founders of united Italy. After serving a prison sentence as a Carbonaro revolutionist, Mazzini founded a new society, called La Giovane Italia, composed of young intellectuals dedicated to the task of liberating their country from foreign and domestic tyrants and the creation of an Italian republic on democratic foundations.

Mazzini dreamed of a "Third Italy," a "Rome of the People," to follow the Roman Empire and the Rome of the papacy. He envisioned an Italy "radiant, purified by suffering, moving as an angel of light among the nations who thought her dead." Nevertheless, Mazzini, unlike Mussolini, was not a chauvinist. His conception of patriotism was founded in love of his own country and scrupulous respect for every other country. Every nation, he believed, has something valuable to offer civilization. There lay in his philosophy the seeds of certain concepts which later sprouted in the League of Nations and flowered in the United Nations. Mazzini was dedicated to the principle that nations should be permitted to exist undisturbed and was profoundly convinced that if this could be achieved the chief cause for war would disappear. He envisioned Italy's mission in world affairs as one teaching mankind "to love and to cherish as an ideal the brotherhood of nations." He even championed such oppressed nationalities at the time as the Hungarians, the Poles, and the Irish and went so far as to organize an international society called "Young Europe." (And Mussolini dared picture himself as the spiritual son of Mazzini!)

Although obliged to live most of his life in exile in England and in France, Mazzini's words, in books and pamphlets and newspapers, reached and inspired the Giovane Italia movement, which, in a short time, counted 60,000 members. It became so strong a force that a new pope, Pius IX, temporarily embarked the Church upon a more liberal tack in a desperate effort to survive the revolutionary winds stirred by the articulate Mazzini.

In the new climate, successful rebellions broke out throughout the peninsula. Many resulted in democratic, liberal constitutions. Charles Albert, who had ascended the throne of Sardinia in 1831, gave his subjects a constitution in 1848. In Lombardy, Milan expelled the Austrian troops and the region joined Piedmont. Venice established a republic and Florence followed suit. In Naples, Ferdinand II, like his father, was compelled to grant a constitution and, finally, in Rome, the Pope was forced to flee before the forces of Giuseppe Garibaldi. Perhaps the biggest single event, however, was the declaration of war against Austria by Charles Albert of Sardinia. Austria was pressed by an uprising in Vienna and was not believed to be able to spare soldiers to suppress the Italian dreams of Liberty and Unity.

But Austria was not as weak as Mazzini and Garibaldi supposed. The armies of Charles Albert could not stave off Austrian offensives led by the able Radetzky, and Charles Albert abdicated in favor of his son, Victor Emmanuel II. Austria offered advantageous peace terms to the new king provided he would repeal the constitution granted to the people by his father. Victor Emmanuel II refused, stating: "What my father has sworn to, I will maintain. If you wish war to the death, so be it. If I must fall it will be without shame. My House knows the road to exile but not to dishonor."

Once more, however, reaction set in. One by one, revolutionary governments were overthrown and everywhere suppression was severe. Thousands of liberals were executed or tortured. The Roman Republic was overthrown and the Pope restored with the help of the French. Louis Napoleon wanted to curry favor with the French Catholics. Pius IX repented his liberalism and became an uncompromising opponent of Italian nationalism and democracy, and the Italians now had another foreign army camped on their soil, the French. The only bright light in the gloom of revolutionary failure was Sardinia. It had been defeated by the Austrians but had remained morally victorious.

Sardinia gave the world, Italy, and the cause of freedom probably one of its greatest men. He was Camillo Benso, Count of Cavour, descendant of a noble Piedmontese family and a hardheaded, clear-eyed liberal. He was a perfect teammate for the honest and sensible Victor Emmanuel II, who, unfortunately, was not gifted with diplomatic skill. Cavour definitely was. It was Cavour's logical mind which really led the Risorgimento. Mazzini made the speeches and wrote the pamphlets. But it was Cavour who translated emotions and aspirations into practical plans. It was Cavour who connived, contrived, and maneuvered until he enlisted the aid of the French against Austria. He gave France Nice and Savoy, later to become, in Mussolini's time, a source of phony contention with France.

By ceding Savoy and Nice to the French—they were overwhelmingly French-speaking regions anyhow—and by sending a small picked force to support the Allies in the Crimean War, Cavour obtained an alliance with Napoleon III to drive the Austrians out of Lombardy and the Veneto and set Italian feet once more on the road to unity. Napoleon later double-crossed the Italians, but his intervention brought about the defeat of Austria and gave new momentum to the Risorgimento. Modena, Parma, Tuscany, and the Romagna joined Sardinia as a result of the Peace of Zurich in November 1859, and Nice and Savoy, following a plebiscite, joined France.

In Rome a man who had supported Cavour, a native of Nice, shouted that he had been betrayed, made a stranger in his native land. His name was Giuseppe Garibaldi, Italy's greatest patriot, whose gallant defense of the Roman Republic against the French won him the love and admiration of republicans throughout the world. A skilled guerilla fighter, he resembled most in American history Andrew Jackson: foolhardy, stubborn, generous, brave, a patriot in every nerve and fiber of his body. He grew to hate Cavour as a calculating schemer but was obliged to admit that the unity of his country could only come through the House of Savoy, which had the distinction of being liberal, democratic, and, above all, of Italian blood. Garibaldi loved a republic but he loved Italy more, and in 1859 he headed a volunteer corps known as the Hunters of the Alps, defeating Austrian forces overwhelmingly superior in numbers in several important engagements.

Garibaldi's most famous exploit probably was his "Expedition of the 1000," a daring body of poorly clad and armed men, red-shirted and wearing slouch hats, who sailed from Genoa on May 5, 1860, to conquer the Kingdom of Naples, a nation of 11,000,000 inhabitants with an army of 125,000. The campaign is an epic, perhaps the epic of Italian history. Italy thrilled first to Garibaldi's successful conquest of Sicily and then, his ranks swollen to 50,000, his defeat of Naples. At the Volturno, Garibaldi defeated an army twice the size of his own. The Neapolitan king fled, and Garibaldi assumed the dictatorship of the entire kingdom.

Now matters became really complicated, and unless the student understands this particular chapter in Italian history, he can never understand present-day anticlericalism and the appeal of Left-wing lay movements, including the extremist one known as communism.

Cavour had looked favorably upon Garibaldi's bold adventure, but now he feared that the great popular hero, not renowned for coolheadedness, might march on Rome. This could mean war with France, a world power, not a mere demoralized, corrupt kingdom like Naples. Cavour counseled his king to invade the Papal States, occupy Umbria and the Marches, and enter Naples, avoiding Rome en route. Victor Emmanuel II accordingly defeated the remnants of the armies of Francis II, already decimated by Garibaldi's legions, and entered Naples in triumph. The Neapolitan kingdom was joined to Sardinia and all other conquered territories. Garibaldi rode in triumph with Emmanuel, then resigned his dictatorship. Victor Emmanuel II became King of Italy "by the Grace of God and the will of the people."

The first Italian parliament met in Turin, on February 18, 1861. Mazzini, Cavour, and Garibaldi had succeeded in creating an Italy, a nation. Missing in the Italian union, however, was Rome. The capital and the states of central Italy were still under the Pope.

But Garibaldi had retired to the island of Caprera, and Cavour, who had always felt that an Italy without its capital in Rome was a headless horse, died. His successor, Ricasoli, shared Cavour's dreams of a "Free Church in a Free State," meaning that the Church should be free to exercise spiritual power but leave temporal affairs to the State. The cry "On to Rome" was raised throughout the land.

Pius IX denounced the new kingdom as a child of revolution and refused to recognize it. He branded Victor Emmanuel II a "usurper." Italians shouted: "Seize Rome." But the government demurred. It feared French intervention on the Pope's behalf. It also feared world Catholic opinion abroad and intervention by all Catholic powers. Rome was defended sentimentally by some 20,000,000 Belgian, Irish, and Austrian Catholics and physically by a fine French corps bivouacked there since 1849.

As was to be expected, Garibaldi became impatient, and in 1862 he attacked Rome against the wishes of his government. He was defeated by an Italian army at Aspromonte, on his way to Rome. Wounded by an Italian bullet, which hurt him far more spiritually than it did physically, Garibaldi retired in disgust. He tried again to liberate Rome in 1867. This time he was beaten by the French and papal armies.

History contrived, at last, however, to operate in favor of Italian unity. Italy joined Prussia in the Seven Weeks' War against Austria and was awarded the Veneto as a prize for its dubious assistance in the Italo-Prussian victory. Then France became embroiled with Prussia, withdrew its troops from Rome, and gave the Italians the opportunity they had been seeking. On September 30, 1870, an Italian army entered the Eternal City in triumph, and in a subsequent plebiscite—134,000 to 1500—the Romans voted to become annexed to Italy. Rome became the capital of an Italy at last united and free of the foreign presence and domination. The papacy, which had ruled for a thousand years, lost its temporal power. The Pontiff was restricted to the square mile or so lying within the Vatican's walls. He was to be released, many years later, in 1929, by a tyrant named Benito Mussolini.

To the "King of the Unification," Victor Emmanuel II, the Italians later erected, in the Piazza Venezia in Rome, a great marble monument, variously known as the "White Typewriter" and the "Wedding Cake." It is an imposing structure, despite its curlicues and furbelows, a white marble edifice which resists the aging process that has turned Rome into a pleasing polychrome of yellows and browns. The monument is also the Tomb of the Unknown Soldier of World War I, a conflict which cost Italy some 600,000 dead, 400,000 maimed, and more than a million wounded.

Following unification and the enactment of legislation granting the Pope freedom in the exercise of his spiritual ministry and temporal power within the Holy See, the Lateran, and the papal villa at Castel Gandolfo, relations between the Church and State appeared to be headed toward peace and co-operation. But the honeymoon was short-lived. New laws abolished the legal character of the religious orders, placed schools and hospitals under civil administration and the churches under the secular clergy. The struggle between the two powers was resumed.

Governments rose and fell in rapid succession in the years following unification of the nation, a period marked by political and economic problems and by the awakening of Italian ambitions as a Mediterranean power.

With British support, the Italians occupied Assab and, later, Massaua in Eritrea. This brought Italy into conflict with Abyssinia. The defeat and destruction of an Italian force of 524 officers and men by a force of 20,000 Abyssinians in 1887, sowed the seeds of the Fascist Ethiopian War. An Italo-Abyssinian war was barely averted through British intervention, and a treaty resulted in the establishment of an Italian colony in Eritrea in 1889.

The breakup of the Ottoman Empire provided Italy with an opportunity to seize territory in Tripolitania and take over the Dodecanese. Italy could ill afford colonies. The Italians poured men and treasure into the development of Libya and Eritrea and, later, Somaliland. They were hardly in a position, financially speaking, to take part in a major world war. Nevertheless, Italy denounced the Triple Alliance with Austria and Germany in 1915 and joined the Allies, in a shift of allegiances that was to be repeated in Italian foreign policy in World War II. By the Treaty of St. Germain in 1919, Italy received the southern Tirol and the Istrian peninsula as spoils. Other spoils, at the expense of Turkey, were never delivered and provided an excuse for Mussolini's friendship with Nazi Germany years later.

Weakened by colonial wars and economically exhausted by World War I, the scene was set for Socialist and Communist agitation and for the emergence, in 1922, of "strong man," Benito Mussolini, himself a former Socialist. Il Duce "marched" on Rome from Milan in a pullman car to break a Left-Right deadlock in the Parliament on October 27, 1922. King Victor Emmanuel III resembled his grandfather in name only. He was a small, weak man who might have saved his nation the indignities of a generation of fascism had he had the courage of a Garibaldi, the integrity of an Emmanuel II, or the diplomatic skill of a Cavour. He wanted peace at any price. He got it, but at a dreadful price to Italian individual liberties. Mussolini's adventures in Ethiopia,

FRANK GERVASI

Spain, and, finally, World War II represent one of the darkest periods in Italian history.

In defense of Mussolini, if defense is possible, it may be said that he was mesmerized by Nazi power only slightly more than many highly placed persons in other countries at the time. In 1940–41 those who believed in the invincibility of Hitler's forces were legion. It was not surprising that Mussolini, exposed daily to evidences of Hitlerian successes, should become persuaded that unless he joined in the maddest adventure of recorded history he would have no place at the peace table when the time came to divide the spoils.

Mussolini was one of those Italians—throughout the country's history there have been some and there are, perhaps, too many still—whose pulses are accelerated by the sight of such symbols of past Roman glory as the Colosseum and the Forum Romanum.

His greatest crime, however, immense as was his delinquency in terms of suffering caused by dragging his country into war, lay in the fact that his regime arrested or reversed those processes which were fashioning in Italy a new democracy. In the opinion of this writer at least, Mussolini's responsibility to history, to Italian history particularly, is enormous; a responsibility shared, however, by a substantial fraction of the Italian population who even today utter nostalgic nonsense about how much "better off" they were under fascism.

The most remarkable fact about postwar Italy, however, is the thoroughness with which the nation has eschewed fascism and its works. Outward symbols of the Fascist heyday are gone. Black shirts and jack boots are mere, and usually somewhat embarrassing, memories for the vast majority of Italians. Some Fascist laws remain on the books, but they are being revised or abolished as rapidly as the still somewhat slow administrative processes permit.

The only major Fascist monument remaining in being is the Lateran Treaty of 1929, which "released" the Pope from his "exile" in the Holy See and restored Church influence in the schools, hospitals—and politics. But if the Garibaldi revolutions failed to dislodge the Church, World War II did succeed in dislodging the Church's most important lever of power, the monarchy. Restoration talk is sheer nonsense, and a monarchist future for Italy is unthinkable. Any effort to restore the King to the Italian throne would most certainly result in bitter and bloody civil war.

The vitality of postwar Italian literature, art, journalism, motion pictures, and political life is astounding indeed. The nation may be said to be living in a Second Risorgimento, and it is not difficult to predict for it, unless another war develops, a brilliant future.

Of problems, economic and social, Italy has many. A burgeoning population produces from 200,000 to 400,000 new candidates for jobs annually. Some 1,900,000 remain unemployed or semiemployed and live on a pittance of a dole provided by the social security laws. But somehow the nation has managed to reduce unemployment gradually from a 1948 total of nearly 3,000,000 to its present figure and to absorb the new labor force produced annually by a fecund people for whom emigration grows increasingly difficult.

Italy's biggest problem, perhaps, is the continued economic gap between North and South. The industrial North prospers; the agricultural South barely manages to eke out an existence, although here, too, there has been progress and more is promised by the new Cassa del Mezzogiorno, Bank of the South, a sort of RFC for promoting industrialization and improving agriculture and communications.

Land reform, the breakup of the big estates, is proceeding more slowly than it should but, probably, as fast as it can, given the limited resources available. The Church still owns approximately one fifth of the arable land, still does not pay taxes to the State, and continues to be a retarding factor. But land reform is not a simple or always economic process. Roads must be built and community centers established with proper housing for men, beasts, and machines, and social services established before a landless farmer and his family can be placed on the land.

Finally, one of Italy's great lacks is leadership. Alcide de Gasperi provided it in the postwar period. But De Gasperi, who must rank with Mazzini and Cavour in Italian history, whatever might have been his shortcomings, is dead. None of the present crop of Italian politicians and diplomats measures up to De Gasperi as a politician, diplomat, and statesman, with the possible exception of Antonio Segni. Signor Segni, however, is getting on in years and is almost certain to retire from active politics in the near future.

Given another Mazzini or Cavour, Italy might indeed provide a "shining light" to help guide men toward "brotherhood of nations." Meanwhile she provides an example of tolerance, hospitality, and warmheartedness which raises her to a level of civilization to which others might well aspire.

SWITZERLAND

Fernand Auberjonois

Fernand Auberjonois, European correspondent of the Toledo
Blade, *has lived twenty-three years in Europe, twenty-three years*
in the United States, and four years as an APO number in the
U. S. Army overseas.

Born and raised in French Switzerland, Auberjonois came to
the United States in 1933 for a three-week visit and never re-
turned to Switzerland to live. He is a naturalized citizen.

He writes professionally in both French and English for maga-
zines and newspapers on two continents. Before the war he was
with the Havas News Agency and the International Division of
NBC in New York. As an intelligence officer with the rank of
major, he was active in several theaters of operations. After the
war he worked first for Time-Life International in Paris, then for
NBC.

Transferred to the State Department, Auberjonois was con-
nected with the Information Program for nearly five years.

Now in his fourth year as European correspondent for the To-
ledo Blade, *Auberjonois works out of his London office and has*
covered every country in western and eastern Europe, as well as
the North African scene, which he had first discovered in 1942 as
liaison officer with General Patton in Morocco.

He is married and has three children and two stepchildren.
Painting is his hobby and he often illustrates his field reports for
the Toledo Blade, *written under the pseudonym of Fernand*
Fauber.

SWITZERLAND

Of normal countries like Switzerland one is tempted to say that they should be seen but not heard. Switzerland is the most frequently visited and least known country in western Europe. Clichés and ready-made judgments cling to her like burrs to corduroy breeches. Each year a million and a half travelers pour through valleys and across mountain passes to see the Swiss landscape. Only a minority can claim to have met the Swiss people.

It is fashionable to regard Switzerland as a beautiful backdrop for a stage play last performed centuries ago. The actors remain in the wings while the audience occupies the center of the stage. Yet the Swiss people exist. They grow in numbers (there are now 5 million of them). They are keenly interested in world affairs. They strive to be as great as their mountains are tall. More perhaps than any of their neighbors, they take life seriously.

How has the Swiss acquired this reputation of being the invisible man of Europe? The answer is that he has done his best to avoid the limelight. He has greased the skids along which foreigners travel, singly or in groups, when they visit his land. He has created oases of comfort—his resorts and hotels—where tourists curl up, relax, and forget all about the natives next door. As he moves along scenic channels, the visitor is encouraged to open his eyes and close his mind.

The great, the near great, and the once great of our troubled world settle in Swiss villas or pensions and live happily until the day when their remains are shipped home on fast trains speeding past neat railroad stations with potted geraniums in every window. Deposed monarchs, film stars on the mend, Arab chiefs in solid-gold Cadillacs, composers, exiled Latin-American leaders, dehydrated or deflated adventurers, seek the ideal resting place in Switzerland.

But the Swiss are great believers in hospitality without intimacy. They spoil their paying guests with good service, pure air, sun, and snow without encouraging too many contacts at the people-to-people level. Familiarity might bring friction, if not contempt. The visitors have come to relax, to forget, or to enjoy normalcy after experiencing tension and convulsion elsewhere. And they seldom realize that their hosts have worries of their own. For the Swiss, like all perfectionists, are great worriers.

Switzerland has been described as one of the very few nations still enjoying direct contact with her past, right back into the Middle Ages—a contact which nourishes a still living tradition. André Siegfried feels that a comparison with France in this respect is striking, even when outward resemblances make the two countries appear quite close. When we go to Switzerland, says Siegfried, we also go back into the nineteenth century. This small country, great by the position it holds in the world, is "the fullest expression of European civilization."

The question whether Switzerland could serve as a model for a unified Europe continues to tease inquisitive minds. One of the major postwar developments in a modern Europe divided by an ideological curtain is the creation of a common market, first step toward political integration. The European Common Market is a babe in arms. It hasn't even begun to crawl. But the birth and early progress of a "Little Europe" is already generating more interest than any other peaceful development in the second half of the twentieth century, with the possible exception of celestial explorations. Of course, the problems of European integration are vastly more complex than those which once confronted early Swiss federalists. But the two structures, one still in the formative stage, the other tested by time and events, are not without similarities.

It is tempting to argue that conditions in a country untouched by armed conflicts or revolutions since the Thirty Years' War are not to be found elsewhere. To say this is to forget that Switzerland has known internal strife, has warred against her neighbors, and once was on the verge of adopting an expansionist policy and made terrible mistakes. There was a time when, conscious of their military might, the Swiss were anxious to conquer territory outside their borders so as to establish buffer zones against Austrian, Italian, or Burgundian princes. Not until their heroic defeat at Marignano in 1515 did they abandon the idea of interfering in the affairs of Europe.

In the subsequent 450 years, Switzerland has found unity in contrast and, one might even say, in contradiction. She is known as an Alpine republic, but her wealth comes from the lowlands. She is neutral, but spends staggering sums for defense. She loves peace, but her sons devote much time each year to war games and military service. She has no coasts or seaports, but her merchant ships sail the Seven Seas. She is Europe's oldest democracy, but her women are denied the right to vote.

How have the Swiss achieved unity out of diversity?

The welding together of linguistic and religious groups has been a slow and sometimes painful process. Four languages are spoken in Switzerland. German, by 72 per cent of the people; French, by 21 per cent; Italian, by 6 per cent; and Romansh, by 1 per cent. Romansh, a language descending from Latin, survives in several of the eastern valleys. German Swiss is quite unlike the German spoken in Germany. The French Swiss have no dialect, but their language differs from that of their French neighbors from the standpoint of intonations and accent.

The French-, German-, and Italian-speaking Swiss formed their association with the understanding that the major function of the federative structure they had created was to protect linguistic and cultural minorities. Had they failed to agree on this point, they would have been absorbed, sooner or later, by Germany, France, and Italy. This explains Switzerland's opposition to the melting-pot theory. The Swiss find strength in diversity.

The nation is united but not unitarian. In recent times, the federal government has become stronger, but further centralization is resisted. And the cantons, with the communes, or townships, remain the more genuine democracy to which the citizen owes allegiance, no matter how deep his loyalty to the national emblem. The essence of democracy resides in the canton.

To understand Switzerland, one must survey political institutions through the wrong end of the field glasses. But is it the wrong end? The Swiss believe that roots count more in the shaping of individual attitudes than any other factor. They cultivate the "home-town spirit" on the assumption that a citizen can best develop his civic sense if he remains aware of these roots. Thus the commune and the canton have become, in the eyes of the Swiss, the first and last refuge. One of the most striking and conspicuous exhibits at the Swiss national fair of 1939 was a display of the flags of Switzerland's 3000 communes.

A Swiss has three citizenships: federal, cantonal, and communal. Communal citizenship is no less important to him than the other two. It is inalienable. And an alien applying for naturalization must first be endorsed by the commune, in the person of its mayor or councilors.

How can unity be achieved in a country stressing the smallest common denominator?

The answer lies in the power of the popular will, which, in Switzerland, forms from the bottom upward. The Swiss put their faith in direct rather than delegated democracy. Each citizen seeks at all times to take an active part in legislative work, through referendum or popular initiative. Complex though it may appear, the Swiss political machinery works because it corresponds to tradition and to civic sense.

It would be difficult to duplicate such a system in younger and vaster countries, where, in order to grow and prosper, the community must cultivate nomadic virtues.

In 1870 there were only three republics in Europe—Switzerland, the Hansa towns, and San Marino. Swiss unity was a fact long before the country adopted its first constitution, in 1848. The Swiss state was born in 1291, when the farmers of three districts on the shores of Lake Lucerne—Uri, Schwyz, and Unterwalden—formed a defensive league against the House of Hapsburg.

Under solemn oath, the three communities undertook to help any member threatened with loss or damage, by providing, without limit or reserve, men and materials for defense or aggression. They were not seeking liberty, but self-government. They did not deny the Hapsburgs' sovereign power, but insisted that authority should be delegated to one of their people. The alliance was to be "everlasting." No time limit was set on its validity.

It is not surprising that this original charter of alliance should be regarded, even today, as more significant than the constitution under which the federal state of twenty-two cantons was established in 1848. The Constitution, revised in 1874 but not radically altered, was drafted by men conscious of their own fallibility. The authors toiled long and hard to strike a balance between federalism and centralism. The document they produced was inspired by the liberal movement then spreading throughout Europe. It bears some resemblance to the United States Constitution, but can be more readily amended if an absolute majority of the people and of the cantons so decides.

In granting autonomy to the cantons, it denied them the right to make separate alliances among themselves or with foreign powers. It guaranteed individual rights, equality before the law, freedom of the press and of worship, as well as the rights of association and of meeting. It is not regarded as sacred or inviolable. The Swiss give priority to the will of the people over constitutionality.

Swiss constitutional experts modeled the country's bicameral system after that of the United States. But differences between these systems are as significant as similarities.

The Swiss are suspicious of personal power. They have set up their executive branch like a board of directors of seven members, whose chairman, the President of the Confederation, is simply *primus inter pares*. This Federal Council, or collegial body of the government, transacts administrative business much like a cabinet. Its members are the heads of seven executive departments. They are elected for four years, by the Federal Assembly, and generally re-elected if they wish to remain in office. Their salary is less than $10,000 a year.

The Federal Assembly consists of two chambers with equal powers and duties: the National Council, elected by the people in the ratio of one deputy for every 22,000 inhabitants, and the Council of States, with forty-four deputies, two for each canton. The entire National Council is re-elected every four years. In the case of the Council of States, the individual cantons determine their own method of selection.

The Swiss, who always seize every opportunity to point out that they do not have a President (only a Chairman of the Federal Council), are also the first to deny that Bern is the capital of Switzerland. Bern is the federal seat, the administrative center of the country.

To carry democratic processes one step further, the citizens of Switzerland have formalized their right to pass judgment on legislation and to initiate new laws. A law passed by the Federal Assembly does not take effect for ninety days. In the interim, if 30,000 citizens call for a referendum, the law can be endorsed or rejected. And by exercising the right of initiative, 50,000 voters can propose constitutional amendments or the drafting of new laws and demand a popular vote on it. This is what the Swiss mean by direct democracy. The system works because of the political acumen, the shrewdness, and the civic sense displayed by the citizenry.

Had Switzerland practiced isolationism in any shape or form, had she entrenched herself behind her natural walls, she would be, today, one of the underdeveloped nations of the world. By definition, Switzerland is a poor country. Her present wealth was acquired through hard work. But it is, also, the result of a curious combination of historical circumstances.

Swiss mercenaries who served on Europe's battlefields, in Asia, and in the New World learned to take a global view of politics and trade. This outlook was passed on to succeeding generations.

At a time when European countries were busy training industrial workers, Switzerland inherited her own pool of highly skilled labor as she became a haven for refugees. Thousands of French, Italian, and Dutch escapees fled religious persecutions, settled in Protestant towns, and introduced silk weaving, ribbon making, and watchmaking in the host country, which, until then, had been primarily an agricultural nation.

Swiss educators influenced the thinking and sometimes the political decisions of many a European ruler. And Switzerland exported men, techniques, and money long before the advent of technical assistance programs as we know them today.

Here are some of the facts worth remembering about Swiss emigrants.

A Swiss, Colonel Henri Bouquet, was George Washington's military instructor. Another Swiss, General Sir Frederick Haldimand, held Quebec against Washington. Albert Gallatin of Geneva drafted the Treaty of Ghent after the War of 1812, had all the frontier forts along the U.S.-Canadian border dismantled, and restored the broken ties between the two English-speaking nations. In all, some 70,000 Swiss officers, including 700 generals, served in foreign armies.

François Lefort was Peter the Great's adviser. Frédéric César de La Harpe tutored Alexander I of Russia. Swiss capital helped launch the Du Pont de Nemours concern in America. Coastal surveying in the United States was initiated by Ferdinand Hassler. Two Swiss scientists, the Agassiz father-and-son team, taught geology and zoology at Harvard. A Swiss was director of the Bank of England; another became chief of a tribe of wildmen in northern Australia. New York's George Washington Bridge was built by a Swiss. A Swiss was Minister of Agriculture, Commerce, and Industry in the Dutch East Indies. Oscar of the Waldorf came from Switzerland.

Switzerland, although self-contained and nationalistic, has developed the most highly internationalized economic system in the world. This had to be. The livelihood of one out of three Swiss citizens depends on exports. By the end of the eighteenth century, Switzerland had become, after Britain, the major industrial country in Europe. She needed markets abroad and began to search for them early.

But the time came, with the rise of mechanization everywhere, when Swiss industrialists were forced to reappraise their methods. Their neighbors, in countries where raw materials were readily

available and capital plentiful for plant equipment, found themselves leading the field in mass production. To meet the competition, Swiss industrialists stressed quality over quantity. Standards were raised to such an extent that the cost of raw materials
became a secondary factor.

What is the situation today? Manufactured goods make up 92
per cent of Swiss exports. Imports include raw materials (35 per
cent), manufactured goods (45 per cent), and foodstuffs (20 per
cent). Yet the Swiss trade balance regularly shows a deficit which
would give orthodox trade-balance watchers nightmares. The gap
is bridged by invisible exports and services—by income from the
tourist trade, by capital investments abroad, by insurance trans-
actions.

In 58 B.C., when the Helvetians—a mixture of Celts, Etruscans,
and Ligurians—harvested their corn, burned their homes, and
moved westward ahead of Julius Caesar's invading forces, Caesar
ordered his legions to bring them back. He needed them to protect
the northern flank of his empire against Germanic invaders.

To guard the crossroads of Europe, with arms or through the
process of neutralization, has been the assignment of the Swiss
ever since—from this day when the curtain of history parted to
reveal them.

It took very little persuading to Romanize the Helvetians. Only
three towns were turned into Roman military camps. Civilian control over this area seems to have been minimal. And, at that
period, only the valleys of Switzerland were inhabited. Aventi-
cum, now Avenches, was the capital. The gold bust of a Roman
emperor was found there, only a few years ago, near the ruins of
the amphitheater.

For the next four centuries peace reigned undisturbed. Celtic
settlements, estates, villas, prospered at the foot of the Jura Mountains and in the Rhone Valley. Under the wings of the Roman
eagle the Helvetians became a relatively sophisticated people.
The Helvetians were then being Christianized.

Then invaders poured into this Roman outpost. The Alamanni,
or Germans, came from the North, the Burgundians from France.

They failed to reach the southern valleys, across the Alps, but brought in two new languages, German and French, to compete with Latin and Rhaetian. From that time on, Helvetia was to become quadrilingual.

Little or nothing is known of the circumstances in which this occupation took place. But the fifth-century newcomers were barbarians. The era of civilization inaugurated by the Romans came to an end. The original Helvetians took to the hills and mountains. The plains were devastated by endless wars pitting Burgundians against Alamanni. The linguistic frontier between the French- and German-speaking populations was established. It has hardly changed since.

During the next turbulent five hundred years, marked by the rise of feudalism and by the appearance on the scene of the only king ever to rule over the Swiss, Christian missionaries converted the Alamanni and founded monasteries, most famous of which was that of St. Gall, later a center of religious music. St. Gall himself was an Irishman.

The whole of Helvetia became a part of the Holy Roman Empire. The Dark Ages were coming to an end. As the threat of tribal war subsided, the bishops of Basel, Lausanne, and Sion could spend more time in their sees.

International commerce flourished. Old towns grew in size. New towns appeared along the main roads linking Germany and Italy. Artisans who lived in these towns were given new opportunities as their feudal overlords devoted much time and money to the Crusades. A brisk business in armor and military equipment developed. With their new wealth bondsmen bought their freedom.

In the land that was to be Switzerland, standards of living soared. Silks, tapestries, spices, sugar, and rice were brought from the Orient.

However, between the main routes of trade leading from the Italian ports on the Mediterranean to the German cities, in a remote mountain area, the people of three agricultural communities —Uri, Schwyz, and Unterwalden—had remained fairly free of outside influence and control. They were not answerable for their actions to any of the overlords whose rule extended over their close neighbors. They owed allegiance to the Holy Roman Empire and the Emperor.

Early in the thirteenth century, the free peasants of the Waldstätten—the "forest communes"—became linked with the outside world when a bridge was built and a new gateway opened leading to the St. Gotthard Pass. They had no dynastic affection for the Emperor. They favored an association with a distant ruler, for this made it easier for them to manage their own affairs. As fate would have it, however, the Empire began to fade into eclipse, and the House of Hapsburg, under Rudolf, acquired rights not only over Austria but over the three cantons on the shores of Lake Lucerne.

On Rudolf's death, the Waldstätten farmers chose freedom. In 1291, they concluded an extraordinary pact of alliance opening with the words "In the name of the Lord, Amen," a military pact challenging the Hapsburgs and pledging mutual aid. The treaty was to endure, by God's will, "forever." No other agreement in the history of Europe has ever included such a clause. And of all the leagues constituted at that time, the Swiss league alone has endured.

What prompted primitive people to proclaim their love of liberty in a feudal age? Fear of intervention was one factor. There were others.

The thirteenth century was the first of the great revolutionary periods that were to mold western Europe. At that time, political passions boiled in Germany and Italy. The communes of Lombardy had already won their freedom. German cities—Cologne, Nuremberg, Ulm, the Hanseatic towns, among others—became free. In England, the Magna Charta was promulgated.

And the Swiss cantons were strategically located on one of the main roads between Germany and Italy, a road along which ideas, not trade only, had been flowing for some time.

The text of the pact signed by the Confederates on August 1, 1291, was not found until the end of the eighteenth century. But the spirit that moved its signers was such that it bound their heirs together for hundreds of years. The signing of this pact also marked the beginning of a long series of bloody battles fought against the Hapsburgs, at Morgarten, Sempach, Näfels, and against the French at St. Jacob and Morat. In practically every encounter the winners were the Schwyzers, later known as the Swiss. The Confederation grew from three to eight cantons by 1400, and to thirteen by 1513.

For the Swiss, warfare had become a lucrative business. Theirs was the only national army in Europe trained by compulsory military service. They had defeated not only the Austrians but also a French king and Charles the Bold of Burgundy. They felt powerful enough to acquire new territories, but the venture upon which they embarked soon proved too costly. The Swiss learned very early that imperialism doesn't pay. Determined to gain a foothold on the southern slopes of the Alps, they occupied the Leventina after defeating the Milanese troops at Giornico. Their next target was Milan. But, at Marignano, in 1515, their infantry was no match for the cavalry and artillery of France and Venice.

The heroic debacle of Marignano put an end for all time to Swiss dreams of expansion. Neutrality became the country's basic policy, even though Swiss soldiers continued to fight under foreign flags.

The hardest thing for a European to grasp is the tremendous contrasts in the American landscape. But these contrasts are even more striking in a small country like Switzerland, where, in a matter of hours, the motorist driving from Germany to Italy on Swiss roads sees fruit orchards, oaks, firs, polar lichens, aloe, heather, pines, and vineyards.

It has often happened that two travelers comparing notes after following different itineraries across Switzerland have come up with two totally unrelated sets of impressions. And this in a country one third the size of New York State, with a population two thirds that of London.

The diversity of the Swiss landscape is due, of course, to variations of altitudes and aspects. But there are also striking contrasts between the various lowland areas; architectural tastes, for instance, have largely been dictated by historical ties.

Burgundy has influenced the planning of many of the small

towns at the foot of the Jura. The farmhouses of the Bernese
countryside are reminiscent—except for their enormous roofs—
of French *métairies*. But the painted façades in villages along
the Rhine can only be of German inspiration. And Italy has
brought color to the narrow streets of Lugano.

What the valleys and provinces of Switzerland have in common
is an abundance of flowers on window sills, in parks, and in farm
gardens. And the Swiss lakes have attracted the builders of towns
and growers of very fine wines. With the exception of Basel, Bern,
and Fribourg, Swiss cities mirror themselves in the peaceful
waters of a lake.

Again, climate and altitude have dictated the choice of shin-
gled walls in the Jura region; and the strange structure known as
the mountain chalet—so different from, yet so closely related to
the log cabin of the American settler—looks out of place when
erected in the plains.

No Swiss will agree with the stranger who finds monotony in
Alpine grandeur and to whose eyes all mountains look alike. For
there are contrasts in flora, fauna, geology, human attitudes, and
in the very smell of mountain air as one passes from one valley
into another.

And the big stone heart of this country, unproductive as it may
be, is the single most important natural bond among people who
speak different tongues and have different outlooks on so many
issues. The St. Gotthard, the core of the whole system of mountain
ranges, is a concrete symbol of national unity. It is the fortified
"redoubt" where a besieged army could hold an invader at bay
despite the loss of all the territory from which modern Switzerland derives her prosperity.

Finally, the land has molded the character of the Swiss farmer,
of the villager whose every move is timed to satisfy the exigencies
of a soil that is rich but demanding.

So we have three Switzerlands (and within these three, many
more) leaving an imprint on the citizens.

—The rugged, wild, romantic Alps, which filled Addison's mind
with "an agreeable kind of horror."

—The farmlands, where a peasant aristocracy of considerable

charm and natural sophistication has been losing manpower attracted by factory life.

—The cities, Switzerland's windows on the outside world, whose
growth in this century has been so impressive that a casual visitor
tends to overlook the very strong influence of tradition on their
inhabitants.

We have a nation born in the mountains, whose population
has expanded toward the plains, toward the rivers that link them
to the seas and oceans. This trend has been constant. It has been
speeded up in the past thirty years by industrialization, European
conflicts, and the depression of the thirties.

Significant changes have taken place. In 1920 the proportion
of the population engaged in farming was 25.8 per cent. By 1950
it had fallen to 16.5 per cent. During the same period the proportion of Swiss citizens living in the canton of their birth declined
from 75 per cent to 67 per cent. The percentage of Catholics
has increased at the expense of the Protestants. More German,
less French, less Italian, is spoken. The delicate inner balance
of the Swiss association of communities cannot but be affected
by these demographic, social, and industrial changes.

The fundamental principles on which the political institutions
of the Swiss Confederation have been resting since the country
adopted its constitution have not been altered.

The Swiss remain faithful to their concept of direct participation by the individual in legislative work. They are still opposed
to centralization, and the federal government has less power than
cantonal administrations. Minority rights are inalienable. No act
of Parliament is valid without the express consent of the voters.
Members of the National Council and of the Council of States
spend only ten to twelve weeks in the capital each year. And they
draw no salaries, only meager per diem and travel allowances.

The state is not always regarded with absolute reverence. Yet
its power has been expanding steadily, for the very simple reason
that decentralization is no longer compatible with the modern
notion of progress.

Legislation by referendum has given the people several opportunities to express their will on crucial questions. In 1935, proposals concerning an over-all revision of the Constitution were rejected. In 1942, the voters turned down a legislative measure whereby the government—the seven members of the Federal Council—would, in the future, be elected through direct suffrage rather than by the chambers. In 1959, the right of Swiss women to cast votes was once again denied by their menfolk, who are perfectly aware that they are only postponing the day when this right will be granted. Yet it is significant that resistance to feminine suffrage emanates mostly from the country's workers and farmers.

The strong state is still, so to speak, on probation and closely watched by the strong cantons. But the federal government has acquired new rights and prerogatives, together with new responsibilities. Whenever an emergency arises, another step is taken toward centralization.

Centralized planning of the country's agricultural output, enforced with remarkable results in World War II, when Switzerland had to count largely on her own modest resources, is now regarded as an acceptable peacetime method of dealing with overproduction in certain sectors. State subsidies to industries and to farmers in times of economic stress would have been condemned by the people four decades ago. But not today, after a depression and a threat of economic strangulation during the war years.

Federal help to private banks is another case in point. And so is the ever growing authority of the federal treasury in fiscal matters. In 1938, the central government's income from direct taxes totaled about 142 million dollars. In 1956, the figure was a little over 600 million.

But new forces have appeared on the national scene: the trade associations grouping producers with similar interests. Their influence is considerable. They received the backing of the people when their existence was threatened by antitrust laws. And they are supported by the labor unions, whose major interest lies in professional rather than political gains.

The inevitability of further centralization and the dangers of centralization are frequent topics of public debates. The cantons cannot extend their powers. They have their own legislative and judicial institutions. They enjoy financial autonomy. They run the universities and the schools. It is true to say that Switzerland has twenty-two capital cities.

The Army, the railroads, the postal services, communications, broadcasting, are dependent on the central authority. But, more and more, the federal government pays subsidies to the cantons and, as a result, acquires rights of supervision.

Did the Swiss find a short cut to peace, unity, and prosperity? Students of history raise this question because of the extraordinary foresight displayed by the founders of the Confederation in signing their unusual pact of alliance. Were the following generations spared the costly political experiments forced upon their European neighbors, whose progress toward democratic aims was so much slower? Actually, Switzerland, like the rest of Europe, learned her lessons the hard way.

It is true that her people became convinced at a very early stage that dreams of aggrandizement can turn into nightmares. But, for hundreds of years, their determination to remain united "forever" was put to the acid test of religious strife and, to a lesser extent, of social conflicts.

The Reformation must be mentioned first as the most disruptive force encountered by the statesmen who kept the Swiss communities together. It began in 1521 with Ulrich Zwingli's sermons in Zurich. Zwingli was merely following the impetus given to the movement by Luther's writings. But he went so far in his condemnation of the Catholic hierarchy that even Erasmus became alarmed and denounced his radicalism.

The crusade against the Roman Church led to a sharp split among the Confederates. There were now two Confederations, the Protestant towns and the Catholic rural cantons. Each followed its own policies, both internally and externally.

The Catholics, once the sworn enemies of the hated House of Hapsburg, were ready to secede. They threatened to ally themselves with Austria and to hand over to the Emperor any territory they might annex by conquest. In the open hostilities which ensued, Zwingli himself lost his life on the battlefield of Kappel. But his new doctrine prevailed. In 1536 the Protestant Church was formally established in Geneva, where John Calvin had only begun his crusade.

Elsewhere in the country the religious conflict was solved in a typically Swiss manner. The final decision rested with the citizens, who voted in their townships and at guild meetings.

But, for many years, the rural communes continued to fight the spread of the reform movement. Religious issues generated great bitterness and caused frequent local clashes. It was not until the revocation of the Edict of Nantes by Louis XIV, when thousands of penniless Huguenots poured into Switzerland, that passions began to abate. The circumstances of this dramatic flight of escapees made a deep and lasting impresssion on the Swiss.

The Thirty Years' War between France and the Empire devastated Germany from 1618 to 1648. Both sides sought the help of the Swiss, but fear of civil war prompted the Confederates to remain on the side lines even though Protestant and Catholic members were tempted by the prospects of possible victories for their camp.

Refusing all inducements to take part in the struggle, the Swiss Diet laid the cornerstone of future Swiss policy: armed neutrality. An army of 12,000 men with guns, controlled by a central war council of Protestant and Catholic leaders, was entrusted with the defense of the country's frontiers.

Neutrality at a time when the rest of Europe was at war gave the Swiss an opportunity to develop their internal economy and external commerce. Prosperity brought an increase in the standard of living of the middle classes. Raw materials were imported in increasing volume. New industries provided the cities with manufactured goods for export.

In the seventeenth century Switzerland became a rich nation. In the eighteenth century she lost her reputation for uncouthness, and outsiders hailed her as an oasis of peace, kindness, and culture. But the high level of stability to which her people aspired had not yet been reached.

The French Revolution was bound to have repercussions in Switzerland, where, as a corollary to prosperity, a patrician society, if not an aristocracy, had emerged. Individual rights were being respected, but a few privileged families had a monopoly on public office. Conservative and liberal parties appeared in the cities. The new ideas of liberty and equality found champions among the intellectuals.

On the eve of the Revolution the confederate state was a loose and complex structure, with its thirteen cantons, its six allies, and its scattered "subject" areas.

In 1789, the Swiss Club of Paris, a group of intellectuals opposed to the patrician rule, was instrumental in spreading to Switzerland the rebellious spirit of the times. Demonstrations in a number of cantons were brutally repressed, but discontent remained alive until news of endless persecutions and executions, brought from Paris by political refugees, began to exert a sobering effect on public opinion.

By 1798 the French government found a pretext for intervention in Swiss affairs and sent troops against the Confederates. Bern was captured and the Confederation of thirteen cantons fell. In the name of liberty, France had brought oppression to Switzerland. And the aim of the Directorate—control over the mountain passes—had been attained with little effort.

Thus was formed, by the use of force, the Helvetic Republic, One and Indivisible. It lasted five years, from 1798 to 1803. No form of government could have been more inappropriate for a country of contrasts, a people who spoke four different languages and practiced two forms of religion.

This, too, came to pass. Napoleon's Act of Mediation restored the confederate structure. But total independence was not regained until the Emperor's final defeat at the hands of the Allies, in 1815. At the second Congress of Paris, Swiss neutrality was declared to be "in the true interest of Europe as a whole."

Swiss history did not end with the Federal Pact of 1815. The

pact marked the beginning of an era of national prosperity and
the slow rise of liberalism. A federal constitution came into effect
in 1848. Since that time there has been an absence of major crises
in Switzerland.

At the end of World War II, Switzerland had an army of half a
million men—one tenth of the country's total population! The
peacetime force is just as impressive if one considers that Switzerland is neutral. At least 350,000 citizens are in training or on
maneuvers at some time or other each year.

To understand Swiss neutrality—which is that of the porcupine
rather than of the ostrich—one should remember that, for centuries, the country's history was written by her regiments. The Army
made Switzerland. The pact sealing the creation of the Confederation was a military agreement.

Military discipline is freely accepted because the Swiss know
that obedience is a quality free men alone can demonstrate. The
citizen soldier is passionately interested in everything military.
Yet no one could accuse him of being a militarist in the pejorative
sense of the word.

Fully aware of their obligation to fight if attacked, the people of
Switzerland undergo an intensive period of training followed by
annual refresher courses. But the permanent establishment consists of only 350 career officers and 200 noncommissioned instruc-
tors.

At the age of thirty-two, a Swiss private has spent fifty weeks
of his life in military service, a lieutenant a hundred weeks, a
staff captain three years.

The citizen keeps his uniform, his light weapon, and his ammunition at home. This would seem to mean that the authorities are
not expecting the crime rate to rise. Nor are they unduly worried
by the possibility of social upheavals.

In two world wars, would-be aggressors knew that the Swiss
would defend themselves. They also knew that they would blow
up the Alpine tunnels and sever vital communications between
Germany and Italy. In classical warfare, fighting against a resolute stand or a slow retreat by half a million men equipped with

modern weapons and familiar with every inch of the ground they defend would be costly indeed.

But what of nuclear warfare—tactical or strategic? How is the new order of things affecting Swiss attitudes toward defense and neutrality? The government has accepted, in principle, the allocation of tactical nuclear arms to the troops. But it is meeting resistance from several quarters, including the Church. Individuals and groups argue that the cost of nuclear weapons cannot be justified. Some experts doubt the usefulness of these weapons in mountainous terrain.

The issue may have to be put to a vote, whose outcome is difficult to predict. In the meantime, the Soviets have made it clear that they would regard the nuclearization of Swiss armed forces as the abandonment, by Switzerland, of her traditional concept of neutrality.

There is no indication, however, that the Swiss will ever reduce their classical armaments and their defense budget on the assumption that the coming into being of the great deterrent warrants such economies.

Switzerland's dilemma has been, all along, that although she considers herself firmly aligned with the West in the defense of Europe's cultural values, she cannot become a member of any groups advocating military sanctions against an aggressor. She joined the League of Nations after being assured that she would not be obliged to take part in military operations or allow foreign troops to cross her territory. But she agreed to enforce economic sanctions against Italy at war with Ethiopia.

This new brand of neutrality, known as *differential* neutrality, was practiced as long as the League showed herself willing and capable of enforcing collective security. When the international organization, whose headquarters was Geneva, wavered in its determination to defend the weak against the strong, Switzerland withdrew and reaffirmed her faith in *integral* neutrality.

But the main lesson of World War II was that the government would find it increasingly difficult, in years to come, to adhere to such a restrictive policy in an age of defensive alliances and of integration. Since the war, Switzerland has given her neutrality a new look, which may not, at first glance, impress the casual observer. Yet the evolution is significant. She has begun to apply the principle of "neutrality plus solidarity." Her leaders are aware that neutrality is not absolutely incompatible with association and with commitments in a variety of fields.

This revision of a historical stand seems all the more necessary now that Switzerland's neighbors are busy creating the nucleus of a United Europe as they lay the foundations of the European Common Market and of the rival Free Trade Area Association.

What is in store for the descendants of the men who, more than six hundred and fifty years ago, gathered in a meadow and swore to remain united forever? Much will depend on the course of world events and on human wisdom or folly. More than ever before, the fate of Switzerland is tied to that of the rest of Europe.

In his book *The Swiss Without Halos,* J. Christopher Herold indulges in a bit of history-fiction and assumes that in the eventuality of nuclear war Switzerland, because of her mountainous terrain, would escape total ruin more easily than others. The author paints this picture:

"Once the Swiss can emerge from their natural shelters, they might easily find that they are the only Europeans left who have preserved the technical know-how of prewar years. They would be in great demand wherever they went. Hunger would force them to help other nations reorganize their resources. About that task they would go with efficiency and a determination of which other peoples would no longer be capable. Swiss engineers, Swiss physicians, Swiss agricultural and financial experts, and Swiss Red Cross workers would roam through the devastated land like a race of supermen. Sensibly and rationally they would survey the potentialities of the ruins, make reports and draft plans for the reorganization of Europe on a solid business basis, with no political nonsense allowed to interfere. They probably would do an excellent job."

So they might. But the Swiss, when they think of the future, tend to worry about less spectacular matters. How, for instance, can Switzerland fit into a centralized, united Europe?

If the new Europe were to be a confederation, the Swiss would, of course, be in sympathy with its aims. But would they be obliged to give up their neutrality, which was never imposed from outside and which corresponds to the wishes of the people? This question may arise sooner than one thinks. It cannot be dismissed lightly.

And then there might come a time when Switzerland would be told that in an era of economic cold war she should practice economic as well as political neutrality. This, for her, would present great dangers.

Sooner or later Switzerland will have to decide whether it is in her best interest to align herself with one of the two rival blocs—the Free Trade Area or the Common Market—in which national resources are now being pooled. At present, she supports the free traders. But can she afford to do so if the spirit of rivalry grows?

Swiss economists are not agreed on the course to follow. Some, however, urge their countrymen to avoid isolation within the European Common Market, which, a few years from now, may be a reality at all points along their borders.

To make full use of Swiss ingenuity and adaptability is the goal the Swiss have set for themselves. But here again they may run into some trouble. Britain trains 57 engineers per year and per million inhabitants. The figure for Switzerland is 82. But the United States trains 140 engineers per million inhabitants, and Soviet Russia's total is estimated at between 280 and 315 per million. All western European countries outside Britain and Switzerland manage to aggregate only 67 engineers graduating from their colleges each year, for every million inhabitants.

The Swiss, while grateful for the fact that they are in third place behind the United States and Soviet Russia in this field of endeavor, are alarmed by the number of scientists they have been losing to American concerns such as Battelle, IBM, or RCA and, more recently, to powerful British combines. Foreign firms are doing a considerable amount of recruiting at Swiss universities. Switzerland cannot export her best brains without weakening herself.

Another question mark: What would happen if, due to the steady rise in standards of living in the free world, Europe's consumers were to demand mass-produced goods in increasing quantities, instead of quality articles? Deprived of raw materials, Switzerland might find competition pretty rugged.

But these are hypothetical questions. And the people of Switzerland are more concerned with facts than with hypotheses. They have had to deal with seemingly insoluble problems before and have come up with the right answer.

Our guess is that, short of a general conflict or a great depression, Switzerland will remain for a long time a showcase of democracy and of stability. Such a showcase is badly needed on the European continent.

The men who are beginning to build a new Europe will find the Swiss blueprints useful, even if not suitable in all respects to their vast project.

The young nations overseas should be encouraged by the thought that Switzerland, one of Europe's most highly industrialized nations, was once herself "underdeveloped."

And in lands where people struggle with minority problems, it should be remembered that the Swiss had no magic formula to help them achieve "Unity through Diversity."

BENELUX

Arthur Settel

Arthur Settel has spent most of his forty-eight years in journalism or closely allied vocations. At thirteen he ran copy for the late, lamented Brooklyn Daily Times. *At seventeen he was a cub reporter. At twenty-one he was graduated from the Columbia School of Journalism. One year later he was in Jerusalem working for* The Palestine Post, *a stringer for a wire service, and a contributor to a long list of American publications. He became Managing Editor of* The Egyptian Mail, *an English-language daily in Cairo, at twenty-five and was concurrently B.U.P. correspondent. He covered some big stories, wrote fiction, sold to* Time, Barron's, *the Toronto* Star Weekly, *and a host of other media.*

Settel was in Germany for seven years on the staff of General Clay as Economic Information Officer, later Director of the Public Relations Division for U. S. High Commissioner John J. McCloy, a post he held from 1949 through 1952. He has been Director of Public Relations for KLM (Royal Dutch Airlines), and a Consultant to the U. S. Department of State, Commerce, and Agriculture and the A.E.C. on International Trade Fairs. He is presently consultant on NATO and international problems to U. S. Senator Jacob K. Javits (Rep., N.Y.). He has been co-author of a number of books and a great many magazine articles, booklets, studies, and brochures. Mr. Settel and his wife and their two sons live in Washington.

BENELUX

Whether you are a businessman in search of a European country with a friendly economic climate, an abundance of skilled labor, and a minimum of red tape, in which to establish your first European assembly plant; or a newspaperman looking for an inexpensive hideaway where you can write that long-deferred world-shaking novel; or an art connoisseur with expensive preferences but a limited budget; or just a tourist looking for a place in which you can have a good time without spending all your money —you could not do better than to put the Low Countries high on your list.

Here, along the northern littoral of the continent, you will find what you want in almost every range of civilized interest, be it investment opportunities, picture-postcard landscapes, jet-age airports, a lucrative market for consumer goods, familiar historic landmarks, and, most significantly, peoples who are probably the most hospitable and friendly on earth: the Dutch, the Belgians, and the Luxembourgers.

A couple of summers ago, I was strolling with my wife along one of the major thoroughfares of Amsterdam. We were looking for a tiny stand-up bar which, oddly, had been built beneath the wing of a beautiful cathedral. It was called The Three Crowns. Nowhere else in the city could we buy a drink which I consider one of the most exciting liqueurs in the whole alcoholic spectrum. The drink is called "Bitter Koekjes." It is made by Lucas Bols and served in The Three Crowns, and customers take the first sip from a standing position without using the hands, tipping over the glass with the lips.

We stopped to ask a policeman where we could find The Three Crowns. He scratched his head, looked knowingly, then said in English: "Follow me." We did. He routed us through a devious path along streets lined with shops and houses of every description, past museums and churches, past canals and parks, across corners jam-packed with a maze of tiny European cars, tramways, and battalions of bicycles and endless streams of pedestrians, all competing for space in this toyland city.

We felt terribly guilty to be taking so much of the policeman's time, but he waved away my protests and apologies. All he would say was "Follow me," and we did for fully twenty minutes. Then at last we found the church, and around the corner, The Three Crowns bar.

"Won't you come in and have a drink with us?" we asked. The policeman agreed to enter the bar, but he declined to touch the liqueur. He stood by politely until we were finished, then shook hands with us, wished us a pleasant stay in Holland, and disappeared into the busy street.

"Imagine a New York cop treating us like that," my wife commented dryly.

We took a trolley, or tramway, as it is called in Europe, and rode through Amsterdam's teeming streets. "Where is the diamond market area?" I asked another passenger seated opposite us. She replied in excellent English, then asked: "You are Americans?" We replied in the affirmative. "Well, then, I must tell you, I have a brother in America. Maybe you know him." Her brother lived with his family in Michigan and, unfortunately, we had never been there. "I wish to go to America, too, someday," she said. We had arrived at our destination and were ready to get off the trolley. "Good-by," said the Dutch woman amiably. "Maybe we meet someday in America." We half suspected we would.

There may be some areas of the world where Americans are despised, due to hostile propaganda and to a few badly oriented American citizens. But Holland, Belgium, and Luxembourg, which I shall hereafter call Benelux, are not among these. Americans enjoy the respect, admiration, and virtually unquestioning co-operation of these three important partners in the free enterprise system to which most of us subscribe. The hospitality of the Dutch, the Belgians, and the Luxembourgers, whether it is extended in a cottage or a castle, whether it is offered to the passenger aboard a luxurious airliner or a visitor to the home of a Maastricht burgher, is warm, sincere, and almost embarrassing.

What nature of men are these, with their kings and queens, their dukes and their duchies, their storied castles and deep roots in history, their tulips and wooden shoes, their sparkling modern factories, their bicycles and jet airplanes, their grottoes and galleries, their folklore, their beaches and their variegated costumes, their business acumen, their festivals, their art collections, and their love of freedom? Who are they, and what is it that makes them pre-eminent in the arts, the culture, the achievements of mankind? What form of government have they adopted as their own? How does one explain the survival of the three royal houses —the House of Orange in the Netherlands, the House of Saxe-Coburg in Belgium, and the Grand Duchy in Luxembourg—while kings the world over have vanished from their thrones and from power? What should we know of their culture? The bases of their economy? The racial strains and the living habits of the peoples comprising the nation?

Let us have a look at the somewhat blurred image of Benelux— through the eyes of a fact-finding newsman. First, some basic data.

The Three Kingdoms have a great deal in common and perhaps even more that is not common. They are linked by the arteries and sinews of geography as well as the highways of history. Belgium has an area of 11,775 square miles, a frontier of 896 miles, a seaboard of 62 miles. The western region—that area west of the storied Meuse River and its tributary, the Sambre—is level and fertile. The eastern tableland of the historic Ardennes Forest is hilly and wooded. The general elevation is under 526 feet; the North averages 60 feet. Slightly more than half (58 per cent) of Belgium is agricultural, 4 per cent for horticulture, 18 per cent is in forests, 17 per cent in urban and industrial areas. The low, reclaimed lands near the coast, which are protected against floods by dikes, cover an area roughly equal to that of the boroughs of Queens and Richmond in New York City, or 193 square miles. Belgium's population of about 9,000,000 (a density of 745 persons per square mile, making it among the most densely populated countries of the Western world) consists of the Flemings, of German stock, who inhabit the North and West, and the Walloons, of Celtic origin, who live in the southern and eastern sections.

Some 2,500,000 Belgians speak Flemish; 3,100,000 French; 1,500,000 speak both; and 300,000 speak some other language.

Belgian cities have distinctive industrial characteristics; the capital, Brussels, which was visited during the 1958 World's Fair by an estmated 10,000,000 people, is world-famous for its beautiful buildings, boulevards, restaurants, and shops. Antwerp, a port city, vies with Rotterdam and Hamburg for the leadership as a shipping center. Liége is famous for its steel industry; Ghent for its lace, its textiles and tools; Charleroi rivals the Ruhr city of Düsseldorf for the coal deposits near by. The picturesque town of Bruges has lost its commercial importance but is worth a visit. On the coast, Ostend serves as a port as well as a tourist center the year round.

The largest segment of Belgium's population is Roman Catholic. There are in addition 50,000 Protestants and 25,000 Jews. The clergy of all faiths are paid by the state. The country enjoys complete religious liberty.

Belgium's greatest foreign trade is with the Netherlands, the German Federal Republic, France, Britain, and the United States. Her largest imports are ores and minerals; textiles and clothing and accessories; nonprecious metals; machinery. Her exports are topped by nonprecious metals; textiles and clothing; ores and minerals; chemicals.

The year 1957 saw 3,456,000 tourists visit Belgium; 1958, over 10,000,000. The national airline, Sabena, flew more than 575,000,-000 passenger-miles.

The country has 22,905 university students, 62 newspapers, 975,829 telephones. His Majesty King Baudouin took the oath on July 17, 1951. The government is Christian Social and Liberal coalition. General Eyskens is Prime Minister.

Luxembourg is famous for its smallness, its castles, its industries, its postage stamps, and the stubbornness of its liberty-loving people. The unofficial national motto of the 350,000 Luxembourgers who reside within the 998-square-mile area of the Duchy is painted across the doorposts of many homes. It reads: *"Mir woelle bleiwe wat mir sin* [We want to remain what we are]."

Geographically, the northern and western regions are a continuation of the Ardennes plateaus, while the eastern sector rolls down to the Moselle River's level, one of the richest wine-producing areas in the world. To the south, the rolling country of Luxembourg is rich in ore. Sandstone and limestone occur everywhere, but there are abundant forests and sandy soil requiring fertilizer. Agriculture, mining, and the manufacture of steel ore, along with wine, leather goods, railway operation, and government service, are the principal occupations of the people of Luxembourg. Their heritage was provided by the Franks, the Celts, and Germanic tribes which traversed the region before and after the Roman invasion. They speak a language of their own—Letzeburgesch—which is strongly flavored by German and French and was not adopted as the official language of the country until 1939.

Other pertinent data: Prevailing religion—Roman Catholic. Government—constitutional monarchy headed by the House of Nassau. Ruler—Grand Duchess Charlotte. Parliament—Council of State, upper house (15 members), and Chamber of Deputies, lower house. Industries—mining and metallurgy, agriculture, crafts, and other professions.

Luxembourg's government is headed by H.R.H. Charlotte Aldegonde Elise Marie Wilhelmine, the Grand Duchess, who chooses her ministers, may intervene in legislative questions, and who has certain judicial powers. Her Prime Minister and Minister of the Interior is Pierre Frieden, a Christian Socialist.

Belgium derives its name from "Gallia Belgica," used by the Romans to describe all of the southern region of the Low Countries. The people won Caesar's praise for their bravery in battle, although they went down to defeat before him. The country had been settled by Belgic tribes of Celtic origin whom the Romans dubbed "Galli." When the Roman legions pulled back from Belgian Gaul in the fifth century, they had left a cultural heritage that transformed the language, religion, and social customs and whose effects are apparent to this very day. The Low Countries became part of the Merovingian Kingdom, stretching from the Weser to the Pyrenees.

The political division of present-day Holland from Belgium was decreed in 1609, when the northern Dutch under Maurice of Nassau wrested their independence from Spain. This division lasted for three and a half centuries, except during an interval from 1815 to 1831, ending with the establishment of the economic union known as Benelux in 1958. It was not racial, religious, or linguistic reasons which determined the dividing line between Holland and Belgium, but strategic and political considerations, and these same factors remain valid today, despite the passing of centuries, as unifying forces rather than divisive ones. Thus the population living in East and West Flanders, Antwerp, Limburg, and northern Brabant speak Dutch and dialects of Dutch, while in the rest of twentieth-century Belgium's nine provinces the Walloons speak French and have developed a proud French culture all their own.

In the fourteenth and fifteenth centuries the country formed part of the Duchy of Burgundy. Afterward, it passed to the House of Hapsburg, and in 1713 it was absorbed by Austria as the Austrian Netherlands. It was annexed by conquest to France in 1794, and in 1815 was united to Holland in the Kingdom of the Netherlands under King William I. The dissolution of that union and the creation of the Kingdom of Belgium is perhaps the central fact in Belgian history, and it compels attention because it explains so much of present-day developments in the character of the Three Kingdoms.

The year 1830 is generally considered the year of Belgium's independence as a nation, but successions of invaders and occupiers of the land both before and after four centuries of submission to other powers, and the characteristics unwittingly borrowed from one another, left deep scars on the people's character.

The Low Countries remained torn between the German empire and the French monarchy, growing simultaneously into greatness as two hostile camps, each claiming the loyalty of certain provinces of Belgium and the Netherlands, and ending up by taking up positions on this terrain for their long and bloody battles, beginning at Bouvines and ending in Versailles.

In December 1813, Holland had shaken off the imperial yoke of Napoleon. By the Treaty of Paris, signed the following May, she was promised additional territory. In 1815 Holland entered into a forced partnership with Belgium. The experience of the subsequent fifteen years of union proved that the monarch to whom the task of forging both nations into one had been entrusted was incapable of accomplishing his task. The nationality of Holland was established as that for the kingdom as a whole, and Dutch became by law the language of the land. Government had its center in Holland, and reforms in the civil and criminal law were in accordance with Dutch and not Belgian views. Taxation was imposed without any reference to Belgian ability or willingness to pay, or Belgian representation in legislative bodies. Nominations to all civil and military posts were for Dutchmen, and anti-Catholicism was the mark of authority. It was a stadholders' regime, wearing the guise of monarchial denominations. All of this despite the fact that the population of Belgium was double that of Holland. That short revolution of 1830, resulting in the overthrow of the yoke of Holland, brought Belgium her freedom. A prince of Saxe-Coburg, founder of the present royal family, was named King Leopold I.

Leopold inherited a country which now had won recognition as an "independent and perpetually neutral state," by guarantee of the major powers. But with it came economic chaos and political upheaval. The new monarch displayed rare wisdom and devotion, which, supported by the energy of the nation, tackled the problems which confronted Belgium. Railways were constructed. The legal system was overhauled. The Army was placed on a sound basis. Electoral reform was introduced. The country's political system and constitution became models for all of Europe. The King's death in 1865 brought the country into a state of national mourning.

Under Leopold's successor, the country's institutions were sorely tested. Prussia's victories in 1870 against France and the latter's "revanchist" feelings regarding the growing strength of Germany prompted Belgium to take emergency measures to build fortifications in Liége, Namur, and along the Meuse. One of Leopold's major interests was colonialism, and he took a deep personal interest in the exploitation and development of the Congo Free State, which was finally annexed to Belgium in 1908.

Albert I, king from 1909 to 1934, led Belgium through the most trying ordeal of her history. Belgian neutrality, which had been guaranteed by Britain, France, Prussia, Russia, and Austria, was violated when Germany's troops crossed the frontier in August 1914 in contradiction to her own guarantee of Belgium's sovereignty. The invading armies shocked the civilized world with their brutal treatment of the noncombatant civilian population. Thousands of innocent people were killed for no apparent reasons, and tens of thousands of homes were destroyed in a wave of ferocity such as the world had not witnessed since the time of Attila. A chill of horror went through Europe when the news of General Von Kluck's order of the massacre of the residents of such towns as Dinant, Aerschot, Louvain, Andenne, Jamoigne, Tintigny, and many others, became known. The facts were proclaimed to mankind by the British government in the now celebrated Lord Bryce Report, and by Sir John Murray in *The German War Book*. It might be worth reminding readers of the German White Book, published in 1915, in which a German staff officer, Major Bauer, recorded that, after the German troops "butchered nearly 700 civilians in cold blood at Dinant, Belgium, 'they manifested a most notable kindness' to the survivors." "All received coffee from the field kitchens," said the major, "and a girl of five years of age who was discovered by the Germans among a heap of corpses of 'women and young lads' was given chocolate and was quite happy." The pattern of German deportment in Belgium in World War I was to be repeated a quarter of a century later not only in the Low Countries but throughout the length and breadth of Europe.

Perhaps some will question my reference to events which took place so many years ago, but if the continuity of history is to be understood, as well as certain deeply inbred attitudes of the people, we cannot gloss over them. The accuracy of some of these historic happenings has been questioned, but the evidence is overwhelming; it comes from the Germans themselves. The general staff made no effort to conceal or even gloss over the events in Belgium, upon which they left an indelible imprint. Thus, when you talk to a Belgian intellectual who was born in the right decade of the nineteenth century, he will tell you: "Remember, we know the Boche. We have made his acquaintance long before the Americans were old enough to walk. Yes, he is our ally against the Russian. We do business with him. He buys our textiles. We buy his machinery. But that doesn't mean we can trust him, or consider him our friend."

For more than a century, from her year of independence in 1830 until 1940, Belgium's central aim in her foreign policy was to preserve her neutrality, to fight and die for it if necessary, and to remain, like Switzerland, above and outside of Europe's fratricidal quarrels. Many difficulties beset the Kingdom on the North Sea, especially during her adolescence as a nation, but most of them were successfully overcome. Although small in area, the people prospered industrially, artistically, and economically. Belgium's ports were a gateway to the heartland of Europe, which emerged from the century with vast new sources of wealth at its disposal. Belgium's dense railway network became the envy of many a large nation and a model for engineers the world over. Belgium's coal mines, their potential greatly increased by the addition of new veins developed in the Campine Basin, provided power for her industrial machinery. Belgium's great steel industry in Liége and the metallurgical plants dotting her countryside, her diamond industry at Antwerp, her leather, glass, and textile industries in Verviers, Courtrai, and Ghent, filled the coffers of the government, elevated the standard of living of the people, and filled their pocketbooks with profits. Added to which was the enormous wealth in uranium and other metals, cotton and diamonds, rubber, tin, and copper, which came from Belgium's Congo Basin in central Africa, which had been bequeathed to the nation by a farsighted monarch, Leopold II.

Twenty-five years and nine months after the invasion of Belgium by Germany in the First World War, and eight months after the outbreak of the Second World War, on May 10, 1940, Hitler's legions violated the Belgian frontier. This second invasion in a single generation followed by a few days a pledge by the German ambassador in Brussels that his country would respect Belgian neutrality. British and French forces raced to the rescue of Belgium's gallant forces, but after eighteen days of bitter fighting, the Allied lines collapsed before Hitler's massive armor and superior air power. The Belgians and Dutch covered the historic evacuation of the British Expeditionary Force at Dunkirk, and King Leopold III surrendered with his army on May 28. Germany's four-year occupation had begun.

The bitter fruits of eighteen days of furor and devastation by the German blitzkrieg in Belgium exceeded the destruction wrought during four and a half years of the First World War: 30,000 dead; 9832 houses razed, 140,860 damaged; 352 factories destroyed, 839 heavily damaged; 100 railroad stations demolished; 1455 bridges blown up; 235 public buildings, including churches and town halls, destroyed; many historic landmarks wiped out; thousands of miles of highway and rail communications reduced to rubble. The celebrated library at Louvain, which was rebuilt and re-equipped with American money after being destroyed in 1915, was again razed by the Germans. Fifty thousand workers were deported to compulsory labor camps in Germany. All production and distribution within the beleaguered country were placed under central control, all crops requisitioned by a newly created Nazi-controlled Corporation of Agriculture. Famine stalked the land. Resistance to the German occupation grew and strengthened. The opposition brought reprisals from General Von Falkenhausen, the Nazi military governor, and Herr Hahn, the civil administrator, who resorted to an old German custom—shooting of hostages, incarceration of 18,000 Belgians in concentration camps, the deportation of a total of 140,000 workers, a cut in the food ration to 800 calories per day. Belgium regained its freedom in February 1945 and the last German was driven from Belgian soil. German plans to dynamite Antwerp were foiled and the port was saved for the victorious Allies.

The sturdy Belgians displayed a high degree of ingenuity, always touched with a sense of humor, sometimes grim, often tragic, in their resistance to the German "brutalitarianism," as they called it among themselves. There was the anecdote, which I heard from an R.A.F. pilot, about the successful bombing attack on Merxem, near Antwerp. The town, which the Nazis had been using as an ammunition dump for only forty-eight hours when the attack came, was cleverly camouflaged. Just before the raid, a light signal was seen from the depot. A wounded sentry later confessed that two Belgian women had employed a ruse to keep him busy while the signal was sent up. The Nazis announced that the man would be executed unless the women were found. General Von Falkenhausen received a letter from "an admirer of Hitler" with a photo of an attractive woman, who was "identified" as the culprit. The snapshot had no name. The Nazis published the picture in the newspapers and offered a reward for information leading to the apprehension of the woman. Imagine the consternation of the German general when over a thousand claims were received for the reward. The snapshot was a photo of a famous American film actress!

The passive resistance of the nation was encouraged by King Leopold, who was a voluntary prisoner of war in the Palace of Laeken, near Brussels, guarded by a German platoon. From its windows, the King observed the R.A.F. bombing raid on the not too distant rail junction of Schaerbeek. Leopold's adamant refusal to accept German offers to restore him to power if he would "co-operate" with the pro-Nazi Rexist party and the Flemish Nationalists gave fresh impetus to the resistance. It was reported that when the Nazi-inspired scheme was laid before the King by Léon Degrelle, Rexist leader, the King rose in the midst of the presentation and said haughtily: "The audience which has been imposed upon me has ended."

The captive people found novel methods of showing their resistance to the old enemy among them, notwithstanding the confiscation of food, arrests, reprisals, and population transfers to which the Germans resorted in their attempt to break the Belgian spirit. Municipal councils were summarily dismissed, thousands of officials were replaced by pro-Nazi elements, and Belgian prisons were overflowing with persons who refused to bow to the conqueror. The concentration camps of western Europe had a high percentage of Belgians, whose worst crime was that they refused to capitulate.

Every opportunity, no matter how trivial, to demonstrate their feelings was taken by the people. Early in the occupation, German posters were torn down. The V-for-victory sign was painted over the walls of buildings. Belgian women openly advertised their feelings on their bookmarks, which were printed over with slogans such as: "*Attendre n'est pas renoncer. Se taire n'est pas approuver* [Waiting does not imply renunciation. Silence does not mean approval]." "*Le jour viendra* [The day will come]." "*Rira bien qui rira le dernier* [He who laughs last laughs best]." The bookmarks were passed from hand to hand.

The Nuremberg *Gesetz*, aimed to curb Jews of Germany, was applied in Belgium. The noose tightened slowly, and the repressions increased in vigor as the war progressed and the German armies felt the taste of victory. The story is told of Antwerp, which General Von Falkenhausen's civil administrator, Hahn, thought was anti-Semitic and would co-operate publicly in shaming its Jewish population. Jewish residents of the town were ordered to wear special distinguishing arm bands, yellow in color, to set them off from the "Aryan" population. On the morning of that day, three fourths of the city's population appeared on the streets, all wearing yellow arm bands. It was their way of expressing their revulsion against the order and a sign of their solidarity. A similar story has been told of towns in Holland and France, Denmark and Norway. All of them are true.

Koninkrijk der Nederlanden, more generally known as the Netherlands, or Holland, has a population of 11,250,000. They occupy 12,850 square miles of land, representing one of the highest population densities in the world.

With its steadily increasing birth rate and bursting population; with one fourth of the country lying below sea level in an area roughly comparable to Massachusetts, Rhode Island, and Connecticut combined; with an eternal war on its hands against the sea and against all too frequent human invaders; with a record of prodigious achievements against almost superhuman odds—the Kingdom of the Netherlands presents a living example of a people who through their energies and productivity have forged one of the richest, most powerful, and most respected small nations on earth. Let's have a look at the statistics:

Holland's farms produce sugar beets and potatoes in abundance; also wheat, rye, barley, and oats—but not enough for the country's needs. Vegetables and fruits abound, and dairy products are a major export and source of foreign exchange.

The Dutch spend almost as much on education (1,161,000 guilders in 1957) as on national defense (1,680,000 guilders), out of a total national income of 28,900,000 guilders. Imports, 4,104,-000 guilders, were exceeded by exports, 3,097,000 guilders. The difference was made up by the sale of services and "commodities." The leading commodity imports: petroleum, coal-tar products; iron, steel, and manufactures; machinery, electro-technical materials. Exports: meat, fish, milk, and dairy products, eggs, petroleum products, textiles, fabrics, iron, steel products, vehicles. The countries which sell most to Holland: West Germany, Belgium and Luxembourg, the United States, the United Kingdom, Venezuela, Sweden, France, Indonesia, Kuwait, Argentina, Switzerland, and Canada. Holland's best customers are about the same, with the Federal Republic of Germany leading the list.

Tourism brings 2,680,000 guilders each year to the Netherlands —almost one fourth of the national income. Most visitors are from Germany (650,786 in 1957), Britain (406,288), the United States (341,943), France (207,767), Belgium and Luxembourg (175,-706), Sweden (105,070).

Independent constitutional life began in Holland in 1568, when seven provinces of the Netherlands seceded from the Hapsburg monarchy and united. The following century, the House of Orange held office as stadholders (similar to chancellors). The Napoleonic era saw Holland first as a kingdom under one of Napoleon's brothers (1805–11) and later (1811–13) as part of France. At the restoration of 1814, Holland became an independent monarchy with the House of Orange as constitutional sovereigns. Holland united with Belgium in the United Kingdom of the Netherlands, which lasted until 1830. The democratic principle of ministerial responsibility to Parliament was introduced under a revision of the Constitution in 1948.

The 1919 and 1922 electoral-reform laws swept away the limited categories of voters designed in 1887 and 1896 to give the vote only to those who were judged to possess the required "aptitude and social condition." The laws conferred suffrage on all persons over the age of twenty-five. Later it was reduced to twenty-three.

The Dutch parliamentary assembly is called the States-General, and it consists of the first and second chambers. The latter has 150 members elected for four years by proportional representation. The first has 75 members, who are elected by the Provincial Councils for six years. All Dutchmen who have reached the age of twenty-three are eligible for election to the second chamber of the States-General; to be eligible for election to the first chamber, one must be thirty years old. The head of the States-General is H.R.H. Queen Juliana Louise Emma Marie Wilhelmina, who ascended to the throne in September 3, 1948. Her Majesty's "Realm in Europe" is the Netherlands; in the West Indies, Surinam and the Netherlands Antilles; in Asia, Netherlands New Guinea.

Under the Statute of the Realm signed by Queen Juliana on December 15, 1954, Holland, Surinam, and the Netherlands Antilles were constituted as a single Realm under the House of Orange, thereby ending the former colonial status of Surinam and the Netherlands Antilles and forestalling the possibility of a repetition of the disaster that overtook the Netherlands East Indies.

Without intensive land-protection schemes, nearly the whole of the North and West of the Netherlands—40 per cent of the total area—would be inundated by Holland's traditional enemy, sea water, twice a day. A large part of the country has been drained by the creation of polders, pieces of land surrounded by dikes from which all superfluous water can be drained into a canal by the aid of pumps. Despite the vast system of sea dikes, such as the Weskapelse Sea Dike on the island of Walcheren and the Hondsbosse and Pettermer Sea Dike to the north of Alkmaar in the province of North Holland, storm tides, combined with the whiplash of the sea, can still create disaster. The greatest natural tragedy to strike anywhere took place in February 1953, when 1835 people died and 450,000 acres were flooded. The result was the formation of a "Delta Commission," which was to seal off the Rhine and the Scheldt estuaries of Zeeland and South Holland. This plan, promulgated in 1955 and the most ambitious engineering scheme ever devised by man, is to create four barrier dams: (a) one, linking the island of Voorne and Goeree-Overflakkee; (b) a second, linking Goeree-Overflakkee and Schouwen-Duiveland; (c) a third, linking Schouwen-Duiveland and North Beveland; (d) a fourth linking North Beveland and Walcheren. The scheme will take twenty to twenty-five years to complete and will cost 2500 million guilders, or $700 million. The first phase of the operation is to build seventeen sluices to the Haringvliet waters, south of Rotterdam.

The Netherlands, Belgium, and Luxembourg have long since abandoned the ancient custom of mutual annihilation which marred their national existence down through the centuries. Today, at the threshold of the seventh decade of the twentieth century, Benelux has assumed a personality of its own, with a common idealism, and common purposes hinging upon identification with the dream of liberty and security which belongs to the Western alliance of which they are members. The Three Kingdoms, like many other smaller powers, have discovered that by speaking with a single voice (and yet preserving their own national individuality) in the councils of the world, what they say is much more distinctly audible. Once part of the German Confederation, Luxembourg threw in its lot with Belgium on December 22, 1921. The Netherlands and Belgium abandoned their traditional rivalry, accentuated for two centuries during the period of the Spanish domination, entering upon a customs rail and consular union which has been toughened by their sharing of common tragedy, common triumphs in the economic sphere, and a common destiny in a world threatened by an atomic war. Under a fifty-year treaty confirming the Benelux Economic Union, signed on February 3, 1958, at The Hague by the Prime Ministers of the three countries, the governments agreed to these conditions:

(1) The free flow of capital, services, and traffic, and the free movement of nationals back and forth across the frontiers;

(2) Adoption of a common commercial policy in relation to other countries, and co-ordination of their policies regarding investments, agriculture, and social and monetary matters;

(3) The establishment of a juridical framework for the economic union, which has been growing in complexity every year for the last few years.

There are a number of other unifying forces encouraging the development of the Benelux concept. All three countries are members of the Council of Europe, which was established in London on May 5, 1949, as a major step toward European unity. The creation in January 1959 of a Common Market, in which Benelux together with France, West Germany, and Italy have determined to integrate their economies, has strengthened the Union even further. The Coal and Steel Community (Benelux, France, Germany, Italy); the establishment of Euratom, which calls for a pooling of resources and information on nuclear energy; the Organization for European Economic Cooperation (the British Isles, Iceland, and the Continent west of the Iron Curtain except Spain and Finland); plus, of course, membership in NATO, have spurred productivity and prosperity for western Europe in general and Benelux in particular. The result is an even greater interdependence of the Three Kingdoms one upon the other.

Measures taken to make the Union a reality include a customs convention and agreements freeing the circulation of capital on investment plans, the sharing of scarce raw materials, and a common policy toward international economic organizations. The sinews of unity are yet to be tested in the cauldron of international conflict, but it is a safe bet that they will prove their durability.

GERMANY

David M. Nichol

David M. Nichol has been a foreign correspondent for the Chicago Daily News since he was first sent to wartime Berlin in the autumn of 1940. For most of the years since then, he has been concerned with the problems of Germany and its European neighbors, including the Soviet Union. He spent two of the critical war years, from the end of 1942 until the end of 1944, in Moscow.

Nichol returned to Germany on a "temporary assignment" from London to cover the closing sessions of the Nuremberg trials in 1946. The assignment was extended, and from 1946 until 1952 he made Berlin his headquarters. Since 1952 he has traveled from the West German capital, Bonn.

Outside Europe and the Soviet Union, he has reported from Canada in 1945–46 and from the Middle East during the Suez crisis and its aftermath. He shared a "William the Silent" award in 1952 for stories from the Netherlands.

Nichol is the son of a Presbyterian clergyman and was born in Canada in 1911. Most of his schooling was in Detroit, Michigan, and its suburbs, and he attended the University of Michigan, completing a master's degree in political science in 1933. He joined the local staff of the Chicago Daily News in 1936.

He is married to Judy Barden, whom he met in Berlin when she was correspondent there for the New York Sun.

GERMANY

The traveler's aircraft lets down at Hamburg, or Düsseldorf, or Frankfurt. There is a minimum of formality with customs and immigration, and he is whisked away along highways and streets bristling with cars and people and belying in a frightening fashion any notions that this is a disciplined or browbeaten community.

The hotel is clean, the service is good, and English is spoken. Neon lights and chromium make the American visitor much at home. There is the feeling and appearance of something substantial, in the people, in their money, in the atmosphere in general.

This is the Cinderella country, the Germany of the smoking factory chimney and the large bank balance, the land of the "golden miracle." No one who saw it in the depths of its collapse in 1945 would have believed it possible. Almost no one intended that this should happen.

German energy and the courage of its leaders are among the unquestioned factors that have contributed to German recovery. So, too, did the breakdown of the wartime alliance between the Western powers and the Soviet Union. The Communist threat to the rest of Europe made it essential that Germany become strong. United States aid to the extent of some four billion dollars provided a foundation on which to build.

In a fairy-tale fashion, even some of the problems which were most worrisome at the end of the war have proved to be disguised blessings. Twelve million refugees have supplied the extra hands without which this recovery could not have been achieved.

Recovery, in turn, has made it possible for most of these people to be absorbed in the communities where they live with almost no suggestion of the radicalism that was feared.

This prosperous concern is the Germany that comes immediately to Western minds. But it is important to note that it is only one of at least three modern Germanys. The standard German encyclopedia actually lists four. Each must be defined and understood if the "German problem" is to make any sense at all.

West Germany, or the Federal Republic of Germany, to give it its official label, has its "temporary, provisional capital" in the Rhineland city of Bonn. It includes about 96,000 square miles, a territory slightly smaller than Wyoming, and a population at last count of about 53 million. This was the region assigned at the end of the war to the forces of the United States, Britain, and France. Its government was established in 1949, after the Soviets refused to permit the creation of a government for the whole of the country.

East of this and separated by a line that has come to be known as the Iron Curtain is the German Democratic Republic, the Communist-ruled zone, which originally was occupied by Soviet troops. It includes about 42,000 square miles, roughly the area of Tennessee, and has a population of less than 16.3 million. The West knows it loosely as "East Germany." Germans themselves normally refer to it as the "East zone." For reasons that will be apparent, they prefer officially to call it "Middle Germany."

In the heart of the German Democratic Republic, some 100 miles east of West Germany, lies the city of Berlin, which is divided in turn into western and eastern "sectors." It is a sprawling complex, covering more than 340 square miles. About 2.2 million people live in West Berlin. Another 1.1 million are residents of the Communist-controlled sector of East Berlin.

The German encyclopedia says Berlin is one of the four "parts" of Germany. West Germany, however, claims West Berlin as one of the Länder, or provinces, of the Federal Republic, and it has most but not all of the rights and obligations of full membership. East Germany has its capital in East Berlin and claims the whole of the city, and this has been the cause of bitter and dangerous crises.

Still farther to the east, beyond the Oder and Neisse rivers, are the territories that were German until the end of the war. They were placed under Polish and Soviet "administration" at the Potsdam Conference in 1945, and only another war could have prevented this—for the Soviets were there—and, in occupation. Poland and the Soviet Union insist this is a final disposition. The West says the question is still to be resolved by a peace treaty, as the Potsdam communiqués plainly state.

Germans call these the "eastern territories." The Poles speak of them as the "recovered lands." Impartial geographers use the label "separated areas." However they may be tagged, they promise to be a source of international unrest and dispute for generations. They have an area of about 44,000 square miles, the size of Pennsylvania, and had a prewar German population of 9.6 million.

As the Soviet armies advanced in the closing months of the war, many Germans fled these regions. After the war, most of the rest of the German population was expelled in a brutal operation paralleled only by the way the Germans and the Russians had shifted the Poles in 1939. As much as possible, the Germans were replaced by Polish settlers from the Polish lands still farther east that were ceded to the Soviet Union in the course of this monstrous game of musical chairs.

Until recently there was still another "part" of Germany, the coal-rich Saar Basin in the West, which the French tried unsuccessfully to absorb. Its return to Germany at the beginning of 1957 was acclaimed as a major victory. It has been a sobering example of the intricacies and the expense of any future unification.

These divisions are the direct outgrowth of Hitler's insane plan of conquest and of his subsequent defeat, and for this the Germans must accept some responsibility. Division as such, however, is nothing new to Germany. It has been this country's frustrating and unhappy destiny, as we shall see, to be fighting itself through long periods and to have been the arena for countless devastating wars among other countries.

The long, slow evolution which produced national states and democratic systems in other European countries was delayed for centuries in Germany. When national union finally occurred, it came with explosive violence. If it should be delayed too long again, a similar outburst is conceivable.

Leaving aside for the moment the question of the "separated areas," the present cleavage is a deep and dangerous one.

For a distance of more than 800 miles the "demarcation line" between West and East Germany runs south from the Baltic Sea and then east to Czechoslovakia. It follows the Elbe River briefly, but for the rest of the way it is marked artificially, generally along old provincial or administrative boundaries that had ceased to have any significance even a century ago.

In the eyes of the Western planners of the occupation this border was intended to remain only an administrative one. But the Soviets had other ideas. They closed the border in July 1946, and it now has most of the dangerous and sullen attributes of related frontiers throughout the Soviet sphere.

Nearly 300 miles of this line are marked by barbed wire. Some of it has high board fences. East German frontier guards watch it from some 500 wooden towers. The border cuts villages in half. It separates families. In one Bavarian community it disrupted the manufacture of dolls, because the eyes were made in a neighboring settlement that fell "to the other side." In at least one place the border cuts through a man's house, and he has been compelled to use only the "west" part of his dwelling, because the Communist guards shoot through his "east zone" windows if he turns on the lights. Officially the man lives in the West and must not cross the boundary without proper permission.

Almost all of the border has a thirty-foot strip, plowed and cleared of trees and undergrowth, which the Germans call the "dead zone." To cross it at all leaves dangerous and easily followed traces. One East German managed it several times with stilts that left prints like those of a wild boar, but in the end he was trapped and sent to jail.

On either side of this line have grown two completely opposed systems of government and society. The very fact of the demarcation line drives each of them into progressively more extreme positions.

The original Allied plan, for example, proposed checks on "free enterprise" in Germany because big business had been notoriously irresponsible under the Nazis. These controls were introduced, but they have fallen away, one by one, until big business today is freer in West Germany than in almost any country in the world. Most economists agree this has been a big factor in West Germany's recovery, but they are dubious about the German tendencies toward concentration.

Similarly, the Communist regime in East Germany has clung to the compulsions of the Stalin period more closely than any other of the satellite areas. The "thaw" after Stalin's death was much briefer and less effective in East Germany than in the Soviet Union itself. The simple fact of West Germany's existence and the anomalous position of Berlin are permanently unsettling for the East German people and their Communist rulers.

Economically speaking, and by its own local standards, each of these competing systems is doing well. West Germany needs little advertising for its success. East Germany, however, is better off than many of its critics will admit or appreciate. Living standards in East Germany still are only about 80 per cent of those in the West, but they are rising, for the time being at least, at the same steep rates.

The onetime Soviet zone was bled white in reparations but has recovered now to the point where it is the biggest industrial supplier for the Soviet bloc outside the Soviet Union itself.

Politically, there is no comparison between the two German governments. West Germany, by any normal standards, is a functioning democracy. Its elections are genuinely free. Its parliament shows encouraging signs of independence, despite the strong hand of Chancellor Konrad Adenauer. From time to time the police are haled into court, and so are important federal officials. Its constitution is liberal and effective.

In East Germany, by contrast, the modern party dictatorship, the most vicious invention of the twentieth century, is riding high. Constitutionally, East Germany also is a democracy, but the constitution is twisted or simply ignored. There is more underlying opposition than in some other Soviet-bloc countries, so the iron fist under the velvet glove is more apparent. But as conformity grows, so the outward signs of the police regime diminish. Conformity is more general as living standards improve and as memories of freedom recede. East Germany has had no direct experience of freedom since the beginning of the Nazi era in 1933.

Militarily, the two parts of the country are in a state of dangerous balance. West Germany's defense forces are geared to NATO, and within a short time the country will have the most powerful land force in western Europe. It will amount in all to about 350,000 men, of whom the bulk will be in the Army.

On paper East Germany's Army is smaller, amounting now to about 110,000 men. But it has been modeled closely on the Reichswehr of the Weimar period to produce a cadre of noncoms and officers. It is supported, in addition, by the armed "workers' battalions" and by the millions of youths, boys and girls, in the "Society for Sport and Technique," one of whose training slogans is "Hatred for the West German militarists!"

Fantastic as it may sound, the ominous phrase of "civil war" is appearing more and more frequently. Gerhart Eisler, who fled from the United States to become one of East Germany's leading propagandists, has compared the situation with that of the United States in 1860. The East Germans, Eisler said, would be fighting the "just war." The "slaveholders," according to Eisler, are the West Germans.

Civil war certainly will not happen while NATO and Soviet forces face each other across this border. But there are few experts who would undertake to say what might occur if the big-power elements are withdrawn.

There is a popular argument that Germans won't fire on Germans. This ignores both German history in particular and the experience of other countries where civil strife has been touched off by differences much less fundamental than those in present-day Germany. The witnesses of the 1953 uprisings in Berlin know that it was East Germans who killed West Germans in that brief, savage exchange across Potsdamer Platz. On the demarcation line between the two parts of the country, one of the problems of the American and British forces sometimes has been to restrain the enthusiasm of the West German border guards. One suspects the situation is similar on the Soviet side.

Walter Ulbricht, the goateed Communist-party boss of East Germany, has warned publicly that civil war would be the result of free elections as the Western world understands these. The Communists simply will not permit themselves to be voted out of office and are prepared to use their armed forces to prevent it.

If "Big Brother's" help is necessary, it is available, as Hungary demonstrated. In East Germany alone, there are twenty-two or twenty-three Soviet divisions, the most mobile and compact force under Soviet command anywhere. It is larger than the combined NATO and West German units in West Germany.

Soviet policy has done everything it can to enlarge and exacerbate the differences between the two Germanys from the moment it appeared that communism was not to be permitted to sweep the entire country, as the Soviets seem to have expected. More recently the effort has been to make this division a permanent and internationally recognized condition under the terms of a peace treaty or treaties.

There is very little the West Germans themselves can do about this except to get on with the job of strengthening the Federal Republic. This is partly policy and partly rationalization. The policy is that a prosperous and vital society in West Germany in the long run will exert an irresistible pull on the Germans of the Communist region and, in some manner which no one can foresee at this stage, will bring about unification. It is rationalization for those who would prefer in their hearts not to be bothered, and there are some.

West Germany's recovery predates the Federal Republic as such. The Marshall Plan for aid to Europe was the prime for the pump, but until Germany had restored some order to its own financial affairs, this would have been wasted. In June 1948 the

German mark in the three Western zones of the country was converted at the rate of ten to one.

Overnight a currency that had been worthless began to have value, and the economy shifted from barter and black market to its modern basis. Since that time, however, the two parts of the country have had separate currencies. Nominally, they are equal. In the only market where they are traded freely, in West Berlin, the exchange is about four to one in favor of the West German mark, but this much-quoted figure is misleading. In terms of its local purchasing power, the East German mark has nearly the value of its West German counterpart, but it cannot be used outside the Soviet sphere. The West German mark has become one of the standard "hard currencies" of the free world—on a level with the American dollar and the Swiss franc.

Currency reform was followed by another fundamental decision which helped to shape the Federal Republic before it was born. Allied and German experts agreed that this new Germany was to interfere as little as possible with free enterprise, but it was to insist that it be genuinely free. Prominent among the men who took this courageous step was Professor Ludwig Erhard. With his rotund figure and the cigar from which he seldom is separated, he has been the symbol ever since of German prosperity.

Ten years after this decision Erhard could report: "The German people in 1958 reached the highest standard of living in its history. This is the proud result of our labors." By 1980, Erhard has said, the present standards will be doubled.

The base on which West Germany has built includes about half of western Europe's coal and a third of its steel capacity, although much of its ore must be imported. There is a powerful incentive, in addition, in the fact that West Germany must produce and export to eat. Even before the loss of the eastern territories the country was far from self-sufficient in foodstuffs.

In ten years exports increased eight times and imports nearly four times, and late in 1958 West Germany moved ahead of Great Britain to become the world's principal trader after the United States. The German mark, an act of faith in its early stages, is covered now more than one and a half times by gold. Stocks of gold and foreign currency in the hands of West Germany's central bank are second only to those in the United States.

Industrial production is approaching two and a half times that of 1936, which is considered to be the last normal prewar year. In figures, wages in 1958 were more than 90 per cent higher than in 1949, and in purchasing power, they were 64 per cent higher. Living costs have increased less than in most other Western countries. The index went up 18 per cent between 1950 and 1958, compared with 20 per cent in the United States, 46 per cent in Britain, and more than 50 per cent in France. Four and a half million dwellings have been built, and six million new jobs have been created.

Savings have increased nearly ninefold, and this is one of the best indications of public confidence in the currency and the country's future. It is all the more remarkable for the fact that twice in the lifetime of most adults their currency and savings have been wiped out.

In this expanding economy people first bought food, for the initial postwar years were lean indeed. Then they began to replace household equipment and clothes. The demand now is for substantial items, such as TV sets, electrical refrigerators, and automobiles.

Churchmen and some other thoughtful citizens have lamented the "materialism" of modern German society. The problem has been the subject of bitingly satirical films, best received in West Berlin, which has shared least in the "golden miracle." Most West Germans are inclined to bristle uneasily at such humor.

The social pattern shows many of the stresses associated with advancing civilization. Heart and circulatory ailments are killing off the "managers" in alarming numbers. Rolls-Royce has made its first inroads on the German automobile market. The Mercedes 300 seems no longer to be sufficiently rare or distinguished. Highway fatalities reflect the increasing traffic.

No less a personage than Josef Cardinal Frings of Cologne, a man of great political as well as religious authority, has counseled his countrymen to learn more of the "art of being moderately lazy." Social workers fear that the five-day week, only now being introduced, may cause difficulties for people who know of nothing to do with their time except to work.

There is a tendency, among Germans themselves and among their critics, to see this restless, ambitious commercialism as something new and not altogether respectable. New it certainly is not. Historians have noted, for example, that the fourteenth century, an "age of fierce violence and expanding wealth," was marked in a similar fashion by "an energetic materialism."

The traders of the Hanseatic League, an alliance of German cities, were well known in the London of the period as "Easterlings," and it is a tribute to their business practices and their currency that the standard money of Britain is described still as "sterling."

The German salesman who scours the distant corners of the world for markets today is a kindred spirit with the German printers who had established three competing presses in Granada in Spain only two years after the Moors had been expelled, about the time that Columbus was discovering the New World.

The most notable lack in modern West Germany is the absence of any physical focus around which its life could take shape. West Berlin, while it remains a part of the Federal Republic for many purposes, has ceased to serve this role, and nothing has taken its place. Even without its Communist-held east sector, it is the nation's largest city.

Eastern Germany is a vastly different picture, of which the Western visitors see only glimpses. For most purposes the area is closed to the free-world tourist; nor is there much to attract him if he were able to go.

Under the insistent hammering of the Communist authorities, the Soviet system of farming and industry has been expanded steadily. The last of the private farmers was collectivized early in 1960 and in numerous villages there was no longer a single independent tradesman or handicraft worker. Ninety per cent of the industry already is state-owned, and shortly the sweep will be complete.

Bit by bit, as the ties with West Germany are cut or broken, the region is oriented toward the East. Its foreign trade is almost exclusively now with the Soviet Union and other members of the Soviet bloc.

Its resources center on lignite, or brown coal, and on the chemical industry which has grown on this base, on machine-tool production, and on closely guarded uranium deposits in the southeast corner near the Czechoslovakian border, the output of which goes to the Soviets. East German chemical production and know-how are budgeted as a major item in the Soviet Union's Seven-Year Plan for outproducing the United States.

In many instances, it has been necessary, because of Communist restrictions on trade between the two Germanys, to duplicate capacities already existing in the West.

In the Stalin period, for example, in common with most other satellites, East Germany established a new steel industry. Its most notable outgrowth is East Germany's single totally "socialist" city, which still is called Stalinstadt and was built near the new mills on the Oder River. In the same area an oil refinery is planned, to be fed from the Soviet fields in the Caucasus by an ambitious pipeline.

Between these two worlds and not wholly a part of either is the city of Berlin. The onetime fishing village on the Spree River had become one of the world's great cities in the period between the wars. Consolidations and its own natural vigor had brought it by 1939 to some 4.5 million persons.

Today it is divided more dramatically than the country itself into West and East, where the much photographed Brandenburg Gate spans Unter den Linden. Its population has been reduced by more than a million, to about what it was some fifty years ago.

The division has been carried to absurd lengths since a Communist putsch in November 1948 established a separate "government" in East Berlin while the Soviets blockaded the West. A telephone call from one side of the city to the other, for example, must be routed over Frankfurt am Main and Leipzig, a total distance of about 800 miles, because all the direct lines have been cut.

Almost the only uninterrupted service is that of the subways, or underground. The trains serve suburbs on both sides of the city, and to halt them would be too damaging to East Berlin as well as to the West. Thousands upon thousands of refugees owe their escape to this route.

East Berlin, in Communist hands, has acquired much of the gray coloration that is an unintended hallmark of Soviet society. There is no more striking demonstration anywhere than the ride which any tourist may make from one side to the other. Western visitors find it impossible to believe that East Berlin is considered by many in the Soviet sphere to be a showcase of Communist achievement, yet this is true. For the government or party bureaucrat in eastern Europe, an outing to East Berlin is a considerable event. East Berlin still draws its supplies from the surrounding territory.

West Berlin, by contrast, is dependent on its supply lines to western Germany, slightly more than 100 miles distant. Not only the Western garrisons, numbering about 11,000, but all of West Berlin must be fed and warmed and maintained by this precarious trade.

The bulk is carried by one railroad, one superhighway, one canal, and three air corridors. The kindest thing that can be said for the existence of this arrangement is that it represents the measure of Allied faith in postwar co-operation with the Soviets, and the extent to which this faith was unfounded. These slender life lines have been preserved only at great cost and hazard. They easily could be the immediate cause of World War III.

In spite of, or perhaps because of, these handicaps Berlin has retained a flavor of its own. The ordinary Berliner has always been a special type, akin in his dialect, his cynical humor, and his political sophistication to the Cockney in London.

During the Nazi period, Berlin became the symbol for the world of all that was horrible in the system, yet the Berliners were the last in the country to be overwhelmed by the Brownshirts. What resistance there was to Hitler centered in the city.

In the worst of the wartime bombings, Berliners told each other: "If you think this is bad, wait for the peace."

No one possibly could have foreseen that they would have to wait so long.

Certainly they have had a much rougher time all around than their countrymen in the West. The Soviet blockade, which the Berliners fought so courageously, postponed the "golden miracle" for about three years, so far as the city is concerned. Production indices still are only about half of the level in the rest of the Federal Republic.

The city is often called a "lighthouse of democracy in a Red sea," and as such it is much appreciated by the West and hated by the Soviets. Less understood is the role it played in providing a warning to the free world. Berlin's resistance to Soviet plans created the interval in which NATO was born and the slow build-up of Western defenses was begun. Like Voltaire's God, if the city hadn't existed, it would have been necessary to invent it.

Ernst Lemmer, Bonn's Minister for All-German Affairs, has pointed out another aspect. West Berlin not only remains West Germany's largest industrial city; it is also "the greatest concentration of energy and skills between the highroad of western Europe, the Rhine River, and the capital of the Soviet empire in Moscow." It is one more of the many reasons why the Communists want to force the city into their orbit.

The famous Kurfürstendamm glistens again with lights. Theaters and opera are excellent. New buildings are going up. Plans proceed bravely for reconstruction of the Reichstag, burned by the Nazis and shelled by the Russians, in the hope that it one day will house again the parliament of a united country. In the waves of crisis that sweep the world periodically because of Berlin, the city itself is often the calmest spot one can find.

The other side of this coin is that it requires outside assistance from West Germany at the rate of about a quarter of a billion dollars annually to keep West Berlin going and that the city would be overrun without the Western political and military guarantees.

To some, at least, it seems already to have the haunting atmosphere of still more tragedy in the future. In terms of the average age of its people, for example, it is the oldest major city in the world, and this aging process is continuing.

Yet defeat and adversity, as one modern chronicler of Berlin writes, have brought the city a blessing it never achieved in its moments of pride and power, a genuine respect and affection.

"In its impotence, it would not survive, without the spiritual vitamins of this sympathy," records Walther Kiaulehn.

One of the first of the postwar song hits in Germany was a nostalgic little thing about "homesickness for the Kurfürstendamm." It appeared while Berlin itself still lay in darkened ruins.

Nazi racial theorists insisted there was something unique and sacred about being "German." In fact, the people of the country are a mixed and varied lot, related in the distant past to most of their neighbors, including the British and the French.

The first resident of whom there is any trace was a being somewhere between man and ape whose lower jaw is one of the treasures of Heidelberg University. The jaw was found in a gravel pit south of the city in 1907 and belongs to the Old Stone Age, perhaps some 300,000 years back. Almost nothing is known of this being, who seems to have been wiped out by one of the glaciers that periodically rolled over Europe.

Much more familiar is Neanderthal man, who appeared some eons later in much of Europe, living a life which a British writer has summarized as "nasty, brutish, and very cold." He takes his name from the valley of the Neander River, near modern Düsseldorf, where most of a skeleton first was found in 1856 and where there is a small but interesting museum today.

He, too, seems to have disappeared, to be replaced in turn by others. But these peoples were two or three whole cultural cycles behind the great civilizations of the Mediterranean and the Middle East and were still in the "noble savage" stage when they first encountered the Romans. In important respects, for which there are geographic and historic reasons, they have lagged behind much of the Western world ever since.

The tribes who became known as Germans, or Germanic, emerged in the pre-Christian centuries in southern Scandinavia and along the southern coast of the Baltic Sea east of the Elbe River.

Experts describe them as "a people of distinct racial type, with a distinct kind of Indo-European language." They did not then or in the future call themselves 'Germans, a label which seems first to have been applied by Caesar. It was revived nearly two thousand years later by German scholars.

The first contact between the Germans and the Romans was fleeting. Two tribes, the Cimbri and the Teutones, stirred perhaps by some unrecorded flood, moved out of the misty North and over the Alps into Italy about a century before Christ, where they were defeated in two battles and disappeared from history.

Yet one of the outgrowths of this haphazard clash was the beginning of a regular Roman army in place of citizen forces. The Romans had a good eye for soldiers, and over the next four or five centuries this army and the Empire became steadily more Germanized.

When Caesar began his notable exploits some fifty years after the Cimbrian excursion, he found that the Celts, who had once covered most of Europe, had been pushed across the Rhine and the Danube rivers to the west and south by Germanic tribes. The Celts held only a small area of what is now Germany, between the angle of these two great waterways.

Except for sporadic forays by the Roman commanders, these river valleys remained the limits of Roman military authority in Germany so long as Rome survived. Rome's influence on German development was to be great, but mostly it was indirect, by contrast with the region of modern France, where Roman customs and language became solidly embedded.

Gradually, in the fifth century, one of the Germanic tribes, the Franks, began to extend its sway over the others, and for the next 400 years they were to dominate most of western Europe. The Franks and some of the tribes over which they exercised this authority are the lineal ancestors of the Germans of today.

The Franks became Christians with the conversion of their king, Clovis, at the end of the fifth century, but most of the other Germanic peoples retained their heathen beliefs for another 250 years. An English monk named Wynfrith was commissioned by Pope Gregory II in 719 to do what he could in Germany, and by the time the Germans killed him in 755, the Church was well established. Wynfrith was renamed Boniface and in due course became a saint. He is buried in the cathedral church of his favorite monastery at Fulda.

There are thought to have been some 5 million "Germans" in the region of modern Germany in 500 A.D. By 1300 these had increased to about 12 million. The Black Death and a series of other plagues reduced this number to about 8 million by 1350. The figure of 12 million wasn't reached again until 1500.

Steady growth followed and the population was about 20 million at the beginning of the Thirty Years' War in 1618. In the course of this man-made catastrophe somewhere between one third and one half of the German people were killed, or starved, or otherwise destroyed in the wake of the marching, marauding armies.

So crippled was the country at the end of this ghastly contest that it couldn't support even its reduced population, and a development began which was to be of great import to the United States. The Germans had no colonies of their own to which they could move, and the founding of Pennsylvania in 1683 as a refuge for the "oppressed and persecuted of all nations" provided a powerful magnet. Louis XIV of France spurred the movement by burning and cutting his way into Germany a few years later. The majestic ruins on the hill above Heidelberg, familiar to thousands of Americans since World War II, are a relic of this enterprise.

What began as a trickle was to become a flood in the nineteenth century. In the period between the defeat of Napoleon in 1815 and the outbreak of World War I in 1914, some 6 million Germans left their country. About 5.5 million went to the United States.

Many of those who left were the enterprising and the progressive and their contribution would be sorely missed, but in numbers alone the drain scarcely was noted. It was a period of unparalleled growth of population. From 25 million in 1815 the country grew to 64 million a century later. France added only about 10 million people in the same period.

The dead of World War I and the loss of about one seventh of its territory reduced Germany to some 61 million in 1921, but by

1935 it had achieved a new peak of 66 million. With the annexation of the Sudeten territories from Czechoslovakia and the union with Austria, the nation numbered 80 million at the beginning of World War II.

The first postwar census showed 66 million in an area reduced by one third in size. Nearly 12 million of these were refugees, driven from the former German territories east of the Oder, or expelled from other countries of eastern Europe, where their families had lived in some cases for hundreds of years.

These new internal migrations were conditioned a good deal by a desperate housing problem and the availability of jobs. Both of these difficulties have been largely surmounted, but one result of this resettlement has been the creation of a more homogeneous population in the West than the country has ever had. The Prussians in the capital in Bonn, for example, are almost as numerous as the native Rhinelanders, and the Bavarian countryside is losing some of its long-standing and exclusively Bavarian flavor.

There is only one national minority of any consequence in West Germany, the people of Danish descent in Schleswig-Holstein in the North. In the early postwar days anyone who could discover a Danish ancestor hastened to proclaim this, for it qualified him for food parcels from Denmark. As conditions improved, so the Danish minority has shrunk. In the 1957 elections the Danish minority party polled fewer than 34,000 votes, less than half of the 1949 figure.

In the Communist region, where there were no real minorities, one has been created, but without much success or enthusiasm. A group known as Sorbs are the descendants of the Slavic Wends, who inhabited the upper Spree River valley when the Germans first began their settlement of the area about a thousand years ago. After the end of the war the Soviets, as big brother to their distant Slavic cousins, tried to revive the Sorbs' language and culture, but little has been heard of this effort for several years.

The German Jews, never a true racial but rather a religious minority, were wiped out under the Nazis through slaughter and flight. A few thousand have returned, but any sizable resettlement is unlikely.

These then are the people of the "German problem," but they do not explain its existence. They are very much like the rest of us and, surrounded by similar circumstances, they become honorable, useful citizens, as the experience of the United States with its millions of immigrants demonstrates so clearly.

A thoughtful historian has observed that "Germany's disaster was in the first place one of geography, in the second place one of tradition." Miss C. V. Wedgwood was writing of the Thirty Years' War, a period of monumental trouble and suffering in Central Europe about 300 years ago, yet few descriptions are more apt or revealing today.

From the very beginning of its long chronicle, Germany has been plagued by at least three geographical factors.

One is the vague and shifting character of its external boundaries. Except along the North Sea and the Baltic, these have lacked any sharp definition. One expert has described them as "wide zones of contact" rather than borders in the normal sense.

These "zones," in turn, have inclined to reflect the political and military constellations of the day. At various times they have included much of the Low Countries, parts of modern France, most of Switzerland, large sections of Italy, all of Austria and parts of Czechoslovakia, and an extremely fluctuating area in what is now Poland and the Soviet Union.

One result is that Germans themselves often find it difficult to agree what Germany is, or what it has been, to say nothing of what it will become in the future. Prince Metternich, the Austrian Foreign Minister, who contrived to wreck one promising interval in Germany's development about 150 years ago, insisted that Germany was no more than "a mere geographical expression." Others have argued that Germany cannot be defined at all in terms of normal geography. Fichte, the philosopher, believed that common or related language was the key, much as do the Greek Cypriotes today.

This absence of natural boundaries has had other effects, some good and some not. One has been to make Germany extremely dependent upon its neighbors for its trade and its livelihood, and, conversely, to make the existence of a thriving and prosperous Germany essential to the well-being of these neighbors.

West Germany today has direct border contacts with eight other nations. Seven of these, or six, if Belgium and Luxembourg are considered as a single customs area, are among West Germany's top ten trading partners.

The single exception is Czechoslovakia. There is every reason to believe that it, too, would share a considerable and profitable trade with Germany except that Soviet policy forbids this. Soviet policy also prevents normal trade within Germany in the sense that the Communist-controlled region of East Germany has been tied increasingly to the Soviet sphere.

Of the remaining four among West Germany's major trading partners, three are near European neighbors, Britain, Sweden, and Italy. The fourth is the United States.

The lack of natural boundaries and this mutual dependence have had important military consequences as well. Defense of the area has been difficult, and over the centuries the north German plain in particular has been a marching place for armies of all description. It is the existence of this military "highway," open at both ends, which adds such menace for Europe and the world to the presence in East Germany of a powerful, mobile Soviet force. Conversely, it is the route through which every Western invasion of Russia has developed.

In its intervals of greatest weakness Germany has been almost as much a threat to the peace as in its better remembered moments of strength, for the neighbors have been too avid to control it, to deny it to others, or to benefit from its energies and resources. These are the circumstances which have brought the United States and the Soviet Union face to face in the territory of a former enemy they had combined to destroy.

The second geographical factor has been the absence of any clear focus within Germany itself, at least until the emergence of Berlin in the nineteenth century. In this, Germany has differed from almost every other western European nation.

The wandering tribes who established themselves in the region some 1500 years ago followed the great valleys of the Rhine, the

Main, and the Danube, and they traded and fought their wars along these routes.

Three quarters of the country was covered with dense forest, which did much to preserve the independence of the tribal regions. These were not brought into normal contact until the "age of the forest clearance," which began in the ninth century and continued for nearly 500 years. This "clearance" program was essential to the development of a populous and industrialized modern nation, but by the time it was completed the political basis for such an evolution had been lost.

As towns were established in the eleventh and twelfth centuries they followed trade routes that were essentially European rather than German. One of these was along the Rhine from the Low Countries to the Alpine passes that led to Italy.

A second followed the northern rim of the uplands in an east-west line through Cologne, Hannover, Magdeburg, and ultimately to Cracow in Poland. It was no accident that Cologne was the first of the big German cities, for it marked the crossing of these two routes, or that the Ruhr industrial triangle, the great steel heart of the country, should have developed as it did. The discovery of coal beneath the Ruhr simply encouraged its growth.

With the rise of sea-borne commerce in the twelfth and thirteenth centuries the harbors on the North Sea and the Baltic took on new importance, and at the peak of its power the Hanseatic League included some 160 cities extending from the Lower Rhine to Riga and Reval in the Baltic countries.

Lübeck served as a model for many of the cities that were established east of the Elbe in this period of German expansion. They were planned settlements, carefully laid out to be eight hours' travel distance apart. It was one of the first and most successful ventures in city planning.

With the coming of the Industrial Revolution other centers of industrial concentration grew around the mines in Upper Silesia, now in Polish hands, and the brown-coal deposits in Saxony, which are the basis in turn for the East German chemical industry, on which the Soviet Union is counting heavily for its Seven-Year Plan.

All these are indications of a vigorous local society and initiative, but there was little to tie these areas together. One scholarly study concludes in restrained language that "physically, Germany is characterized by a lack of structural unity and natural coherence." A German writer calls it "a land without design."

Nor was nature overly generous in the parceling of resources. Germany possesses about half the coal of Europe, but its extensive steel industries depend almost entirely on imported ore. There is some oil and some water power, but these are supplementary quantities. In its present crowded and truncated state it must import nearly half of its food requirements.

The third geographical factor is related to the second. Not only does Germany lie athwart the principal trade and military routes of Europe; it has been its peculiar and fateful destiny to lie as well, for most of its history, between two opposing worlds.

These worlds themselves have changed in character with the progress of the centuries, but the position of Germany at the core of these tensions has been permanent.

For a period longer than the entire existence of the New World since the time of Columbus, Germany was part of the disruptive boundary between the learning and culture and military strength of Rome and the pushing, vigorous, barbaric society of the Germanic tribesmen.

A thousand years ago it was the barrier between Europe and the marauding Huns, who settled in Hungary and accepted Christianity only after their defeat by the Germans. With more or less success Germany has stood since then as a buffer region as well between the world of the Slavs and the Latin civilization of western Europe.

In the early Middle Ages, Germany was the battleground for emperors and popes with tragic consequences. In the sixteenth century it was divided along still another axis, between Protestants and Roman Catholics, and it persists to this day, roughly half in one of these worlds and half in the other. In no other modern Western nation do religious rivalries play such a considerable although sometimes concealed role.

In the eighteenth and nineteenth centuries Germany was the

stage for a bitter contest between Austria and the emerging power of Brandenburg-Prussia for control of all Germany, and in our own time the plowed strip, the barbed wire, and the wooden watchtowers mark the line of the Iron Curtain through the country's heart.

From some of these encounters at least, the Germans would have been spared gladly. But the perverse destiny that located them where they are has made this impossible. Germans speak and write often of their "historic mission," but one suspects they would exchange it in a minute for assurances of genuine peace.

In their difficult position only a people of consummate skill in government and diplomacy, acquired through centuries of practice, and shaped by the regular correction of past mistakes, could hope for a peaceful existence.

Instead, it has been Germany's destiny to come to grips with modern statehood and with the processes of democratic government so tardily that the world still is unsure that these have been mastered or are genuinely esteemed.

The alarm of the world is understandable, for the memory of what can happen when this nation's unquestioned powers and energies run off the rails as they did with the rise of Hitler is still too near and too hideous to be erased easily.

Most nations have experienced phases of aggressiveness and then have settled down to become respected members of the international community. Europe has been ravaged in turn by Turks, Spaniards, Swedes, and Frenchmen, before the Germans. Germany's turn came late, as has much in German national development, and when it came the Germans enjoyed an ominous advantage.

In the period between the defeat of the French at Waterloo and the emergence of a "German problem" as such at the turn of the twentieth century, the Industrial Revolution had made immense strides in Germany. Scientific advances and manufacturing techniques had enormously increased the country's capacity for damaging its neighbors. In the hands of a people more practiced in democracy this need not have led to disaster, just as a similar development in the United States has been essentially nonaggressive.

But means and controls seemed to grow at different rates in Germany, and there were some important areas of society quite outside normal checks. Big business became an arrogant world to itself in many ways, and so did the Army. The visions of power and the urgings of a nationalism so thwarted for centuries that it neared the psychopathic were altogether too heady.

The darkest bloom in this exotic garden was the police state itself. Modern communications, brilliantly exploited propaganda, the lonely vulnerability of individuals in a complex world, the bloodthirsts of the mob so thinly covered everywhere by civilization, and the total absence of any moral restraints or standards among the Nazi leaders combined to make the Nazi dictatorship possible. The fledgling democracy of Weimar simply couldn't withstand the pressures.

Once the Nazis were installed and prepared to use all the massive compulsions which the armory of scientific dictatorship includes, it was too late to do much about them, even for those who might have wanted a change. The number of these is fewer than the Germans would like to admit, but larger considerably than it has ever been believed outside the country. The Communists, in the meantime, have added their own convincing demonstrations of the way in which a people may be imprisoned by a determined minority.

The roots of Germany's awful disaster are buried deep in the country's past.

Charlemagne, the Frankish king who was crowned emperor in Rome in 800 A.D., ruled most of western Europe and northern Italy and, before his death in 814, had pushed the defenses of his empire into the borderlands of the Slavs.

Charlemagne's empire was divided into three areas. The western portion, in due course, became France. Its middle areas, a strip from the North Sea to Italy, over the years were contested bitterly. Some portions became sturdily independent, such as the Netherlands and Switzerland. Others, including Alsace and Lorraine and the Saar industrial basin, have changed hands and have figured prominently in the wars of our own time. The eastern portion of Charlemagne's empire was about that of West Germany today.

It was more than 100 years after Charlemagne that a Saxon duke, Henry the Fowler, was elected king of the several tribes, in 919. This, rather than Charlemagne's transient empire, was the beginning of modern Germany.

The next four centuries were a formative period of great importance in much of Europe. England and France made interrupted but cumulative progress toward nationhood in the modern sense. In Germany, by contrast, the bright hopes had been destroyed completely by the latter part of the thirteenth century.

The unification that came to the other great powers of western Europe so long ago was not to happen in Germany until the nineteenth century. When it did occur there, in 1870, under the Prussian Hohenzollern crown, it was accompanied by violence, a fusion like that of hydrogen, releasing immense energies and reverberating to this day.

Prussia has been admired, feared, and despised in turn, and when the Allies decreed it out of existence in 1946, it was already a corpse, another of Hitler's victims. Under Frederick the Great, one of the truly remarkable and enigmatic figures of history, who ruled Prussia from 1740 to 1786, it came to symbolize "militarism," yet Frederick preferred to play the flute and to write in French.

Prussia placed high value on the sterner qualities of mortal existence, on frugality, discipline, honor, capacity for sacrifice. On these it built a system of government, courts, and civil service that was one of the most honest that ever existed, and one of the most efficient. Yet it brought a ruthlessness and a cynicism to its international dealings that has often been equaled by others but rarely exceeded.

Elsewhere in Germany, until the end of the eighteenth century, little had happened for nearly 300 years to change the patterns of individual existence. Kings or dukes or petty sovereigns ruled with no popular checks or concept of representative government, and the philosophers, writers, and scientists who flourished in the eighteenth-century "enlightenment" seemed peculiarly divorced from politics.

Only in Württemberg in southwest Germany had an assembly, or "diet," established itself, and the benefits of this early exercise in democracy are clearly apparent. It is one of the most progressive and best-managed areas of the country today, and the only center in West Germany of classic liberalism.

The American and French Revolutions stirred Germany only vaguely, with the result that the Napoleonic era, which followed in the early years of the nineteenth century, was all the more shattering and bewildering. The French conqueror humbled Prussia. He decreed the empty shell of the Holy Roman Empire out of existence. He abolished and consolidated free cities and principalities until by the time of his defeat at Leipzig in 1813 there were only 39 of these authorities left, compared with nearly 400 a generation back. Germany's natural unity was now at least a physical possibility.

The collapse of the society in which the Germans had vegetated so long did more, however, than merely alter internal borders. It produced a body of genuine reformers and ideas, associated mostly with Prussia, and a feeling of German nationality that found expression first in the liberating war against the French. For all its hardships, it was a promising period, a time for fresh beginnings. In a few crowded years, under the lash of Napoleon, Germany had made the long passage from the Middle Ages to the threshold of the modern world.

A people more practiced in political thinking and less exposed geographically might have progressed further. But Europe was frightened of revolutions and Prussia was too weak to proceed on its own. The Congress of Vienna, under the guiding hand of Prince Metternich of Austria, created a loose German Bund, or confederation, designed to check Prussia's expansion on the one hand and to clamp the lid firmly on liberalism wherever it might appear. It succeeded in both of these aims for another half century, but the struggle exhausted Austria itself.

The German Bund had a Bundestag, or parliament, but it was crippled alike by the veto accorded to each of its members and by the prevailing atmosphere of political reaction. Instead of loosing constructive energies, it imposed what one historian describes as "a permanent obstacle . . . against the legislative development of the future German United States."

Thwarted politically, Prussia was beginning to stir economically, although the full impact of the Industrial Revolution would not make itself felt until after 1871. A customs union was established in 1818 to bring together the scattered pieces of Prussian territory and soon attracted other members. This was the beginning of Germany's modern unification.

A fresh wave of revolution swept Europe in the spring of 1848. Once again hope soared for constitutional government. There was serious rioting in Berlin, and the Prussian king was forced to promise civil liberties and to wear the black, red, and gold colors of the uprising. A German National Assembly was elected and met in Frankfurt.

Action would have carried the day, but the Assembly debated endlessly. The impetus was lost, and the promises of freedom were recanted in Berlin, Vienna, and Prague. A constitution actually was completed in the spring of 1849, but it never became effective. Friedrich Wilhelm of Prussia, firmly in control of his own capital again, dismissed the proferred German crown as a thing of "filth and clay."

The failure of this Assembly has been described as "one of the great tragedies of German—and of European—history." One person in every forty among the people of Germany fled to the United States from the repressions that followed. Reform would not have another chance until the end of World War I, and then it would be confused with treachery and defeat.

When unification occurred it was the work of another great and disputed figure, Otto von Bismarck, who became First Minister in Prussia in 1862 and in the most coldly logical fashion fought three short wars to establish a new German empire. One with Denmark settled the border problems in the North. A second crushed Austria, Prussia's rival for 200 years for German leadership. A third humbled France, which had connived and fought for centuries to prevent any German union and was slow to recognize its inevitable approach. The Empire was proclaimed in the famous Hall of Mirrors in Versailles in 1871.

Bismarck was a "militarist," in the sense that he used armies to achieve his ends, but with the distinction that he knew where to call a halt. He was a conservative, yet Germany owes its highly developed social insurance system to Bismarck. It was the first of its kind in the world, and one of the basically important discoveries of the nineteenth century.

Bismarck was a one-man government and foreign office, and immensely successful, yet he seems not to have grasped the fact that no one could succeed him. He was confident of his own ability to control the armed forces and refused to share any of this responsibility with the Parliament. After his dismissal in 1890, there was no one who could exercise such authority. The Army became the "state within the state," with disastrous consequences.

Bismarck's juggling of foreign affairs was so personal and so complicated that it was years before many of the details of his promises and arrangements were known. This inability to share his plans with others was the cause of much of the subsequent blundering that brought on World War I.

Creation of the Empire did nothing to increase the political stature of individual Germans, but it transformed their society in every other respect. Almost overnight the country became a modern industrial power. Germans had long been leaders in music and learning, and now this heady progress brought demands for what were felt to be other attributes of greatness, among them colonies and a major navy. Moderation was a suspect virtue; liberalism a despised philosophy. The clash that led to World War I was almost inevitable.

Out of that terrible conflict came a revolutionary Russia, a belt of new "nations" in eastern Europe, the first appearance of the United States as a power with European interests—although it was slow to recognize this—and a wholly unworkable peace.

Within Germany it brought the overthrow of the monarchy. A country that had passed up some opportunities and had been prevented on other occasions from developing normal representative government had now to create such an instrument under the most adverse circumstances.

The Weimar Constitution of 1919 was the result. It outlined

a logical federal system, which owed much to the ideas of the Frankfurt Assembly of 1848 and, in turn, to the United States Constitution.

"It failed," records a British historian, "less because it was a bad constitution than because it was adopted in the shadow of defeat and operated in the midst of very bad times."

To the normal problems of reconstruction was added a ruinous inflation that wiped out the middle class while it increased the power of big business. To many others, Soviet communism seemed still to hold great promise, and in southern Germany, Adolf Hitler, the Austrian corporal, was preaching his doctrines of hate and revenge.

In the second half of the twenties it appeared that some stability might after all come to Germany, but the depression wrecked these hopes.

Nazis and Communists alike were committed to the destruction of the infant republic rather than to any changing policies within its framework, and both of them gained as the economic pressures increased. The two parties combined quite openly and in the end achieved the overthrow. The highest vote the Nazis ever received in a free election was slightly over 37 per cent, but it sufficed to hoist Hitler into power, January 30, 1933. Germany's first nation-wide experience of democracy had survived only fourteen years.

Short as was this period, the life of Hitler's "Thousand-Year Reich" was even shorter. It combined the worst features of classic dictatorship with the weapons of the modern police state. It was and still is the cause of untold suffering. Its racial policies, not only about Jews but about most other peoples as well, were execrable. Its concentration camps are unforgivable.

Yet, if a politician's success is to be measured by the extent to which he approaches his own fixed goals, then Hitler displayed near genius, particularly in the early parts of his career. He crushed his domestic opponents and mobilized the unquestioned skills and energies of much of the nation. He bluffed and confused and divided his foreign adversaries. His successes won him following even among many who had at first been dubious. His defeat in the war that broke in 1939 was by no means as automatic as is sometimes now assumed. It required the combined strength of the three most powerful nations of the world—the United States, Britain, and the Soviet Union—to roll back the German tide.

At the peak of his power Hitler controlled an area greater than had any German ruler before him. For a few brief years Germany was one of the most unified, highly centralized nations in history. The vague dreams and stirrings of a thousand years had materialized in a hideous nightmare.

Hitler's official enemies were nations, but his attack was much broader. It aimed at the destruction of a way of life he despised and at the introduction, as Sir Winston Churchill said, of "a new Dark Age made more sinister, and perhaps more protracted, by the lights of perverted science." As the scales tipped from victory toward defeat, Hitler's twisted visions became more apocalyptic. If the Germans were incapable of following his lead they deserved the utter, total collapse for which they were headed, and which did in fact occur. The end of the war in May 1945 was also the end of a world.

Statistics convey only poorly the picture of Europe in the following summer. The continent was in ruins from the cathedral square of Coventry in England to the distant bluffs of the Volga River at Stalingrad, and the heart of this ruin was Germany itself.

Some 19 million soldiers and 18 million civilians had been killed, starved, murdered, or otherwise lost. The hatreds which grew from this appalling slaughter were savage and unbounded, and they focused on Germany.

The cry was for controls and punishment and some assurance that the peace would not be disturbed again. American planners who had the ear of President Roosevelt talked in terms of creating a "cow pasture." Communist plans were more sophisticated. They wanted to create a Soviet-type society and, in the process, to collect 10 billion dollars in reparations.

Among Germans themselves 6.5 million soldiers and civilians had died. A large percentage of the men who survived were prisoners. Families were scattered and hungry. The principal cities were crushed. Neighbor turned on neighbor, and only the presence of Allied troops prevented an additional bloodletting. The physical and moral disintegration was complete.

It was a farsighted prophet indeed who could see in this the outlines of a "new chance" for the German people. Almost no one did, yet it was to prove just that.

More than a decade later I talked at length one day with a German officer who had been a member of the General Staff and was now engaged in rebuilding a German Army.

"What would have happened," I asked, "if the bomb plot against Hitler in 1944 had succeeded and the Allies had been prepared to negotiate with a new government?"

His answer was careful and astonishing.

"I think it was necessary," he said, "that Germany should experience the full measure of the disaster. There is no one now we can blame except ourselves, and perhaps we have learned."

Germany's "new chance" did not depend in its early stages on the Germans. The Western powers were prepared to agree with the Soviets on a system much harsher and more punitive than anything that World War I had produced, and were ready to sign a treaty guaranteeing, for twenty-five or forty years, Germany's helplessness and poverty. It was the Soviets who prevented this.

Soviet behavior in the closing months of World War II in eastern Europe had begun to create doubts. In that bright and hopeful summer of 1945 the Potsdam Conference nearly failed. Early in 1946 the Soviets apparently decided they could acquire the whole of Germany if they played it right. Joint Allied military government was doomed from that moment, although it tottered along until 1948, when the Soviets imposed their blockade on West Berlin.

It was the Berliners who blew the whistle. The Allied airlift was a spectacular operation. It made it possible for the Berliners to keep their freedom. The decision was that of the city's people. The progressive unveiling of Soviet aims in Europe was opening other eyes as well. NATO was created in the spring of 1949 as a direct result of the Soviet threat.

Throughout the period of the airlift a Parliamentary Council of sixty-five members had been sitting in Bonn, and in May 1949 it completed the draft of a "basic law," by which the three western zones of Germany became the Federal Republic. One quarter of the Germans were in Soviet hands, but the rest at least would have the opportunity of liberty. This also was their own decision.

The Communist attack in Korea in 1950 removed many more lingering doubts. With considerable emotional misgiving, the Western world decided it would try again to make a partner of the German people. Geography and the rivalries of the neighbors once more were major factors in Germany's future.

From Germany's standpoint at least, it was fortunate, as a German editor wrote in 1959, that the Allies had been unable to agree on the peace in 1945. Sober historians may record one day that it was also fortunate for the Allies. In retrospect, the kind of a peace they were planning seems unbelievably naïve and unworkable. The existence of the heart of Europe cannot be ignored, no matter how much one might wish on occasion to do so.

The Marshall Plan, as early as 1947, "the most unsordid act in history," was one expression of this dawning realization. Germany alone was to benefit to the extent of about 4 billion dollars. Side by side with this, Soviet policy in East Germany forced the dismantling of many controls in the West.

Soviet refusal to account for the occupation currency it had printed from American plates was a major factor in the decision to reform West Germany's currency. Soviet refusal to give West Germany access to the food-raising regions in the East meant that West Germany's industrial ceilings had to be lifted so that food could be imported. Soviet charges that the West divided Germany are true only to the extent that the Soviets forced the West to act. Three quarters of a loaf was better than none.

The early years of this period were bewildering and sometimes a little absurd. One day, for example, the Germans were prohibited model aircraft because these were "too militaristic," and the next they were being chided by the Allies for not making sufficient progress with a new defense force. There was considerable irritation that youngsters who had been taught the "evils of militarism" didn't rush to volunteer for service.

German ideas were changing, but so were ideas about the Germans. Bit by bit it came to be recognized that not all Germans had been practicing Nazis and that there was an element of "liberation" in the Allied advance. The history of the Nazi period is still far from clear, but it came also to be suspected that the Western powers might have intervened much sooner, and at almost no cost, at the time of Hitler's reoccupation of the Rhineland in 1935, or even at the time of Munich in 1938. It was not a comforting idea, and it goes far to explain Western unwillingness to bow now before similar Soviet blusterings.

For all this new understanding it was three years before the British military governor could offer a gentle reminder that the majority of Germans were Christians and deserved to be treated as such, and this caused a storm of protest.

It was only much later that a British historian, surveying the course of the centuries, could observe that "perhaps the country and the people who have suffered most from Germany's past and the deficiencies of her leaders at different periods in her history have been Germany and the Germans themselves."

This more objective view spreads slowly. A single generation is scarcely sufficient to wipe out the memories of occupation and mistreatment among many Europeans. Yet it is an astonishing fact that a German visitor in Paris today often is better received than one from Britain, while during the Poznan Fair disturbances in 1956 the rioting workers went to extremes to safeguard West German businessmen and correspondents, whom the Poles seemed to regard as fellow allies in the struggle against the new Soviet tyranny in Europe. Communist East Germans, by contrast, stayed carefully out of the way.

With this has come a revised appreciation of the functions of military occupation in Germany and of the Western defensive alliances which have grown from it. The fundamentals of democracy may be "taught," but true skill can be acquired, as in music or painting or any of the other fine arts, only by patient practice and the painstaking study and correction of one's own faults in an atmosphere that permits such concentration. Viewed in this light, the occupation was necessary, but largely negative. Real progress began only when the Germans undertook to manage their own affairs. For ten years NATO has provided the Germans with this precious opportunity by holding at bay the one force that is committed openly and blatantly to the destruction of these liberties.

Curiously, because he is something of an autocrat himself, Chancellor Konrad Adenauer seems to have sensed this more clearly than some of his colleagues and opponents. The inviolability of NATO, the importance of Germany's growing ties with the United States, and the reconciliation of the ancient Franco-German rivalries and distrusts were the core of his program from the time he first took office in 1949 by the slender margin of a single vote in Parliament. The German people seemed to sense this as well. Dr. Adenauer's party increased its backing in succeeding elections until in 1957 it attained a clear majority over all the others, a measure of support no German leader ever had received in a free vote.

The best yardstick of West Germany's success is a comparison with Weimar. Civil disturbances after World War I were not brought under control until 1923. Ten years later Weimar's social and political structure was in tatters. The republic was defenseless before its enemies.

In 1959, at the end of a comparable period after World War II, West Germany's economic expansion was slowing slightly but continuing. Individuals and families were sinking new roots. Parliament worked and was gaining stature. The press was freer than it had ever been in the past, and jealous of its obligations. The trade-unions, by U.S. standards, were almost too cautious. The radicals, to right and left, were small and disorganized groups. The country gave every appearance on the surface of being a going concern.

Long acquaintance sometimes brings an uneasy feeling that these still are no more than surface appearances and that the molten material beneath this crust has not yet assumed its final shape. But each passing year makes the survival of this better Germany more likely. It already reacts to crises in a vastly different fashion from most of its predecessors, and so far it has been spared any stresses to which it is not yet equal.

The uneasy and the openly opposed can find damaging examples of voices from the awful past and of people who have managed despite their questionable records to remain in high position or to re-establish themselves. It is worth having a look at the record and remembering that some of these people are disappearing from the scene through natural causes while the Germans themselves are hunting down others.

In 1952, long before the outlines of the "golden miracle" were apparent, West Germany agreed, as "a spiritual purging," to pay nearly three quarters of a billion dollars to Israel. The treaty has been observed scrupulously, despite Arab threats and complaints, and the payments have been a major item in the support of the struggling country. Money can never replace lives, but it represented an admission of guilt and a desire for atonement. The East German Communists, by contrast, flatly refused to recognize any such obligation and have used this refusal with damaging effects to West Germany in the Middle East.

The much publicized "new anti-Semitism," is not new at all, but has been brought into the open by German publications and German courts. It is worth recalling, too, that West Germany is the only country in which people actually are sent to prison or must flee to some more congenial atmosphere like that of Cairo for making "anti-Semitic" remarks.

West German rearming is another cause of concern. But there are fundamental differences between the rearming that is taking place now and that which occurred between the wars.

For one thing, the Bundeswehr, or armed forces, is in the hands of the political leaders for the first time in German history. There is no "state within the state," and there need not be if the politicians are up to their trade. This is a matter of experience.

For another, the rearming is proceeding openly, by treaty and with the aid of allies, and not secretly and in violation of agreements.

For a third, the day of national wars in Europe is passed. No single nation can any longer hope to oppose the massive alliances that have grown on both sides. A "little war" in the center of Europe is inconceivable short of some arrangement which withdraws outside protection from both parts of Germany and leaves its opposing armies to fight it out in disastrous civil strife that could be confined within the cockpit of Germany's borders only with the greatest difficulty, and perhaps not at all.

There are some obvious threats to this growing stability in West Germany. Two need not materialize, but might. One is the possibility of a major economic depression of the kind the Soviets predict so hopefully for the free world. The chances of such a catastrophe appear to diminish as Europe moves toward a common market, a program in which Germany has taken a powerful lead.

The second would be an attempt by the Western world, in agreement with the Soviets, to impose new controls or sacrifices which were not shared by all the others in the alliance, or to restrict in any way the liberties and the opportunities the West Germans have been promised so solemnly and encouraged to accept.

Because of its element of discrimination, this second probably would be more dangerous than the first. Either might touch off a wave of bitterness and nihilism sufficient to damage much sturdier plants than democracy has yet produced in Germany.

There are at least two other hazards, which are unavoidable.

One of these is the transfer of leadership after Dr. Adenauer's long rule. The stern old chancellor has been a pillar of stability, but his very pre-eminence has dwarfed and stunted some of those around him. The Christian Democratic Union, the political party Dr. Adenauer created, is a mixture of North and South, Catholic and Protestant, industry and labor, which will require the most skillful handling if it is to survive. Past elections have shown a steady trend toward a two-party system, similar to that of the United States and Britain. The breakup of the C.D.U. would signal the return to the multiparty coalitions more common in Europe, and often unmanageable, as they were in France.

It is entirely possible that sufficient new leaders will be discovered, but there is a statistical handicap. A large number of those who might have made the race are lying in German soldier cemeteries in one or another of some fifty different countries. Wars have a way of killing off many of the best while those who plot and connive and exploit are less exposed. Not until roughly the year 2000, and then only if some new disaster doesn't intervene, will Germany have a normal quota of men under sixty.

The second of the unavoidable problems is a nagging one and probably the most important of all. It is almost certain that sooner or later Germany will be reunited. If the 17 million people in East Germany cannot be pried from the clutch of their Soviet masters, then the 53 million in the West may be shaken loose from their Western ties. It seems impossible that both the West and the Soviet world can be winners in this contest, however reluctant either may be to face its implications.

It is argued now, as it has been possible to do so about almost any given period in Germany's past, that there are many Germans who don't care whether their country is unified, and that most of the neighbors oppose it. Yet if there is one sustaining theme in Germany's chronicle it is this yearning to come together. At intervals it has been submerged, but it has never disappeared. When it has been too long and too recklessly frustrated, it has erupted in savage and destructive violence, aimed often at its tormentors. The Catholic Church, the once powerful Austro-Hungarian Empire, France, and Germany itself have been multiple losers as a result.

At this stage it is impossible to foresee or even to suggest how this reunification can be brought about, but some of its consequences are much clearer.

If it should be achieved under Soviet auspices the gain to the Soviets in industrial potential and skills might tip the balance for all time against the Western world. The rest of Europe almost inevitably would fall into Soviet hands.

Equally, if the Germans can be brought under a single roof in freedom there would be grounds for hope that the Soviet challenge to free peoples everywhere was beginning to ebb.

Until one or other of these solutions occurs, Germany will remain the unfinished business of almost everyone, as it has been for a thousand years.

SCANDINAVIA

Thomas A. Reedy

Tom Reedy has covered news from City Hall to State House to National Capitol to world problems for more than a quarter of a century.

A native of Reading, Pennsylvania, he left local papers to join the Associated Press in Harrisburg in 1936. Six years later he was transferred to wartime Washington, and his first assignment there was regional coverage of Minnesota, Wisconsin, and the Dakotas, which were often called "Scandinavia." He had no idea then that eighteen years later he would be in charge of Associated Press operations in Scandinavia.

Through the war years, Reedy was variously assigned to Congress and to government departments, with some high-pressure desk duty and some general tasks, including features. At the White House for the Associated Press he handled the break on the dropping of the first atomic bomb and also the surrender of Japan.

Toward the end of 1945 Reedy joined the Associated Press Foreign Service in Germany, covered the Nuremberg trials, the Berlin blockade and all its subsequent cold-war developments, including the Big Four conferences of Berlin and Geneva. In 1956 he was assigned to Stockholm as Chief of Bureau and later was appointed Chief of Scandinavian Services with responsibility for Sweden, Finland, Norway, Denmark, and Iceland.

SCANDINAVIA

The very word "Scandinavia" leads one to think of Danes, Norwegians, Swedes, and, indeed, even Finns as being something homogeneous. Nothing could be further from the truth. When you consider this part of the world, the best advice possible is to suggest that you forget the word "Scandinavian" and take things as they are in each separate area. Forget that all Scandinavians are blond, tall, this or that. Just as there is no such person as a typical American, so there is no such thing as a typical Scandinavian.

There are some threads which run through the entire Scandinavian peninsula and even stretch into Finland, but they do not dominate, they do not control, and very often do not influence any final concepts. The Dane will do it his way, the Norwegian as he sees it, the Swede will or will not do it as he views it, and the Finn has his own ideas. Thus, it is futile to learn a lesson in one nation and believe for a moment that it applies *in toto* to its neighbor. One might as well compare the Pennsylvania Dutch with the First Families of Virginia.

The best way to read Scandinavia is from left to right, just as you read any other book. And it is quite a book, crammed with romance and dry fact, the past and the present, habits which antedate civilization and others which seem a jump ahead of the most modern of communities.

In the left-to-right operation, you begin with Denmark, ease over into Norway, thence to Sweden, and finally to Finland. By doing so, the lessons of an extremely rich past and how it was refined into today's outlook are learned in the proper chronology.

Travel from Copenhagen to Helsinki bridges many chasms in history, and what the traveler sees en route demonstrates the folly of thinking that different languages and customs do not mean barriers. They most certainly do, and no single word such as "Scandinavia" can eliminate them. Only the most educated Norwegian or Swede can really understand Danish. The Swedish minority in Finland would like to believe that they speak the same Swedish as those in Sweden, but it is simply not so. The Finns claim the Swedes "sing" when they speak, their voices rising at various points of a sentence. The Swedes contend that the Finns, not they, "sing" in their diction. The Laplanders, who run their reindeer herds across the entire Scandinavian peninsula and into the Soviet Union, claim that all these other folk "sing" their speech, save themselves, but in fact they do the same thing, in another way.

Each has its own tradition, in some ways ancient and in others fairly modern. And it is reflected in daily life. The purpose of showing something about the daily life in this chronology is to illustrate the complexities and how they came about.

Since we are left-to-righting, let's start with Denmark.

DENMARK

It required a Shakespeare to find the melancholy Dane. If there has ever been a race of roisterers, living, drinking, carousing, sailing, and fighting in high good humor with a belly laugh about it all, it is the Dane. Other Scandinavians call the Danes plunderers and the Danes do not really deny it. Indeed, if you call them such a thing in modern business today, so long as it is accompanied by a grin, they will react with a little bit of honest pride.

Today the Dane drives his bargain over the table and he does it so well that, hemmed in from all sides, with a tiny piece of land and scarcely more than three million inhabitants, he has forged his habitat as a crossroads of the world.

Kastrup Airport links Europe with California by way of the North Pole. It is the landing spot for jets from Moscow. Copenhagen Harbor receives shipping of the North and Baltic seas. Causeways and ferries bring what seems like all Europe to the Danish capital in search of holiday.

Aside from the world's greatest dairy products, about all the Dane has to sell is himself, and he does a mighty job of that. Consequently, the visitor is king and that is a complete reversal of Denmark's ancient role in history. A thousand years ago the "visitor" was hung up to dry on the walls of old Harald Blue-tooth's Viking fortress at Trelleborg.

One gets the impression that even though civilization has come to the Viking Danes, they insist on retaining some of the wild freedoms of their past.

The nation is a curious admixture, with Social Democrats in power and with the driving spirit of private enterprise really pro-viding the energy which makes the whole operation highly profita-ble. This marriage of what might seem like conflicting interests grew from the desperation of Nazi occupation during World War II, when all Danes joined forces against a common foe. Hitler created the marriage, then Stalin and his cold war kept it together in such fashion that the Danes are a vital link in the North Atlantic Treaty Organization. They are dedicated to the principle that a few local fights at home can be set aside if some big bully has to be dealt with.

The genial Dane likes everyone save the Germans, and there is no point in disguising that fact. He simply refuses to forget the Nazi legions which stormed into a defenseless and peaceful country in 1940, even though the Wehrmacht actually treated Denmark with kid gloves in comparison with its conduct else-where. Yet Danes died and they do not forget. The German who comes to customs counters in Copenhagen gets a going-over while any other traveler gets a big hello. The German occupation pro-vided the spark for further endearing the monarchy, a really benevolent one, to the Dane. In the early days of the catastrophe, the late King Christian won his people anew by riding his horse entirely alone through the streets of Copenhagen, utterly ignoring the German conqueror, until one day when he saw a Nazi swastika being raised on a public building by some SS troops. The

King ordered the SS officer to haul it down, asserting that only the Danish flag belonged there.

"If you do not do it, I shall send a soldier up to do it for you," he said quietly.

The officer sneered. "Where will you get a soldier?"

"I am the soldier," replied the King.

The bewildered German hauled the swastika down and went for further orders from his superior. All Denmark thrilled, and the Resistance was just a little tougher that night.

Nowadays the monarchy is a far cry from its Viking inception, but it serves a high social purpose and is just as much a part of Danish life as shrimp sandwiches and beer.

The smallest of the Scandinavian countries, Denmark is the richest, and this came first from the sea—every Dane is a sailor even now—and then air contact with all the world. The link with Britain is fantastically strong, but there is nothing new about that. Almost a thousand years ago, the Danes plundered the English kingdom of Ethelred the Unready, settled down there, and then provided Britain with one of its mightiest monarchs, the Dane Canute. Over the centuries the seafaring traditions of both nations bound them together. Across the sea in northern France are Denmark's original cousins. It was the Danish Viking who seized Normandy, and it was Danish blood that stood by William the Conqueror in the establishment of Norman rule in Britain.

The Dane views his Norwegian neighbor to the north as a slightly unlucky and unblessed ward to be chided, scolded, but protected. He views the Swede as slow, slightly stupid, lucky in his natural wealth. Back of a lot of this is envy but also a mighty big chunk of respect. When the Swedes and Danes battled each other in the days of Erik the Victorious, there was no quarter given. They fight today commercially, even inside the workings of their own Scandinavian Airlines, and in the Nordic Council, and there's plenty of commercial bloodshed and very little quarter.

Emotions of the dim past seem to grip the Dane and motivate his daily conduct. For instance, one of the best ways to get into a rousing battle with any Dane on the street is to tell him he is being pretty cheap about the Icelandic sagas. These are the writings of the Vikings who left Denmark, plied into the North Atlantic, and settled Iceland. Some went on to Greenland and even to the North American continent. Iceland claims the sagas, since they tell of these voyages, and indeed the Icelander is almost the only one in the world who can still read them, because the language has remained pure. But the Dane says he will hang on to them forever, and why?

"They were Danes, weren't they?"

The way to take Denmark is to let it take you. Copenhagen is the gateway. It's a raincoat town. However brilliant the sun, the clouds come scudding off the sea without warning and the wise man expects showers. As the Dane says, if you do not like the weather, stick around fifteen minutes; it will change.

The capital is crammed with remarkable restaurants and places of entertainment. Every night seems like the windup of a convention. The Danes encourage it as one of their most fruitful industries.

Outside Copenhagen is another side of Denmark, all within a radius of 125 miles. At Roskilde is the medieval capital of Denmark, and beneath the twin-spired cathedral lie the bones of many Danish kings of long ago. Near Slagelse is the unique Viking fortress of Trelleborg, which garrisoned 1000 warriors in the days of Harald and Sven Forkbeard (father of Canute). At Korsör, reached by ferry, is Danehof, the oldest castle in Scandinavia. South through Funen's countryside with its beautiful manor houses leads eventually to Odense and the birthplace of Hans Christian Andersen, Denmark's famed spinner of fairy tales. His childhood home is a museum.

NORWAY

To hear the Norwegian tell it, his country is just a heap of rocks, but there are few peoples in this world so fiercely wrapped up in their own land and, though he is steeped in travel, the Norwegian never really is quite happy till he comes back home once more.

This ancient love of his own makes the Norwegian anxious to

prove it. He feels there are some things he possesses which cannot be matched elsewhere: the fiords and the mountains of the North and West, the midnight sun in June, the snapping salmon which when smoked tickle a palate thousands of miles off, the ski slopes with snow atop the peaks and summer swimming at the base.

There is a great bond with Britain. British influence has been of commercial variety for generations, and the ties grew even closer in World War II. The Americans are admired and in some degree envied, but it is the Briton who is respected, listened to, and believed. The German is thoroughly distrusted, in some degrees genuinely hated. A symbol of this feeling toward Germans is a stone wall beside the old royal castle in downtown Oslo, facing the harbor. At one end of the wall there are a number of chips. They were caused by German bullets executing Norwegian underground patriots during the Nazi occupation. Next to it are a set of similar marks. They were caused by Norwegian bullets executing the Quisling traitors after the liberation. That old, mossy wall is the real monument of those times of great misery, tragedy, and considerable daring.

Britons and Norwegians parachuted in, sneaked in aboard little boats, and made life miserable for the Nazi legions. These two will always remember that, and it is largely British influence which brought Norway into the Western Atlantic Pact alliance and keeps it there despite some misgivings from time to time.

There are quite a few "different Norways," but all interest starts with Oslo, the big harbor built for safety from marauders off the Skagerrak and directly north of the tip of Denmark. The town sprawls like Los Angeles and is still growing, since the Norwegians believe in elbow room, not skyscrapers. The Hotel Continental is at the center of interest, within sight of the palace of King Olav and the Norwegian National Theater. The main street, Karl Johans Gata, links the palace with the Parliament, called the Storting, with a long, tree-lined esplanade which always seems to resound with the tunes of a brass band. The fronts of the buildings do not seem very attractive, but in most of them are passageways to courtyards where one can usually find something old, interesting, or quite handsome.

222

To appreciate Oslo one has to bear in mind the way it is today as well as what happened to create it.

There are dramatic living symbols of today, such as Jan Baalsrud, who lives in Oslo and is the author of *The Great Personal Experience,* which has become a best seller and a great film. It relates how Jan himself parachuted into Norway with the British Commandos and then endured a most magnificent and unbelievable experience at working his way toward liberty. When one knows that Jan broke off his own toes, frozen stiff, one by one, and then was buried in snow for weeks awaiting succor, it is almost impossible to imagine a cup of tea with him in such peace and quiet as Oslo now affords. Yet he will receive you with extraordinary patience. Then you will understand what kind of a man it was who survived this experience, and only then can you be sure of something 'way down deep in the Norwegian character.

Where did it come from? Well, go back as far as you like to the Viking period and it is not hard to see and even feel the fires of the forges that built such a man. The Norwegian, Oslo style, does not forget it for a moment. While the Danes and the Swedes on either side have more to show for it, the Norwegian contends that his Viking was a good deal more effective. And in these modern times, the Norwegian is the only one who can produce some genuine evidence. His neighbors have all sorts of burial mounds and castles which require many words to describe, but only in Oslo can you find a real Viking ship.

Somehow or other, this magnificent piece of wood, built with such excellent engineering skill that it could withstand whatever there was in the way of weather or sea, refused to die in Norway. Modern excavators found one of these tenth-century masterpieces, dug further, and found two more. Thus we have now the Oseberg ship, the Gokstad ship, and the Tune ship, dug out of the mud of the Oslo Fiord together with the effects of the warriors who sailed the high seas before the Christian world was a thousand years old.

The Oseberg ship helps toward understanding how the men of those times covered thousands of miles of ocean and survived. Buried with the Oseberg was a collection of household articles and garments which show how the Viking lived and under what conditions. The Norwegians are especially proud of their assembly of things buried with Queen Ase, for whom the Oseberg was named. "The Death of Ase," part of Grieg's *Peer Gynt Suite*, is set in just that time.

Still within the sea motif is the Norwegian polar-exploration ship *Fram,* in which Fridtjof Nansen pierced the North Polar regions before the turn of the century. It sailed also through the Arctic seas north of the American continent and, for all its tiny thousand tons, illustrates once more that iron men could do quite a lot with wooden ships even in an advanced age. To know the *Fram* is to know about Nansen and Roald Amundsen, Norway's greatest explorers of both polar regions.

Nansen lived out his life in Norway, but Amundsen disappeared and so he seems a more romantic figure. But Nansen gave something more to the world in creating the so-called "Nansen passport" after World War I, a concept that those who were displaced and stateless nevertheless should have some document to show their validity. The nations of Europe accepted the idea, and the Nansen passport became the badge of honor for the "DP" of an earlier age, a device that the best brains of a generation later were unable either to improve upon or to adopt to anyone's satisfaction. Nansen explored more than ice and snow. He delved into the world's sociological conscience.

SWEDEN

Göteborg is the home of the Swedish-American shipping lines and a typical port city, and the first thing you do is check in with the Park Avenue Hotel. All you have heard about the slow Swedish tempo seems alien, and in Göteborg it is. On a small scale Göteborg is much like San Francisco, and only after the visitor passes the outskirts of the city does he discover the real Sweden. This impression begins with the Göta Canal to Stockholm.

South of Göteborg lies Malmö and the part of Sweden called Scania. This was the leaping-off place of the old Vikings and still bears the unmistakable air of the Danes. Malmö is a former Danish city and, indeed, the Malmöite looks on Copenhagen directly across the water as a sort of suburb. They ply back and forth on the ferry all the time, buying cheap butter on the Danish side and selling American cigarettes in exchange. The Swedes call it "the butter run."

All through Scania, on the Baltic, are the old castles of bygone imperial grandeur, constructed in an area of mild climate, always about two or three weeks ahead of severe Stockholm on the east coast.

But Stockholm is the "center" of Sweden, a remarkable city which grew too big too quickly on what started out to be only seven islands. Now it is a maze of bridges, and the Swedes like to call it the Venice of the North. To see it by night from the air is a fantastic sight, the lights of the curving bridges and traffic clovers forming a network of gleaming jewels. About the only other city which strikes one so forcibly by night is Rio de Janeiro.

From the Bromma Airport helicopters fly to the roof of the Foresta Hotel, which stands atop a big cliff on the island of Lidingö overlooking the most beautiful stretch of water and forest imaginable. Next door is the home and gardens of the late Carl Milles, one of the twentieth century's greatest sculptors, and the gardens abound with examples of his work.

The Swede is different from other Scandinavians, perhaps more relaxed and yet with more elements of leadership. His country is rich in iron ore, in forests, in medical and scientific research, in engineering, in ceramics and glassware, and whatever he puts his hand to is done eventually as well as anywhere in the world. This is one pride of a country with a population of only seven million, always suffering from a limited labor supply.

Stockholm presents the contrasts of modern enterprise and early-nineteenth-century forms and their graphic reflection of the country's individuality. Here is located the Nobel Foundation, established by Alfred Nobel, whose tremendous fortune from the discovery of dynamite is used for annual awards to pioneers in medicine, chemistry, physics, and literature and in promoting peace.

Not far from this unique shrine of modern industry, the waters lap up to the steps of the Royal Palace, a big pink building. It houses one of the world's most popular royal families, but one with no Swedish roots at all.

This dynasty dates from 1810, when the Swedes invited Bernadotte, one of Napoleon's marshals, to the throne.

That era also marked the start of Sweden's neutrality in Europe's conflicts. The Swedes had battered the Russians, the Germans, the Poles, and others for centuries and seemed to have had their fill of it. But today every Swede is a reservist, and the armed forces' training high in the snowy mountains is the toughest in existence. The air force of 1500 jet fighters is all pointed East, every Swede regarding the Russian as his natural enemy. They are neutral, yes, leaning West.

Not having engaged in armed combat for a century and a half weighs on the Swedes. Many seem to wonder if their neutral role in World War II was correct. But that, too, is part of the Swedish desire to be liked and admired, as against his refusal to be an extrovert openly asking for favorable opinion.

For a nation that had been introverted for many centuries, the Swedes seem finally to have hit a hurry-up stride to catch up with the rest of the world. Consequently, if anything good is made elsewhere it shows up in Stockholm, regardless of the import cost. It is part of a special pride.

Position means everything to a Swede, so give up any idea of looking up Sven Andersson in the telephone book—that chap you met once in Dubuque. You must know his "title," as this is how it is listed alphabetically. He is Engineer Andersson, or Director, or Disponent, or some such thing. This illustrates the length to which the Swede goes in regularizing his life and his manners. He tips his hat to all and sundry. He shakes hands all day long. He says "thanks" in so many different ways it is hard to keep track of all of them. But he's the best industrial-management man in existence.

Once he says "all right" to a business deal, though, no matter the extent of the Arabian tactics that have gone before, you need no fountain pen. That deal is sealed and will be met. As part of his correctness, it's interesting to see what other Scandinavians say about the Swede. Take the words of Willy Breinholst, a Dane, who wrote the following in a privately published booklet, *Scandinavians—That's Us.*

"Among the Scandinavians the Swedes are easily the best dressed. They will dress up in tails just to go out and get the evening paper. Swedes are so fussy that they will always shave before going to the barbershop."

For a good day in Stockholm, a morning tour in a motorboat "under the bridges," which means around the islands which make up the city proper, is pleasant. Lunch ought to be taken at a place on the edge of the city surrounded by some woodland, and there are many. The best is Stallmästaregården, on the water, and famed for its cuisine. An afternoon walk through the Old City, which is the keystone of Stockholm, is apt to cost you some money, because the little shops are enticing. It lies directly behind the Royal Palace and is the land Birger Jarl chose eight centuries ago as a haven from marauding tribes. This was not the heart of Sweden as a nation then, but the old Viking chose well. After such a walk, and a freshener in the hotel, the evening can be most charming. Go to Drottningholm, directly to the royal summer palace (*drottning* means "queen" in Swedish), and see a theater that is today unique. It is an eighteenth-century theater attached to the palace but long since thrown open to the public. Here only eighteenth-century music and opera are presented. The atmosphere is retained to such a degree that the opera "machinery" of that time, old wooden things, are used even today. You do not have to care about opera, or even eighteenth-century music, to realize that this is something special and worthy of retention.

FINLAND

Most American tourists who put Finland on their list and finally reach it come armed with the sole knowledge that the Finns paid their World War I debt. If you are one of those, don't mention it to the Finns. They're sick and tired of hearing it, and there are in fact some other things better worth knowing. Actually Finland's payment of her debt, which got such wide publicity every year, characterizes something deeper inside the Finn, and the visitor will elicit a smile of genuine warmth if he so much as mentions it. That is the trait known as *sisu,* and it defies translation into one single word. The definition to a Finn is "fortitudinous staying power and tenacity in the face of adversity against insurmountable odds." The Finn has this to a degree that never fails to surprise. Ask the Russian who was on the Finnish front two decades ago. He knows about it.

Sisu keeps the Finn going under harsh conditions. It keeps him going, too, at the festive board and over the bowl of wassail. When all others fall by the wayside, the Finn wants "one more for the road." He's an all-out man in all respects.

On leaving Sweden for the final leg of this northern-tier "armchair journey," the best way to approach Finland is by boat in navigable times of the year.

The visitor seeing Finland for the first time gets a mild shock when he reaches Helsinki. This is truly eastern, a strange mixture of Finnish and Russian. The people are small in height; the architecture is mainly of the period when Finland was a duchy under the czars. The churches are topped by minarets, and each onionlike bulb denotes that here is a different land from anything in the so-called West. In winter, the city is gray, forbidding, freezing. In summer it is bright, gay, and completely transformed.

Helsinki is 400 years old, but it seems modern and is constantly teeming with some new constructions. Finnish architecture is unique and stands proudly along with the best in the world. There is hardly a park which does not have some masterpiece in bronze which is so graceful and enticing that you wonder why someone doesn't steal it.

The very breath of the East wafts through Senate Square in downtown Helsinki. There is the statue of Czar Alexander II, who is known as the "benevolent czar." Under Alexander, Finland had autonomy except in foreign affairs. The fall of Nicholas II in 1917 kept the Russian Bolshevists so busy that Finland took the occasion to declare its independence completely, so in that sense it is a pretty young country even though the original Finns came up from somewhere around Hungary more than seventeen centuries ago.

Behind the statue is the "Great Church," a glorious example of Russian architecture. The more modern buildings around it, mostly government headquarters, are unable to pierce the atmosphere or spoil it.

Every visitor to Finland is intrigued by that ceremonial bath, the *sauna*. Most foreigners feel like Mark Twain once said, that if it weren't for the honor of the thing, he'd just as soon pass. It is not to be ignored in any case, as an American journalist discovered on one occasion when he wanted to interview the Prime Minister during a government crisis.

He was invited to the *sauna*, and there was the Prime Minister and his whole Cabinet, naked, sweating out in the literal sense something other than political problems. The interview was conducted in highly dignified fashion, nonetheless, without pencils and notebooks and pockets. Only a true *sauna* man can be nonchalant in such an atmosphere.

The *sauna* is a bakehouse for humans. It is heated up to 212 degrees Fahrenheit and men sit in it and sweat. Women attendants occasionally spread water on the heating unit and the steam rises. They take birch branches and beat you with them, gently but with enough authority to bring life to dead muscles. Then you are hauled out to another room not nearly so hot, dunked in various tubs of hot and then cold water, scrubbed vigorously, and then the remains of the man who started this exercise is tossed back into the oven for another bake. On the second trip out, the patient is about finished, and he is robed and laid on a bed to sleep for half an hour.

The Finn has had his *sauna* for so long that he has invented variations that the foreigner almost never hears about, much less sees. The avid *sauna* man tosses a bit of schnapps onto the heating unit, for example, and that fills the room with alcoholic fumes that, breathed in, are more potent than a whole bottle of whisky. Many, or rather most, slip from their *sauna* during the winter directly into the snow outside their homes and roll around in it for a moment or two. Then they go back into the steam room and let their flesh tingle with the contrast.

It must be said for the snow exercise, it is not at all as shocking as it sounds. The idea of it may well have been the Finnish desire to show that their *sauna* is a little different from the old Roman baths and the later Turkish baths. There wasn't any snow in Rome or Istanbul.

RUSSIA

Irving R. Levine

Irving R. Levine spent four years in Russia as correspondent for the National Broadcasting Company. Now Mediterranean Director for NBC based in Rome, Mr. Levine is heard regularly on NBC radio and seen on television. Author of the best seller Main Street, U.S.S.R. *and of the first full-length guidebook to the Soviet Union,* Travel Guide to Russia, *Mr. Levine also writes for many American magazines. While in Moscow from 1955 to 1959, he also served as special correspondent for* The Times *of London.*

Born in Pawtucket, Rhode Island, Irving R. Levine graduated from Brown University, Phi Beta Kappa, and received a master's degree from the Graduate School of Journalism at Columbia University. He served in World War II as a lieutenant in the Signal Corps in the Philippines and Japan.

Mr. Levine worked on the Providence Journal *newspaper and joined International News Service in 1947 as a foreign-news editor in New York and went to Vienna as Bureau Chief a year later. He worked in Paris, Sofia, Prague, and Frankfurt before being transferred to Korea in 1950, covering the war and truce talks as well as stories in Japan, Hong Kong, Thailand, Indochina, and Formosa.*

He was the recipient of the annual fellowship for a foreign correspondent awarded by the Council on Foreign Relations in 1952 and has since won many awards.

Mr. Levine is a contributor to an earlier Overseas Press Club book, entitled Off the Record. *He is married to the former Nancy Cartwell Jones.*

RUSSIA

If by some fictional circumstances a person were granted one hour, and only one hour, to spend in Russia he would be wise to spend it in Red Square.

No other single place in Russia reflects so much of the country's past, its present, and even its future.

The vast rectangle is not *typical* of Russia. For one thing, in majestic beauty and grandeur, the Kremlin, which borders one side of Red Square, happily contrasts with the characteristic drabness of present Russian construction. The square's older landmarks convey an atmosphere of the princely state of Muscovy that provided the nucleus of the original Russian state. And the humanity that flows through Red Square is a reminder of the expansion of that Russian state. The motley crowds include Ukrainians and Uzbeks as well as Russians, because, of course, a cluster of smaller, heterogeneous countries around Russia's frontiers has been brought under Moscow's control.

At the north end of the cobblestoned expanse of Red Square (whose dimensions are 1300 feet by 430 feet) rise the four slender spires of the State Historical Museum. In its more than twenty rooms maps and remnants trace the residents of Russia from prehistoric to proletarian.

At the opposite end of the square, in a combination of colors and shapes that should be cacophony but somehow is symphony, stands St. Basil's Cathedral. Its nine bulbous, painted cupolas are crowned by golden crosses of the once politically powerful Russian Orthodox Church. The cathedral is now a museum of the atheistic Soviet State. Czar Ivan the Terrible had this cathedral built to commemorate his victory over the Tatars—the cruel invaders from Asia who conquered vast regions of what now is Russia, as had other waves of invaders before them.

The Kremlin itself was in fact built as a fortress against such attacks, and that is what the word means. Home of the Czars, scene of fighting during the 1917 Revolution, it now is the seat of Soviet government. Its red-brick, crenelated walls, sloping gently and punctuated by nineteen towers (which bear such names as Savior's Tower, Water Tower, and Nameless Tower), might remind our one-hour visitor of an ancient Italian walled city. And correctly so, because Italian architects, brought in, ably blended their Italian genius with traditional Russian qualities.

At the foot of the Kremlin wall is one of Red Square's newer but equally significant landmarks—the mausoleum of red-granite blocks that was constructed to perpetuate the body of V. I. Lenin, "father" of the Revolution, who died in 1924. More recently, in 1953, the embalmed body of Joseph Stalin was given a place in a glass casket next to Lenin's. This has become a shrine of the new order, visited as reverently and by as great numbers as were ever the nine chapels of St. Basil's.

Opposite the Kremlin wall and the tomb, across Red Square, windows look out from Gosudarstvennyi Universalnyi Magazin, the State Department Store, generally known by its initials, GUM (which rhymes with "boom"). Displayed in these windows are dresses, men's suits, shoes, crystal ware—distinguished by increasing availability and high prices. Built in the first third of the nineteenth century by putting a glass arcade roof over rows of merchants' stalls, GUM was converted to government offices during Stalin's era but since Stalin's death has been restored to its former function. More than any other part of Red Square, GUM with its bustle of shoppers, often pushing each other unconscionably, reflects the energy and peasant directness of everyday Russian life.

On May 1 (the international labor day which the Communists have adopted as their own) and on November 7 (the anniversary of the revolution that brought the Communists to power) GUM's gray stone acquires a bright plywood façade. Signs, boldly painted with slogans, confidently predict the eventual world triumph of communism and the fulfillment of whatever Five- or Seven-Year Plan is then in progress. If our one-hour visitor were in Red Square during the spring or autumn holiday he would be swept along by the thunderous parade of military equipment and soldiery that moves under the eyes of the Kremlin's leaders, who stand on an upper ledge of the Lenin-Stalin Mausoleum. The military might is followed by ordinary civilians, marching fifty and more abreast, carrying flowers and placard slogans and portraits of the current leaders and those deceased ones who are still in favor. It is an annual ritual of renewal of allegiance by the populace to their state, its leaders, and the Communist Party—the only political grouping permitted in the land.

On the five principal towers of the Kremlin red-glass stars gleam at night. These ruby-red star symbols of communism replaced the imperial eagles of the Romanov czars after the Revolution. The symbols of the premises have changed along with the occupants (from the early 1700s the czars had their capital at St. Petersburg, now Leningrad, and only occasionally lived at the Moscow Kremlin), but a form of tyranny has prevailed both under the eagles and under the stars.

The present form of government is frankly described by its leaders as a "dictatorship of the proletariat." The proletariat, the laboring class (including urban factory workers, rural farmers, and intellectuals who come from both factory and farm families), is supposedly the sole wielder of power. Actually, not the laboring class but the Communist Party is the basic repository of power. The Party's size has varied. During World War II, for example, it was considered desirable to expand the Party, and new members were admitted rapidly and rather readily. After the war, though, a more traditional course was again resumed—the Party was kept small, manageable, disciplined, a carefully selected and supervised organization of men and women.

The membership of the Party in this land of 215,000,000 people is less than 4 per cent of the total population. The explanation offered by the Communists is that the Party has only the interests of the laboring class at heart, and in mind, and the Party consists of those individuals most competent to lead the nation to a better, more prosperous life.

Organized into units at every enterprise—whether at a ball-bearing factory or a ballistics institute—the Party members elect delegates to periodic Congresses of the Communist Party. These convene in the Moscow Kremlin in a huge hall, part of which once housed the czar's throne room. These important Congresses —there had been twenty-one of them by 1960—set the course of the Communist compass. For example, the Twenty-first Congress approved major revisions in the nature of Soviet economic planning—switching from Five-Year Plans to Seven-Year Plans, with goals of proportionally enhanced magnitude.

It is at these Congresses, too, that a Central Committee is elected, a body varying in size but usually totaling about 130 members. This high body, in turn, elects a Presidium. The Presidium also varies in number, but 15 is customary. The First Secretary of the Central Committee is Chairman of the Presidium, and in this role he is the most important man in the Soviet Union, the leader, the dictator.

With only one political party, there is no room for an opposition, loyal or otherwise. Thus, there is no place in the Soviet system for a minority voice in public affairs. In debates in the Central Committee or in the Presidium that precede a decision, there is opportunity for personal opinions and persuasions to be expressed. To reach a position on the Central Committee or on the Presidium, a man (or woman) must have undeniable ability and talent, besides other characteristics, among which ruthlessness is not excluded. Men of this caliber have their own ideas on such problems as whether the management of factories should be decentralized in order to give greater authority to factory managers in day-by-day production. Similarly, on foreign policy, individuals of Central Committee stature have ideas on whether it serves Soviet interests to invest huge resources in the Middle East.

However, once a decision is reached—and such decisions are determined finally by a majority vote in the Presidium—unanimity is expected and almost always achieved. There is no tolerance of argument after a decision has been made. Such argument or dissension is considered disloyalty, or worse, treason. According to the nature of the particular era, such "opposition" has been dealt with by execution or exile or demotion.

It is the Communist Party that really governs Russia and the fourteen other so-called republics that make up this enormous country. The Party, by having its members and its units on every level and in every realm of activity, has the apparatus for effective action. However, there is a government, too. Almost invariably personnel in the pinnacle positions in Party and government are the same. It is commonplace for the same man to occupy the posts of First Secretary of the Central Committee of the Communist Party (Party Chairman) and Chairman of the Council of Ministers (Premier). This is a natural tendency in a one-party system.

The Soviet Union has its ministries, its legislature (the Supreme Soviet, which is supposed to meet twice a year and sometimes does), and its local-level equivalent of city councils and mayors. But in these—with an occasional intentional exception for making the point that it is not essential to be a Party member to get ahead—the Party and the government overlap wherever it is necessary for control.

Under its constitution the U.S.S.R. also holds elections. Only one candidate is listed for each office. The voter has no choice of candidates. Nevertheless, great efforts are exerted by so-called Party "activists" to produce a large turnout of voters, and customarily more than 99.5 per cent of eligible voters cast ballots. Almost all ballots (with the exception of a few write-in votes) are cast in favor of the Party-approved candidate. Although predetermined by the very nature of the election, the results are published with great pride in newspapers (all of which are run by the Party, or the government, or their appendages). In a sense, like the parades through Red Square, the elections are contrived perennial demonstrations of allegiance.

Proponents of the Soviet system claim that this is democracy. They argue that it is democracy for the working people. There is only one party because it alone satisfies the needs and aspirations of the laboring class. Democracy and freedom are denied only to those who would deny the laboring class their hard-won status and restore them to the position of the exploited class. So runs the Communist apologia for their system of government.

If our hypothetical visitor were in Red Square during almost any winter's day, snow would probably be falling, and he could watch a cleverly designed, efficient loading device mounted on a truck, scooping up snow. Mechanical arms at street level avariciously claw snow into open containers on a horizontal conveyor belt. The containers dump the snow into the back of a truck. Working near the mechanized device are women, barrellike in heavily quilted jackets of blue, incongruously wearing white work aprons. As is the case in almost every phase of the Soviet economy, it is mechanization and manual labor side by side.

The Soviet economy has made enormous strides since the Revolution of 1917, when the decision was made to raise Russia from an agrarian economy. Russia was to be industrialized at whatever the cost in human dignity, creature comforts, and personal freedom. Progress is seen in every quarter. If our sixty-minute visitor would lift his eyes from Red Square's wonders he might catch a glimpse to the southeast of one of Moscow's thirty-floor "multistory" buildings (this word is preferred to "skyscraper"). There are sputniks, of earth and sun, and fast planes, jet and turbojet. Dams have been constructed across the Volga and Russia's other great rivers; in some cases, the capacity of one of these dams exceeds the sum total of all of Russia's electric-power output before the Revolution. Resources have been invested, too, in schools, libraries, and kindergartens (where working mothers leave their children for the day six days each week on the way to the factory).

Yet, it was with accuracy that Britain's Prime Minister, Harold Macmillan, explained on the state-operated television station during a trip to Moscow that "we in Britain still produce twice as much as you per head." This placed Soviet industrialization and level of efficiency in context. And it was with equal perception that a British journalist, observing the shoddy construction of acres of ten-story apartment houses on the fringes of Moscow, wrote that "it is a depressing sight to see slums being built before your very eyes."

The resources of the Soviet Union are tremendous. One is almost tempted to say unlimited. In some cases, the natural resources are still so lightly tapped that it has been possible for Soviet planners to speak realistically of increasing oil output by 200 per cent in the period of one year. The U.S.S.R. is now the second-most-industrialized country in the world, ranking only behind the United States. Soviet leaders describe the Soviet Union's "main economic task" as surpassing the most advanced capitalistic countries in per capita production.

All resources—ore deposits and forests and water power—are owned by the state, as are all the means of production. The manpower, resources, and money that will be invested at any period of time in the development of these resources are prescribed in State Economic Plans—formerly of five years' duration, and now of seven. It is a planned economy in every sense. The plan, worked out by an army of technicians, prescribes everything from how many lathe operators will be trained to how many television sets will be produced. Resources available rather than demand (as in capitalistic economy) is the determining factor of output.

It is no simple matter to plan ahead for seven years or five years or even one in an economy as complex and extensive as that of the U.S.S.R. The complexity of the task is compounded by the human factor. Depending on their stake in the matter, individuals tend to influence the Economic Plan in one of two directions. There are those, including many factory managers, who try to submit conservative figures and estimates in the hope that the Plan's targets will be kept low. The factory manager's motives are transparent. A low target figure is easy to fulfill and surpass, and thus the manager's chance of establishing a reputation for himself is strengthened. On the other hand, there are those individuals—the economists and the politicians—who stand to benefit by presenting the leadership with the most ambitious of Plans. Their tendency is to seek swollen figures and to intensify the work

load in order to achieve their lofty goals. The net result is to com-
plicate the task, gargantuan at best, of trying to plan—on the basis
of the means really at hand—the production of needles or nuclear
reactors.

There is yet another complicating factor in a planned economy
in a fast-moving technical age. The planners may decide on the
basis of accurate figures that a certain number of, say, chemical-
plant technicians will be needed during the next seven years.
Technical institutes are created and staffed to educate such personnel. The appropriate number of promising youngsters are admitted to the educational institutions. Then a new breakthrough
of knowledge in the chemical field makes it possible to bypass
the very steps in the chemical process for which the youngsters
are being trained. The job becomes obsolete. So do the institutes
and their staffs. Problems of this nature do arise under long-term
economic planning, but in general such planning has raised Russia
to the status of a formidable industrial power and is gradually
providing more of the necessities of life, and even some creature
comforts, for its people.

The people in Red Square, it might quickly be noted by the
man we set down there at the outset of this chapter, come from a
variety of national stocks. Most are Russians. The Russian Soviet
Federated Socialist Republic (Russia) is by far the biggest of the
fifteen republics that comprise the U.S.S.R. Russia occupies five
and a half million of the more than seven and a half million square
miles from the Baltic Sea to the Pacific Ocean, from the Arctic
Circle to the frontiers of Asia, that is the Union of Soviet Socialist
Republics (the "U.S.S.R.," or the "Soviet Union"). More than 60
per cent of the population of the U.S.S.R. lives in Russia. Russians
comprise well over half the country's populace. Russian is the
principal language spoken in the U.S.S.R., but there are sixty other
tongues, and one hundred dialects, some of which are different
enough to be considered separate languages themselves.

Besides Russia, the Soviet Union consists of: the Ukraine,
Byelorussia, Azerbaidzhan, Georgia, Armenia, Uzbekistan, Turkmenistan, Tadzhikistan, Kazakhstan, Kirghizia, Moldavia, Lithu-

ania, Latvia, and Estonia. The people of the Ukraine and Byelo-russia are most like the Russians, but the people of Kirghizia, Uzbekistan, Tadzhikistan, and Turkmenistan, in central Asia, are Asian rather than European. They look more like Orientals—which they are—than like the Russians. Their languages have roots in Turkic or Persian rather than in Slavic, from which Russian and Ukrainian were derived. The Soviet Union is a complex nation racially, as it is in many other ways, but the process of "Russifica-tion," or of "Sovietizing," if you prefer, is very gradually eliminat-ing extremes of difference.

The Russian language is now taught in schools all over the coun-try (although the regional tongue, in most cases, also is taught). European-style clothing, or the rather baggy Russian variation of it, is being worn with ever greater universality in Yakutia and Bukhara as well as in Red Square. However, even in the queue that wends through Red Square from the Alexandrov Gardens at the foot of the Kremlin wall into the Lenin-Stalin tomb, it is possible to see the traditional native ankle-length cloaks of many-colored stripes worn by visitors from Tashkent to the Moscow Mecca.

There are a number of theories to explain the origin of the Russians. Exhibits in the State Historical Museum at the foot of Red Square seek to convey the impression that Russians can be traced in an almost continuous thread from prehistoric man, whose arrowheads and beads have been found in the Caucasus Moun-tains, along the eastern Black Sea coast, and in the Crimean Pen-insula of the Black Sea—areas on and near the land bridge that connects Russia with the Middle East.

However, a more convincing theory, accepted by many (but not all) students of the subject, is that a great migration north-ward occurred some 1500 years ago from the general area of what are now the Balkan States. The peoples involved were Slavs, a large ethnic and linguistic group of humanity whose roots are obscure. The Slavs probably participated in the westward expan-sion into Europe in earlier eras by those peoples known as Sar-matians, Goths, and Huns. The reason for the Slavic movement is unknown, but it may have been caused by pressure from Asian tribes coming across Turkey.

Traced by language similarity, three groups of Slavs stemming from this source are identifiable. The Western Slavs include the Poles, the Czechs, the Slovaks, and groups in eastern Germany. The Southern Slavs include the Serbs, the Croats, the Slovenes, the Macedonians, and the Bulgarians. The Eastern Slavs include the Russians, the Ukrainians, and the Byelorussians.

In the ninth century certain tribes of these Slavic peoples organized themselves into the first state of the Russian region. This was around the present city of Kiev, capital of the Ukraine. (Slavs had migrated to this region in the seventh century but it was not until two centuries later that their tribal society evolved into forms of state.) At about the same time (or perhaps even earlier, say some historians) a state similarly was organized by other advanced tribes at Novgorod. These beginnings of the Russian state are said by some historians to coincide with another event. It was in the ninth century that the Varangians, Scandinavian warriors and traders, found their way into this region. It is understandable that they would, because the flat steppes and waterways formed a natural route from Scandinavia and from what is now Poland and Germany to the great capital and trading center of Constantinople. Legend has it that one of the Varangian leaders named Rurik was asked by the tribes around Novgorod—lying one quarter of the way from Leningrad to Moscow—to establish a state. It may be that the Varangians *imposed* their organizing ability. However, it is widely accepted that the Slavic tribes had no experience in organization of this sort and sought the advice of a foreigner for their own advantage—a practice that has been repeated in subsequent times (Czar Peter the Great in the 1700s sought architects and technicians from the Western world, and so did the Communists in the 1930s and later). Rurik set up the Novgorod state in 862.

It is considered likely that the name given by the Slavs to the Varangians with whom they came in contact was "Rus" or some variation of that root, and from it the name Rus, and later Russia, developed for the country as a whole.

The ruler Rurik was succeeded by Oleg, who expanded the area of his domain. Oleg finally conquered all of the Eastern Slavs and in 882 shifted his capital southward to what is now the city of Kiev, on the tree-covered, hilly banks of the Dnieper River. At the time of Oleg's acquisition of Kiev, it was already the center of a thriving, walled princely city. It had received its name from the prince Kiy, leader of the Polyani tribe of Slavs. As early as the eighth and ninth centuries Kiev had already become an important center for administration, trade, and handicraft for the Polyanis, who maintained trade ties with other Slavic tribes. Situated on an important river trade route and having access to the sea, Kiev was visited by merchants from Byzantium, Scandinavia, Arabia, and Armenia. Merchants from Kiev, it is said, traveled to India and China.

Kiev grew in prosperity and military strength under Oleg and his successors, including for a time a woman named Olga. This Olga, a name in wide use today, may be considered a remote precedent by Soviet women as they engage in all manner of enterprise, from sweeping streets to serving in the nation's version of a legislature.

Under the ruler named Prince Vladimir I, who reigned from 980 to 1015, an important event occurred in the land of the Rus. Its repercussions have been felt, both before and after communism. It was under Prince Vladimir that Christianity came to Russia. The date given by historians is either 988 or 989. Vladimir had asked the hand of the sister of the Emperor at Constantinople in marriage. The Christian emperor was reluctant to grant her to this Kiev prince who was considered a barbarian and a pagan. Constantinople set a condition—Vladimir must accept Christianity. This, Vladimir did. There is a less reliable, but perhaps more disarming, account of how the Orthodox faith of Constantinople spread to Russia. Ancient documents of the twelfth century, called the Russian Chronicle, a history kept in Kiev, written by a monk named Nestor, reports that when Vladimir decided to bring religion to his realm, he sent emissaries to the capitals of the Moslems, the Christians, and the Jews. Also, he invited theologians to come to Kiev to tell about their faiths.

For a time Vladimir was attracted by the Jewish faith, and then by the Moslem faith. However, when he learned that it was forbidden to Moslems to drink alcohol, Vladimir set aside any ideas of adopting Islam. Then, as now, the joy of the grape was a part of Russian life too much enjoyed to be abandoned. The ambassadors of the Prince who returned from lands of the Greek Orthodox religion were greatly moved by the pageantry and music and ritual. The elaborate decorations and artwork of the cathedrals left an enormous impression, which they brought back to their ruler. It was like being in heaven, they told him. Vladimir decided to adopt this religion that brought heaven to earth.

Whichever story is true, the adoption of the Orthodox faith greatly strengthened ties of the Kiev state with the powerful Constantinople. Constantinople's influence is seen even now throughout Russia in many ways, including the Byzantine architecture of church cupolas and in the art forms of that era.

Kiev's prosperity grew in commerce. Agriculture was a main occupation of the lands of the Rus, as it is today even in industrialized Russia in terms of people employed. Furs, hides, honey, wax, and slaves were Kiev's chief exports. However, disputes developed with princes of other Russian cities, and in 1169 Kiev was stormed by one of these rulers, who moved the capital to the city of Vladimir, 100 miles east of Moscow and 500 miles to the northeast of Kiev. The conqueror was Andrei Bogolubski, son of the prince Yuri Dolgoruki (George of the Long, or Grasping, Arm). A statue of Prince Dolgoruki in mail and mounted on a horse is seen now in a square across the street from the Moscow Soviet building (the city hall), because he was the founder of Moscow in 1147—the city which later was to become the heart of Russia and of the Soviet Union.

The deathblow to Kiev's greatness was struck by the Tatars, ferocious Mongol fighters, the so-called Golden Horde, which between 1237 and 1240 overran Kiev and the other cities of Russia, with the major exception of distant Novgorod. These Mongols were tenacious conquerors and held sway over this region for almost 250 years. The nature of their rule differed with different cities. Although the Tatars captured and burned Moscow, they later appointed the Moscow princes (or grand dukes, as they came to be called) as their collectors of tribute from the other cities of Russia.

By 1380 the grand dukes of Muscovy had so prospered and grown in strength in this role of tax collector that a duke named Dmitri was able to wage a victorious battle against the Tatars well south of Moscow on the plains of the Don River at a place called Kulikovo. Dmitri won the battle but not yet the war. This was not a decisive encounter. It did not force the withdrawal of the Golden Horde, but it did greatly encourage the Russians in their struggle against the Mongol conquerors. In fact, the Muscovy rulers felt their backs secure enough against the Tatars that they were able to turn to conquest of their own, and they gradually absorbed the other Russian princely states, including Novgorod. In 1480 Ivan III, Grand Duke of Moscow, felt strong enough to refuse to pay tribute to the Tatars. Ivan was a bold man in many ways. He had married the niece of the last Byzantine Emperor, Constantine XI. Constantine had lost Constantinople in 1453 to the Turks, who of course were Moslems, and with Constantinople went the last of the great Empire. Centuries before, when the capital of the Roman Emperor was transferred to Constantinople, this city became known as the second Rome. Now, Ivan III, claiming lineal descent through marriage, proclaimed Moscow as "the third Rome," center of the Orthodox faith and heir to the imperial glory of Byzantine.

Ivan III's son, Vasili (Basil), continued his father's conquests, and Vasili's son, Ivan IV (known as Ivan the Terrible), assumed for the first time the title of czar (stemming from the word "Caesar") in 1547. Ivan the Terrible sent his armies against the khans (princes) of the Tatar-occupied cities of Kazan, 450 miles east of Moscow, and Astrakhan, double that distance to the southeast at the mouth of the Volga River on the Caspian Sea. The rule of the Tatars over the Russians was thus ended, and it was replaced by the rule of the Prince of Muscovy, who was now recognized as the Czar of all Russia.

The prolonged rule of the Tatars, even though gradually diminishing in scope and strength, left its mark on the Slavs. There was some intermarriage, and it has been said that "if you scratch a Russian you find a Tatar." However, this is often meant to refer to the Asiatic cruelty of the Tatars, which is said to have rubbed off on the Russians, rather than to racial characteristics.

There has been much intermarriage among the people of some regions of the U.S.S.R. for instance, natives of the Baltic states of Latvia, Lithuania, and Estonia have frequently married with Russians. Although Soviet theoreticians and propagandists claim that there is no color bar or racial discrimination of any sort among the Soviet people, there has been less intermarriage by Russians in the central Asian Soviet republics of Kirghizia, Kazakhstan, Turkmenistan, Uzbekistan, and Tadzhikistan than might be expected in a region where millions of Russians have been sent as colonizers.

However, the flow and ebb of the Tatar and other invasions and mass movements of humanity have left their marks on Russia and Russians.

Our imaginary visitor might not be in Red Square for many of his sixty minutes before, very likely, he would be approached by a passing Russian or two, attracted by his obviously foreign clothes and unfamiliarity with his surroundings. Russians are usually friendly toward foreigners. Usually, too, they are intensely curious. Often they are suspicious.

The suspicion is understandable, and, in fact, it is surprising that it does not manifest itself more often than it does. Traditionally, Communist newspapers carry frequent warnings to Soviet citizens to beware of spies. The picture is drawn in Soviet publications of a bee-busy imperialist hive of espionage agents seeking to fly away with succulent bits of information from easily stung Russians.

It is a suspicion born, too, of history. The Russian has reason for a hereditary wariness toward the foreigner. In ancient times his land was overrun by Tatars and Teutons. At the time of the Revolution and the subsequent civil war, foreign soldiers, including those from the United States and Britain, landed in a brief and unsuccessful attempt at intervention against the Communists. World War I brought German armies to Russian soil. During

World War II the Nazis' mechanized divisions rolled over the flat
Russian land to lay siege to Leningrad, to within almost artillery
range of Moscow, and into the streets of Stalingrad.

These periodic and usually disastrous invasions have left their
mark on the Russian people in characteristics other than suspicion. Russians have learned to hate war. The ordinary Russian
wants peace. It does not take many days in Moscow or many con-
versations with Russians to become firmly convinced of the unanimity of this desire for peace. The Russian knows, for one thing,
that only through a prolonged period of peace—which he is not
entirely sure he will enjoy—can he acquire the housing, the variety
of clothing, the abundance of foods, the television sets, and the
shorter working hours that lie just over the Red horizon—or so he
has been promised.

The Russian's passion for peace as well as his unsophisticated
peasant directness make him a friendly individual in spite of his
inbred and indoctrinated suspicion. This friendliness may manifest itself in a Russian's walking several blocks out of his way to
make sure that a visiting tourist arrives at an obscure address he
is seeking. The suspicion which is never far below the surface of
amity may burst forth when a visitor wanders off the beaten tourist track, or when he lifts his camera to take a photograph of an
old house that the sensitive Russian considers unworthy of the
Soviet system.

This sensitivity is as much the result of deprivation as of suspicion. The Russian is aware of the nation's multitudinous shortages.
He very likely shares one room—or, if he is extremely fortunate,
two rooms—with his wife, two or three children, and perhaps even
a mother-in-law. Even in new apartments it is customary for several families to share an entry hallway, a kitchen, and a bathroom.
Being a proud and patriotic people, it is natural that Russians
should harbor an acute sensitivity, especially in the presence of
foreigners, about the shortcomings and inadequacies of their way
of life.

The view of the Soviet citizen toward the outside world is naturally distorted. Few Russians have the opportunity to travel
abroad. Those who do are usually permitted to go only to other

Communist countries. Only a minor proportion of the Russian people have opportunities to see for themselves what life is like in
the non-Communist world. *Pravda,* meaning "Truth," and *Izvestia,*
meaning "News," and the many hundreds of other daily newspapers, magazines, and the government-regulated radio present
a picture of the outside world that serves Soviet propaganda purposes. Although Russians are told that the goal of their Economic
Plans is to catch up and surpass the United States in various
branches of production, they are also told rather incongruously
that life in the United States is grim. There are stories of dire
unemployment: the working class is depicted as exploited at the
hands of greedy capitalists. Workers are said to be forced to purchase refrigerators and cars on an installment plan in order to
place themselves in eternal bondage to their employers. Strikes,
which are not permitted to Soviet workers, are pictured as manifestations of the sorry lot of the American wage earner.

The salary of the Soviet wage earner is small, but it must be
appraised by Soviet standards. Rent, which may consume 30 per
cent of the American's monthly salary, never totals more than 5
per cent of the head of the family's wage in Russia. The housing
may be poor, but it is inexpensive. Furthermore, the Russian has
no need to set money aside for medical care: the State provides
free medical care, surgery, and hospitalization. There is no compelling need to make provisions through insurance or other savings
for old age. There is a government pension (for men at sixty years,
for women at fifty-five) to which the worker need not even contribute. Education for youngsters is provided at government expense. In most cases, several members of the family work, including the woman of the house.

An elevator operator in a hotel earns 400 rubles a month ($40,
at the exchange rate granted to visiting Americans for their dollars). A chief librarian in a neighborhood library earns 1200 rubles
($120) per month. A skilled lathe operator in a smoothly running
factory receives 1900 rubles ($190). A popular circus clown earns
6000 rubles ($600) a month. These sample wages may seem de-
pressingly low, and by American standards they are. By the standards of some western European countries they are less shocking.

Compared to some Asian countries the amounts are, indeed, respectable. It all depends on the context.

It is dangerous to generalize about the people of any nation.
Certainly, this danger applies equally in the case of Russia. But,
while acknowledging the risk, it may be said that although the
Russian people want change, few want a return to the pre-
Revolutionary status. The Communists have improved conditions. The Russian sees that he is eating better now than he did
a decade ago, and he hopes that the promises of still better conditions to come will materialize. There were few such hopes under
the czars, and the Russian does not enjoy the opportunity for
fair comparison with the Western world.

The foreigner in Red Square may be approached by the Soviet
variety of the black-market operator—a new genus that has flourished only since Stalin's death and the admission of large numbers
of tourists. These operators will pay a high price for the visitor's
coat or his shoes. The quality is certainly better than often haphazard Soviet workmanship. But it is more than quality that the
black-market operator is paying for. The fact that it is *Western*
makes it valuable. There is a small group of people in Russia—
rich in rubles—who will pay exorbitantly high prices for an article
of clothing that assumes a disproportionate value simply because
it is from England or France or America. Such an illegal operator
may even resort to reciting phrases to the Westerner that he thinks
will please the "capitalist's" ears and make him more amenable
to selling his possessions. The Russian may curse the Kremlin leaders, denounce the system.

But such individuals do so for a commercial purpose, and they
must be suspect. Most Russians—and again this is a generality—
have something, and often many things, with which to be dis-
satisfied. It is not uncommon to hear a Russian complain bitterly
about the high prices of poorly sewn garments. But then, even
official Soviet newspapers scold government factories for the poor
quality of goods. It is not uncommon to hear a Russian complain
about the cramped conditions of his housing, about the dreadful,
time-consuming lines in stores, and about the heartless red tape
that complicates the most commonplace contact with Soviet bu-

reaucracy. But these are particularized complaints. These do not take the generalized form of calling for the overthrow of the regime. In fact, it seems that most Russians disassociate themselves from the political machinations of their government. They realize that they are powerless—even by so much as the power of a single legitimate vote—to alter the path or personalities of politics.

What's more, and this is probably the least dangerous generality of all, most Russians love Russia. It is an emotion that found dramatic expression in Boris Pasternak's rejecting the opportunity to leave his native land, and, in fact, pleading for the privilege to stay. It is an attachment difficult for the foreigner to comprehend. But the fact is that in Paris or New York or London it is the colony of Russian émigrés that longs most achingly for the soil of its homeland. Other nationalities seem to acclimate and, in part, forget. But seldom do the Russians. It is a loyalty to a country with a long and often tragic history, with an often cruel climate. It is devotion to a rich language, an emotional heritage that has produced heart-choking music and brooding literature, to an endlessly vast land.

It seems only fitting that Red Square should be one of the largest in the world. Gigantic size is a characteristic of Russia (and of the Soviet Union) that has influenced the proportions and dimensions of man-made creations. By way of comparison, Japan —a country about equal in size to the state of California—builds on a delicate, small scale. Miniature gardens and stunted trees blend with the Japanese scheme of nature; it is just the opposite in the U.S.S.R.—an expanse that covers one sixth of our planet. This enormous land has had its effect on the nature of the people. It is partly responsible for the Soviet enthusiasm for size for the sake of size. A rule of thumb of Soviet life sometimes seems to be that if something is good it will be twice as good if it is twice as big. This has resulted in revolving doors at the skyscraper Ukraine Hotel in Moscow that are almost too heavy and tall for a woman to push, and that once in motion can crush the unwary. The penchant for huge proportion stems, too, from a national sensitivity about having been a backward country for so long. To overcome this inferiority, buildings in Russia must be bigger than anyone else's, even if of grotesque proportions that are an inconvenience rather than a service to the humans who live there. The lust for size finds expression in construction of the deepest subway in the world, the heaviest sputniks, and in the cultivation of radishes as big as carrots. Such radishes lose their characteristic flavor to girth.

The vastness of Russia is responsible in some measure, too, for the fatalism and mysticism of the Russian, although the influence of the Orthodox faith must not be discounted. A man may stand on the flat Russian steppes and see only horizon in every direction. A schoolboy realizes that he can never hope to travel the length and breadth of this great continent. A peasant feels powerless as he watches the annual snows, blown by winds out of Siberia, pile higher than his head on the fields through the long winter. In December in the northern latitudes, the sun drops quickly in a fiery red ball into the western horizon by three in the afternoon. In June it is possible to read without artificial light by the midnight sun.

All of these are factors that make man seem at the mercy of nature. The elements on and over this flat, never ending terrain seems to minimize the potency and importance of the individual. The history of the Russian political system has not served to counteract this fatalism, this hopelessness, this natively Russian attitude of what-can-the-individual-do? If there is a Latin attitude of "mañana" born of climate and national personality, then there is a Russian attitude of "nichevo"—the attitude of "never mind," of "what's to do about it?" It is an attitude best represented by a gay and yet resigned shrug of the shoulders.

Russia stretches over two areas of the globe which man, in his search for categories, has termed "continents." Russia is both European and Asian. It is often difficult to tell where one begins and the other ends, both geographically and in the personality of the people.

Only a low mountain range, the Urals, separates the European continent from the Asian continent. It is a dividing line that gradually diminishes before it reaches Russia's southern frontiers and it is a barrier easily breached or bypassed. Russia, now as in ancient times, lies open geographically to those with the spirit of conquest. The Tatars swept into Russia from the east in their time, and Napoleon from the west in his. Mud and snow and a hostile populace provided barriers, but terrain offered none.

This geographic insecurity has been a factor which has motivated the Kremlin's rulers—czars and Communists both—to push the frontiers of Russia outward toward the mountain ranges that now comprise some of its frontiers. Where mountains do not exist for frontiers, the Russians have sought friendly buffer states. After World War II this found expression in the Soviet insistence on conditions that would keep Bulgaria, Romania, Hungary, Czechoslovakia, and Poland in the hands of those who, bolstered by the Soviet Army, would not be hostile. The anxiety for security is understandable, but the process of expansion that it sets in motion is self-perpetuating. When frontiers do not consist of natural mountains and river barriers, then there is a tendency—as there has been in Soviet military and geopolitical thinking—to acquire more buffer states to act as buffers for the buffer states already in hand.

Because much of the Soviet Union lies in northern latitudes (in fact, a belt of considerable dimensions lies above the Arctic Circle), there is a short growing season in most of the country. Size has not meant compensatory fertility for Russia. There are great stretches of barren tundra in the North and equally sterile desert in an extensive area in the South. However, an irregularly shaped band of land, roughly 3000 miles long and varying in width from 250 miles to about 1000 miles, is endowed with a rich black soil, as productive as nature has provided anywhere in the world.

This black-soil region extends from the Carpathian Mountains in the West to the Altai Mountains in the East; it runs north of the Black Sea and dips below the foothills of the Urals, tapering off into Siberia. The Ukraine, the traditional breadbasket, is blessed with this type of earth. However fecund the black-soil belt is, it has produced insufficient crops to satisfy Soviet needs. Like most of the U.S.S.R., even in this region the rainfall is not dependable. It has been necessary to cultivate additional areas, where a brief growing season, undependable rainfall, and inferior quality of soil result in marginal agricultural production. However, the total average under cultivation is now so great that in some years Russia has a grain surplus.

Despite its enormous amount of land, Russia has known hunger. History has recorded drought and famine. In the early 1930s it was human nature rather than unfriendly elements that resulted in widespread hunger. This was the outcome of an overly intensive attempt by Communist authorities to force farmers to amalgamate their privately cultivated land with other farmers to form "collective farms."

In more recent years, with active opposition to collectivization having become archaic and with improved agricultural methods, Russia's food picture has gradually brightened. Under a bold program inaugurated by Stalin's successors, principally Nikita Khrushchev, hundreds of thousands of people have migrated into Siberia and Kazakhstan to create farms of "virgin land"—areas where the soil and rainfall previously had been considered too unpromising for settlement. The project has been expensive in manpower and machinery, but it *has* produced food.

The movement of men across Russia's vastness has determined to a great extent the forms of government under which Russians have lived. Evidences of some of the forms are visible in Red Square and its neighboring buildings. The jewel-studded, sable-fringed crowns of the czars and their thrones can be seen in the museum and in the cathedrals of the Kremlin grounds. Above the green dome that shelters the round Sverdlov Hall of the Kremlin— once the princely senate chamber of czarist days—the red flag of the Soviet state flies twenty-four hours a day.

It has been the fate of the Russian people to live almost uninterruptedly throughout history under one form of dictatorship or another. It has been said that a people deserves the kind of government it gets. Certainly the Russians may seem unusually submissive to the forms of tyranny that history has imposed on them. Yet, it must be said that Russian history recounts heroic struggle against foreign occupiers, peasant revolt against serfdom, revolution against selfish czars. It has been the particular misfortune of the Russian people that in their strivings to free themselves from one sort of tyranny they have almost invariably been led by tyrants of another sort. It is not that the Russians have not fought for freedom; it is rather that they have failed to achieve what they fought for.

The Russians deserve something better. Their earliest beginnings showed seeds of democracy long before many nations that are today considered free and democratic. The northern ancient city of Novgorod with its considerable outlying lands bestowed a rather highly developed form of liberty on its people. Nearly 1000 years ago the people of Novgorod practiced a kind of town meeting which theoretically could be assembled by any free citizen ringing the town bell. Unlike other principalities—cities governed by princes—Novgorod hired its prince as a kind of primitive city manager. Gradually, however, as was to be the case subsequently in other eras and other places of Russia, democratic theory broke down and autocracy developed. Instead of any individual being able to summon the town meeting, the prerogative became that of a council. A unanimous vote was necessary for major decisions. This left no room for a minority. A decision was sometimes taken by a duel on a bridge between leaders of two contending opinions. The loser toppled into the water and the issue was thus settled. The pressures of foreign invaders—in this case the Germans and Swedes—led to further disintegration of Novgorod's democracy. Finally, Novgorod became a part of the Moscow realm of autocratic rulers at the end of the fifteenth century.

Among the factors that have shaped the governments endured by the Russians, the rise of the Mongolian Tatars out of the Gobi Desert in the east cannot be overlooked. The conquest by the Tatars in the early 1200s came at the very time that the embryonic Russian nation was taking shape. The various princely cities of Russia were beginning to amalgamate into a nation. A Russian culture was just taking root. As one historian has described it, the advance of the Tatars took Russia "out of the orbit of Europe." For a long and formative era Russia was under Asiatic control and influence. The insignificant geographic divisions lost meaning altogether.

The Tatars taught the Russians many things. It may be said that the Asiatic horde, in devastating the land by military conquest and cruel taxation, toughened the Russians. The Muscovy princes had to acquire a wiliness, a cleverness, a quality of artful deceit, to retain their precarious positions under the Tatar sword. The Muscovy princes retained autonomy over their domains by delivering periodic, punitively heavy payments of treasure and crops to the Mongolian invaders.

The Tatars imported their ingenious cruelty into Russia. Previously, theft was punished by a fine. The Tatars cut off an arm to punish a thief.

After one particularly notable battle, Asian invaders built a wooden floor, put a half dozen captured princes and seventy minor leaders under it, and then seated themselves on the floor to eat their victory feast. The captured Russians were crushed beneath the weight.

It was Tatar battle technique to put conquered troops in the center of their attack formations and to fight themselves on the flanks, where hand-to-hand combat was less likely to ensue. Often the Tatars would feign a battle retreat in order to lure the enemy into a gantlet of fire by their concealed archers. These Tatar practices and principles left their mark in the formation of the Russian national character.

The Tatars were responsible for the first stirrings of the spirit of a national mission—a characteristic that manifested itself in the empire expansion of the czars and in the more recent phenomenon of the Messianic-like determination to spread communism. The mission that consumed the early Russians was to free themselves of the Tatar yoke. Clever Moscow princes played on this theme as a means of rallying the people and also making them forgetful of their grievances at the hands of the princes themselves. The "mission mentality" found expression later when Ivan III bestowed on Moscow a world mission as the "third Rome," inheritor of the cultural, religious, and imperial power of Byzantium.

This trait of government finds its expression under communism.

Although denied fruits proportional to their labor, the Russian people are told by their leaders that other peoples will adopt their system of government. Communism will spread, it is said, by peaceful means throughout the world. Communism is presented as the best of all possible systems and the one which is rapidly gaining numbers as workers of the world shed their shackles.

Among other factors that have been significant in shaping the successive forms of Russian government, the Church ranks high in importance. It was the Church leaders who tried originally to rally rival princes against the Tatars. Seven centuries later, during World War II, the Church, weakened by atheistic oppression, was an important force in rallying religious elements of the population in the battle for national survival.

The Church was important in czarist politics, and in fact on occasion was instrumental in the very selection of the czar. It was a religious figure of warped mind, Rasputin, who exerted harmful influence on the Czarina in the closing days of the Romanov family, thus contributing to the political bankruptcy of Imperial Russia.

Coronations of the czars were religious ceremonies. The pomp and circumstance of the Moscow, and later the St. Petersburg, court were often religious in nature. With the diminution of the role of the Church under communism, ceremonial elaborateness has survived in another form. Under communism, the processionals through Red Square have a quality of almost religious fanaticism.

The cupolas of gold and of silver on the cathedrals that can be seen from Red Square rising above the Kremlin's walls are well-preserved reminders of the religious faith that was so powerfully influential in Russia's past. To the Communists' credit, their revolution did not destroy many of the historical monuments and treasures of the past. In fact, as greater resources become available for such luxuries, increasing attention is being paid to restoring churches (as museums, of course) and other ancient edifices that had been permitted to fall into disrepair. The golden crosses of

Ivan's Belfry still rise against the gray Moscow sky as the highest point within the Kremlin's walls.

In Red Square, St. Basil's Cathedral, constructed during the 1550–60 decade by order of Ivan the Terrible to celebrate his victory over the Tatars at Kazan, stands as a monument to the ebb tide of Tatar supremacy. St. Basil's is a museum, but some churches, synagogues, and mosques still are used for worship, which is discouraged if not now suppressed.

There are other structures that are reminders of foreign conquerors. In Samarkand, one of man's oldest known cities, now a part of the Soviet republic of Uzbekistan, there are remarkably well-preserved relics of Timur the Lame, or, as he is sometimes called, Tamerlane, one of the mightiest of the Mongol khans. Tamerlane's tomb, a graceful mosquelike building with Persian lines, raises an elongated dome of brilliant glazed bluish-green enamel against the bright central Asian skies.

Napoleon's ill-fated invasion of Russia has left its mark in historical monuments, too. The Borovitsky Gate, through which Napoleon entered the deserted Kremlin, while Moscow around it burned, is now the principal entrance for tourists on sight-seeing tours. In one of Moscow's fast-expanding outskirts a one-room log cabin has now been converted into a museum and an extra room added for memorabilia where General Kutuzov conferred with his generals to plan the defense of Moscow against Napoleon— a defense which was never attempted.

Much of Russian history is written in the buildings and monuments of Leningrad on the banks of the Neva River. Founded by the ambitious and able Peter the Great in 1703 under the name of St. Petersburg (and briefly renamed Petrograd two centuries later), this majestic city served as the capital with a few interruptions until 1918, when the seat of government was moved back to Moscow.

Peter the Great had transferred the capital to St. Petersburg in an effort to cut Russia from its "oriental" past and as part of his obsessive program to "Europeanize" his country. Although the "head" of Russia, the capital, was moved to St. Petersburg, the "heart" of Russia, the emotional attachment of the people, remained with Moscow. In the decades that followed, Russian history was made in St. Petersburg, and Moscow sank into a quiet, almost provincial existence. This existence was shattered by Napoleon's invasion of Russia in 1812. The Russian people, it may be said, then consciously realized what they had subconsciously sensed all along—that Moscow was indeed the heart of the nation. Probably no blow was more deeply felt or served so well to unify the spirit of the Russian people as the capture of Moscow by Napoleon. That is why the Communists, after taking power in 1917, acted responsively to popular sentiment in transferring the capital to Moscow. Once again, the head of the Russian Government was in the city that was the historic heart of the Russian people.

Stalingrad stands as a monument to the German defeat in World War II. Situated on the banks of the Volga, some 600 miles southeast of Moscow, Stalingrad was almost entirely destroyed in weeks of brutal house-to-house, room-to-room, hand-to-hand combat. It was at Stalingrad that the German momentum was slowed and stopped and the enemy forced to retreat in disarray. A museum portrays the heroic defense, but the miles upon square miles of new buildings stand as a more eloquent testimony to this decisive battle of the war.

An impressive canal that connects the Don and Volga rivers is the work of German prisoners of war, many of whom were captured at Stalingrad, and so are some of Moscow's thirty-story buildings.

A hint of the lavish life lived by families of royal blood during the czarist time—men were still serfs or slaves as late as the nineteenth century in Russia—is seen in several great estates that are preserved as museums. Archangelskoye, an hour's drive from Moscow, for example, was the stately home of the Youssoupoff family. Prince Felix Youssoupoff with several colleagues participated in the assassination of Rasputin, an incredible episode for the twentieth century, even for Russia! The assassination took place in the Youssoupoff home in St. Petersburg; the hope was to bring the royal family to its senses in the conduct of World War I and in the governing of the country, by ridding the Czarina of the distorted influence of Rasputin. The assassination succeeded only after several mishaps, but the event failed to produce the desired salubrious effect.

Families of great wealth, drawn from vast landholdings and royal position, as in the case of the Youssoupoffs, or from the manufacture of textiles or sugar in other cases, were often diligent collectors of art. The state acquired many of their collections after the Revolution, and the Pushkin Gallery in Moscow and the Hermitage (the czars' winter palace) in Leningrad are among the world's richest repositories—ranking with the Louvre and the National Gallery. Rembrandts and Gauguins and Picassos in exciting abundance span much of the history of art of the Western world. There is the Tretyakov Gallery in Moscow, where the works of famous Russian artists—Repin, Shishkin, Polenov, Vereshchagin, and others—are hung. Episodes of history can be seen on canvas. "Apotheosis of War," painted in 1871, shows a pyramid of sunbleached skulls depicted against a background of sand and a ruined ancient city. Originally the painting was called "Apotheosis of Tamerlane," the central Asian conqueror of the fourteenth century, but later the artist renamed his work, dedicating the ghoulish painting to "all conquerors—past, present, and future." Works hung in the Tretyakov Gallery often have a political edge of this sort. The criterion seems to be that the painting be politically favorable to communism or at least politically neutral. Thus, seascapes, forest scenes, and wildlife qualify for a place on the Tretyakov's walls as creditable Russian art.

The same yardstick applies to literature which survives from Russia's pre-Revolutionary past and is studied and republished today. Russia's literary heritage is proud and powerful. Leo Tolstoy's *War and Peace,* Feodor Dostoievsky's *Crime and Punishment, The Idiot, Brothers Karamazov,* and *The Possessed,* Alexander Pushkin, Anton Chekov, Turgenev, Gogol—these are names to hold in awe. In music and in ballet as well, the creative genius and energy of the Russian people have found rich expression.

In lesser works, too, is seen the heritage of the past. Folk tales are an example. It is not surprising that many survive and are republished under the Communists, because in old Russian folk tales the prince, the merchant, or the government bureaucrat was often represented as the villain or the fool, and the simple muzhik (peasant) as the long-suffering, ill-appreciated hero.

One folk story is entitled "How One Simple Peasant Fed Two High Officials." It is a charming tale of two czarist officials who found themselves on a desert island. Having served all their lives in a useless government registry office, they were completely unequipped to fend for themselves. "What on earth shall we do?" exclaimed one functionary through his tears. "To write a report now would hardly do any good." The officials knew neither how to gather berries, nor how to fish, nor how to trap wildlife. Said one to the other: "Who would have thought, Your Excellency, that man's daily food in its original state flies in the air, swims in the water, and grows on trees?"

In a happy coincidence of the sort that abound in folk tales, the pair of hopeless officials stumbled upon a muzhik, "sleeping under a tree, with his belly upward and his fist beneath his head, quite obviously and audaciously shirking work. Their indignation knew no bounds. . . . The muzhik rose to his feet and saw that this was no joking matter. These were very stern officials. At first he wanted to show them his heels, but they pounced on him and held on like grim death. After that he got busy."

The resourceful peasant "climbed up an apple tree, plucked a dozen of the ripest apples for the officials, and took a sour one for himself. Then he dug in the earth and produced a few potatoes. After that he rubbed two pieces of wood together and obtained a fire. Then of his own hair he made a net and caught a grouse. Finally he kindled a fire and cooked such a variety of good things that it even occurred to the officials that they might spare a morsel for the lazy lout, too."

Finally the peasant built a boat and rowed them across the sea from the desert island to their apartments on Podyacheskaya Street in St. Petersburg. During their absence, the officials' pensions had been piling up and they found themselves richer than when they had left.

Concludes the folk tale in its tongue-in-cheek tone: "But don't

go thinking that they forgot the muzhik; they sent him a thimble-
ful of vodka and a silver coin: there, muzhik, go and enjoy your-
self!"

Presumably, in reading the folk tale today, some Soviet citizens
identify themselves with the put-upon muzhik and compare their
lot with that of ineffectual officials of today.

During the comparatively short span of Soviet rule a number of
important names in literature have appeared. Mikhail Sholokhov's
trilogy, *Quiet Flows the Don*, has gained great fame as a sensitive account of the life of a Cossack (czarist frontier-region cavalry) village in the civil-war era. Nikolai Alexeyevich Ostrovski,
although blind for much of his adult life and dead at the age of
thirty-two, wrote several important works, including *Born of the
Storm*, and *How Steel Was Tempered*, which has sold 12 million
copies in more than 300 editions in the U.S.S.R. It, too, has a
civil-war theme.

World War II also has left its mark on Soviet literature. The
effects of the costly war are seen, in fact, in many phases of Soviet
life. The terrible suffering left scarcely a family untouched. Great
numbers of people were evacuated from Moscow and other
threatened cities to remote Kazakhstan and far eastern regions.
Under siege for 900 days, Leningrad's population sustained
hunger and the hourly threat of death by artillery. About 25 million soldiers and civilians perished during the long war. Perhaps
a third or more of the nation's Jewish population was extermi-
nated by the Germans. Cities were leveled.

The effect is seen in Soviet policies, economy, and attitudes.

The people, as has been explained, hate war. An inordinate
number of crippled and disabled persons are seen. Men often wear
service ribbons on the breast pocket of civilian suits.

The economy was set back by the need to repair the war damage before new expansion could be undertaken. What is more, the
war enhanced the historic Russian fear of attack, and in this case
not without cause. The result has been a renewed concentration
on heavy industry and weapons at the expense of consumer goods.
As so often in Russian history, the needs of the people have assumed second-place priority.

The war, though, with the diminution through defeat of the powers of Germany and Japan, and despite victory of the powers of Britain and France, placed Russia on the threshold of becoming one of the world's two "super powers." The Soviet Union has crossed this threshold swiftly and, for better or worse, stands today as a giant among nations.

In reading Russian history it is difficult to avoid a feeling of futility that wars cannot be avoided in the future any more successfully than they have in the past. The history of Russia, like the history of the world, seems in perspective to be a series of wars momentarily interrupted by periods of blissful optimism that war will not come again. Wars have been fought between nations with fewer causes for dispute and with less differences in concept of how man's life should be lived than is the unfortunate case between the United States and the Soviet Union.

It is said, of course, that there is greater hope now than in the past that war will be rejected as a course of action because technology's developments of atomic and hydrogen bombs has made war unthinkable. This is a comforting thought, but perhaps not a very realistic one. After World War I it was similarly thought that the horrors of poison gas would force man to find other means of settling differences than through battle. This proved a false hope. In eras past, the development of the machine gun, of the rifle, of armor, must have made war seem as suicidal as it does today. In Napoleon's time, for example, an army of 600,000 men that entered Russia was reduced to the body of 50,000 men that got back to France as a unit. Yet, Napoleon fought again, and so have men before and since.

However, man's nature cannot accept the inevitability of war. Whether or not there will be a war depends in large measure on Soviet policy.

What is Soviet policy toward the United States?

Russia's foreign policy is simple, clear, and consistent. Nikita Khrushchev, the most vociferous of Russian leaders, expressed that policy at many times in many ways. Once, at a reception at the Polish embassy in Moscow, he turned during his speech of the evening toward Western diplomats who were present and said with characteristic graciousness, "We will bury you." Khrushchev and other Soviet leaders also have said that now capitalism and communism must coexist, must live in peace together.

This may sound contradictory. Yet, the Soviet desire to coexist peacefully now and to bury the capitalist world later is entirely reconcilable. The core of communism's leadership consists of fanatic believers that communism is the wave of the future. These men believe that capitalism is doomed. These beliefs are buttressed by a phenomenon which is not unique to Soviet diplomacy. There is often a disinclination on the part of ambassadors serving abroad to submit reports and recommendations that are at variance with the policy of the government at home. It would be a rare Soviet ambassador indeed who in his reports from Washington would attempt to dissuade his superiors in the Kremlin from believing that they are correct in anticipating the eventual economic collapse of capitalism.

Convinced as are communism's leaders of communism's steady economic progress, of its world mission, and of the anticipated decline of capitalism, they may feel perfectly secure to wait for this to occur rather than to try to bring it about by outright force. Russia knows that, at best, war is a two-edged sword. Even the victor in a war must anticipate devastation as the price of victory.

Consequently, Russia wants to coexist in peace. Or in partial peace. Or, perhaps, most accurately, without atomic war.

Russia has demonstrated that she *will* practice "brinkmanship" to try to accomplish objectives, that she will practice policies that stop just short of atomic war. The period since World War II has experienced an unnerving number of instances to underscore this. The names of Korea, Indochina, Quemoy, Lebanon, Suez, Berlin, stand as reminders of how close to war the world has come.

Russia has demonstrated, too, that, as is true for America as well, there are certain objectives for which Russia will fight. The brutal Soviet action in crushing the Hungarian uprising indicates that the Kremlin leaders would risk World War III if necessary to hold on to their Communist buffer states.

Withal, it is clear to even a brief visitor to Red Square and its

Soviet environs, and it becomes more abundantly clear the longer one stays in Russia and the more Russians he talks with, that the Russian people do not want war.

This is a fact which the Soviet leaders, even as unresponsive as they may seem to public opinion, cannot totally ignore. To the extent that a Soviet dictator is vulnerable to the approval or disapproval of the other members of the Presidium and the Central Committee, to that extent must he realize that war is the one thing—unless Russia were attacked—which might coalesce into an effective opposition whatever elements may be potentially hostile to his leadership. Politically speaking, war is not a trump card in any Soviet power struggle.

Members of the Soviet leadership are aware that almost every Russian personally has suffered from war. For instance, a hotel maid named Vera, forty years old, is not married although she would like to be and is quite attractive. Periodically, in her quiet and emotional way, Vera wrings her hands over the fact that there is such a shortage of men because of the war. Several members of Vera's family were lost in battle. Vera's brother lost the toes of both his feet.

Another Russian, an engineer, served ten years in the Army. He was decorated three times and wounded four times. He once spent twelve days crawling a mere ten miles through cranberry marshland under intermittent enemy fire. His colleagues and himself, cut off by a German breakthrough in those early days of the war, had only stagnant water to drink and the bark of bushes to eat. This Russian fought, too, on the Leningrad front, and he claims to have seen cases of bodies disappearing from the morgue because, he says, some people resorted to cannibalism.

This sort of war experience breeds pacifists. The Soviet leaders know this.

Thus, the Kremlin makes no secret of its intention of—and its confidence in—spreading communism everywhere it can, by any means it can, short of all-out war.

But a more dangerous period than even now may lie in the future. If the Soviet leaders a generation or two from now come to realize that their slogans about the spread of communism are invalid, how would they readjust to this?

Would they resort to war—especially if they then hold some slight superiority in missile capability—in order to try to *make* their slogans come true? After all, in a generation or two those who experienced the horrors of World War II firsthand—the Veras and the former soldier—will have been replaced by youth of fighting age to whom battle might be less repugnant.

However, there are factors at work that give cause for a more optimistic outlook. As time passes we are likely to find, as is already happening, that there is less revolutionary fanaticism in Russia. As Russians acquire more goods, better housing, more material advantages, and more property, their stake in security and in international stability increases. Their interest in protecting and retaining what they have will grow.

Even a dictator must take into account the sentiments of his people, because ultimately the dictator is dependent on those people to produce and to fight.

Even Russia's leaders cannot completely ignore the fact that the Soviet people want peace.

And in that single fact lies some slight cause for optimism that Red Square will remain a tourist sight and not become a missile's target.

POLAND

Flora Lewis

Flora Lewis, a foreign correspondent since 1945, has spent half a dozen years in eastern Europe. She is married to Sydney Gruson of the New York Times, *and together, usually trailing three children, they have covered stories in Europe, the Middle East, and Latin America.*

Miss Lewis was born in Los Angeles and educated there, starting newspaper work on the Los Angeles Times *and then, after a year of school in New York, joining the Associated Press. Like most correspondents, she concentrates on politics and the people who make politics, but she has written about almost everything, from cabbages (how to make borsch) to kings (royal weddings).*

In recent years, she has worked primarily on reporting the background to the news and the social, political, and plain human scene against which it develops. She is the author of A Case History of Hope—The Story of Poland's Peaceful Revolution.

POLAND

Despite haphazard, melodramatic, or even frivolous ways in which countries acquire their national anthems, the music and words often cast a revealing shaft of light on the people who stand to attention at the song. Poland's hymn is a striking example. The words to its brave, romantic, and yet melancholy air begin, *"Jeszcze Polska nie zginela poki my zyjemy* [Poland is not yet lost, while yet we live] . . ." The song was written in 1796, while Polish legions fought their way through Italy with Napoleon Bonaparte in the hope that his revived strength would support and protect a revived Polish nation. But Napoleon fell, and so did the attempt to maintain an independent Polish existence against the combined power of three mighty neighbors, Russia, Prussia, and Austria. For a century, until all three were too enfeebled by World War I to keep the stubborn Poles down, there was no Poland. The state was drowned again in the maelstrom of World War II, and when it finally emerged it was as an ironic victor, chained to the heel of its "liberator," the Soviet Union.

And yet, the Poles still stand furiously straight and sing that all "is not yet lost," rejoicing that bitter centuries have given them such a talent for subtle wit and satire that they can chant at least this much with impunity in the face of their Soviet and Communist masters. They are incurable romantics, but not visionaries, so they do not even bother to sing of some happy day when their land will be the realm of their dreams. At the moment, it is far from that, although not so far as it was in the first decade after World War II. Even its Communist leaders speak of "this unhappy land," revealing with a certain surreptitious honesty the chips and cracks behind the fixed tooth-paste smile of normally smug Communist propaganda.

There was a period, until the upheaval of October 1956, which brought the national-minded Communist Wladyslaw Gomulka back to power, when so much public honesty was impossible. It is a measure, and an important measure, of their unrelenting persistence in the struggle for national expression that Poles once more achieved the right to complain. As a result, the country's Communist government is distinctively Polish, different in certain vital ways from other Communist governments and imbued with a surprising amount of the die-hard, sometimes querulous and flamboyant individualism that marks the Polish spirit.

The past, political geography, the people and their intense nationalism, the stubborn austerity of the top leaders, and the sardonic, poetically cynical energy of the intellectuals make communism in Poland differ from its theoretically monolithic image in the rest of eastern Europe. In Poland, it is rather more flexible, more questing, more civilized, Polish Communists like to think, than anywhere else, including independent, fiercely nationalist Yugoslavia. The paradoxical aim is to achieve a sophisticated dogma, one that acknowledges the facts of national life and does not seek to gild the thistle but to blunt at least its most painful spikes.

If the stolidly pious peasants and blunt-tongued workers give the substance of Poland, the intellectuals give its flavor. Poetry, lyric and satiric literature, are its proudest products, little known in the West perhaps because of lack of translations but not for lack of resources to draw upon. It has become traditional that the somewhat disheveled, always excited men and women who babble around café tables of Warsaw and Cracow should set the tone of the nation's thought. It has been that way for generations. And though it pressed fiercely to set a simple new mold, the Communist regime failed to break the tradition and has had, after all, to change its own tone. Now it is a Communist government that endorses a certain measure of individual, civic, and religious freedom, one that looks for compromise solutions. Nevertheless, it is

Communist. The country's economy is planned; industry and services are state-owned except for droplets of private enterprise too small and too fragmented to affect the whole. Agriculture, since Gomulka, has been returned to small holders' production, but the state still holds the guiding strings through control of credit, prices, farm supplies, and the market.

Communism rode into Poland in 1944 and 1945 on the hefty shoulders of the Red Army, and it was quick and ruthless in staking out its claims. Agriculture, always before the mainstay of the nation, was disdainfully neglected in the frantic rush to fashion a heavy industry and a proletariat. Important boundary shifts added a new coal basin, and Poland tried to live on coal and steel instead of wheat and ham. At a painful price, industrialization was advanced, but the disequilibrium was an important factor in the ferment that led to Gomulka's return.

Since 1956, the effort has been to balance national development of industry and agriculture. Now Poland exports bacon and butter, coal and freight cars, but its people must still scratch for a cramped, inadequate living. When the world price of coal drops sharply, the national purse is drained. Too weak still to stand the buffeting drafts of the open market place, the country is forced for economic reasons as well as political pressures to seek the protection of closed Soviet-bloc trade.

No country in the modern world can live well exclusively on its own resources, without benefit of rationalized trade and a broad market. Poland, populated by a sturdy but apathetic 28 million, has neither the balanced resources nor the intensely organized energy to spurt ahead without strong support. So with coal, steel, machinery, and textiles from its mines and mills, and grain, sugar, and pigs from its farms, Poland has striven desperately to make good the wartime devastation and inch forward its living standards. This has imposed a considerable economic dependence on its trading partners. Neither in the Soviet bloc nor in the free-market countries has Poland the good fortune of possessing a strong hand for bargaining.

This was not always so, for the Poles are a people whose history has been a series of drastic swings—between power and impotence, glory and despair, well-being and misery. Their volatile temperament matches this story of extremes, for they soar as easily to heights of giddy exuberance as they plummet to depths of melancholy. It is said in Poland, "There is only one thing normal in this country—being abnormal."

Their origins are lost in the murky past of the great Slav family, an ethnic group that eluded the Greco-Roman illumination of our common European past. Some historians say that Slavs, wandering down from some mysterious northeastern homeland, had already begun to settle on the fertile eastern European plains 2000 years before the Christian Era. Others date their arrival as late as the sixth or seventh centuries. The westernmost tribes found a better living in the rich flatlands than they had known roaming through the dark eastern forests, and for their choice they came to be called the Polanie (field dwellers). The few scraps of knowledge handed down about their tiny scattered communities show them to have been an independent-minded people, impatient of authority, and preferring to live dispersed than to submit to social regulation.

But when the Germanic tribes in middle Europe had overrun Rome and touched the Atlantic barrier to expansion, their energy spilled eastward, and the Polanie felt the first push of a *Drang nach Osten* that has pounded them spasmodically for more than a millennium. In defense against this pressure, they organized loose confederations and, at last, in 963 A.D. a single nation evolved under a single ruler, Mieszko I. The Teuton bands that Mieszko was elevated to repulse marched under the banners of the Holy Roman Empire, claiming, as others later learned to do, that they fought but for the greater glory of God and hungered for conquest to bring souls and lands to the service of Christ.

Their appetites were insatiable and their arms effective. The pagan ruler of Poland could not defeat them, but he found a canny way to hold them off and to strengthen his people. In 965, he married a Christian princess, Dubravka of Bohemia, and the following year proclaimed the conversion of himself and his nation to the Church of Rome. That was the decisive date in the whole future development of the Poles, a date whose thousandth anniversary will be celebrated in 1966 by great and prolonged national festivity of much immediate significance. For the result was to turn the Poles' faces to the West and their backs to the East. From then on, the gulf deepened between them and their Slav brothers in Russia, who spoke much the same language, ate much the same food, but worshiped at the altar of Byzantium. With the Church divided between Constantinople and Rome, the border between Russia and Poland was the border between East and West.

Poland prospered in the centuries that followed, uniting late in the fourteenth century with Lithuania, whose Baltic barons had been the last pagans on the continent of Europe. The battle of Grunwald (Tannenberg) in 1410 confirmed her status as a major European power with the climactic defeat of the relentless Teutonic Knights. The pattern of pressure consolidated and intensified the feeling of national identity. There was little mixture of racial strains and little absorption of neighboring cultures, for the clergy devotedly nourished Polish culture in resistance to Germanic influence.

With the eruption of the Reformation, this national task of Polish Catholicism was redoubled. And it was all the more effective since Poland avoided western Europe's racking wars of religion, its people uniting around the church which distinguished them from the national enemies—Orthodox Russia, Protestant Prussia, and Protestant Sweden. But perennial problems of succession to the Polish throne and internal political bickering weakened the state, if not the spirit of the people. By the end of the eighteenth century, Poland lost all that had ever been won by conquest and political diplomacy and was too feeble even to keep the heart of the nation. In three successive partitions, Russia, Prussia, and Austria gobbled Poland off the map of Europe. There was nothing left but memories, the lively flame of tradition devotedly fed by the Church, and a new and deep emotional attachment to France, the enemy of Poland's enemies.

But political geography limited the French inspiration to an ardent intellectual blossoming. The libertarian ideals of the French Revolution echoed slyly or boldly through Polish literature, depending on the wakefulness of the censor. Nevertheless, the dead hand of the authoritarian Russian and Prussian monarchies, and somewhat less of the Austrian, petrified social development. The wealthy, the educated, the traveled, absorbed French taste, French elegance, and produced that image of the madly heroic, gallant, reckless Polish soul, almost preposterously refined in manner but totally uninhibited in emotion, foolishly generous and mulishly stubborn, that remains the archetype of the Polish upper crust. The peasants, bogged in their muddy villages, clung taciturnly to the Roman Church, which was their only link to a power outside the alien rulers. Living thus in the past and the future, the people disdained the present and nursed their ancient dislike of imposed order, their distrust of authority.

When at last the Western victory in World War I revived Poland, after 113 years of oblivion, there was no civic tradition on which to build, but a wealth of old enmities and hatreds. Revolution in Russia only intensified hostility between the two neighbors. Defeated Germany, hating and fearing France, saw in Poland only the other, the less powerful, side of a French pincers meant to turn the Germans in upon themselves forever. It was not so much prophetic of the fourth Polish partition, between Russia and Germany in 1939, as it was expressive of the deepest currents in European affairs when General Hans von Seeckt wrote a secret memorandum to Chancellor Friedrich Ebert in 1922:

"The existence of Poland is intolerable and incompatible with Germany's vital interests. She must disappear and will do so through her own inner weakness and through Russia—with our help. Poland is more intolerable for Russia than for ourselves."

Von Seeckt was gone before Hitler came to power, but it was he who launched the renewed German Army, the renewed German cult of might, and set the course that others pushed to World War II.

There was, in that mere score of years between holocausts, no cause for Poles to change their attitudes or habits of thought. There was neither time nor temptation to cultivate the gentle moderation of character, the happy marriage of thought and action each tempering the other's wildest flights, which constitutes the Anglo-Saxon ideal of a stable civilized society. Nothing had ever revealed to Poles the virtue of tolerance, nothing prepared them to practice it, and they did not. Their strength of character is lined everywhere with the grain of prejudice and superstition.

Between the wars, that violence of unthinking emotion expressed itself in roughshod oppression of ethnic minorities, especially in anti-Semitism. It was no mere snobbish stance of an elite, for the worst and toughest prejudice came from the countryside, a miasma that emanated from the Polish soil. There were Ruthenian, Ukrainian, Byelorussian, and other minorities in Poland between the wars—they, too, fared badly. Like the dark, raw peasant vodka, Polish nationalism does not mix and is meant to be gulped, not sipped.

The land as well as the history contributed to the extremes of the Polish character. For the most part, in central Poland, it stretches flat and full, open to the howling frozen winds that sweep from the east. In winter, rural Poland is made of banked snow, in spring of mud, in summer of dust. Only autumn is gay and soothing, the traditional "golden autumn." Strong drink, strong emotions, are called upon to relieve the emptiness of the horizon in wood, twig, and wattle villages, gray under a leaden sky.

But it is good land, and the people who settled there had a good road to carry away their produce when they began to trade— the broad and quiet Vistula. In the South are mountains, in the East are forests, in the Northeast lovely twisting lakes, but all Poland is traced by rivers. Their watershed supports the fields and the woods, and if the climate blusters harshly, the land gives a sturdy support.

The geography that has mattered to Poland is not physical geography, however, but political. There are no protective barriers but rivers against the ceaseless drive of other nations. There are no clear and permanent lines that mark the limits of the Polish ethnic realm; in that sense, no fixed frontiers. In its medieval glory, Poland stretched far to the west and east. Victories and defeats have changed its borders drastically. The Poland of 1918–39 was a monstrosity of the drawing board and a hodgepodge of cultures, with its gooseneck "Polish corridor" stretching up for a gulp of sea air on the Baltic, its grumbling minorities surrounding the Polish cities of Lwow and Vilno.

After World War II, Poland was shifted west, a brutal, almost surgical operation of the political geographers that caused as much malignancy as it removed. The Soviet Union moved up to the Bug, the line drawn as the Russo-German border in the 1939 partition, and swallowed both Lwow and Vilno. With those proud old cities, Poland lost its petroleum industry, and its poorest and most primitive peasants. East Prussia, cut off from Germany by the corridor before the war, was shared out between the Soviet Union and Poland. Russia gained more coast line and the largest city, Königsberg (now Kaliningrad). Poland gained a larger share of magnificently wooded, lake-strewn territory.

And in the West, Poland took most of German Pomerania and Silesia, setting its new border on the north-south line of the Oder and Neisse rivers. The Oder-Neisse line brought a long Baltic coast, ending the semiclaustrophobic feeling of the old corridor, a rich if thoroughly devastated coal and industrial basin, some good agricultural land if less than had been lost in the East, and a terrible, terrifying problem of security.

Under the authorization of the Potsdam Agreement, the Poles quickly set about throwing ethnic Germans out of what they call "recovered territories," so that the lands are now effectively and thoroughly Polish. But the Germans who fled still speak of those areas as "home." West Germany still claims the lands beyond the Oder-Neisse, West German maps still show them as German "under temporary Polish administration," and West German school children study Silesia and Pomerania in their lessons on geography of the German homeland.

So Poles have recurrent nightmares of a German drive for armed revenge. They are excruciatingly vivid and graphic nightmares, linked inevitably with how the Germans treated Poles in World War II. The official Nazi policy toward Poland was that it should serve as virgin territory for German colonization, and that its present inhabitants were a sort of subhuman species destined only for slavery or extermination. It was to have been a kind of

Wild West, with tanks instead of covered wagons, whose Indians might choose only between submission and extinction.

Germans have always looked down their noses at the flighty, temperamental Poles, pouring all their respect for their own stolid, stiff efficiency in the scorn with which they use the phrase *polnische Wirtschaft* (Polish economics) to mean any kind of sloppy work. Poles have always felt unnerved and depressed by Germans, sensing something mechanical, inhuman, joyless in their methodical, organized, group approach to life.

But the Russians, whom the Poles disdain as crude, primitive, insensitive, managed by Stalin's devilishly brilliant stroke of map drawing to make sure that German-Polish hostility will not fade, that it will thrive for many years to come. With the border changes, Russia insured that Poland could never ally herself with Germany against the Soviet Union, and that Poland must depend on Soviet protection for her territorial integrity. The new political geography, quite as much as the Communist regime, did far more to change Poland's traditional posture of face to the West, back to the East, than anything since Mieszko's conversion a thousand years ago.

Within her new borders, Poland feels uncomfortably squeezed. It is the political pressure that hurts, however, for the land amounts to 120,818 square miles and its 28 million people are not seriously cramped for space. Those former migrants of Polish stock who have settled in France, England, Canada, and the United States left home not to look for room to live but to look for a living. From the early days of the nation until the nineteenth century, there were no important waves of migration out of the Polish plains. When it started, it was the result of economic pressures. The peasants lived in crushing poverty, traditionally symbolized by the old habit of cutting a match in four pieces to make it serve longer. For millions the only escape was departure. A very large source of migrants was in the southern mountains, whose tough and stringy people have never managed to scrape more than a bare living from their craggy farms and skimpy flocks. It has made those who stayed behind an oddly privileged group now, for, as they have the most relatives abroad, they receive the most parcels. People come from all over Poland to the muddy street bazaar of Nowy Targ in the lower Tatras, for that is where shining, glittering goods from the West can best be bought.

Their unruly spirit and their unsheltered land have shaped the development of the Poles' government. Very early, when most of Europe was ruled by absolute monarchs, they achieved an unusual degree of consultative government. The power of the medieval kings was limited by the landed nobility, which extended its rights to the election of the king. Sometimes wise and sometimes foolish, sometimes brave and sturdy and sometimes feeble nonentities, the Polish rulers were never strong and powerful autocrats. And yet Poland's feudalism was not on the classic pattern, for the dangers of hostile and marauding aliens always forced enough co-operation to keep the provincial aristocracy from massacring each other.

Nor, as in England, did the assertion of decentralized baronial rights lead eventually to establishment of a democratic tradition. The very weakness of central authority each time the rather short-lived kings were elected encouraged the intrigues and interventions of Poland's neighbors, for it was a land of enormous strategic importance to each of them. And the result was Poland's collapse in the partitions.

During the century when home government was suppressed, imposed government differed according to the traditions of each imposing power. Czarist Russia, the most autocratic, ruled fiercely through a governor in Warsaw, brutally suppressing all movement for liberal reform and seeking vainly to Russianize the people. Some of Dostoievsky's stories reflect how even the intelligentsia of St. Petersburg considered the Poles as upstarts who must be kept firmly in their place. Arbitrary, reactionary Russian officialdom put the idea into practice with a heavy hand.

Imperial Prussia, stirring with modern ideas but accepting those of the machine and organization and rejecting challenges of the spirit, ran an orderly government in the western part of the country that took pains to stifle the Polish yen for liberty without crushing the people. Under Prussia, a habit of civic obedience was instilled among a minority of Poles, while the majority deepened its conviction that disobedience was the greater national virtue.

The Austrian Hapsburgs, who ruled the south of Poland, had already lost their imperial dynamism. Their fusty, bumbling functionaries provided the least harsh of the governments partitioned Poland knew, but it was tatty, stagnant government, incapable of development, and contributed no fruitful social or political innovations and no inspiring traditions.

It seems appropriate that the Pole who sparked his country's resurgence was Ignace Paderewski, a brilliant, bright-hearted pianist with all the artist's range of tenderness and fire, but none of the political leader's cool shrewdness. He was a wonderful, lovable man, genial in his art and in his humanity, but he was no engineer of governments. Newborn Poland was quickly caught up in war with the newborn Soviet Union, and the idealists' vision of a healthy, democratic parliamentary government faded before it was fairly stamped on the country. There were parties aplenty, but they turned out a wealth of bickering, intriguing politicians and a dearth of sound statesmen. The triumph of the Bolsheviks next door aroused the Right to extreme and energetic reaction, and the people to demands for social reform and responsible government. What they got was a man on a white horse—Marshal Jozef Pilsudski.

From Pilsudski, who took over in a bloodless coup in 1926, until the Stukas started World War II over Warsaw in 1939, Poland had governments that were more or less dictatorial. The country never achieved any solid democratic foundations, or scarcely even ephemeral democratic appearances. It was not a time or an area in which democracy flourished. By the thirties, Stalin had launched his devastating collectivization campaign and then his bloody purges that made the Soviet Union a land of terror. Hitler took power in Germany and made Poland's western neighbor a land of shrieking, arrogant brutality. Some Poles were Fascists and openly sympathized with the perverted ideas stamped with the swastika, but Hitler was too overtly anti-Polish to undermine basic reliance on the long-standing ties and the military alliances with Britain and France. The ten-year non-aggression pact between Hitler's Berlin and Warsaw did not really change that situation. Internally, the Polish government was autocratic but not totalitarian like its neighbors west and east.

The war revived a purer Polish patriotism. Inside the country, there was the expectable number of whimpering collaborators, but no important quislings. The government fled to London and reformed as a government in exile around the widely popular figure of General Sikorski. Sikorski died in a mysterious wartime plane crash, and Stanislaw Mikolajczyk, leader of the Peasant party, succeeded him. Under London's orders, an active, dare-devil underground army was formed in Poland, and its directorate was all the Polish authority that existed on Polish soil. When Hitler attacked Russia, after the long quiet on the Eastern Front that followed Poland's defeat, a Communist underground army was also organized in Poland and, later, a rival Communist government in exile was set up behind the advancing Red Army.

Long before Poland was liberated, the question of its future government began to strain and shred the wartime grand alliance. Many hours of the crucial Roosevelt-Churchill-Stalin meetings were devoted to the postwar fate of Poland. The Western chiefs managed to extract some promises from Stalin that Poland would have a chance to decide for herself in free elections. But Stalin did not very seriously pretend that he meant to keep the promises. "The problem of Poland is inseparable from the problem of security of the Soviet Union," Stalin wrote President Roosevelt in 1944.

Stalin's insistence on shifting the Polish borders in his favor argued on grounds of the Soviet Union's vital security. But it was soon clear that Moscow's idea of minimum security included a government in Warsaw that Moscow could control. The Western Allies demanded, and secured, the right of the London Poles to return to Warsaw and form a provisional coalition government with Moscow's Poles until elections could be held. But from the time the Red Army stepped onto Polish soil, the Russians concentrated on insuring that the Communists would run Poland.

From then on, it was only a matter of steps. The Poles were not fooled; nor basically were the Western statesmen. But there was nothing they could do. For the Communists, who controlled all the levers of power, it was simply a matter of consolidation. Bit by bit they beat down the die-hard rebels who took to the woods to fight them, and they purged all posts of responsibility of opponents and unreliables.

By 1949, only four years after the war, the Communist regime was so thoroughly established that it went on to purge itself—ousting loyal Communists who showed too much Polish patriotism and too little "proletarian internationalism," the euphemism for complete subservience to Moscow. That was the period of the rupture between Yugoslavia's Tito and Moscow. Poland became an unquestioning satellite. Its government developed then along the lines Moscow traced for satellites. The differences betwen Poland's Communist government and that of other eastern European people's democracies were trifling compared with the similarities.

But after Stalin's death in 1953, the feeling of separate Polishness began to reassert itself. Once again, as in the nineteenth century, civic freedom and independence danced in Poles' dreams as inseparable twins who could be won together or not at all. Exhausted from a life of continuous fear and hardship since 1939, the people stirred slowly. But the Communists themselves were impatient to release their pent-up pride of nationality. The ferment grew in many places, each bursting bubble of expressed dissatisfaction feeding many more. The crisis came in October 1956.

The 1956 upheaval did not even attempt to release Poland from communism. Even the wildest-eyed Poles realized that any such hopes must be futile. The bitter defeat of Hungary, which started, like Poland, to assert itself and wound up trying to break completely free, proved that the best Poland could hope for was reform. That was achieved, and to a startling degree. It converted Poland into something of a freak among Communist states—not independent like Yugoslavia with its favorable political geography, but still a country with a discernible voice of its own.

Gradually, the facts of life of modern power politics eroded away some of the gains. It is still as true as when Stalin proclaimed it, that no Polish government can oppose Moscow and get away with it.

Certainly, the communism in a velvet glove under which they now live is not a form of government that pleases most Poles. But in modern times, at least, Poland has never had a form of government that her people could find eminently pleasing. When it comes down to concrete details, they are hard put to say just what might satisfy them. Nor, it must be said, are they likely to be asked by anyone with the will and the power to fulfill their wishes. Her history has drawn no happy blueprints, built no firm foundations, for a freely acceptable form of government for Poland.

Yet the monuments of the past that have been left intact to Poland exist mostly in the minds and hearts of her people, all the more deeply rooted perhaps for the wanton destruction of a more tangible, visible ancestral heritage. The demolition of Warsaw in World War II was a calculated effort to wipe the city off the earth and out of men's minds as well. Nothing was expressly spared, although the German teams charged with razing the city after the defeat of the Warsaw uprising in 1944 necessarily left standing the few dowdy buildings where they went to rest each night after the day's methodical destruction. Specialists, crammed with knowledge of the history of art and architecture, saw to it that anything of real value was carefully and completely blown.

When the Poles returned and began the aching task of re-building their capital city, they deliberately chose to put back the landmarks they had known and loved. There were some who urged a radically new city plan, incorporating the latest inspirations of modern art and technology. But conscious choice as well as necessity dictated piling the rubble back up as it had stood before. Thus the city's distinct quarters were preserved, and many of its churches, its favorite monuments, were carefully remade from old plans and photographs. The Old City, once the heart of Warsaw, was gaily and lavishly reconstructed to look as it was in the seventeenth century, its architects following the precise and lively detail of the old paintings by Canaletto. When thousands of families still huddled in heaps of bombed-out debris for lack of other shelter, Warsaw builders put up another column to King Sigismund III, who had made the city Poland's capital, and lovingly refashioned the dome of Alexander's Church at the Square of Three Crosses. No one grumbled about that—the city's spirit placed the physical re-creation of its historical continuity ahead of its creature comforts.

But the war years and the postwar years could not afford Warsaw much brightness. It was left a threadbare, graceless city with only a few spots of half-hidden loveliness to illuminate it, like the flashing eyes in the ravaged face of an old and ill-used beauty. Its physical spoliation did not reduce its place in Poland, however. Warsaw has remained the headquarters of Polish wit, flair, and madness even though its rival, Cracow, preserved the outer mold much better.

Cracow, in the South, fortunately escaped serious war damage, so that its scene is still set with the handsome backdrops of its history. Until the seventeenth century, Cracow was the capital. On a hill above the Vistula, narrow and pastoral-looking here compared with the wide gray river that hurries past Warsaw, stands Wawel, the old royal castle with its marvelously lively ceiling sculptures, its great tapestried halls, and its empty echoes of dead glory. Still now, every hour on the hour, a live echo of the past rings from the top of the tall, narrow tower on the Rynek, the great market square in the center of the city. A trumpeter blows the strains of the call that a boy was blowing from that tower to warn the city of danger, and the call always stops unfinished on the last note the boy had sounded before an arrow from the invading Mongol armies pierced his throat.

The tower is at one corner of the Rynek. In the center is the great market hall, built to house the wares of the Hanseatic merchants, who came regularly to trade in the Cracow of the Middle Ages. Now its stalls and shops offer Polish textiles, the flowered skirts and velvet bodices of the traditional costume worn in the nearby Tatras, carved wooden boxes, and gimcrack mementos. Diagonally across the square from the tower is the cathedral, squat and sprawling from the outside, soaring and gleaming within with the rich ripe beauties of the famous Veit Stoss altar-piece, returned now after a generation in exile. And down a side street is the cracked, unostentatious university building in whose courtyard the Pole Copernicus sat and pondered the paths of the heavenly bodies and of this lumpy earth.

All this gives Cracow a musty air, an air of living tranquilly in the past that is not shared by many Polish cities. Katowice, in the heart of the Silesian coal basin, sprawls awkwardly under a coat of industrial grime. Lodz, in the central plain south of Warsaw, bustles about its spinning machines. Poznan, mid-point on the straight east-west line between Warsaw and Berlin, buzzes with commerce and clangs with the sound of metal cutting metal in its factories. Gdynia and Danzig, on the Baltic, merged now into a single great port, look out on the cold sea and haul away the trade it carries. Not much shows of a long past.

In the countryside, it is the towering mounds of dirt-brown sugar beets, the insolence of white geese, the wrinkled trunks of great lime trees, and the smooth elegance of poplars that hold the flavor of the centuries. The villages look neither very old nor new, although it seems appropriate that the oldest institution in Poland has its seat in Gniezno, little more than a village not far from Poznan. For the Church, whose Cardinal Primate traditionally has his archbishopric in Gniezno, is the core of peasant Poland.

The religious heritage, so powerful and so enduring, so bound with the ideal of nationhood, has yet not been responsible for the brightest offerings of Polish culture to the European spirit. They flowered particularly in the nineteenth century, precisely the period of national suppression. The great names of Polish litera-ture—Mickiewicz, Slowacki, and Krasinski—are of this time, and they thunder with the yearning for national existence, independ-ence, freedom not just of the immortal soul but of the conscious Pole in his homeland. Even the lyrical genius of Chopin built on old Polish themes with an ever recurrent nostalgia for Polishness, although the composer chose to sing his joys and sweet laments in self-exile from his native soil.

Those nineteenth-century songs and poems have a special meaning for Poland now, because once again the nation feels burdened by alien impositions and once again it must look to the talents of its writers and artists to find expressions that defy enforced silence. That tradition has given Polish intellectuals a special skill for saying things not permitted to be said, and a willfulness based on the feeling of a special responsibility to speak for those who dare not. More specifically, it has plunged them inextricably into politics.

There are no ivory towers in Polish intellectual life, not just because the total ideology of communism forbids such retreats, but because Polish intellectuals would quickly wither and die of bored frustration if they closed their minds to their nation's affairs. Life in Poland now is hard and uncertain, beset with terrible quandaries and tossed by seemingly endless storms. Yet no one who knows them is surprised when Polish intellectuals flee to the West seeking freedom to be themselves and, finding it impossible, go home sheepishly to suffer. Their excited palates have lost all taste for tranquillity and easiness; cut off from turbulence, they no longer feel they are themselves or, at any rate, they don't enjoy it.

Whether they live and breath turmoil, as the intellectuals, or plod on through drudgery, as the rest of the nation, Poles are acutely conscious that for them sheer existence is fragile. When they hear others talk of what will be in fifty years, or a hundred years, as Czechs sometimes do, they strike their heads in awed despair at what seems such smug lunacy. It is not easy for a Pole to speak confidently of next year, it is difficult to speak of five years hence, almost impossible to speak of the next generation, so uncertain is the outlook. Perhaps in no other country are people more sharply aware of the great destructive forces in this world and of their immediacy. Poles do not need big newspaper headlines and growling speeches to remind them that they live dangerously.

That may well be the most important effect of World War II on their country, the war that changed all their historical alliances, tied them willy-nilly to the tail of Moscow's kite, and completely reordered their society to the pattern of the Communist revolution. Even communism in Poland is beset with uncertainties. No one knows just where it is going, how it will eventually look. Transition, development, adaptation, are the key ideas, and they must be understood in terms of a country whose destiny lies mainly in the hands of aliens it cannot hope to control, and which knows it.

In this sense, the drastic changes in the social order, the economy, the political structure of the country, come to look more like the unhinging of things as they were than the arrival of a new, clear-cut system of things. Communism wiped out the old aristocracy, but for some time it had been withering more or less decoratively on a fading vine. The new aristocracy is the top ranks of the Party, a shifting, far from stable group. The new bureaucracy is perhaps the most firmly entrenched of all classes. Like all bureaucracies, it tends to stagnate, but it, too, is at the mercy of currents that sweep in varying directions. The workers and peasants are restless, unsatisfied, resorting too much to vodka to still yearnings they find it hard to name, or rather that they give a thousand piecemeal names, like a radio, a pair of handsome shoes, travel, an apartment. They want things most of them never wanted before, but they have no confidence that energy and persistence will ever be rewarded.

Even the Communist leaders in Poland now seem to have lost their righteous assurance that the way to perfection has been found and only time and effort are needed to finish the journey. And yet the essence of communism is its ideological completeness, its claim to contain all the right answers to all possible human questions. In such a system doubt is far more unsettling than blatant opposition.

So the outlook for Poland is murky. Certain facts are hard, beyond the ability of Poles to change. These are essentially the military, political, and economic power of the Soviet Union. That power does not permit, and in the foreseeable future will not permit, Poland to choose freely its friends, its ideals, and its way of trying to achieve them. Poland must remain Communist so long as Moscow commands it.

Moscow's commands are no longer so detailed and so specific as they were when Stalin snapped them out, and Poles have found that Moscow, too, is subject to influence and change. The fundamental achievement of the Polish upheaval in 1956 was to establish the nation's right to work out its own problems within the limits laid down by Moscow, and to establish the nation's desire to broaden those limits wherever that might be possible. Since their startling defiance in 1956, the Poles have been fighting a rear-guard action against erosion of that right and desire under the weight of Soviet ambition. They have not succeeded as well as they had hoped; they have not failed as badly as they had feared.

The most realistic hope available to the Poles is that their path of compromise will enlighten and influence their patrons. World war, which might or might not destroy Soviet communism, would certainly destroy Poland, and responsible minds in Poland know too well the strengths of Soviet communism to suppose that it might simply collapse of its own weight. Reform, then, seems the only possibility. If Poland can make its own reforms work, it can hope that the spirit of reform will spread.

It sounds presumptuous, perhaps, for weak and struggling Poland to imagine itself capable of finding and leading the way. But there are worthy grounds for the presumption. The craving of Poles for a better standard of living is shared by all their neighbors. The yearning for free self-expression, for truth and honesty and decency in civic life, may roil Poles with a special intensity, but it is not peculiar to them. Poland wants these things for itself, but it is convinced that others living oppressed want them, too, and that they in turn will take up the banners of freedom and well-being as Poland's advances provide encouragement.

It is not to be expected that the Poles will soon again amass the enormous reservoir of reckless determination that was expended to make the 1956 revolt. Such bold and dangerous initiatives exact a heavy price in nervous energy. A nation cannot hold a steady course by exploding violently at every threatened deviation. But the cravings that were responsible for the initiative have not diminished in intensity. If once again a Polish lunge for greater freedom should appear to have at least a slim chance for success, the Poles still have the will to try. They learned, from their own experience and even more from Hungary, what is to be lost by trying when there is manifestly no chance.

When might a chance come? That depends primarily on the Soviet Union, although a whole conjuncture of national and international developments would have to be involved. It is patent that Moscow will not willingly present the Poles with opportunities to make decisions that Moscow finds inimical. But there are hypothetical possibilities, none of them currently probable, that might divert the Kremlin's attention sufficiently for the Poles to attempt once more to help themselves. One is a new indecision within the Soviet leadership over the problem of succession when Khrushchev goes; another is a ferment inside the Soviet Union against a life that is regimented and cramped despite great improvements; another is national and ideological dispute within the Soviet bloc, particularly between Moscow and Peking.

The past shows that the chance for initiative is greater when cold-war tensions are somewhat relaxed, less when the power blocs of East and West are growling mutual threats and tightening their alliances as they would tighten the bucklers of their shields. Since Poland cannot escape its ties to Russia, its chance for more independence can come only when a calmer world situation makes such ties less vital to Moscow.

Meanwhile, Poland's task is to strengthen itself for what seems inevitably a long pull. The statesmen of the West have shown intelligent understanding of Poland's aims and abilities in their support for the effort to raise living standards. The support has been relatively meager, but it is better than previous indifference. For if Poles can demonstrate that it is possible to maintain even a measure of freedom, and a measure of well-being, within the bear hug of communism, they will be feeding the flame that threatens tyranny. Perhaps the next time the purifying flame leaps high it will be in Poland, perhaps it will be elsewhere. No one can say. What matters is that it is being kept alive inside the darkness.

CZECHOSLOVAKIA

Flora Lewis

A biographical sketch of Miss Lewis can be found on page 268.

CZECHOSLOVAKIA

Of all the countries that have taken the veil of communism, Czechoslovakia is the one Americans know best and find it most difficult to lump mentally with "East." How is it possible, people ask again and again, that such a sturdy, Western, middle-class democracy could have fallen to the Communists? And yet, Czechoslovakia is the only country whose Communist regime gained power without force of arms, neither the arms of violent domestic revolutionaries nor of overwhelming foreign legions. It must be said immediately that the Communists did not drive to Hradcany—the ancient castle overlooking Prague that is the presidential seat and the symbol of government—on ballots. They moved in as a minority, but they moved in with a minimum of fuss and overt opposition.

And it must be quickly said that, so far as anyone can measure, the Communists and their loyal adherents seem still to be very much in the minority, doubtless considerably shrunken from their numbers at the moment of their triumph. But they clearly have no intention of moving out, and the population appears to have adjusted to the fact that they cannot be shoved. Therefore, the regime looks stable, at least as secure as that of neighboring countries still extending hospitality to the Soviet Army, and more secure than some.

There are many reasons. Perhaps the major one is that the Czechs are an orderly people, tidy, careful, who shun the goads of impulse and are willing to take the long view. They look both ways before they cross the street, unlike the Poles, who leap first

and then consider. Unkind visitors have compared their spirit to
the national dish—*knedlíky*, a thick, nourishing bread dumpling,
solid, unimaginative, sometimes soggy and generally bland. No
bitter critic would deny their generous endowment with the domestic virtues. It is typically Czech to be hard-working, honest,
hospitable, reliable, law-abiding, substantial. No ardent admirer
would draw on the national character for the incarnation of
gallantry, daring, grace, and the peppery spices of life.

The two major groups in the country, as its name implies, are
Czechs and Slovaks, racially alike but different in temperament as
the result of centuries of separate development. They compress
the definition of the difference in their liquid pleasure. The
Czechs drink beer (their Plzen brew is world-famed), they grow
hops, and they say "beer soothes and satisfies, the more you drink
the better you feel and the less you argue." The Slovaks drink
wine, they grow grapes, and they say "wine excites gaiety." But
the Czechs, more advanced in every material way, tend to dominate the country and to give its composite character their comforting malty flavor.

Under communism, the brew has tended to go flat. The sentimental, richly indigestible central European schmaltz that Czechoslovakia once evoked has been melted down to a dull gray
margarine. The government functions with an efficiency that
other Communist states envy, and with a dreary regularity of
pressure that leaves little room for surprises. Since they grabbed
control in the coup of 1948, the Communist rulers have held the
country on a tight rein, relaxing but a millimeter or so when neighbors relaxed a few inches and stiffening at the first small signs
that the population sought to take up the slack.

Carefully, coolly, to a degree that has driven even calculating
Russian wits to mockery, the regime has clung to Moscow's apron
strings. Of course, the Kremlin has set the line and demanded
that its viceroys in Prague observe it, but sometimes there have
been hints that the Soviet leaders were surprised with the
thoroughness of Czechoslovak Communist obedience. It shows
through the Russian joke about the time Soviet Premier Nikita
Khrushchev was off on one of his jaunts and his plane got hope-

lessly lost in a sea of clouds. Finally the pilot saw a break and dove down to land. As Khrushchev stepped out of the plane, people came rushing up to bow and kiss him, almost smothering him with displays of devotion. "Where are we?" he asked his companions in amazement. "Who can these people be?" And the story goes, his comrade quickly answered, "I don't know the name of the place, but it must be somewhere in Czechoslovakia."

Czech jokes are generally not so piquant. That is due partly to the completeness with which the Communist regime has managed to suppress subtleties of expressive opposition, partly to a tradition that leans more toward drama and warming song than to sharp satire. The most popular and most expert cultural achievements of the country are in the fields of music and sport. It is true that those are forms of expression least subject to public involvement with politically prohibited yearning and opinions, which makes them safest during periods of oppression. Whatever the reason, they are forms in which Czechs have a special excellence, and they are especially dear to Czech hearts.

The name Dvořák is a common one, and there is likely to be someone who bears it at almost any sizable gathering in Prague. But ask if the person happens to be kin to the famous Czech composer, and the answer given is "No, I'm no relation to Anton Dvořák, but of course I'm a musician, like all Czechs." The particular addiction to music is neither new nor limited. Mozart dedicated *Don Giovanni* to the city of Prague, and the opera had its first performance there. When the Hapsburgs glittered in Vienna, it was taken for granted that the court musicians would be Czech. Nor has the pain of the postwar period diminished the pride and practice of music. Without stooping to statistics, which sometimes belie facts anyway, it can be said that in no capital city is the per capita output and consumption of music so high and so fervent as in Prague.

Perhaps the only more important calendar than that of musical events in the national affection is the sports program. Ice hockey is the national favorite. Children swarm across the village ponds in winter and adapt it to the city streets all year, with barrel staves and lumps of coal when better equipment is lacking. The gymnastic societies, particularly the remarkable national organization of Sokol, can bring hundreds of thousands onto a field to swing their arms and bend their backs in a perfect rhythmic unison that they have practiced once or twice a week for generations. An international hockey or football match in which the Czechoslovak team has a chance can catch the country in a frenzied excitement that makes baseball fever at World Series time in the United States seem no more than one degree above indifference.

But otherwise, when there is no sport and no music, the chords of the Czech soul no longer seem to vibrate audibly. The country works like an electric clock, with no ticks, no chimes, to break into the drudging regularity and heighten the sense of the moment, but only the faint buzz of an undercurrent that sinks below conscious existence by the weight of its own monotony.

Work it does. Czechoslovakia has long been noted for its people's industry, and although a totalitarian morass inevitably swamps initiative and craftsmanship, people still work hard and well. The standard of living is well above that in any other Communist state, probably somewhat above what it was before the war, although the social upheaval and specific shortages like housing make that hard to measure. There is even room for argument on how living standards compare with such a state as Austria. Certainly, Austria looks brighter, smarter, far more lively and more satisfying; it is *possible* to live much better in Vienna than in Prague, but not everyone does. The revival is a fairly recent development, however. Communism has ruled for just over a decade in Czechoslovakia, and during the first half of that period living standards were severely and purposely depressed to squeeze more capital for the state from the people's labor. After Stalin's death, the pendulum was slowly reversed, and after the Hungarian and Polish revolts in 1956, the effort to satisfy the population's material wants was accelerated.

The basis for the country's relative well-being in the tatty company of other Soviet-bloc consumers lies in the balanced economy it had achieved before the war. There was already a solid industrial development, which shared the country's labor force equally with agriculture. Industry depended on trade, both for raw materials and for export markets, but it was a fairly balanced industry, ranging from heavy machinery, railroad goods, and one of the world's largest armaments plants to textiles, glass, shoes, beads, and trinkets. Nor did the industrial plant suffer severely from wartime destruction, in comparison with what happened in some neighboring states. Therefore, it was not necessary to extract enormous investments for rapid industrialization from an exhausted postwar peasantry in the way that characterized Communist development elsewhere.

Nevertheless, the Communist regime has put more emphasis on further industrial expansion, and more and more Czechoslovakia has come to serve as a pool of capital goods for the Communist bloc. Almost as important to bloc-development schemes is its pool of technical skills. Since the war, as they did before, Czech engineers have ranged through the world's outlandish places, installing sugar mills, building bridges, setting up electric-power stations.

Aside from plant and know-how, the resources for industry consist mainly of Bohemia's deposits of brown coal, a smoky, inefficient fuel but comparatively cheap, and the hard coal of Moravia and central Bohemia. The old Joachimsthal mines—whose silver was minted into coins that bore the region's name and thus gave rise to the word "dollar," via the Austrian "thaler"—turned out to be rich in uranium. Long before the peculiarities of uranium were discovered, it was known that the waters of the region carried mysterious minerals whose properties were exploited in western Bohemia's famous and cosmopolitan spas. The Curies got the pitchblende from which they discovered radium from those mines. Now the Russians obtain great quantities of ore for their atomic production, but Czechoslovakia has not sought to make any important use of this natural resource for its own industry.

Agriculture is diversified, with important industrial crops such as hops and flax and sugar beets, as well as grains and table vegetables. Between the wars, most of the great estates were broken up by land reform into medium- and small-sized freeholdings. Now, the government boasts, three quarters of the farmers have been corralled into collective farms and the aim of complete collectivization has been energetically—sometimes forcefully—pursued.

As in other Communist states, the advent of Communist power worked a drastic upheaval on every part of its people's lives, so that the key date in Communist Czechoslovakia is February 25, 1948, the date of the *coup d'état* by which the Communists vaulted from the step of junior coalition partner and strongest party in the country to total mastery. And as in most of the other states, a difference marked the years before and after Stalin's death, a difference of degree. Violence tended to diminish, living standards tended to improve, but the Czechoslovak regime has been one of communism's most conservative. Its changes have been held to a pace so slow and gradual that they were perceptible only to the most patient eye. Furthermore, in some fields, particularly culture, a retrogression appears to have set in.

The people of the nation learned, and accepted, patience long ago. There have been periods of triumph and glory, of proud dominion over neighboring lands, but for much of their existence the Czechs have been underdogs, lying low and sneaking through history cautiously. It was so often dangerous to flaunt the fact of their being that they developed secret hearts where feelings could be nursed without showing. They told themselves: "We've been here a long time; we'll be here a long time after those who stomp and flash their power have crumbled to nought but dusty flecks on memory." People who take the long view seldom flare up with emotion. A painful history taught the Czechs to hold their tempers and to show the world a calm, impassive, docile face.

They did not start that way. Their origins lie in the misty past of the Slavonic nation, but they were the first Slavs to pop assertively onto the stage of recorded European history. The lands they took over in the fifth and sixth centuries A.D. had once been settled by Gauls and Celts who seem to have vanished completely except for the Celtic tribal name Boii, which endures in the name Bohemia. They were lands traversed by fertile river valleys, richly veined with minerals, luxuriantly cloaked in piny forests alive with game. That is, they were lands worth conquering and worth defending.

So the Western Slavs who settled in Bohemia, Moravia, and Slovakia were endlessly set upon, by intermittent waves of Asiatic warriors erupting from the East and by the vigorous Germanic tribes pushing from the West. They developed early a feeling of national unity and a will to resist invasion, a will that sometimes sprouted into bursts of conquest but more often had to be concentrated on withstanding attack. As early as the seventh century, they formed the first Slavonic state, ruled by the Frankish merchant Samo, but it collapsed with his death. The state's revival is set down only on the vaporous scrolls of legend, but before the end of the Christian Era's first millennium, it was cemented into history.

The story of their nation's birth is enshrined in the myth of Libuse—honored in Smetana's opera, in tapestry, and in painting as the beautiful and wise princess who dreamed of a great and happy kingdom with its capital in Prague. Libuse, the legend says, married the plowman Přemysl and thus founded the Přemyslide dynasty. There were times when the lands ruled from Prague reached down to the bright Adriatic, to the frontiers of Byzantium, to the edge of the gray Baltic.

It was the intrepid Orthodox apostles from Salonika, Cyril and Methodius, who themselves brought Christianity to the empire and thus made it one of the first Slav groups to adhere to civilized Europe's faith. But another Asiatic incursion—this time of the fierce and dashing Magyars—cut communications with the beams of eastern light that radiated from Constantinople. It was a decisive development. Bohemia turned its eyes toward Rome, adopted the Latin rites, and linked its future to the West in allegiance to the Holy Roman Empire. Slovakia, conquered by the Magyars, lay inert and hapless. With the conversion of their Hungarian overlords, the Slovaks were also attached to the faith of Rome, but they no longer participated in the cultural, economic, and temperamental evolution of the Czechs. Originally there was no distinction between the two. Magyar conquest brought about the differentiation of the Czechs and Slovaks out of the Slavonic nation in the center of the European land mass.

That was in the tenth century. Prince Vaclav, the good King

Wenceslaus of the Christmas carol and Czechoslovakia's national saint, pursued the newly imposed trend of looking West, not East, and brought his people into ever closer relations with their Germanic neighbors. They were not always comfortable relations. Sometimes the Germanic will to supremacy engulfed the sturdy, stocky Slavs; sometimes, through the intricate politics of the Holy Roman Empire as much as through the force of arms, Prague was the seat of dominion. But in this ebb and flow, the learning of German monks, the artistry of Italian craftsmen, the graceful engineering of French architects, moved freely into Bohemia and Moravia and merged with the stream of Slav development.

Although there seems to have been relatively little dilution of the Slavic racial strains below the level of the aristocracy, there was a thorough permeation of cultural life and of temperament. The thrift, the industry, the solidly sensible outlook of the Czechs, who scorn romantic bravura in favor of efficient organization, have no counterparts in the characteristic images of other Slavs. They seem to reflect an absorption of Germanic mental habits, an over-layer of Teutonic precision and tidiness without the underlayer of grandiose Teutonic reverie.

More intimately involved with the life of western Europe than were any other Slavs, the Czechs were also more acutely torn by the strains and upheaval that racked the continent. They shared richly in the early flowering of the Renaissance, and wholeheart-edly, if ruinously, in the Reformation. Under the influence of Wycliffe, the Czech Jan Hus preached fargoing religious reforms at the very beginning of the fifteenth century. Hus, rector and professor at the University of Prague, combined his teachings with political and social reforms and an assertion of Czech nationality against pervasive Germanic influence, which was becoming dominant. The austere fire of his spirit was consumed in flames—he was burned at the stake in Constance on July 6, 1415—but not before his demands for purification and regeneration had kindled an ardent belligerence that was to spread until it eventually laid much of the continent in ashes.

The Hussite movement which followed his death erupted into an armed insurrection in the Czech lands. The people flocked to its banners and a great spiritual ferment swept the nation. It produced the famous slogan "Truth prevails," to which the Czechoslovak Republic pledged itself once more when the nation was reconstituted. The ideas were not so linked to national revival, however, that their appeal was limited to those who used the Czech tongue. Martin Luther was inspired by them. The terrifying amalgam of spiritual passion, cruelty, idealism, pride, greed, faith, torture, dignity, hope, and destruction that was the Reformation and the wars of religion was unleashed on Europe. But the Czechs, who were the first to rise, were the first to be shattered. The Turks stormed the doors of central Europe, and in 1526 Ferdinand Hapsburg was elected King of Bohemia as the Christian nations momentarily drew together to repulse the imminent menace of the infidel. Thus the Counter Reformation gained its footing in Bohemia, intermittently persecuting Protestants with zealous aggression and tolerating a quiescent coexistence.

After that, there was only a final gasping outburst of Czech self-assertion. It began when a delegation of Protestant Czech noblemen threw two representatives of the Catholic Austrian emperor from a window of the Hradcany Palace above Prague. That famed defenestration led to the Thirty Years' War, but the Czechs succumbed to a crushing defeat at the battle of White Mountain two years later. The Austrian victory was secured with a drastic fury that nearly wiped out the nation forever.

For the following 300 years, the Czechs were reduced to submissive vassaldom, their language and their identity perilously preserved only in the rustic folklore of peasants. That disaster left a deep imprint on Czech character, producing a pacific stubbornness, a resignation, a thick absorptive wrapping of pliability around a slim hard core of reserved determination that was never to be shed. The centures gnawed the pillars of Austrian power that had imposed Czechoslovakia's collapse long before that power toppled. The result of those 300 years was the Good Soldier Schweik.

Schweik was a comic invention of the Czech writer Jaroslav Hašek, who created him shortly after the First World War, when the Hapsburgs had been swept away and Czechoslovakia, once more united, took its own tint upon the map of Europe. A pudgy, angelic-faced rascal, the unwilling soldier represented to Hašek's countrymen the mirrored image of their own hearts and minds drawn sharp with brutal comedy. Schweik was a sly and tricky character, steadfast only in his search for undisturbed, untrammeled comfort of body and mind, but Czechs do not disown his pretension of being a roguishly ignoble national hero. They laugh at him, and they admire him, and they say with a half-ashamed, half-delighted wink, "There is a lot of Schweik in all of us." Schweik's triumphant weapon against his bombastic persecutors was relentless amiability. He grinned, and served, and agreed until he agreed them out of their wits and wormed himself out of their grasp. His devilish, insidious, inventive patience may not have been the way of honor, but it worked wonders as the way of survival. It was a strategy of active submission—not trying to struggle to the top of the heap, but wriggling around the bottom in secret contempt until the top dogs lost their balance and fell crashing from their proud heights. Now that Moscow and its Communist viceroys rule their country, Czechs have not lost their esteem for Schweik.

Another effect of deep consequence resulting from the Czechs' Armageddon at White Mountain was an infusion of large minorities in the population. Along with the reimposition of Catholicism, Austria made harsh efforts to Germanize the Czechs. Most of the Czech aristocracy and intelligentsia were killed or exiled, the population was decimated, and Germans and Austrians moved in to take their places. They established themselves more or less throughout the province of Bohemia and Moravia, for the lands were reduced to a mere province, producing a jumble of ethnic geography but without actually assimilating the Slav peasantry or merging with them into a common culture. Except for the smallest villages, there were people of Germanic origin everywhere, but they concentrated in the cities and in mountainous border areas that enclose the western end of the country. Some Germans had moved in to settle on the border long before, during the thirteenth century, but now they dominated the region. The ill-defined area, never an administrative unit, came to be called the Sudetenland, after the name of its mountains.

The two people most responsible for the revival of a Czechoslovak state out of the European jigsaw of 1918 were Tomáš Garrigue Masaryk and Woodrow Wilson. In accordance with Wilson's principles of self-determination and his concern for minority rights, Czechoslovakia's borders were drawn on a basis of compromise among ethnic lines, ancient claims, and twentieth-century politics. In the part of Silesia assigned to Czechoslovakia, there was an important Polish minority. The Carpatho-Ukraine, the skinny eastern tail of the new polliwog-shaped country, was populated largely by Ruthenians and Ukrainians. Under the special minority treaties, Germans, Poles, Ruthenians, and other groups that dotted the land had special rights, and these led to endless bickering. Like the rest of central Europe, Czechoslovakia had a stew of nationalities. But no matter how the pot boiled, each morsel kept its own flavor and there was precious little melting down.

Wilson's noble ideals of tolerance and indulgence had soured by the time the uneasy "eternal peace" that lasted a scant twenty-one years gave way to World War II. Much more drastic weapons were applied to the minorities problem after 1945. The Soviet Union sliced off the Carpatho-Ukraine and swallowed it. Most of the Germans were deported. The Nazis had already killed most of the Jews. Border adjustments were made with Poland, making the frontier coincide more neatly with the ethnic line. Czechoslovakia was left with a more homogeneous population than it had had since the days of the Premyslides—only the rivalry between Czechs and Slovaks was left to sow ethnic strife. The disgruntled German deportees provided a new source of quarrel, for they found it hard to renounce Hitler's annexation of the Sudetenland in the Reich. But they could only carp and complain from beyond the German borders, and with time their whining demands subsided into mere professional politicking of patent futility.

So far as Czechoslovakia is concerned, the country's frontiers are now satisfactory. An exception must be made, of course, for

Slovak separatism, intensified by the Nazi wartime creation of an autonomous Slovak state disconnected from the Nazi "protectorate" over occupied Bohemia and Moravia. But with the progress of economic integration, and under fierce Communist suppression of "bourgeois nationalism," which in the Slovak case means separatist yearnings, the pressures for division of the country have diminished to an unobtrusive mumbling.

If the political distinctions are fading, however, nature has made ineradicable differences between the Czech and Slovak lands. The country lies flat across the middle of Europe, its 14,000,000 people squeezed into 49,358 square miles, a little less than New York State. It is a thin and long country, so that a traveler following precisely a single line of latitude across it can see with clarity the change from a land warmed by Atlantic breezes to a land bundled against the harsh air of the eastern steppes. The mountains of the West are green and amiable, rolling down into the bright valleys and gentle horizons of Bohemia. The Tatras rise higher in the North, marching eastward to join at last the stern Carpathians. But south of their protective wall, the surging Bohemian fields give way to the broader plains of Moravia, good, even soil that flows in comfort to the edge of the dark Slovakian forests. There, in Slovakia, the land breaks sharply, jutting craggy peaks and steep valleys where soil cannot sprawl but must cling if it will stay to mantle earth's rocky crust. With each step eastward the going is tougher, the winds more vindictive, the path more forbidding. Winter is colder in Slovakia, life is poorer, all that will draw nourishment there must be hardier and more tenacious.

Shoved away at the bumpy end of the line, Slovakia has always been somewhat isolated, cut off from the swirling currents of Europe by its mountains. But all of Czechoslovakia is landlocked in the most graphic sense, surrounded by ranges, now lower and now higher, that ring it like an uneven fence. Geographically, it is the very solar plexus of Europe, equidistant from the Baltic, the North Sea, the Black Sea, and the Adriatic. Many of the great rivers of Europe, the superhighways of the ages, spring as freshets and streams rolling down Czechoslovakia's slopes. The Elbe, the

Oder, the Vistula, the Vltava (more widely known abroad by its German name, Moldau), rise there. The Morava, the Váh, the Hron, the Tisza, whose waters swell the mighty Danube as it pushes across Europe just south of Czechoslovakia, have their source in this compressed watershed that feeds so many distant seas.

Like the rivers themselves, their spreading valleys have been paths for the march of people. Bismarck once said that he who controls Bohemia controls Europe, for Bohemia is the crossroads of the continent. Technology has changed modern strategy, and politics has made of Prague an Eastern city on the fringe of the West instead of a Western city on the approach to the East. But it still looks in both directions, still stirs itself to be a central point from which the many arms of commerce can reach out and touch the entire world.

Because of this crossroads position, the landlocked Czechs have always tended to look abroad rather than to concentrate inward upon themselves. It has been a disadvantage—constant exposure to conquest and alien pressure—and an advantage. Contact with so many, varied peoples brought them early the cultural and economic benefits of exchange. It is a small country, but trade enriched it and encouraged earnest development of both its natural and human resources.

Repressed by the centuries of Hapsburg overlordship, Czechs streamed abroad in search not only of a better living but also of adventure and opportunity for self-development. Many returned. They are a people who have seen something of the world. In the nineteenth century, Slovaks, too, emigrated in large numbers, driven by hungers that their Hungarian masters' neglect did nothing to appease.

Their worldly contacts gave the Czechs some small substitute for the experience in self-government which their history denied. The three centuries of national oblivion constituted the period when the nation-state was taking shape in other countries, when traditions that underlie modern government and administration were accreting. From the end of the Kingdom of Bohemia until the end of the First World War, they had no chance to practice the art of ruling.

What was left of medieval and Renaissance tradition was comparatively liberal. There had been periods of great cultural flourishing in Bohemia. The Hussite campaign had instilled a deep, if sometimes buried, awareness of freedom and of the puritanical respect for a clean spiritual independence. The Counter Reformation succeeded in reimposing Catholicism, but it never stirred again the velvety mysticism and the sensuous lightness of heart toward this mortal life that characterize so many Catholic peoples. There had not, of course, been democracy in the modern sense, but there was an egalitarianism in Hus's teachings and a sense of self-imposed restraint which are part of the philosophical roots of the democratic outlook.

The fact that all the nobility was alien after 1620 sharpened the feelings of hostility toward autocracy. Also, the development of industry and commerce produced a class of burghers, that middle class with something to lose and something to gain whose existence is so conducive to moderate government.

The kind of government which Czechoslovakia chose when at last, in the twentieth century, it had a chance to choose was also conditioned by timing. The Austrian monarchy, which had been so fierce at first, had long since been running downhill. In the middle of the nineteenth century, Czech revival began first with literature, then music, and lastly politics. By then, Austrian rule in Bohemia had grown so slack, so bumbling, so fusty and dusty, that no wild-eyed revolutionaries were required to challenge it. Czech intellectuals developed a national council, political parties mushroomed, and the step from tutelage to power was only a pace. It was no accident that Tomáš Masaryk, the country's founding father, was a professor, not a soldier or a plotter.

Under Masaryk, Czechoslovakia adopted an eminently democratic constitution, guaranteed all manner of freedoms, and set about contriving social reforms to give the citizen the protection that modern society demands. Theoretically it was a model state, the model of democracy that looms in the minds of those who ask how could it go Communist.

But the facts were stubborn and pugnacious. Severe world depression rocked the new state with bitterness. The old landed estates were for the most part broken up, but there were greater and more powerful concentrations of industrial wealth set against unemployment. City poverty may be several degrees above rural hunger on some absolute scale of indigence, but it is always more racking and more degrading.

Political parties proliferated, and the politicians haggled and quarreled as though they'd been born to the caucus room, but their antics scarcely inspired popular devotion to their excessive variety of banners. The minorities question plagued every search for harmony, and the pestilent problem was greatly exacerbated with its direct links to the precarious international situation between the wars.

Czechoslovakia sought to base its security on alliances and on the sweet vision of European concert that found its incarnation in the spastic, disconcerted League of Nations. Nothing availed against the menace of Germany, a menace that growled louder and louder for many uneasy years before it pounced.

During those years, a regular 10 per cent of the electorate voted Communist. Bolshevism had no allure for the rest of the people, but there was a much broader spread of warm sympathy for the Soviet Union. In part, it was the old Pan-Slav affection for Mother Russia, an echo from the heartstrings of a Slavic people so long under Germanic and Magyar thumbs. In part, it was admiration of a machinery-minded people for enormous Soviet industrial construction. And especially, it was a common fear of Germany, a fear that crystallized sharply at Munich, when the Soviet Union seemed willing to go to Czechoslovakia's aid but France and Britain refused.

The choice for Czechoslovakia at Munich was to submit and to be swallowed, or to resist and to be chewed to bits. The first course—the one Neville Chamberlain acclaimed as "peace in our time"—brought the country out of World War II with a comparative minimum of destruction, but with a broken spirit. Czechs, who almost all regretted not having fought for their freedom when it was challenged from outside in 1938, could not bring themselves to fight each other over freedom in the brief, chaotic days of the 1948 coup, much less to lunge out for a lost freedom when their Hungarian neighbors arose in 1956. The moment of decision had been shunned and the will to decide frittered away. Never again were the issues to be so clear. Czechoslovakia settled down at mid-century with the long view for consolation—the times of past brilliance were visibly memorialized in the magnificent buildings that had endured so many changes of regime, and their stones looked solid enough to outlast more changes however long it takes. Libuse's prophecy of a great and happy nation, Czechs told themselves, still holds out a distant hope.

Tangible reminders that a nation, however oppressed, can survive the despair of its people are planted handsomely all over Prague and in many other parts of Czechoslovakia. Although it has all the facilities of a modern city, central Prague is a breath-taking museum of marvels men have wrought in stone throughout the centuries. Once the seat of the Holy Roman Empire was in Hradcany Palace, and the palace, with its lace-vaulted ceilings, its solemnly spired cathedral, its somber halls and crooked lanes, its doll's-house cottages for the retinue of emperors, is still there.

The bridge that Charles IV built in the fourteenth century to span the Vltava, with its time-blackened tower gate and its saintly procession of heroes and martyrs in graceful surveillance of the living city, is still there. The awesome clock on the tower of the Old City Hall still ticks off the minutes, the days, and the seasons with a flash of glowing color and an hourly repetition of the cycle of eternity as it has done for hundreds of years. Whenever there is a festive occasion, Prague's best monuments are illuminated, and it is possible then, looking up to fairy castles and domes shimmering in the darkness, to see that time is much greater than the cares of the moment. Wherever the eye falls, there is a green-and-gold cupola, a plume, and a pennant of metal marking ancient exultation, a gaslit arcade hiding shadows of the ages. Prague is a uniquely beautiful city, crowded on the Vltava's steep banks in a way that spreads panoramic loveliness around the turn of every corner.

Little besides this antique splendor was vouchsafed to Czecho-

slovakia by its past. Czech culture was erased at the start of the
seventeenth century, and it only began to revive in the middle of
the last century. The first national expressions took a musical form
—and that is why the works of Smetana and Dvořák, the National Opera House with its inscription testifying that the nation
exists, arouse such emotion in Czech hearts. Literature erupted
later, first in pastoral poems and tales of country life, then with
Alois Jirásek in historical epics. There was a burgeoning of cultural activity with independence, producing a creative community of whom Karel Capek was best known abroad. Franz Kafka,
though he lived in Prague and had a Czech name, was a German,
wrote in German, and thought mystical, questing, restless German ideas which do not assort themselves to a Czech point of
view. Czechs do not claim Kafka as one of their contributions
to world literature.

Nor is their religion a heritage of national continuity. Now, 75
per cent of the people are Catholic, but religion is more of a personal force than a bond of community. The deep emotional pull
that keeps Polish and Hungarian eyes always turning to Rome
has far less compulsion in Czechoslovakia. The Protestant minority
lives comfortably in this climate of temperate devotion. Hearts
have cooled from the days of vicious religious battle, and reverence though perhaps not piety has cooled as well. In the place
of institutionalized passion, their past developed in the Czechs a
civic sense, an ethic of orderly, decent behavior, a taste for moderation, and an ability for adjustment and compromise, which
were essential to the calm of a shattered and jumbled nation.

When Czechoslovakia was liberated at the end of World War
II, its President, Eduard Beneš, saw the need for moderation and
compromise as greater than ever before. Soviet troops, accompanied by some Czech legions, moved westward across the country
shoving back the Wehrmacht. The United States Third Army,
under General George Patton, reached Plzen and could easily
have gone on to free Prague but for the high-level political agreement which had drawn beforehand the lines where advancing
Allied armies were to meet. Perhaps it would have made little

difference in the end if Patton had been allowed to make the triumphant liberator's entry into the capital. But the fact that he was not reflected acutely the position in which the Czechoslovak government found itself when it returned from exile.

The Soviet colossus loomed on the east with a power it never had before. The Red Army, although it withdrew soon enough from Czechoslovak soil, remained in Poland and East Germany on the north and northeast, in Hungary and Austria on the south. Only on the short southwestern border with the American-occupied zone of Germany did the Czechs have direct contact with the Western powers. At the first general election, in 1946, the Communist Party received 38.1 per cent of the vote, and the parties of the Left together won a majority. Both internal and external politics demanded good relations with the Soviet Union. As in many western European countries, the Communist Party was included in the governing coalition, and Czechoslovak leaders sought to make their country a living example of coexistence, a key span of that famous "bridge between East and West" that rose as solid as a politician's metaphor.

It was, of course, a bridge of illusion, as well as of sighs. The Communists took over the police, infiltrated the administration, and in three years made their snatch for power. Devotees of historical speculation can mine a wealth of might-have-beens from the rich lode which the situation presented. Beneš vacillated, the Army waited for orders, the bewildered people looked numbly for leadership that never came. In a few days it was over, and then it was simply a matter of tidying up and making the country a people's democracy—that is, a Soviet satellite.

Starting late, the Communist regime hurried to catch up with its brethren. The first period was painful, but resistance was disorganized from the start, people told each other resignedly that once more Czechs were constrained to making the best of a bad thing, and the regime managed quickly to consolidate its power. After that, it was simply a matter of development along the lines laid down by Moscow with a certain number of practical deviations accorded because of the country's advanced industrial capacity. Like others, the Czechoslovak Communists had their round of bloody purges and then settled down to becoming a technological hub of the Communist world. The leaders showed a certain canniness in their economic relations with other Communist states and, after Stalin's death, a cleverness in manipulating economic indulgence and political orthodoxy so as to get the most possible from their own people at the least cost to absolute control.

On the surface at least, every evidence is that Czechoslovakia is resigned to its fate. Certainly, there has been no sign that it is ever likely to provide the source for a challenge to Communist orthodoxy, either through reform or outright resistance. Once again, the predominant spirit is Schweik's—lie low, make out as best you can, and hide the patient flame that burns in the heart. Beneath the surface, every evidence is that the flame still burns.

As in several other Communist countries, the greatest urge to tame tyranny, so long as ouster is not possible, seems to well in the youth. It is not a remembrance of a better past, but a dissatisfaction with the present, and the eternal pressure of youthful ideals for a better future, that works this yeast. Outright suppression, indoctrination, careful controls of education, can limit the growth of this ferment, but they have not been able to kill it. Intellectuals, too, especially young poets and painters and the like, gasp for a breath of freedom and a chance to let their minds wander across the wide world.

For the time being—and everyone expects it will be a long time beyond the horizon of the visible future—Czechs are convinced that there is nothing they can do. They looked on with a combination of great, mute sympathy and a rather smug disapproval of foolhardiness when the Hungarians revolted. They watched, with awe and skeptical disbelief, when the Poles struggled, and they decided with Schweik that sacrifice is pointless. Survival is the thing, for glory fades and only from life can the seed of hope ever spring.

There was an eastern European story at the time of the upheavals in 1956, probably apocryphal, since it put the psychological facts so patly, but alleged to be true. It concerned a Polish and a Czech architect, both delegates to an international congress in the West. In that foreign atmosphere, they held a conversation more open than it might have been at home.

"What's the matter with you Czechs?" asked the Pole. "Why do you let the Hungarians and Poles do all the struggling for freedom? Don't you care about it?"

"Oh yes," replied the Czech, "we do. We want freedom more than anything else in the world, with all our hearts. But you don't understand. In my country it is forbidden to demonstrate against the government."

The story reflects the bitterness of Czechoslovakia's neighbors at a time of martyrdom, but it also reflects both Czech yearning and Czech restraint.

In the meantime, the country's economic development is progressing; certain reforms in such fields as health and social welfare have been achieved to the benefit of the population. There are dark spots and a few light ones on Czechoslovakia's landscape, but mostly there are great gray stretches, bleak but tolerable. Czechoslovakia does not seem likely ever to lead a parade for freedom, nor even to join in the vanguard. But if the parade ever forms up and really seems to be going somewhere, it cannot be doubted that Czechoslovakia will swing joyously into line. What the future holds will not be decided in Czechoslovakia, but the people console themselves with a thought upon which other eastern Europeans are not so sure they can rely. They are quite certain that Czechoslovakia has a future.

AUSTRIA AND HUNGARY

Frank Bourgholtzer

Presently diplomatic correspondent for NBC News in Washington, Frank Bourgholtzer has been correspondent and commentator for NBC for thirteen years. As White House correspondent, he covered the hourly progress of the major part of the Truman administration, including the 1948 upset election victory, the Wake Island conference and later dismissal of General MacArthur, the attempted assassination at the Blair House. When General Eisenhower gave up his NATO assignment and returned to America to run for President, Bourgholtzer was assigned to cover him on a twenty-four-hour basis, beginning June 1, 1952.

In March of 1953, Bourgholtzer went to Paris as Bureau Chief and subsequently held the bureaus in Bonn and Vienna, where he and his family lived in half of a small Schloss. This overseas assignment included coverage of such events as the Berlin uprising in 1953, the Berlin foreign ministers' conference, the coronation of Queen Elizabeth II, the defeat of the European Defense Community by the French Parliament, the summit conference in Geneva, the Hungarian Revolution and subsequent events in the satellites, especially Poland, with time out to cover the 1956 Republican and Democratic elections at home.

Before joining NBC, Bourgholtzer spent three years with the Wall Street Journal *and worked for various weeklies and dailies in Indiana. He is a native of New York City and a graduate of Indiana University, married and the father of two boys.*

AUSTRIA AND HUNGARY

The Russian soldiers who defeated Hitler's men in the East, whose orgies were described by their propaganda officers as "liberation," crossed into Austria from Hungary at the town of Köszeg and, on Easter Sunday 1945, occupied the village of Gloggnitz, at the foot of the Semmering Pass on the main highway south from Vienna.

After two days, the village's elder statesman set out, coatless but carrying his walking stick, to find the Russian local commander and plead for a respite from the Red soldiers' depredations. It was a fateful stroll down the village street, involving a succession of near miracles which led directly to the true freedom, independence, and prosperity of Austria.

The old man was Dr. Karl Renner, senior member of the Social Democratic party of Austria and first Chancellor of the Austrian Republic after the First World War. The rise of Austrian nazism had forced him from active politics in 1934. He had retired to Gloggnitz and had been living there ever since. On Easter Tuesday, as he stepped out to find the Russian command post, he was seventy-four years old.

The first Russians Dr. Renner met, instead of molesting him or sending him back home, sent him to another village, a mile and a half away. There he encountered Russian officers who recognized his name, and they dispatched him in an army truck to the headquarters at Hochwolkersdorf, between Sopron and Wiener Neustadt. There he met Russian officers who not only knew of him but respected him and devoted the evening to discussing the possibilities of a new civil regime for Austria. The discussions went on through the following day. By the time Dr. Renner was allowed to return to Gloggnitz, the Russians had promised him full support in setting up a provisional government and had breezily accepted his stern admonition that he would in no sense be a Russian agent, but would be responsive only to the will of the Austrian people.

The direct result of all this was that Austria received immediately a central government, inspired by a singular leader, who made good his promise to be the agent of no foreign power. The Russians tried hard to capture Austria for communism, as they tried elsewhere, but they were destined to fail from the moment Karl Renner decided Russian soldiers were a menace, took up his walking stick, and stepped out onto the lane in Gloggnitz on Easter Tuesday 1945.

At about the time that Renner was being taken by Russian truck to Hochwolkersdorf, other Russian Army vehicles were transporting a Hungarian provisional government from Debrecen to Budapest. This provisional government had been set up in Debrecen by the Russians after their political officers had roamed the countryside in search of former opposition politicians, who had been forced to retire, or hide out, because, in both countries, regimes of the extreme Right had taken power.

In Budapest and in Vienna the provisional governments at first appeared remarkably non-Communist. The Debrecen Cabinet, moved intact to Budapest, contained two Communists, two Smallholders, two Social Democrats, and one Peasant party member, plus five nonparty members, one of whom later turned out to have been a Communist previously. The Renner Cabinet in Vienna contained three Communists, four Social Democrats, four People's party members, and two nonparty members.

The Communist leadership in each country was turned over to men who had been thoroughly schooled in Moscow, flown into Budapest and Vienna at the earliest possible moment. Mátyás Rákosi was Moscow's top man in Hungary, and Johann Koplenig was the leader in Austria.

In the next four years, parallel pressures were applied to Austria and to Hungary, and in 1949 both countries held vital general elections. Practically all the eligible voters in each country went to the polls. In Austria, the two big coalition parties—People's party and Socialists—gained 144 seats. A Right-wing bloc had 16 seats and the Left bloc, including Communists, only 5. In Hungary at this same time there was only one ballot and one party. The Communist Party joined with some Communist-front groups to form a so-called Hungarian People's Independence Front and received 95.6 per cent of the vote. The Communists had won Hungary and, although it took them a few more years to realize it, they had lost Austria.

A completely satisfactory explanation of these diametrically opposed results from parallel policies has not yet been offered. They are partly explained by the different situations which prevailed in the two countries, and partly by the long run of history, which was the context of the events.

Without a doubt, a vital part of the explanation is the fact that the Austrians had Dr. Karl Renner and that he chose the moment and the reason he did to go looking for the Russians.

Never, since Árpád's Magyar tribes decided to end their roaming and settle down between the Danube and the Tisza, and the first Babenberg came along to give Austria a national character, has the Austro-Hungarian border been so well-defined a dividing line between Asia and Europe. Neatly plowed rows of earth are planted with explosive mines instead of grain, all the way from Freistadt to Bratislava to Maribor.

In the midst of the twentieth-century revolution, Hitler rechristened Austria with the name "Ostmark," originally bestowed by Charlemagne to signify the eastern reach of his empire. It was both a symbol and a practical element in Hitler's version of *Drang nach Osten*, the push to the East which set up Stalin's more fateful roll-back of the West.

A visitor in Austria's western provinces, at a ski lodge beside Kitzbühel's Hahnenkamm, or loafing in the sun beside one of the lakes of Salzkammergut, feels only the most tentative suggestion of this "East wind," feels it, probably, only as an accent to the basic Alpine sense of isolation. But, in Vienna, in the lobby of Sacher's, or at the Opera, or afterward at the White Chimney-

sweep tavern, one knows that the border is not far away. At a
municipal *Schwimmbad*, where the only beer served is the city-
owned, therefore "socialized," *Stadtbraue*, or on the Kärntner-
strasse, where coffeehouse is giving way to espresso, it is clear
that the spirit of Mozart and Haydn may remain, but the age of
Franz Josef has vanished.

At Nickelsdorf, the pastorale that is Burgenland is a taste of
old Hungary, but once past the Hungarian customs agents, the
road to Budapest beckons through the forest ahead, and the
striped gate drops down behind. Then the unparalleled atmosphere of the Communist People's Republic becomes an oppressive
reality.

In Budapest, although the hand of Austro-Hungarian Baroque
stylists is evident everywhere, the arm of the new Eastern master
is firmly around the country's shoulder.

Hungarians and Austrians are alike in their consciousness of
the long-term currents of history. This is a European characteristic. Central Europeans appreciate that the current flows forward
into the future, that their position tomorrow will no more be that
of today than today's is that of yesterday.

Today's Hungarians and Austrians have widely divergent de-
sires, problems, pleasures, hopes, and prospects. They are like
apartment-house neighbors, each aware that the other is beyond
the thin partition, privy at times to the family arguments by virtue
of the fact that sounds carry, but thoroughly cut off from participation in each other's affairs. The tragic days of the Hungarian
Revolution in 1956 made this divorce of interests brutally clear.
Austrians watched the struggle build, burst forth, and die,
watched with truly aching hearts and desire to help, but could
do no more than care for the wounds of those who came, defeated,
seeking shelter and asylum.

Someday, the balance of pressure will change the nature of
the border once again, perhaps to repel the Russian toward the
east, perhaps to yield further westward. Austrians know this. Hungarians know it. This is the common knowledge that shapes the
way of life everywhere in central Europe, will shape it in the

future as it has in the past, ever since their ancestors put down the roots that led to their existence today.

The phrase *"Biegen, aber nicht brechen"*—"Bend, but do not break"—is supposed to describe the plasticity with which Austrians have sustained their individuality through ages of buffeting from East and West. It is about as valid as two other popularly ascribed national characteristics: *Gemütlichkeit,* the effusive, native charm which sometimes seems insincere, but isn't, completely; and *Schlamperei,* an attitude of regret at something spoiled, expressed with a sigh as "Ah, well, there's nothing to be done about it" (*"Nichts zu tun"*).

The Austrians of today are the German core of the old Empire, and the trend of events is making them more rather than less German. The iron curtain that cuts off Czechoslovakia, Hungary, and Yugoslavia has barred the normal intercourse which, in the past, intermingled all these and other racial strains.

Politically, the Republic of Austria was set up after World War I under the "self-determination of peoples" principle that dismembered the Hapsburg Empire. The Constitution of 1920, providing for a parliamentary form of government, has been reinstituted, minus certain features added by the Nazis. The nine Austrian states, or *Länder,* have their own local governments and are united in a federation with its national parliament in the capital, Vienna, plus a President elected by universal suffrage. The power and operation of government are in the hands of a Chancellor and his Cabinet, chosen by the usual parliamentary methods, but with a special Austrian twist.

This peculiarity stems from two political realities that have controlled Austrian affairs since the end of the Second World War. One is the near parity of the two main parties, the Catholic, conservative Austrian People's Party, and the Socialist Party of Austria. The other, which is passing now, was the desperate need for unity in the face of occupation. Instead of the stronger party taking all the power, the two main parties have united to share the power and to share the jobs. The Austrian bureaucracy is divided at every level in proportion to the relative electoral strength of the parties at each election. This system, known as *Proporz,* is an outstanding example of the *biegen* part of the alleged Austrian slogan.

During the first fifteen years after liberation by the Russians from the East and by the Western Allies from the West, the People's party held a slight edge, although, curiously enough, all three Presidents have been Socialist: Dr. Karl Renner, Dr. Theodor Körner, elected when Renner died, and Dr. Adolf Schärf, elected when Körner died. This parliamentary edge was reduced in the 1959 elections, and the Socialists broke the monopoly the People's party had held on the two offices of Chancellor and Foreign Minister. Socialist Bruno Kreisky took over a reorganized foreign ministry from Leopold Figl, but Julius Raab of the People's party remained as Chancellor.

Music is, far and away, the basic element of Austrian cultural life: the Opera, the Philharmonic, the Volksoper, the Salzburg Festival, the Boys' Choir, not to mention the *Schrammelmusik,* the folk music of the mountaineers and of the Slav and Hungarian admixtures, and the cabaret satirists. Vienna and Salzburg welcome new performers of ability, but only in performance of the classics. Austrians are skeptical of modern music.

In the Age of the Common Man, that symbol of Austrian culture—the Vienna Opera—deserves a second look. The fact is that only a small fraction of Austria's population really patronizes the Opera—or ever has. This fraction goes to it so intensely that the fever of participation is spread among the nonparticipants, but most Austrians never even see the inside of the Opera House. The entertainment of the people is the cinema, and there is a special Austrian variety, known as the *Heimatfilm,* a sort of hayseed rococo. Increasingly, there is television.

At the height of the Empire, Austria was already involved in industrialization, while the surrounding nations, kept in the position of raw-materials suppliers, complained that Vienna treated them as colonies. Since the sloughing off of the Empire, she has moved more rapidly toward industrialization, but away from production of fully finished goods, because the change of fortune put her into a competition, for which she wasn't ready, with western Europe's experienced industry.

There is a psychological explanation for the progress in Austria's economy. Thirty years ago, it was considered to be utterly without hope of achieving viability. Today, it is considered, and is, completely workable. The causes are three: first, the contribution made by Hitler, who built up Austrian industry when he was planning in terms of a thousand years; second, the American Marshall Plan aid, which restored this base after the Second World War and helped to modernize it; and third, a point of view which, after 1945, became as firmly optimistic as it had been pessimistic in 1918–38.

Austria has great wealth in water power, which is being increasingly developed, and a relatively new resource in oil. Her industries include iron and steel, chemicals, pulp and paper, machinery and vehicles, electrical machinery and equipment. The trend is steadily toward iron and steel semimanufactured and capital goods. Tourism is a growing industry.

The shape of today's Austria was ordained, if not foreseen, in 1918, when the Hapsburg Empire was dismembered. The chaos which followed, including revolutions in 1918 and 1934, and the Anschluss with Germany, were part of the struggle to identify and regain a national equilibrium, and much that happened then was transitory.

It is proper to consider that today's Austria is as new as her rebirth in 1945, in the sense that "little" Austria managed to transform the burden of the past into a heritage for future guidance.

More than one observer of Hungary has remarked that the history of Europe, if not of the world, would have been vastly different had there been as many Hungarians as there have been Germans. The same has been said of others, notably the Serbs, but the implication is valid, if the generalization isn't: Hungarians make their presence felt.

There are close to 10 million Hungarians, and it is easy to hold the misconception that their cohesion is basically racial. Their Magyar heritage comes directly from the Asian tribes moving eastward through the Carpathians, with this land as their goal. But the tie that really binds Hungarians together is the Magyar language, a unique tongue that makes 100 per cent Hungarians from

Czechs, Austrians, Slavs, Spaniards, Italians, or any others who find themselves absorbed into the culture.

A revolutionary spirit is strong in these people, but, for the most part, it has been revolutionary in the nationalist sense. The Magyars habitually, traditionally, and constantly resisted foreign encroachment and domination. At one point, they resisted it so successfully that their borders reached from Poland to the Adriatic Sea, and Vienna was their capital. Today Hungary is a people's democracy, a form defined by Hungary's most famous Communist, Mátyás Rákosi, as a "dictatorship of the proletariat without the Soviet form." In other words, the Communist Party, known in Hungary as the Hungarian Socialist Worker's Party, runs the country.

The Central Statistical Office in Budapest, in its summary of Hungary's present situation, puts it this way: "In Hungary's political and social life, the most decisive role is played by the Hungarian Socialist Worker's Party, which exercises political control over the work of the state, economic, and social bodies."

The form resembles Western parliamentary systems in that there is a Parliament, elected by universal suffrage, which chooses a Council of Ministers to operate the government. There is, however, only one list of candidates at election time. The Chairman of the Council of Ministers is Premier. A Presidium, whose chief officer is the President of Hungary, is chosen by the Parliament as its permanent representative between the traditionally brief parliamentary sessions.

Political power is managed by the First Secretary of the Party, who may also be Premier, or, in some people's republics, may be President. János Kadar, the Russians' choice to restore communism after the 1956 Hungarian Revolution, held the party leadership as well as the post of Premier for some time, then relinquished the premiership but retained the position of ultimate power, the party direction.

The Party puts its thumb on every aspect of life, cultural pursuits especially, in the name of building socialism. Despite the recent efforts of the Russians to instruct them in culture, Hungarians still believe, as they always have, that they combine the best influences of East and West in their creative arts. However, the communist concept of art as a social tool, to be used in the national, or party, interest, is not entirely foreign to Hungary. The theme of national independence has been a constant current in Hungary's cultural as well as her political life.

The middle centuries of the past millennium produced this deeply rooted nationalism, as Turk and Hapsburg played tug of war with the Hungarian nation. The Turks contributed little or nothing to the Hungarian culture, but the Hapsburgs contributed much, particularly in music and architecture. Haydn was a familiar figure in Budapest and was employed, for most of his life, by the House of Esterházy. Beethoven composed two works especially for the opening of the Budapest Municipal Theater in 1812.

The heights of Hungarian creativity have been reached in poetry, and the most striking figure has been Sándor Petöfi, hero of the wildly romantic episode surrounding the composition of his famous lines: "Rise Magyar." Petöfi read his poem from a platform in front of the National Museum on the fifteenth of March 1848, celebrated as Hungary's Day of Liberation until the advent of the Russians.

The Communists have had some statistical success in spreading the base of culture in Hungary: more books published, more libraries, greater attendance at concerts, theatrical performances, operas, art galleries. Their regime has been in constant battle with the intellectuals and the artists, however, and there has been no sign of a new flowering of Hungarian culture under the Communists. It remains to be seen whether recurring Communist drives against the nonregimentable gypsies will have any permanent effect on the gypsy music, which has carried Hungarian folk music through the years and all over the world.

Communist domination is making a fundamental change in the Hungarian economy, as might be expected from a system based in economic philosophy. A most significant influence is the concept of "socialist division of labor," which means that Hungary is expected to devote its productive energies to those things which it can most efficiently contribute to the entire Moscow-directed camp, abandoning production of and importing from the other people's democracies the things others can produce better or are assigned to make on a specialty basis.

Historically, Hungary has had no natural resources to speak of, a condition modified in the nuclear age by the discovery of uranium in the neighborhood of Pécs. The greatest resource has been its great plain, the Alföld. Some 55 per cent of the population was engaged in agriculture before the war, and, even now, about 45 per cent of the population is out on the farms. Industrial production is a larger element, monetarily, in the national economy, however, with most of the industrial manpower concentrated in what are known as the "engineering industries," in mining, in textile manufacture, and in food processing.

The "socialist division of labor," which decrees, for instance, that Hungary shall make buses, but not passenger automobiles, dates from the great turning point in Communist postwar history, the Twentieth Congress of the Soviet Union Communist Party. Hungary's present economic, political, and social position dates from the "liberation" of Hungary by the Red Army on April 4, 1945, a date which the Communists prefer to Petőfi's as the "national day." It was only in the elections of May 15, 1949, that, all opposition parties having been eliminated, the so-called "Peoples Front" won 95.6 per cent of the votes, and the new constitution of the "People's Republic of Hungary" was adopted. This is the controlling political date of today's Hungary. Its geography was established at the Trianon, in the peace treaty after World War I.

At the height of what Austrians now remember as their "occupation" by Hitler's German government, following the Anschluss, a Viennese remarked snappishly that it was a mere accident that Germans and Austrians spoke the same tongue. It is this "accident" of language, all the same, that defines the entity of postwar Austria, just as it is primarily language which unites the Hungarians.

Both countries have controlled considerable areas of Europe, in their days of aggrandizement, and both Vienna and Budapest have sought, at one time or another, to force German or Magyar on the subjected peoples. When they were cut down to size, after

World War I, territorial losses also cost them portions of their German and Magyar populations. Essentially, however, Austria and Hungary are the remnants of an empire defined by the limits of population which speak German, in the case of Austria, and Magyar, in the case of Hungary.

Racial purity has not been maintained with the language bond. Restless tides of humanity, pulsating for centuries across central Europe, have produced, in both areas, intermixtures of racial backgrounds, Teutonic, Slav, Latin, and Asian, including Magyar.

In Austria, the purest remnants of the Germanic tribes are found in the deepest valleys of the Alps. In Hungary, isolated peasant villages often present an uncomplicated strain of Magyar. The cities of both countries are thoroughly conglomerate.

One of the earliest kings in the region which is now Austria left a mark in history by the outrageous flamboyance of his tastes. It is recorded that he once exacted tribute from Byzantium in the form of a solid-gold bed. This monarch was an Avar. At that time the river Enns was the dividing line between East and West. The Avars ruled an area extending from the Volga to the Elbe and, in this neighborhood, to the Enns. They moved into this Austrian territory when the Lombards moved on south to Italy.

On the other side of the Enns, about the year 500 A.D., the Avars had as neighbors the Bajuvarii, later known as Bavarians, descendants of an earlier Germanic tribe, the Marcomanni.

In common with many of the people of Europe, the Austrians owe to Charlemagne a basic historical debt. The Bavarians, fearing Charlemagne intended to destroy them because of their prosperity, appealed to the Avars for help. Charlemagne moved too fast, however. He conquered Bavaria and gave it to his brother-in-law; then went on and destroyed the Avars.

When they fell, the Avars fell hard, leaving virtually no trace for the historians. It is believed that their last settlement in Austria was in the neighborhood of Petronell, a village on the road from Vienna to Bratislava, bordering on the Danube, near the present Czech border. There is nothing to indicate that the Avars left a mark, racially or otherwise, on today's Austrian population.

There is a Slav proverb: "He vanished like the Avar, neither son nor nephew of his was left."

Preceding the Avars and the Bavarians, there had been the Romans, for whom the Danube was a northern boundary, and before them, Celtic tribes. The Roman emperor Marcus Aurelius died at Vindobona, now Vienna, in 180 A.D. A hundred years or so after the Avars, the Magyars made their first appearance. In a brief foray they managed to wipe out most of the Germanic population before they disappeared again into the East. They were driven back by the Bavarians, who formed the basic stock, racially and linguistically, from which today's Austrians derive. The Magyars, a collection of nomad tribes descended from the Huns, roamed western Asia until the time came for them to make their fabled march westward toward a promised land.

All around Austria, by the year 1000 A.D., central and southeast Europe was settling down into a racial and linguistic pattern, the Bohemians and the Poles to the north, the Southern Slavs to the south (*jug* means "south"). The meeting point of all was Vienna, and all these racial strains appear in the population of Vienna. The people of Austria's border country are similar to those living on the Czech, Hungarian, Yugoslavian, or Italian borders. In Vorarlberg, the people are very much like the Swiss.

Less permanent influences came to the Austrians from Asia Minor, in the Turkish invasions, during which Vienna was twice besieged, and from the West, when Napoleon set up headquarters in the Schönbrunn Palace.

Establishment by the Russians of a rigidly enforced political dividing line, the Iron Curtain, has set up an influence which runs counter to the centuries-long trend of intermixed races and cultures. Movement back and forth to Czechoslovakia, Poland, Hungary, Rumania, and even over Tito's "little Iron Curtain" to Yugoslavia has been severely restricted. The only open borders are with Germany, German-speaking Switzerland, and Italy. There have been waves of refugees, but these, except for the Hungarians in 1956, often have been German-speaking minorities, such as the Sudetenlanders, and as a result, the German character of Austria and its population is in the process of intensification.

The beginnings of Hungary were of a different order from that foreign conquest in which Charlemagne designated his Ostmark and thereby delineated Austria. The region was known, even before the Magyars arrived, as the land of Attila the Hun. The first great Hungarian leader, Árpád, was the spiritual descendant, and was presumed to be a blood descendant, of Attila.

Árpád's tribes were Asian horse-breeding nomads who roamed the steppes in search of grazing land and hunting grounds and fought to win one another's possessions, but never established land frontiers to enclose specified territory. Many tribes were related: the Huns, Avars, Kirghiz, Tatars—and Magyars. All, at one time or another, raided the West, defeated and subjected parts of it, then melted back into the Asian scenery. The Magyars were the only ones to travel West and remain.

Their racial background explains their name. The basic race, living between the Ural and Altai mountains, had two main branches. The Ural Finn-Ugurs were one, and the primitive Altai nationalities, made up of East Turks, West Turks, and Mongols, were the other. The West Turks produced the Ogurs, and their intermingling with the Finn-Ugurs produced a nation called "Megy-Eri," the word *megy* meaning "men." "Megy-Eri" became "Magyar." The people also called themselves "Onogurs," which later evolved into "Ungers," "Ungres," "Hungarians." They inhabited western Siberia.

After the death of Attila, and the rapid decline of the Huns under his successors, the Onogurs began moving south from Siberia and settled for a while in the land the Greeks called Lebedia, between the Caucasus, the Don, and the Kuban.

In 881, Árpád led his Magyar tribes westward toward the land Attila had occupied. The Huns had occupied it for some two hundred years after the inconsequential passage of some Germanic tribes, and before the arrival, two centuries later, of the Avars. In 896, Árpád's Magyars began occupation of the country.

They arrived to find the area between the Danube and Tisza rivers virtually uninhabited. It had been traversed, in all directions, by nearly everyone during the migration periods, and some, like the Huns and Avars, had stayed for a time but left no heirs.

Their graves have yielded evidence of their culture, but, so far as Hungary is concerned, no populations remained to perpetuate it. There probably were some scattered settlements, and the residents probably were Slavs, whom the Magyars assimilated.

Árpád's warriors immediately set about raiding the West. They struck into Bavaria, and south into Lombardy. They sought not to conquer land but to capture booty. Among the treasures carried back to the new Danube-Tisza homeland were Bavarian and Lombard women. Men prisoners were taken, too, for their crafts and talents. These captives mingled Western blood into the Magyar race. Later Magyar leaders led raids farther and farther west, reaching Bremen, Burgundy, and Italy.

A court materialized around the monarchy and attracted many foreigners from Germany and Italy, and, in fact, privileged classes of foreigners were established in the cities.

Colonization was a frequent process in Hungary, and it, too, modified the make-up of the race. In addition to what might be called normal colonization, there were emergency periods when German or Slav immigrants were brought in wholesale to make up for drastic population losses in wars and pestilence.

There was one episode, early in the history of Hungary, when Béla IV decided to seek contact with original Magyars who, legend claimed, had remained in Asia rather than follow Árpád to the West. Two monks were sent on a mission. One returned with a report that he had found the original Magyars, and that they were coming to Hungary to escape the imminent conquest of the world by Genghis Khan. Béla welcomed 40,000 nomad horsemen of the same racial stock as those who originally had arrived with Árpád. The newcomers agreed to help fight off the Tatar invasion, but the result was disaster. The Hungarians had, by now, settled into the land as peasants, and they had only antipathy for these newcomers, nomads who recognized no property boundaries, no property rights. Common ancestry was no palliative, and when the Tatars finally came, the 40,000 Kumans joined them instead of fighting them. In the end, however, they were settled, all together, in the Alföld.

The story of John Hunyadi helps to explain the Hungarian essence. Hunyadi, the son of a vassal, became commander in chief of the armies, scored a remarkable series of military triumphs, and, in the middle of the fifteenth century, was named regent of Hungary at a moment of national crisis. A Magyar historian has written: "They considered him a Magyar because of his appearance, his mentality, his language, and his behavior." Hunyadi actually had been born in Walachia, possibly from a Magyar-Walach union, and one legend said he was actually an illegitimate son of Sigismund, the German emperor. "In any case," the historian wrote, "he himself lived and worked like a Hungarian."

After Hunyadi's time, Hungary knew centuries of depredation. The Turks set up a pasha to rule in Buda. Under the Turks, parts of Hungary lost not only their populations but their very resemblance to populated areas. Farmlands became marshy wastes. Liberation by Austria brought a new suppression, which was even worse. There was mass colonization by non-Hungarians, including tens of thousands of Serbs in the southern areas. Throughout the oppression, the Magyar identity was preserved most jealously in Transylvania, which is, today, not even a part of Hungary.

In 1956, many of the Soviet troops who came to put down the Hungarian rebellion turned out to be Mongols, modern-day neighbors of the area where the Magyars began.

Joseph Wechsberg, writing in Fodor's guide to Austria (one of the best), nominates a line from *Fledermaus* to be Austria's national anthem: "*Glücklich ist, wer vergisst, was nicht mehr zu ändern ist.* [Happy is the man who forgets what can't be changed]."

Wechsberg, in the same piece about Austrian attitudes, describes the "typically Austrian emotion called *Raunzen.*" Says Wechsberg: "A *Raunzer* always has something to complain about. He's got no money or too much of it ('You know the troubles you've got nowadays when you make money'); he's either too fat and sick, or too slim and healthy ('I wouldn't mind being sick for a while, so I could take it easy'). Even the weather is always prefaced by 'too' in Austria: it's either too cold or too hot, too wet or too nice. Austrians are genuinely unhappy when there is nothing to complain about. If the present is bright, they console themselves with the thought of a terrible future."

A visitor to Austria is tempted to look for the exported impression of the country: the blue Danube and the jolly peasants, the overwhelming romance which has been associated with Franz Josef. One who looks for it will find it, the magnificence of Austria's past being so much greater than the present that no Austrian can resist at least an occasional look backward. However, it is probable that the Austrian, when he looks backward toward glory, looks beyond Franz Josef, at least to Maria Theresa.

The late Karl Renner, in a New Year's message, said the Austrian people in 1945 wanted: "self-reliance and independence; no Anschluss at all, neither with the East nor the South, neither with the West nor the North." Author Richard Hiscocks feels that "this change did not mean that the Austrians lost pride in their German cultural heritage, but it did mean that they became increasingly conscious that the German culture of which they were proud could be traced back to an age when the Austrians, not the Prussians, set the tone and determined the character of the German contribution to European civilization."

That age reached its fullest flower under Maria Theresa.

All Austrians living today have known hard times. They have personal memory of heartbreak, privation, betrayal, and indignity. Only in May 1955 did the Austrian of today's living generations acquire the right to throw his weight around. From the time of the First World War until the signing of the State Treaty in 1955, Austria was in subjection to forces beyond her control, political or economic. This history has left a mark, a certain underlying bitterness and suspicion. It is difficult to find a Viennese today who isn't just finished with a lawsuit or just about to start one; in the midst of a lawsuit or about to be sued himself.

Between the wars, there was hopelessness in the attitude of millions of Austrians, but that is gone today, and most Austrians are aware that they have been lucky, all things considered, in the handling they have received from history. There is a realization, now, that the Republic of Austria can survive as a nation. For possibly the first time in all their history, the people of Austria have a

sense of national identity, a sense of being Austrian. This adjustment to circumstance is restoring to Austrians a basic dignity
which was hidden for a while, if not lost.

The sleepy pace so long associated with Vienna is almost gone.
The tempo is picking up. The little, old-world streets are obscured
nowadays by the blaring horns, flaring tempers, and bumper-
locked conglomeration of a traffic jam.

Escape from the city is more than ever necessary and the Vienna woods are still there. The Viennese are in them every weekend. As walkers, they are very German. Many families have acquired automobiles, but the acquisition does not dampen their
enthusiasm for walking; it merely extends their range.

There are community gardens in all sections of Vienna, and
many Viennese have their own garden plots in them, some situated magnificently on the slopes of the Kahlenberg, overlooking
the entire city.

Skiing is the Austrian national sport, but the people indulge
in other sports as well, especially water sports in the huge playground made from the old winding course of the Danube, left
when engineers cut a straight river channel past Vienna.

Carnival is a high point of every year, and the Fasching in Vienna achieves a uniquely elegant dignity with the Opernball. This
is a public affair in the Opera House, to which men wear full-dress
civilian clothing or military uniforms, with all their medals, and
the women wear the year's most pretentious gowns. Crowds of
Viennese who don't go gather outside just to watch the arrivals
and departures.

The quickening pace in Vienna hasn't fully outdistanced the
coffee shop, with its sidewalk tables and old-fashioned interior,
where it is stylish to dawdle over the newspapers, sipping coffee
or tea, a glass of wine, or a beer. The changing times are recorded
in the espresso, the chrome-and-plate-glass rival of the coffee shop.
The tradition is somewhat the same, relaxation over a cup of coffee, but the customers are younger, and they have added a juke-
box in the corner.

There is no way to modernize the *Heurige*, the small, intimate
tavern in Grinzing, or Sievering, or Nussdorf. It is in the *Heurige*

that the Austrian really lets down his hair, after a few liters of the owner's wine and a few of the old songs, like *"Wo Bist Du Mein Schönes Wien?"*, *"Silberne Kanderl,"* or *"Draussen in Sievering."* Strictly speaking, the *Heurige* is a room in which a vintner is licensed to serve his own product for a certain number of days a year. Many have been commercialized to the point where they serve full dinners, as well as wine, and remain open all year round.

The focal point remains the new wine, the *Heurige,* which is mild and light and full of dynamite for the uninitiated. It is full of dynamite for the initiated, as a matter of fact, which is one of the main reasons for the continued popularity of the *heurigen Abend.* It is part of the way of life.

In the provinces, especially in the villages, life is far simpler. In the Alps, there are the folklore celebrations, surrounding such events as the return of the grazing cattle from the mountaintops after a summer in the care of a young cow girl. Religious holidays are observed with great attention and symbolism, especially Easter and Corpus Christi, the latter being the occasion for blessing the fields. At Christmas time, there is the tradition of Krampus, the black devil who comes on December 6, with St. Nicholas, to see which children have been good and which have been bad. St. Nicholas rewards the good children with presents, but the bad ones may even be carried away in a sack by Krampus. The Christmas tree is a custom still new to Austria, and it has a tradition in some parts of the country which says the tree must be cut and stolen from a neighbor's land, without his knowledge or permission. This is the kind of tradition the Austrians usually ascribe to Hungarians.

If one thinks of Austrians in the musical imagery of Johann Strauss, which is an oversimplification but not untrue, then Hungarians may be appreciated in the music of a gypsy orchestra: soulful and heartbreaking at one moment, breathlessly gay in the next, then bursting with fiery emotion; in every mood, intense. The gypsies actually play the folk music of several eastern European lands where they have roamed, but the best-known gypsy music is Hungarian folk music, and the Hungarian folk music is best portrayed by the gypsy band.

Where the Austrian only recently acquired national identity, associated with the land and its boundaries, the Hungarian has been a creature of national identity for a thousand years, through eras of partition, foreign rule, occupation, revolution.

Hungarians established a special relationship with their king only seven years later than the English produced their Magna Charta, and, while Hungary's famous Bull is not quite the document one might expect from this comparison with Britain's bill of rights, it is part of the background of every Hungarian that his ancestors were among the first in the world to speak out for freedom.

Historians in Hungary always have made a great deal of Hungary's position on the extreme eastern flank of western Europe, and most Hungarians have grown up believing that it is their destiny to guard Western civilization from the encroachments of the East. It is a vital part of the Hungarian character that he thinks of this service to the West as largely unappreciated and ignored. In today's people's republic, this attitude is bad politics, inasmuch as the great force in Hungary's political, social, and economic life is the big brother to the east, Soviet Russia.

One clearly sees the Hungarian characteristics, good and bad, in the cataclysmic event of modern Hungarian history, the anti-Russian revolution of 1956, which spokesmen of the present regime refer to as "those unhappy days."

Foremost, of course, in the story of that revolution, was the picture it gave the world of pure, shining bravery. Earlier, the picture of the East German youth throwing rocks at a Russian tank, in the Germans' brief adventure in defiance, was symbolic. The symbol became a national act when Hungary's turn came. A tiny country defied the full armed strength of the almighty Soviet Union, defied and defeated it, and tasted the sweet fruit of victory for a brief moment while the oppressor lay stunned.

The Hungarian is a brave, fierce fighter, especially when he does battle in the name of Hungarian independence, in the image of Kossuth and Petőfi.

He looked to the West when that revolution broke, and this, too, was typical. He remembered the centuries of battle with Hun,

Tatar, and Turk, and once again identified himself with the Western world in his struggle against the Russian dominion.

There were other, less admirable, traits that were apparent during the 1956 rising. A capability for cruelty stood out in the stories of secret police tortures that was matched by the contemptuous, hate-saturated treatment of secret-policemen by the mobs, released from fear of the regime.

There were the refugees.

Some who fled were genuine freedom fighters, youngsters, who knew they were marked for extinction momentarily if they stayed. These were a tiny portion of the flood. A good many who fled were persons who had been living on the brink of arrest, or had been in and out of political prisons, and who knew they had shown their hands too plainly to remain. But most of the refugees were people who had taken no real part in the revolution, and who left with a sense of resignation, much as they had previously compromised with the regime in order to get along with a minimum of trouble.

One eloquent young Hungarian writer has described the event in terms of a century of compromise with freedom in Hungary. "One way or another," he writes, "you step in the swamp and you begin to sink. The hundred years of dirt just collects and collects on the inside of you, and there is no way to get rid of it. It just collects. Until, finally, the opportunity is suddenly there. It is not just a question of killing Russians, or the AVO. Have you ever seen people escaping from a burning building? It is about the same thing. The hell with life, with clothing, with cold, with the neighbors, with position, with money. The important thing is to get clean."

Today's Hungary is a place where the orgy of self-cleansing has been stopped. The regime can prevent an attitude of defiance, and it can smother resistance, but it cannot wholly remove the traces of satisfaction that accompany such a bath, even among those who in reality scarcely dipped their toes into the water.

It is basic in a people's democracy to attempt to organize the attitudes, living habits, and general way of life of the whole population. This is the ultimate goal of the revolution. The pattern of everyday life in Hungary is, therefore, shaped by efforts to organize youth into Young Communist Leagues, athletes into athletic clubs, factory workers into a variety of recreational and educational groups centered in the factory, also labor unions, government workers, housewives—everyone. Hungarians are occupied either with participation in group events, arranged by the state, or with calculated steps to avoid participation in them. There are, for instance, some 4400 sports groups in Hungary, with more than half a million members.

Before the two wars, Budapest was known as an even gayer capital than Vienna, less restrained. History has given an international profile to Budapest. Today's international aspect is Russian.

Of all Hungary's industrial workers, 47 per cent are in Budapest. Of the undergraduates in Hungarian universities, 72 per cent are in Budapest's 14 institutions of learning. There is the Opera, the Academy of Music, 16 theaters, and about 100 cinemas.

"Night by night," says an official description of Budapest, "the coffeehouses, the espressos, restaurants, night clubs, and other musical places of entertainment with rich programs are the centers of a bustling night life." This is how Communist Budapest sees itself.

Revealing clues to modern life in Hungary come in the Hungarian press itself when it views with alarm certain trends among the population. Example: young people who drift from one collective farm to another, staying only as long as the return is satisfactory, moving on when it falls off; example: the constant difficulty of suppressing "moonshiners" and illegal wineshops; example: the thousands of young people who have left secondary schools, only to become idlers, because they have not been admitted to universities. All these testify both to the breakup of old social customs and to the failure of new forms to win faithful converts throughout the population.

Hungarian Communists have great difficulty with their writers. Harsh treatment has not completely stamped out the publication of works which are unflattering to the new life, such as these lines of Ferenc Jankovich, decried in the party paper as decadent and surrealistic. Translated loosely, they are:

"Gray is everything when I look around me,
Gray it is when I lie down,
Gray like paper, gray like graphite,
Gray like the fear, without substance—dreamlike gray.
Oh, everything, everything is gray."

For sheer topographical magnificence, the land of Austria is a wonder, and the land of Hungary is less than ordinary. Yet, Hungarian historians have worked up the most enchanting legends about their land, and the way their Magyar forebears were drawn to it at just the magically proper hour of history. There is no parallel Austrian legend.

More than 90 per cent of Austria's land is mountainous. This is clearly the most decisive influence on the course of Austrian history, on the shape of her economy, the make-up of her people. The universal image of the Austrian is a fellow in *Lederhosen* and Tirolean hat against an Alpine background. The Alpine influence has been in two directions: the mountains have been a barrier to the passage of migrating peoples but at the same time have attracted migrations by channeling the transients through the passes.

The most famous of Austria's mountain passes is, of course, the Brenner, 4495 feet high, between the massive Stubai and Zillertal Alps, the only thoroughfare for more than a hundred miles to either side. Others are the Arlberg Pass into Switzerland, and the Semmering Pass south of Vienna.

The mountains of Austria are in three parallel ranges, running from west to east. The central range is the highest, with peaks up to 11,000 feet in the Tirol, Salzburg, and Carinthia provinces. The mountain chains link Austria with their extensions in Yugoslavia, Italy, Switzerland, and Germany. On the terraces are many *Einzelhöfe*—or isolated farms—small hamlets, and villages. Farmers grow grain on the gentler slopes up to a height of 4000 feet. The mountain streams, fed by snow field and glaciers, give

Austria a great potential in water power. There are many peaks above the 9500-foot snow line—the Piz Bruin at 10,880 feet, the Wildspitze at 12,382 feet, and the Gross Glockner, Austria's pride, at 12,461 feet.

The river Enns flows down from the Salzburg mountains, running northward to join the Danube at Linz and to separate Upper and Lower Austria. Near its starting place, the Mur also begins, and flows east and south, joining the Drava near Maribor and, via the Drava, reaching the Danube not far from Belgrade. Still another river, the Salzach, is brought to life in central Austria, to flow north toward Germany, joining the Inn north of Salzburg and the Danube at Passau.

The fertile valley of the Danube crosses the northern part of Austria, leading eastward to the Vienna basin. At Vienna, the mountains end, and the great Hungarian plain begins, Austria's share of it being the Burgenland. Wealth and power have been associated with the area from the dawn of history. One of the world's most famous salt mines is at Salzburg. The mountain passes channeled traders on the ancient amber route through Austria.

The Austrian Alps seem to have served as an abrasive on the many transmigrations. Bits and pieces of humanity have rubbed off and settled in the valleys, to make up a population united, after Celtic, Latin, and Teutonic influences, in a language prevalently High German, but disparate in racial strains.

The border between Hungary and Austria has remained relatively unchanged throughout the past thousand years, but in all other directions, the Hungarian borders have varied wildly, at times extending all the way to the Adriatic Sea, and northward, embracing Slovakia, and eastward, embracing Transylvania and much of modern Rumania.

The boundaries today enclose a land that, in general, is a plain surrounded by mountains.

The variations in Hungary's land are associated with two great rivers. One is the Danube, which swings in from the west as far as Budapest and then makes a sharp right turn to head south. The other river is the Tisza, which, appropriately enough, flows in from the east and makes a left turn at the Russian border to turn south toward Szeged. The two rivers actually meet in former Hungarian territory, now Yugoslavia, above Belgrade.

West of the Danube the part of Hungary closest to Austria is Transdanubia, once called Pannonia. A tradition of culture, based on relatively settled conditions and agricultural prosperity, goes back to pre-Roman days. The climate in this Transdanubia area is the best in Hungary.

The Kis-Alföld is an area of advanced farming, with wheat, rye, crops for fodder, and cattle raising. Then there is a highland belt, including the famous vacation resort area of Lake Balaton, where forestry, mining, and some fishing are the activities, and there is a tourism potential. The third division of Transdanubia is along the Yugoslav border, also a highland region, with more advanced agriculture and mining than in the central uplands. This part of Hungary, which extends to and includes the capital, Budapest, feels itself most aligned with the West.

The rest of the Hungarian plain is known as the Nagy-Alföld, or "The Great Hungarian Plain." It is in two sections, one on either side of the Tisza. The area between the rivers is featured by a line of dunes and marshy hollows, alkaline soil with poor drainage, an unpromising land that probably was a factor in discouraging those who preceded the Magyars. East of the Tisza, the land becomes a true steppe, suitable for cattle grazing and cereal grains. Here, on the steppe, is where the Hungarian "farmer towns" grew up, towns that acquired a special character from the fact that their enormous populations were entirely made up of agricultural workers employed on the vast farms of the Alföld. Szeged is the largest of these. Others are Debrecen and Kecskemét.

The Roman traces that exist in Hungary are found in the Transdanubia area. Acquincum was a flourishing Roman town, near where Budapest is today. Pécs, at the base of the Mecsek Mountains, was Sopianae to the Romans. Sopron, a cartographical wart protruding into Austrian Burgenland, was Scarabantia; Szombathely was Sabaria. The Romans came to the Danube, but the marshlands to the east blunted their interest in going further.

The Huns swept through from the other direction, and Attila

was buried in the bed of the river Tisza, along which he had
established his capital.

The Avars took up residence, then disappeared after Charlemagne crushed them, and the land of Hungary stood empty until
the Magyars came to occupy it for good.

It is a land of 35,902 square miles, about 1 per cent of Europe's
area. It lacked the room for the Magyars' nomad ways. As a result,
they gradually took up agriculture and the breeding of livestock.
Hungarian historians insist that the Magyar tribes had resolved
to settle in Hungary long before their arrival and, once arrived,
would let nothing deter them from their mission.

More than 90 per cent of Hungary's land is suitable for cultivation. This, plus the subservient role which Hungary played to
Austria through most of its history, made agriculture, and to some
extent, mining, a main feature of Hungarian economic life.

Hungary is poor in natural resources, and this, too, hampered
industrial development until the First World War brought drastic
political and social changes. Along with all the other standards
that crumbled, the Hapsburgs' power evaporated, and Hungary
was cast into its twentieth-century role. The changes were crystallized after the second war, and Hungary progressed—if that be
the word—from her independence of Austria to dependence upon
Russia. Hungary became a supplier of the Soviet Union, a people's
democracy converted to industrialization in the pattern best
calculated to promote the long-term interests of the Communist
empire.

The most widely celebrated event in all Austrian and Hungarian history was a military victory in a city which, today, is most
emphatically neither Austrian nor Hungarian. This oddity is a
helpful clue to the history of these two countries.

It was in the year 1456, on the twenty-second of June, that one
of Hungary's favorite heroes, John Hunyadi, went into battle
against the Turkish army of Sultan Mohammed II and annihilated
the Turks. Hungary celebrates this as the Battle of Nandorfe-
hervar. The city is better known, today, as Belgrade, Yugoslavia.
The victory was considered so important in the defense of Chris-

tendom that Rome ordered bells to be rung in every church throughout the world to celebrate it. They've been ringing in response to this order for 500 years, and still ring daily at noon in many countries of the world.

Hunyadi himself died as an aftermath of the battle, a victim of the plague, which the Turks had brought to Belgrade. At this time, one of history's stranger characters, Ladislas Posthumous, was the nominal ruler of Hungary, Bohemia, and Austria. This area included what, today, is called Yugoslavia and much of the rest of what later was called the Balkans.

Ladislas was named "Posthumous" because he was born after his father, Albert, the first German king to reign in Hungary, had already died. A vastly complicated struggle for power, including the murder of an Italian count, Ulrich Cilli, the evil mentor of young Ladislas, ended, finally, in the accession of John Hunyadi's second son, Matthias, as King of Hungary. Matthias eventually conquered Austria and set up his court in Vienna.

This is a fair sample of the whole history of government in Austria and Hungary up to 1919–20, when the Treaties of St. Germain and Trianon were signed, and the modern era for both countries began.

The struggle between the two dates back to the very first appearance of Magyar tribes in the West, when there was no Austria as such. The second appearance of the Magyars was when Árpád brought them from Asia and became the first Hungarian ruler in 896. A successor, Zsolt, beat the Germans at the Lechfeld, but his successor, Taksony, was decisively defeated by the emperor Otto I, also at the Lechfeld.

Otto II turned the Ostmark of Germany over to Leopold of Babenberg in the year 976.

In 997, István, known in the West as St. Stephen I, became Hungary's king, and Pope Sylvester II bestowed the kingly crown upon him in the year 1001.

These two, Leopold and Stephen, were the real founders of the forms of government which Austria and Hungary maintained until the period of the First World War, in this century.

The Babenbergs produced a series of Leopolds, plus the colorful Henry, whose favorite oath marked him for history as Henry

Jasomirgott. The Hungarians disposed of the last of the Babenbergs, in battle, in 1246.

Rudolf of Hapsburg, thought to be the least likely to succeed
and therefore the least dangerous, was chosen to succeed the
Babenbergs. The Hapsburgs held power from 1273 until 1920.
For much of this time they were also the emperors of Germany, a
normally honorary but not insignificant simultaneous title for the
rulers of Austria.

Hungary never managed anything like the continuity of ruling
family that the Hapsburgs provided, but there have been two
symbols of continuity. One was St. Stephen's crown, which became a romantic symbol of power in Hungary. The other was the
so-called "Blood Agreement," made by the Magyars at the time
that they chose Árpád to lead them from Asia to the new land. It
established the principle that the leader, or king, was to be a "first
among equals," a principle that, with other basic elements of
freedom, was reiterated in the "Golden Bull" of 1222. The kings of
Hungary, over the years, came from all over Europe, however:
Germany, Spain, Poland, Bohemia, Turkey, and even, from time
to time, Hungary.

It was a Hungarian king, John Szapolyai, who delivered Hungary over to the Turks in July of 1529, on the field of Mohács,
where the Hungarian Army had been wiped out by Turkish artillery three years earlier. This was the beginning of 150 years of
Turkish domination in Hungary, but it was also the beginning of
400 years of German-Austrian domination.

The Hungarians were counted among the more loyal subjects
of the Hapsburgs when that family's male line ran out and the
succession passed to Maria Theresa. Louis Kossuth made what
has been called the inaugural speech of the Austrian Revolution,
in 1848, when he addressed the Hungarian Diet on March 3.
Throughout that great year, nothing happened in Budapest
without an echo in Vienna. The results of 1848 were more immediate and more profound in Austria, yet the names which are
remembered are, curiously enough, revolutionary names for the
Hungarians, but reactionary ones in Austria: Kossuth, the poet
Petöfi, the statesman Széchenyi—as contrasted with Prince Met-

ternich, who fled to England when the revolution began, and the eighteen-year-old Franz Josef, who took the crown and held it for sixty-eight years. Karl Marx visited Vienna in 1848 but found it not yet ready for his ideas. Later on, other German socialists visited Austria—Wilhelm Liebknecht, Hermann Hartung, Johann Most—and helped to organize the Austrian Socialist party.

The Hapsburgs seemed to survive the Revolution of 1848 rather well, but they lost to Bismarck their influence in Germany, a defeat sealed later at Sadowa. They were excluded from Bismarck's German federation. The Dual Monarchy with Hungary was the consequence. In 1867, Franz Josef was crowned monarch of Austria and Hungary, and separate parliaments and ministries for each country were set up. Austrians dominated the arrangement, but Hungarians occasionally rose high in the combined state: Count Gyula Andrássy became Minister of Foreign Affairs for the dual state; Count István Tisza, as Prime Minister of Hungary, nearly succeeded in restraining Austria from declaring war after the incident at Sarajevo; Admiral Miklós Horthy became the King's first admiral.

Nineteen eighteen was another year of revolution, and this one drove the Hapsburgs from power. The Social Democrats formed the strongest bloc in the national constituent assembly, and their leader went to St. Germain to sign the treaty which set the physical boundaries of Austria, the same boundaries which exist today. The Socialist leader was the first Chancellor of the Republic, the same Dr. Karl Renner who returned to power in 1945 to build an Austrian government out of the ruins of the Second World War.

The power passed from Franz Josef, when he died in 1916, to the Archduke Charles, who served out the final two years of Hapsburg rule. The Socialists held power, with Renner and Otto Bauer as the two leading lights, until the Christian Socialists, forerunners of today's People's party, outran them at the polls. Even then, the municipal government in Vienna remained Socialist and put through social legislation which came to be considered a model for progressive democracies.

The Socialists did not prosper. Economic chaos gave way to

gradual improvement, but not enough to produce any faith among the people that Austria had a future worth considering. The attractions of fascism were strong, and in 1934 there was a five-day civil war. The government turned artillery against the workers' para-military groups in the Karl Marx housing project. It was a low point for Austria, surpassed four years later, when the ill-used republic vanished in Hitler's Anschluss.

The Resistance, which did not exist when Hitler took over, was generated by Hitler's rule, and especially by the disaster of war, which it very quickly brought with it. The Socialists and the Conservatives, who had fought each other in public life, became fast friends in the underground, and, not infrequently, fellow sufferers in Hitler's concentration camps.

Their dedication to their own views did not change, but a respect for the other's views was born out of a respect for the other's person.

This acquired instinct for co-operation may have been a treasure, to Austria's credit, worth the tragedy which the Second World War brought in human and property loss. It is the key to the coalition government which served Austria through the occupation and into the present period of the Second Republic.

In the breakup of the Dual Monarchy, Hungary lost two thirds of its territory and three fifths of its population. The Rumanians, who wanted, and eventually got, Transylvania, emphasized their point by occupying Budapest. The Czechs and the Serbs moved into the areas they desired.

In October 1918, mutinous troops had carried out a revolution in Budapest. In November, Béla Kun arrived from captivity in Russia and organized a Bolshevik revolution. By the early part of 1919, the Hungarian Socialists had joined Kun's Communists. In March, a Soviet state was proclaimed, with Kun as People's Commissar for Foreign Affairs.

The Hungarian Bolshevik state was a failure in almost every aspect of its endeavor, but most especially in its efforts to force immediate and total collectivization of the peasants. Armed trains, manned by released convicts, traveled through the countryside.

The "Lenin Boys" conducted a reign of terror, but the farmers simply stopped sending food to the cities. The Soviet government resigned on August 1. Kun and his fellow commissars fled to Vienna and were later sent back to Russia. Vice-Admiral Horthy arrived with an army and took over Budapest.

Hungary retained its monarchy but accepted a pledge from the last Hapsburg, Archduke Charles, already deposed as Austria's king, renouncing participation in state affairs. The Parliament dissolved all links with Austria. Horthy became regent, ruling in the name of the nonexistent king.

The final two years of the war had seen in Hungary a leftward surge of the body politic greater than anything which had happened in the preceding fifty years. This played to the initial advantage of Béla Kun. Eight of the eleven people's commissars in Kun's Soviet state were Jews, and most of the local representatives of the Soviet also were Jews. This contributed strongly to the subsequent anti-Semitism in Hungary. Horthy's movement called itself the "counterrevolution," but it repeated the Communist reign of fear and came to be known as the "white terror." It began to co-operate with the Fascist movements in Italy and Germany, and Hungary progressively came to be a Fascist state, too.

There were degrees of resistance. At the outbreak of war, when Hitler decided to use Hungary to jump off against Yugoslavia, the Hungarian head of government, Count Teleki, committed suicide in protest.

At the end of the war, most of Hitler's allies managed to switch sides and gain some credit for good behavior. Hungary was unable to turn, and finished with full war guilt. The monarchy-regency ended with the arrival of the Russian troops, and the Hungarian People's Republic was created in 1949.

The Russian Army had barely taken Budapest, and was still seriously engaged with the Germans only ten miles away, when Russian military-government teams began erecting statues all over the city.

This puzzling Communist passion for monuments is, perhaps, linked to the fact, which is striking to any tourist in Europe, that

nearly all the tangible monuments of the past were erected by one
or the other of the two absolutist powers of European history: the
Church and the Monarchy. Time has diminished the power of
the Church, and has nearly obliterated the Monarchy as an institution. Their power in the past was such, however, that their
monuments are a comprehensive guide to history.

Vienna's most important monument today is the Stefansdom,
the Cathedral of St. Stephen, which, some say, is one of Europe's
most important Gothic structures. It was a parish church in the
year 1144, later burned, and was replaced with the foundations of
the present cathedral. The West Front of the church, of classic
Romanesque architecture, was constructed in 1259 by direction
of the Bohemian king Ottokar. This was the Ottokar whose
burgeoning power so alarmed the Electors of the Rhine that they
sought out Rudolf, the first Hapsburg, to guard the German claims
to Austria.

At the time when the Stefansdom began building there was an
interregnum between the Babenberg and Hapsburg lines, and
Rome and the Emperor Friedrich II were quarreling over the
disposition of the Babenberg lands. Ottokar profited from the dispute to seize Austria. Then Rudolf of Hapsburg, when he was
designated, drove Ottokar from Austria and established the
supremacy of Vienna over Prague. In time, the Hapsburgs became
the symbol of Rome's temporal power, regularly taking the crown
of Holy Roman Emperor along with the Austrian rule.

Hungary's founding is reckoned from the year 1001, when
Stephen became a Christian and was crowned Hungary's first
king. As Imre Kovacs has written, it "dramatically symbolized the
conditions for survival set by Christian Europe: join the Christian
faith, or be destroyed."

Religion was the basis for the interminable trouble with the
Turks which occupied so much of everyone's time in Austro-
Hungarian history. In fact, the very lack of ancient monuments in
Hungary—and there is a great scarcity of anything pre-eighteenth
century—is at least partly due to the violent destructiveness of
the Turks.

In addition to their basic representation of the infidel, the Turks contributed to the spread of the anti-Church Reformation. Long before Martin Luther, the Hapsburgs had been forced to face the powerful influence of Jan Hus. As one historian has phrased it, "Hus may be said to have handed on to Luther the torch which kindled the Reformation."

The Hussites were thoroughly triumphant in Bohemia, and their teaching that all men were equal and that all property should be held in common spread dissension to neighboring Austria and Hungary. There were popular risings, in which "heresy and communism were inextricably intermingled." Inquisitors arrived from Rome to burn out the heresy, but the influence remained. When the Turks took over Hungary, they permitted religious freedom and gave the Reformation a freer rein than was provided elsewhere. In Austria, the emperor Maximilian remained true to Catholicism himself but permitted Protestantism to spread through the old estates, and by the time he died the Protestants formed a great majority of the people in most of his lands.

The Counter Reformation, inspired in central Europe from the Jesuit university founded at Graz, coincided with the final repulse of the Turks, and, in Hungary, the liberation was combined with social and religious pressure, which oppressed the country but served the end of restoring Catholicism. The Hapsburgs' ascendant line stamped out the Hussite influence with the victory at the White Mountain in Bohemia.

The result of all this emotional, religious, and social turmoil was the eruption of Austrian Baroque, the dominant element in the monuments of both Austria and Hungary. In the Graben today stands one of the most striking monuments ever erected, the Pestsäule, or Pestilence Monument. The Graben, so called because it covers the ditch into which mounds of bodies of the victims of the plague were thrown in 1713, is now Vienna's most fashionable shopping street.

The Pestsäule depicts nine angels being swept up to heaven, accompanied by cherubs, on a column of clouds, on top of which are the three persons of the Trinity. One of the subsidiary figure groups in this fantastic monument is "Faith Triumphant over the Pestilence," and the despicable figure representing the Pestilence also represents the Protestant leaving the "True Faith." One critic of Austrian Baroque suggests the Pestsäule as a test: "If you find it a work of art, you are going to be very happy with Austrian Baroque."

Johann Bernhard Fischer von Erlach, one of Austria's greatest names in architecture, created the Pestsäule. His great triumphs include the Karlskirche, also dedicated to deliverance from the plague and considered a major treasure of Baroque, and the Schönbrunn Palace. Fischer also designed parts of the Hofburg, the city palace of the Hapsburgs. One can hear opera today in the Redoutensaal of the Hofburg, see the Spanish riding school in its arena, hear the Boy's Choir in its chapel, visit its national museums and libraries. A well-placed Austrian or a distinguished foreigner can even rent a room in the Hofburg to hold a reception, or can borrow some of the old Hapsburg furniture.

Other monuments in Vienna include the Ballhausplatz, where Prince Metternich held sway, location of the Congress of Vienna in 1814–15, of the office of Chancellor Dollfuss, in which Nazi thugs murdered him in 1934, of the balcony from which the Anschluss was proclaimed in 1938. It is the Chancellery today.

All the Baroque is not Fischer von Erlach's. He had a distinguished contemporary, Lucas von Hildebrandt, who also built a monument to the victory over the Turks. His is the Belvedere Palace, constructed for Prince Eugene, hero of the Turkish wars. Eugene joined with others to help the Polish king Sobieski drive the Turks from their siege of Vienna in 1683, and in 1717 Eugene finished off the Turkish threat with the capture of Belgrade. There is no lack of monuments to Eugene, and the Belvedere Palace—consecrated in 1955, when it was used for the signing of the Austrian State Treaty—is the greatest.

Vienna has another monument, perhaps greater even than the Stefansdom, and that is the Vienna Opera. It is a great monument because it is much more than just a building; it is a living institution, and it proves its greatness by a daily performance, ten months of the year. Architecturally, the Opera is part of the style that dominates the Ringstrasse, a style even more Austrian than the Baroque—Biedermeier. Like the Stefansdom, it was severely damaged during the last war, and, like the Stefansdom, its reconstruction was of high symbolic value to the Austrian recovery and rebirth. The Stefansdom is a monument to the continuing dominance of Catholicism in Austrian life. The Opera is a monument to the strong current of music, which is really Austria's greatest contribution to the world. The names which go with it are the very best: Mozart, Haydn, Beethoven, Schubert, Lehar, the two Johann Strausses, Brahms, Bruckner, Hugo Wolf, and Mahler. It is a measure of the vitality of Austria's musical heritage that one of Vienna's favorite *Heurigen* is the Beethoven House in Heiligenstadt, where the new wine may be drunk under the same roof that sheltered the composer as he wrote the *Pastoral Symphony.*

Monuments of a different sort are: the Prater, Vienna's great public park, originally a game preserve for the Hapsburgs, whose Spanish branch inspired this corruption of the Spanish word *prado;* the Danube River port, in which a straight-line channel for the river was cut, protected harbor facilities constructed, and a magnificent playground created from the old meandering river course; the Karl Marx Hof, the Socialist monument—one of the twentieth century's first model housing developments, distinguished in history by its becoming a target of Nazi-Fascist artillery in Austria's brief civil war in 1934.

History has been unkind to Hungary's monuments. The Tatars, Germans, and Turks disposed of nearly all the achievements of the Magyars, and what they missed the Magyars destroyed in counterattack. Maria Theresa restored the Royal Palace, but most of the buildings in Budapest go back no further than the inauguration of the Dual Monarchy under Franz Josef's Double Eagle.

King Béla IV started building the first Royal Palace on the hill where the ruins now stand. That was in the thirteenth century, after the Tatars had drifted back to the East.

It was finished in the fifteenth century, by King Sigismund, and was said at that time to be the greatest and most splendid anywhere in Europe. Its splendor increased in the reign of King Matthias Corvinus, who also fortified both Buda and Pest with strong walls. But the Turks burned it all down and stripped it of its treasures. Maria Theresa had it rebuilt in Baroque rococo. The struggle for Budapest between the advancing Russians and the retreating Germans in 1944 smashed the whole area, true to the tradition of the city. In 1956, revolutionary fighters used the ruins as a strong point, and Russian artillery added a little more to the wreckage. The Kadar government promised to restore the area, palace included, to its historic appearance, much as Poland has restored part of the Old City of Warsaw.

Budapest's National Museum and Opera are examples of the Biedermeier influence in Hungary. Most of the rest of the public buildings are versions of Baroque.

In the town of Debrecen, near the Russian border, stands the Big Church of the Calvinists, with a statue of Louis Kossuth in front. Kossuth read the declaration of Hungarian independence in this church in 1849. In 1944, the Russians used it to convene the first provisional government.

In Pécs, near the Yugoslav border, is the cathedral which was started in the eleventh century, and is considered the finest example of Romanesque architecture in Hungary. Pécs is also the home of Hungary's oldest university, the fifth oldest in Europe, founded in 1367. The parish church in Széchenyi Square began as one of the largest Turkish mosques in Europe.

At Višegrad, where the Danube makes a U-shaped curve, a castle has been unearthed which was a royal residence of King Matthias.

There are a few great names in Hungarian culture which qualify as monuments: Liszt, Bartók, Petőfi. For the most part, however, Hungary shares her monuments of the past with the Austrians, with whom she was so intimately associated for so long.

The most profound single consequence of the Second World War for both Austria and Hungary was their liberation by the Red Army of the Soviet Union. The stimulation of Austria toward achievement of Western democracy and the enlistment of Hungary in the Communist camp were reactions to the same Communist stimulus.

The Russians taught Austrians and Hungarians that the single-minded Communist drive is irresistible to a war-ravaged nation, without help from the outside. Austria and Hungary taught the Russians that free elections are an intolerable menace to Communist ambitions. The Communists have not made the mistake of trying them since that time.

A central government was installed by the Russians in each country, and in each country the central government proved to be a powerful instrument of national revival. The Communists managed to subvert it by a variety of devices in Hungary. They failed in Austria, for a variety of reasons.

For Austria, the selection of Dr. Karl Renner as head of the central government was the first big step toward freedom. The second was a big-power deal in which the Western Allies agreed to accept the Renner government as an all-Austrian government, provided that it be modified to include representatives from the Western-occupied zones. There were two other items in the trade: the Russians won agreement to take formerly German-controlled assets in eastern Austria as a part of the German-assets settlement; the Russians accepted a "veto in reverse" in the Allied control council. Instead of providing that any one of the four control powers could veto any action of the Renner government, the agreement specified that all four powers had to disapprove unanimously. Since unanimous action on any subject was an unlikely occurrence, this meant almost a free hand for the Austrian central government. For many years, the reparations deal appeared to be an insuperable impediment to Austrian independence, but, in fact, the concessions on the other side permitted Austria to establish a vigorous, independent government which threw off all the efforts of the Communists to subvert it. The last major effort, a general strike in 1950, received the support of the Russian occupation forces, but failed signally, despite that. A major cause of the Communists' failure in this strike was the militant opposition of the Socialist party, which endured the shellfire of the regime in the Karl Marx Hof in 1934.

Of the desperate situation in Austria between the two wars, the Viennese are alleged to have said: "In Germany, the situation is serious but not hopeless; in Austria, it is hopeless, but not serious."

By some magic, the hopelessness did not reappear after the Second World War. Instead of pessimism, there was optimism. Instead of the spineless acceptance with which Hitler was welcomed, there was a quixotic bravery in rejecting the Communists. The terrible national complex of guilt which swept Germany completely passed Austria by, and, instead, Austria managed to take on the protective coloring of the innocent, though ravished, maiden.

The challenge Austria faced after the second war, beyond the political ambition of the Communists, was the economic question of whether Austria could become viable. For this, the German influence was helpful. The Germans, intending to keep Austria in their thousand-year Reich for the full term, had built up a number of industries. To this base was added the Marshall Plan assistance, which came quickly, not after the people had already lost their self-respect, as happened with the League of Nations loan after the first war.

Austria's size accentuates the importance of foreign trade. Circumstance has forced it to swing from East to West, a necessity which began when the Empire fell apart and the "successor states" of Czechoslovakia, Yugoslavia, Poland, and Rumania, along with Hungary, turned their eyes inward and Austria became an outsider. The Communist conquest in all these former Austrian lands has hardened this between-wars resistance to trade with Austria. It has also put an end to Austria's former position athwart the highway to eastern and southeastern Europe and the Middle East. Austria now is the end of the line.

The statistics say it forcefully: In 1937, western Europe shared 45.3 per cent of Austria's foreign trade. In 1955, it was 74.3 per cent.

The socialization of industry has been extended since the end of the war. One reason was the influence of Nazi Germany, which created a state-organized industry that the Austrian government felt could be taken over only by the government.

A government statement gave this summary: "In 1946, a federal law was adopted providing for federal ownership of many of the formerly German-owned industries and enterprises, and certain others, including substantially the entire coal, iron-ore, and iron-and-steel industries and a large part of the nonferrous-metals and oil-and-natural-gas industries, as well as a number of enterprises producing machinery and vehicles, electrical machinery and equipment, and chemicals and chemical products."

The government estimates about 25 per cent of total industrial employment in Austria is in nationalized industry.

The case of Yugoslavia has shown that there is no halfway position with the Communists, even among themselves. By failing to include Austria in their socialist camp, the Russians perforce turned Austria over to the West after the Second World War.

One profound result of this fact has been the general acceptance by the Austrians of their status as citizens of a small, independent nation. They seem ready, at last, to build on the basis of no-empire. The maturity of this postwar outlook is reflected in the Austrians' resistance to accepting another extreme. There is much talk of the danger of *Verschweizerung*, an uncomplimentary term meaning "Swissification" literally, but translated practically as "isolationism."

The Bolshevists bobbled their chance in 1920 to take over Hungary, under Béla Kun, and they nearly bobbled it again in 1945. There was a basic difference, however, the second time. They had the Soviet Army at hand to backstop their errors. Their experiment with free elections was not fatal, therefore, although it took them four years to achieve the creation of the "People's Democracy."

Rákosi himself referred to it as the "salami method"—carving away the opposition, a slice at a time. This was possible because the coalition government was a shadow government. The real power was in the Communists' hands, and the real process of government was carried on through Communist-dominated trade-unions, Communist-organized "national committees" which had been formed in many localities, and Communist-controlled police in every city. The decisions were made in the Soviet embassy.

The Smallholder party was the first target. The Communists

badgered it, infiltrated it, and finally claimed a conspiracy involving Béla Kovacs, the party leader. Kovacs was imprisoned, and new elections were called. As in the first free elections, the Communists again were soundly trounced, even though they had encouraged formation of six rival parties to confuse the electorate. They had received only 17 per cent of the vote the first time. This time, even with vote frauds managed by László Rajk, they garnered only 22 per cent. But they went to work in earnest then on each party, bullying the leaders, discrediting those that were weak, isolating those that were strong.

The process is described clearly enough in the Communist statement which followed the third national elections in 1949:

"Since the elections of 1947," said the statement, "the political and economic structure of Hungary has undergone a thorough change.

"The opposition parties, which at the elections of 1947 received a proportion of the votes, have since disappeared from the political scene. . . .

"It became evident," the statement continues, "that behind their anti-Communist and anti-labor slogans, the agents of capitalists and large-estate owners, the saboteurs of production and nationalization, were seeking cover. The leaders of these parties fled from the country, deserting their followers, and the parties themselves were dissolved."

What remained, principally involving the Communists and a thoroughly cowed Socialist party, joined in the "Hungarian People's Independence Front." They put up a single list of candidates. The people, no longer distracted by the opportunity of choice, gave the Communist list 95.6 per cent of their votes. Hungary was a people's democracy.

The most powerful political force by which the mold of history has been bent in this industrial age is Marxism, in its many interpretations, manifestations, incarnations, and countermovements. This long-range development is a major clue to the present, and probable future, of Austria and Hungary, taking into account the two other significant forces in modern Europe: the growing power of the Soviet Union and the intimate involvement of the United States in Europe's democratic security.

Austria, for the moment, is a modern parliamentary republic, working in the direction of sociological, economic, and political inclusion in western Europe.

Hungary is a modern "people's democracy," a socialist state under the formula of Lenin, controlled by a national Communist Party and dominated by Russia.

Considered on its own terms, Europe appeared to reach a turning point, in socialist development and in Russian power, with the revolutions of 1956 in Hungary and in Poland. They represented, in Europe, the generation of counterforces destined to check or seriously modify the Communists' course. Europe might very well have been expected to stabilize itself along the demarcation line of the Iron Curtain after 1956. A period of mellowing accommodation might then have developed on both sides of the line.

Europe cannot, however, be considered in a vacuum, even less today than at the time of Attila, or Genghis Khan. The same forces of socialism, and of Russian power, are agitating the rest of the entire world. Europe cannot remain unaffected.

Nevertheless, both Austria and Hungary are studies of the de- of the Iron Curtain after 1956. A period of mellowing accom- nism which Russia seeks to impose on the world, and the anti- communism which is a hallmark of Western Socialist parties. The evidence is strong that, while the People's party has been a stout champion of freedom and a vital force in Austrian postwar re- covery, the Socialists have been the rock upon which Russian communism has foundered.

All the Austrian political parties, of course, grew out of the same upsurge of desire to recognize and deal with the needs of the people, a desire which became urgent not so much in 1848 as after the economic crisis of 1873. It was in 1882 that the so-called "Linzer Programm" was adopted, calling for nationalization of railroads, introduction of a progressive income tax, establishment of standard working hours, and reduction of female and child labor.

One of the leading lights of this meeting was Viktor Adler, the founder of the Social Democratic party. Adler was an organizer, not a theoretician. He took his theory straight from Marx and Engels, called himself in a letter to Engels the *Hofrat* of the revolution. Adler favored, therefore, an internationalism which made socialists especially sympathetic to the monarchy's most vexing problem, the nationalities.

Karl Lueger, also intimately associated with the Linzer Programm, and considered the founding father of the Christian Socialists (today's People's party), proposed a United States of Austria, modeled after the United States of America, to deal with this problem.

The problem was that Vienna ruled an empire in which most of the people were non-Germans. They were Slovaks, Rumanians, Croats, and Serbs, not to mention, of course, the Hungarians. The increasingly violent nationalism of these nationalities set up the fateful situation at Sarajevo. Their demands, after 1878, established the environment in which the Austrian political parties took shape, and enabled them to give concurrent expression to the demands for social progress which were arising everywhere in the Western world.

In this period, Karl Renner published several volumes on the subject of nationalities, and even Stalin visited Vienna and composed a treatise on *Marxism and National Questions*.

The First World War brought revolution to Vienna. The Hapsburg dynasty was rejected, definitively. The Socialists had a majority in Parliament, and Renner was chosen Chancellor. He made the peace at St. Germain. The Christian party soon took the power away from the Socialists in the national government, but the Socialists maintained control of the municipal government in Vienna. Throughout the period of the nazification of Austria, therefore, the Socialists were in the opposition, yet were able to make a record of social reform in Vienna.

Their revolution of 1934 was regarded, at the time, as a failure of their whole position, which, indeed, it was. In retrospect, however, the picture of militant Socialists at the barricades, and the great symbolism of the Socialist-built Karl Marx housing project as the scene of resistance, have given the Socialists a particularly firm hold on the Austrian working population.

The Austrian Socialist leadership, since World War II, has been the most vigorous in Europe. It proved itself in the Communist drive of 1950, when a general strike was plotted and the Communists went into high gear. The Socialist party ordered its members to have nothing to do with the strike, and they obeyed, even in the Russian zone, where the Red Army was in occupation. In Wiener Neustadt, a completely industrial suburb of Vienna and a traditional center of Left-wing agitation, the Communists used undisguised terrorist methods to force the workers to join their strike, and even went so far as to attack and capture the city's post office and telephone exchange.

Wiener Neustadt was just twelve miles from the Soviet Military Headquarters for Austria, but Interior Minister Oskar Helmer, a Socialist, sent police reinforcements from Vienna. They restored order and recaptured the post office. The Russian commander hastily intervened, but the government show of courage and strength had done its work. The big push was a failure.

The Russians were not surprised, six years later, when Minister Helmer organized the reception of Hungarian refugees at the Austrian border during the 1956 revolution.

Austria's Socialists have shared the administration of the country, through the coalition with the slightly stronger People's party. This experience with responsibility has given them an advantage over some of their sister Socialist parties in Europe. Sooner or later the coalition is certain to break up, and one party or the other will have to go into the opposition. Such a development probably would serve to strengthen, rather than weaken, the parliamentary democracy of the Second Republic.

The Communist Party in Hungary lacks the courage to call itself a Communist Party. It is the Hungarian Socialist Worker's Party.

After the Russian Army liberated Hungary from the German armies, the Socialists were the first to be attacked. They were forced to sign an agreement with László Rajk to co-operate with the Communists. Then, after the Smallholders and the other non-

Communist Hungarian parties had all been badgered, intimidated, or finessed out of existence, the Communists turned on the Socialists and eliminated all who displayed independence of thought or expression. Even then, it was deemed expedient to go through the motions of merging the Social Democratic party's remnants with the Communists. The result was called the Hungarian Worker's Party. After the 1956 revolution, it became the Hungarian Socialist Worker's Party.

It seems probable that Hungary will experience a gradual consolidation of Communist power, and a gradual economic improvement, as the entire Russian bloc expands its production base. The 1956 revolution will serve the populace both well and ill. It was a lesson to the Communist leaders that they may never feel secure in their control and will always have to take into account the feelings of the populace. It was also a lesson to the Communist leaders that, when a decision must be taken to crush opposition, they must eschew moderation.

YUGOSLAVIA

Leon Dennen

Leon Dennen is a foreign correspondent and literary journalist who has been reporting on Europe and the Middle East for almost three decades. He is the author of Trouble Zone, The Soviet Peace Myth, and Where the Ghetto Ends and has translated from the Russian, among other things, Vladimir Mayakovski's drama The Bed Bug and D. Dallin's Soviet Russia's Foreign Policy. A diplomatic correspondent of the Newspaper Enterprise Association, he has also contributed articles on foreign affairs and literature to numerous magazines in the United States and abroad.

Born in New York City, Leon Dennen was educated in the United States and Europe. He speaks Russian, French, German, and other languages. His knowledge of Russian and other Slavic tongues has given him an advantage in obtaining one scoop after another about conditions and plans in the Communist world.

In 1958 Dennen was cited by the Overseas Press Club for the "Best American Press Interpretation of Foreign Affairs."

YUGOSLAVIA

Two dates and two places stand out in Yugoslavia's history.

The one—the assassination of Archduke Franz Ferdinand by the Serb terrorist Gavrilo Princip in Sarajevo in June 1914—led to the breakup of the Austro-Hungarian Empire and the emergence of Yugoslavia as an independent state.

The other—Communist Party Chief Tito's defiance in Belgrade of the June 1948 order of the Kremlin to adhere to the official Communist line—established the precedent of national communism free of Soviet dictation.

Both these events were of world significance as well as crucial and decisive for Yugoslavia's history and future.

They underline the distinctive character and nature of the country and its people. Even as a Communist state, supposedly organized along rigid and regimented lines, it is shot through with the paradoxes that make it uniquely Yugoslavian.

Foremost among these paradoxes is the fact that it is the only Communist country which is treated as a bitter enemy by Moscow. Then there is its anomalous position as a Slavic country bordering on the Mediterranean, a peasant nation with a strong new industry, a military power (proportionately it has the largest army in Europe) desperate for peace, a fiercely independent people who lead highly regimented lives, and a country with a leader who is a dedicated Communist with a taste for gaudy uniforms, Rolls-Royce automobiles, luxurious yachts and villas. A European country—with the largest Moslem population in Europe. A poor country officially dedicated to austerity—which offers tourists the highest possible luxury. A Communist country which has defied Moscow on the principle of independence and freedom—and which has imprisoned Milovan Djilas, one of its founders, because he wished these things for himself.

Yugoslavia occupies the northwest corner of the Balkan Peninsula and resembles a mountainous core extending from the northwest Dinaric Alps to the rugged Balkan Mountains on the Greek-Bulgarian frontier. The only gateways through these mountains are the Morava and Vardar valleys, which link Salonika with Belgrade, the capital of Yugoslavia. However, no significant elevations separate the country from her neighbors to the north, where the lands are low and the plains rich and fertile.

In size Yugoslavia approximates the state of Oregon. Her frontiers sweep to the east coast of the Adriatic and, reading clockwise, she is bordered by Italy, Austria, Hungary, Rumania, Bulgaria, Greece, and Albania.

A country of many rivers and sparkling lakes, Yugoslavia also lays claim to more than 300 miles of the "blue Danube," which, though frequently gray and muddy rather than blue, is certainly rich in historic events.

Yugoslavia's beautiful coast and excellent harbors have no hinterland, so that her exports must travel east for Western markets. About 70 per cent of her population is still dependent on her comparatively poor soil for its livelihood. Even though she has rich mineral deposits, their location is often inaccessible and they vary widely in quality.

Modern Yugoslavia is a complicated, multicolored mosaic of peoples and cultures, with four major languages (Serbian, Croatian, Slavonian, and Macedonian).

There is no real racial majority, but twelve minorities. There are nine languages (three official), two alphabets, three religions, and uncounted cultures.

Yugoslavia (the land of the Serbs, Croats, and Slovenes) has existed only since 1919. It was politically united from six separate governments and represents all the typical Balkan faults and virtues.

Yugoslavia is not really a nation in the European sense. It is a confederation of 17 million people speaking separate languages, with different cultural and artistic traditions, professing different religions, and possessing fierce and often mutually exclusive loyalties.

Yugoslavia's peoples have a colorful past filled with heroes and scoundrels, conquests and defeats, and inspiring struggles for freedom.

The Yugoslavs, or Southern Slavs, arrived in their present home on the shores of the Adriatic some 1400 years ago. This was part of the great Slav migration which began in the sixth century with gradual movement from behind the Carpathians to, first, mountains and then broad valleys and little plains. Within a century or two they were converted to Christianity, some by missionaries of what later became the Greek Orthodox Church, while others by missionaries of the Roman Catholic Church. This double conversion set the pattern for the country's pluralistic culture and future problems.

The most far-reaching effects on Yugoslav history occurred when a fundamental dividing line was caused by the part of Yugoslavia which had belonged to the Byzantine Empire falling under the repressive Turkish regime and being cut off from Western influence for centuries. The Catholic Croat and Slovene culture, even the alphabet, is that of the West; while the culture of the Orthodox Serbs, Montenegrins, and Macedonians is that of Greek Orthodoxy (including the Cyrillic alphabet) strongly influenced by five centuries of Turkish occupation.

The Slovenes occupy the northwest corner of the country on the Austrian and Italian borders. Because they were under German or Austrian domination for a thousand years, Slovenia has the highest level of literacy, industrialization, and general culture in the entire country. Never conquered by the Turks, they enjoyed a comparatively beneficent administration as part of the Hapsburg domain. They are Catholic, and their major cultural influences were German and Austrian. They speak a separate and distinct language of their own.

The Croats, neighbors of the Slovenes, are also Catholic. Except for a short period of independence in the Middle Ages, they formed part of the Kingdom of Hungary until the end of World War I. Their culture, accordingly, was heavily influenced by Austria and Hungary, although they share the Serbo-Croatian language with the Serbs and Montenegrins. The Dalmatian coast of Croatia, however, was for centuries in close contact with Venice, across the Adriatic, and possessed a number of wealthy trading cities. Here the Venetian influence, particularly in architecture and music, is very evident.

The Serbs, who formed the nucleus of the Yugoslav state created in 1919, are of the same ethnic stock as the Croats, whose language they share, but their history is considerably different. In medieval times, Serbia rapidly became an independent state. At its height in the Middle Ages, it had conquered Macedonia, much of northern Greece and Albania, and for a short time was the most powerful in the Balkans.

The medieval Turkish onslaught on Serbia culminated in the bloody battle of Kosovo in 1389, which utterly destroyed Serbian statehood and independence. Nevertheless, the fierce Serbian nationalism smoldered through the centuries under Turkish domination.

The Montenegrins are the valiant inhabitants of the mountainous area along the Adriatic coast of the Albanian border. Although they, too, for a time were subject to Turkish domination, they resisted so fiercely from their inaccessible mountain peaks and valleys that in 1799 the Turks recognized their independence.

The Macedonians are a cultural and ethnic jigsaw puzzle. Covering the area where Albania, Greece, Bulgaria, and Yugoslavia meet, there are elements of each culture to be found, even though the area and the people have a character of their own.

Bosnia-Herzegovina, one of the federated republics of Communist Yugoslavia, lies between Serbia and Croatia and has been a bone of contention between them throughout their history. The language spoken is Serbo-Croatian, and the population is either Serbian or Croatian, but only here did the long Turkish domination lead to large-scale religious conversion to Mohammedanism, and this has left an indelible cultural imprint. Even today, almost one third of the population remains Moslem.

Yugoslavia's modern history began with the establishment of the small principality of Serbia in 1815, following repeated revolts against the Turkish authorities.

By the beginning of the nineteenth century, Turkey had become known as "the sick man of Europe." The Sublime Porte was approaching the end of its long decline from the days when victorious Turkish armies had rolled the forces of Christendom back to the gates of Vienna. Although it still held much of the Balkans, nationalism and discontent with Turkish rule were rising and spreading among the peoples held captive for centuries. Of the future Yugoslav peoples, tiny Montenegro had already gained independence, and the formation of the Illyrian Provinces by Napoleon in 1809 had united the Slovene lands with much of Croatia and Dalmatia and established schools using the Slovene and Croatian languages.

The most serious threat to continued Turkish domination arose in Serbia, whose fiery and valiant people revolted and gained control of Belgrade and its surroundings and held them against the Turks until 1813. In 1815 the Serbs erupted again, and the Turks granted them autonomy under a Serbian hereditary prince. Montenegro and Serbia were now the two small nuclei of Yugoslav nationalism, if Yugoslav in this instance is taken to mean the nationalism of the various groups eventually to be united in that state. This nationalism was no longer directed solely against the Turks but to some degree against Austria-Hungary, which obviously intended to swallow up into its empire any lands freed from the Turks. Further, the Hapsburgs were far from happy with this rising nationalism, which had begun to infect the Slavic people under Hapsburg rule.

In 1875, Bosnia-Herzegovina revolted against Constantinople, and the new and tiny states of Serbia and Montenegro declared war against the formerly mighty Turks, each hoping to incorporate new territory from the eroding Turkish Empire. The Congress of Berlin in 1878 settled Balkan history for the following few decades. While both Serbia and Montenegro gained some territory, the powers who settled the fate of the Balkans had no intention of encouraging Balkan nationalism except at the expense of the Turks, and Austria-Hungary not only was allowed to occupy and administer Bosnia and Herzegovina, but was permitted to garrison troops in the strip of land separating Serbia and Montenegro.

In 1908, Austria officially annexed these two provinces. Serbia and Montenegro, who had successfully opposed Turkey, now mobilized for war against the mighty Austro-Hungarian Empire. They were only deterred by the lack of aid from czarist Russia, which had encouraged them but was not ready to support them in a major European war.

The confused and tangled intrigues of Balkan politics were further complicated by the constant machinations of Russia, Austria-Hungary, resurgent Italy, and England. Each power supported or opposed the nationalism of the various Balkan peoples only depending upon its own interests. Russia generally supported the Slavic peoples' aspirations, because of her own hopes of acquiring further chunks of the breaking Ottoman Empire, and as a counterbalance to the Austro-Hungarians. The other powers, worried that czarist Russia—whose "Pan-Slavism" was gaining ground in the area—would become the heir to Turkey, favored the status quo to a degree while supporting the claims of the peoples under Turkish domination for religious freedom and social and economic equality.

During the shifting alliances of the First and Second Balkan Wars in 1912–13, Austria forced both the Serbs and the Montenegrins to evacuate Albanian territory occupied by the Austrian Army. This convinced the Serbs and the Montenegrins that Austria was their major enemy.

Serbia, Montenegro, Greece, and Bulgaria combined against Turkey in the First Balkan War. Their success led to the Second Balkan War, for the victors quarreled over the spoils. Bulgaria, which had played a prominent role, felt she deserved more territory. When she didn't get it, she declared war against her erstwhile partners Serbia and Greece. Thereupon, the major powers applied pressure—Russia on Bulgaria and Austria-Hungary on the others. One result was an uneasy truce, with Balkan unity disrupted and replaced with mutual Balkan dislike, intrigue, and

militarism. Another result was a *rapprochement* between Bulgaria
and Turkey. The successful wooing away of Bulgaria from Russia
resulted in Bulgaria's joining the Central Powers in the imminent World War I.

Nevertheless, the Balkan Powers' victory in the limited but
bloody struggles of the Balkan Wars gave them huge new chunks
of formerly Turkish territory. Newly victorious, these nations were
gripped by nationalist fever. They had proved their valor at arms,
and they intended to do everything possible to advance their
aims. Serbia provoked Austria-Hungary by spreading nationalist
propaganda among the Southern Slavs within the Austro-Hungarian Empire and supporting their nationalist groups and
organizations.

Serbia is credited with being responsible for the actual start
of World War I. It was a Bosnian revolutionary, supplied with
Serbian arms, who assassinated the Austrian archduke Ferdinand
in Sarajevo in 1914. Austria, waiting for an opportunity to settle
accounts with this upstart power, used the assassination to present
crushing demands on Serbia under threat of war. When the Serbs
refused to accept the Austrian ultimatum without reservations,
Austria-Hungary declared war on Serbia, and soon it was to in-
volve most of the world for four years, the effects of which
changed history and are still not yet over.

In the initial campaigns of 1914–15, the Serbs outfought the
Austrians with the courage which long had made them famous,
but when the Austrians mounted a major campaign supported by
the Germans and Bulgarians, the Serbs were defeated. But even
then the Serbian armies did not surrender. In a terrible retreat
across the mountains in the middle of winter, the surviving armies
reached the Adriatic coast and were evacuated to Corfu. They
later joined the Allied forces at Salonika and eventually spear-
headed the Allied forces which drove the Central Powers back
from all Serbian territory.

Serbia emerged from World War I as the Kingdom of the Serbs,
Croats, and Slovenes, uniting most of the Yugoslav peoples in
one nation and more than tripling its area and population.

A host of new problems plagued this new and greater Yugoslav state after 1919. The seizure of territory around Fiume by Italy, territory to which it felt entitled, was a minor problem that left only a residue of Yugoslav resentment against Italy. Much more important were the economic and political problems which faced the country in the interwar period. The country was poor and underdeveloped. Despite some economic progress and a modest industrialization, primarily intended to make the country militarily self-sufficient in keeping with its new status as a major power, the economic and social system remained much the same as it had been for decades, even centuries.

From 1919 on, Yugoslavia's political history faithfully mirrored all the ills of eastern European political life for the next two generations. While theoretically a democracy, Yugoslavia's democracy in operation left much to be desired. The peasants, who formed the overwhelming bulk of a semiliterate population, were not interested in any political problems except those having a bearing on their land or village. Their loyalty was more to their family and their own national groups or religion than to the new Yugoslav state.

Corruption was widespread, and the diversity of peoples and loyalties within the new state led to mutually obstructive tactics rather than any nationally supported constructive program. Pan-Yugoslav nationalism had been a constructive force while the component peoples were struggling to free themselves from "foreign" rule. But the continuing Serbian, Croatian, Slovenian, and other nationalities within the new state were its most divisive force.

The new state had a federal government through a constitution which allowed limited national autonomy. In practice, however, the Serbs actually dominated the country as the largest single component state, controlling the army and the government. And it was the King of Serbia who ruled over all of Yugoslavia with very wide powers. This aroused bitter resentment among the Croats, Slovenes, Montenegrins, and Macedonians. In the case of the Croats, it went so far that they set up their own parliament and defied Belgrade when one of their leaders was assassinated on the floor of Parliament.

Such lese majesty was met by stern measures, and in 1929 King Alexander abolished Parliament and all political parties, proclaiming a royal dictatorship.

This attempt at "order" did not lessen the turbulence of Yugoslav history. Many of the Croats supported a fascist-type Croat party, Ustase, which was dedicated to Croat independence and which was responsible for the assassination of King Alexander in 1934. The new king, Peter, was only a child, and Prince Paul assumed power as the head of a regency.

Meanwhile, the menace of Nazi Germany increased over Europe. When the war began, Yugoslavia at first was able to maintain a precarious neutrality. While Prince Paul was not a Nazi sympathizer, the exigencies of *Realpolitik* had dictated the conclusion of pacts with Bulgaria, Italy, and Hungary, all in the German camp. Finally, in March 1941, when it looked as though the Axis was well on the way to victory, he formally joined Yugoslavia to the Axis Pact.

This step was strongly opposed by most of the patriotic anti-German and anti-Italian Yugoslavs. They supported a small group of Serbian officers who courageously overthrew Prince Paul the day after he joined the Axis. Young Peter was proclaimed king. Even though the new government promised to adhere to the Axis agreement, Hitler was not appeased and reportedly swore vengeance on the "perfidious Serbs."

Belgrade was promptly bombed by the German Air Force, and the country was simultaneously invaded by German, Italian, and Hungarian troops. The badly organized and poorly equipped Yugoslav Army fought with its usual valor, but courage alone was of little value against Panzer divisions and the Luftwaffe. The remains of the battered Yugoslav Army surrendered. The Axis nations occupied and dismembered Yugoslavia; different parts of the country were held by the Germans, Italians, Hungarians, Bulgarians, and even the Albanians. Serbia and Croatia were recreated as puppet states, the latter under the fascist Ustase, whose leader, Ante Pavelić, outdid even his Nazi mentors in atrocities, mass slaughter of suspected Serbs and Croats, and the liquidation of Croatia's few Jews.

Although the Army had been defeated, a fierce, courageous, but disorganized mass-resistance movement against the invaders began in the hills and woods. The heart of this first resistance consisted of the Serbian Chetniks, led by Draža Mihajlović, a colonel in the regular Serbian Army. The Chetnik exploits were widely publicized in the Allied world, and young King Peter, who had fled to London, appointed Mihajlović Minister of War and Commander in Chief of the Royal Yugoslav Army.

The Chetniks were fundamentally Serbian nationalists, supporters of King Peter hoping for the restoration of the *ancien régime* after eventual Axis defeat. Accordingly, after German reprisals had resulted in the slaughter of thousands of helpless civilians, they decided to curtail their operations and wait to strike in full strength when the Allied invasion would come.

After the Nazi invasion of the U.S.S.R., a second formidable resistance movement, led by Tito, began to harass the occupiers. These Partisans differed from the Chetniks in everything but courage. The Partisans desired to engage as many Axis troops as possible, so that they could not be used against Russia on the Eastern Front. Unlike the predominantly Serbian Chetniks, they attempted to create a national Yugoslav resistance movement which would lead to a Communist regime when the war was over. The Partisans grew stronger every day, largely due to their unquestioned courage and attacks on the hated invaders.

Although the Chetniks and the Partisans worked together for the few months from the German invasion of the U.S.S.R. until October 1941, their mutual distrust and entirely different political objectives soon led to a break. By November of 1941, the two resistance groups, while both fighting the occupiers, were engaged in the first skirmishes of what was soon to become a civil war against each other.

By 1942 Tito's Partisans had been organized into the "National Army of Liberation." Consisting of volunteers until November 1943, it had one of the highest records of casualties and heroism of any army in the history of warfare.

The mountains and forests of Yugoslavia were ideally suited to the guerrilla warfare of an army without heavy armament. This lack was their major weakness. The Partisans received supplies by air and sea from England and the United States. By the time Italy collapsed in September 1943, the Partisans were strong enough to disarm several Italian divisions, which gave their forces added military muscle.

Russia did not deliver any supplies to them whatsoever until March 1944. Even then, they were meager, more of a token than any real help. The major Soviet "contribution" to the Partisans was in the form of "advice," which more closely resembled outright commands.

Tito was unique among Communist leaders during World War II. He was a national hero and at the same time was able to channel patriotism along Communist lines. At the conclusion of a victorious war, the Yugoslav people almost unwittingly had been brought under complete Communist control. The Anti-Fascist Council of National Liberation was a Communist-controlled front organization set up late in 1942. The Partisan forces fought under its orders. But this council was soon transformed into a Communist-controlled legislative body, and the National Committee of Liberation was given the powers of temporary government with Tito as Premier, Minister of Defense, and Commander of the Partisan armies. The postwar Communist shape of things to come was indicated as early as 1943, when the National Committee of Liberation passed a resolution forbidding the return of the King to Yugoslavia.

Throughout the war, and long after, Tito faithfully carried out Moscow's orders in the international political field. In September 1944, when the Nazis were reeling back from southeastern Europe pursued by the Red Army, Tito, who had been conferring in Naples with Churchill and the Allied commanders, secretly flew to Moscow for orders without even informing the Allies that he was making the trip. Shortly thereafter, the Russian forces entered Yugoslavia and joined Tito's Partisans in a fierce battle for Belgrade, which was liberated in October 1944. The National Committee of Liberation moved to Yugoslavia's capital, and the Communist complexion of postwar Yugoslavia was to all intents and purposes a *fait accompli*.

Tito's war against foreign invaders was over. A new Communist war against all opposition to communism now began. Not only the Chetniks and "collaborators" suffered persecution, but anti-Communist democrats, Socialists, Catholics, and Royalists. Anyone who was a known or even suspected anti-Communist began to live in terror of the Communist secret police patterned after the Soviet NKVD. Mihajlović was quickly tried and executed, and the late Catholic Primate Archbishop Stepinac was sentenced to sixteen years of hard labor in a Communist "trial." These were but two prominent examples of the thousands of drumhead trials held in 1946 to crush any potential opposition and to consolidate Communist power.

On November 11, 1945, the Communist Party staged the first of its rigged "elections." Opposition was not allowed, non-Communists were disenfranchised, the Communists alone counted the votes, and fraud and force were major ingredients. It was hardly surprising that the Communist People's Front won all the seats in the Assembly. The first act of the Communist Assembly was to abolish the monarchy and to establish a Communist Federal People's Republic. A new constitution was passed, which legalized the regime, and Communist political, social, and economic dogma became officially the law of the land. Democracy and private enterprise were eliminated.

What makes Yugoslavia unique among Communist countries is her position in world affairs, and most particularly her relations with the Soviet Union. It should never be forgotten that the Yugoslav government (1) remains as firmly Communist as ever and (2) that its whole international policy since the end of World War II has been based on one single-minded premise: an attempt to remain both Communist and independent of outside domination. The Yugoslav position toward the East or the West at any given time has depended entirely upon Moscow's attitude toward Yugoslavia.

When Tito was Moscow's fair-haired boy, no one exceeded Communist Yugoslavia in aggressive vituperation of the capitalist West in general and the United States in particular. Only when Stalin attempted to cast Tito and all his works into outer darkness did Yugoslavia grudgingly accept Western aid and support and attack Soviet policy. Yet even in the face of every possible degree of Soviet insult and intimidation, the Yugoslavs defended themselves against their giant adversary more in a tone of sorrow than of anger.

It may be difficult for the Western democrats to understand why the U.S.S.R. and its puppets have spent so much effort, anger, and propaganda attacking "Titoism," which is, after all, officially dedicated to the same economic and social philosophy. The reasons are more basic than simply a question of discipline. The Kremlin realizes that despite the uncompromising adherence of the Tito regime to its own brand of communism, its continual existence is perhaps the greatest ideological threat to Soviet domination of world communism. Titoism may yet be the catalyst which will result in an internal ideological explosion shattering the complicated formula Moscow has laboriously developed and maintained for over forty years.

There are many lessons for the rest of the world, Communist and free alike, to be found in the paradoxes of Yugoslav history since World War II.

From 1945 to 1948, next to the Soviet Union itself, Yugoslavia was the most aggressive and expansionist country in Europe, seeking to expand its borders in all directions—at the expense of Italy, Austria, Greece, and even of Communist Bulgaria and Albania. In the cases of Italy and Austria, they were supported at first by the Soviet Union as a blow at the West. This support was to terminate abruptly after Tito's break with Stalin. In the cases of Albania and Bulgaria, and a potentially Communist Greece, Tito hoped for a Balkan federation with himself as Communist dictator. Even before 1948, Stalin opposed any such increase in Tito's power and prestige.

The history of the Tito-Stalin rupture goes back to World War II, when the Yugoslav Partisans were continually promised, but never received, aid from the U.S.S.R. In the immediate postwar period, Tito accepted all the UNRRA aid he could get, which virtually saved Yugoslavia from starvation, and started her battered economy on the road to reconstruction. Tito, nevertheless, obeyed every order from Moscow to minimize the importance of Western aid, to encourage hatred and suspicion of his Western benefactors, and to entrench communism at home and support Moscow abroad.

The major base for the Communist attempt to gain control in Greece in 1946 was the material and political support for the Communist regime in Yugoslavia. Tito's forces also shot down in that year two unarmed American transport planes, presumably following Stalin's policy directives, which could have led to serious consequences.

But no matter how slavishly the Yugoslavs followed Moscow's orders, no matter how little help they received from Stalin, or how much they were expected to give, it did not seem to be enough for the Kremlin. As a result, there was growing annoyance with the Tito hierarchy, although official Yugoslav policy remained adulation of Stalin and unquestioning obedience to the U.S.S.R.

Not only did the Yugoslavs feel that the Soviet Union had not given them the determined and resolute support to which they were entitled, but the Soviet Union seemed determined to turn Yugoslavia into a captive satellite along the lines of the eastern European nations "liberated" by the Red Army. This was doubly galling to a proud people with a tradition of fierce independence who had achieved victory over the Nazis and Fascists through their own courage and force of arms.

When the Soviet Union proposed the formation of a series of joint Soviet-Yugoslav companies which would not only have given the Soviets control of the Yugoslav economy but would have milked it for the benefit of the Soviet Union, disillusion set in even among the convinced Yugoslav Communists. Soviet military advisers were sent to the Yugoslav Army and attempted to reorganize it on the Soviet pattern. They almost openly attempted to subvert it and infiltrate the country with Soviet spies and agents. It became clear to Tito that he either had to assert some measure of independence or allow his country to become a Soviet satrapy.

In February 1948, Stalin had expressed his strong displeasure with Yugoslav independence in Balkan activities. In the same month, he canceled a proposed trade treaty and informed Tito that all Soviet advisers were to be withdrawn. He accused the Yugoslavs of every possible Communist ideological sin and perversion. The Yugoslav leaders continued to pay lip service to the U.S.S.R. and its "great leader"—but increasingly, if regretfully, they refused to accept the orders and tutelage of the Soviet Communist Party.

Stalin finally decided that the time had come to eliminate Tito. A meeting of the Cominform was called to discuss the Yugoslav "errors"—a meeting to which the Yugoslav leaders were invited. Prudently, they declined the invitation. To have accepted would have been tantamount to participation at their own demise. The Cominform puppets duly met in January 1949 and called upon the Yugoslav Communists to replace their leaders with "healthy elements," meaning Communists totally subservient to Moscow.

Stalin seems to have thought that this would be the end of Tito and that the Yugoslav Communist apparatus, either through fear or the moral authority of the "fountainhead of all wisdom," would rise against the Yugoslav leader. This was perhaps the wily Georgian dictator's worst political mistake in his long history of political double-dealing and deceit. To his and the Communist world's incredulous surprise, not only the Yugoslav Communist leaders but the ordinary members and officials of the Party and government stood by Tito in the face of the strongest possible intimidation and threat of force.

In the months prior to the Cominform resolution which signified Moscow's declaration of ideological war on Tito, the correspondence between the two countries had become increasingly bitter. The Russians had declared that the Yugoslav Party was "undemocratic" and that the Yugoslav leaders were "questionable Marxists." The Yugoslavs replied with some of their own complaints, including that of the Soviet Intelligence Service recruiting agents in Yugoslavia. But the one Yugoslav phrase addressed to Moscow which reflected the general, but never enunciated, feeling of all non-Soviet Communists was: "No matter how much each of us loves the U.S.S.R., he can, in no case, love his country less."

The greatest resentment on the Yugoslav side came from the Russian answer to Tito's remark that the operation of the Yugoslav Communist Party was not the business of the Soviet ambassador. The Russians wrote: "The Soviet ambassador, who represents the friendly power which liberated Yugoslavia, not only has the right but the obligation to discuss all questions with Yugoslav Communists."

This bald assertion that the U.S.S.R. had the right to meddle in domestic affairs may have shocked the Yugoslavs, but it was the pointed statement that Russia had "liberated" them that really infuriated Yugoslavs of all political hues.

After the break, the Tito regime published the Russian-Yugoslav correspondence, and at the next Yugoslav Party Congress, speakers from Tito downward defended their position strongly, even though they did not say one harsh word directly against Stalin or the U.S.S.R. Amazingly, only two high-ranking Yugoslav army officers and a few Communist diplomats in Moscow-controlled eastern European capitals defected. Faced with this unexpected setback, Stalin pushed the appropriate buttons in the Kremlin, and the captive countries launched all-out attacks on Tito's Yugoslavia. Communist Albania, which had been in the position of a subsatellite to Yugoslavia, which had largely organized and controlled the Albanian Partisans' war effort, denounced all her agreements with Yugoslavia.

Soon all Yugoslavia's Communist neighbors were pursuing similar policies in the economic field and began political warfare and the actual use of force. Anti-Tito broadcasts beamed to Yugoslavia, frontier incidents, including shootings and border crossings, as well as reconnaissance flights over the Yugoslav borders, were all part of this campaign.

Propaganda warfare reached new heights (or lows), in which Tito and his associates were called everything from "despicable traitors and imperialist hirelings" to "worthy heirs of Hitler." All the weapons in the Soviet arsenal—propaganda, subversion, economic and political warfare, and constant insult and as much injury as possible short of actual full-scale military attack—were employed by the U.S.S.R. and the entire Soviet bloc against Tito's Yugoslavia. It was said that the mere mention of Tito's name in Stalin's presence was enough to set the dictator off into paroxysms of rage.

Perhaps the most important consequence unforeseen by Moscow was the danger of similar "Titos" arising in the various captive nations. Boiled down to the essence, "Titoism" means nationalist communism not subject to outside dictation. This was a development neither Stalin nor his successors would allow. In the captive states of eastern Europe until Stalin's death, the charge of Titoism was sufficient to purge the Communist Parties' leadership of all members even vaguely suspected of not being sufficiently subservient to Moscow, or of even considering the interests of their own countries ahead of that of the Soviet Union.

Throughout eastern Europe in this period, many of the leading Communists were tried and executed on false charges in a bloody echo of the Stalin purges of the 1930s. Wladyslaw Gomulka of Poland was an exception. He was not executed, but simply banished from political life and held under arrest. It was in Hungary that the most vicious and obviously phony trials were held. László Rajk and many others were tried and executed at the orders of Mátyás Rákosi, the most hated and servile to Stalin of all eastern European Communist leaders. In Czechoslovakia, Bulgaria, and Albania, too, the charge of Titoism was sufficient to condemn to death or imprisonment anyone suspected of possible independent communism, or anyone the controlling Stalinists wished to eliminate out of personal motives of jealousy or fear.

There can be little question that Western support saved Tito's Yugoslavia from economic collapse or even a Communist invasion from the East. The United States realized that the existence and growth of Titoism was beneficial to the West, but was firmly opposed to any Communist or nondemocratic regime.

The United States pursued a careful policy toward Yugoslavia. At first, small loans were made, Yugoslav frozen assets in the United States were released, and emergency loans for foodstuffs were granted when Yugoslavia suffered a disastrous drought in 1950. Further, the United States made it clear that any Soviet-dictated attack on Yugoslavia by remote control from Moscow would not go unpunished. Military supplies were made available to the Yugoslav Army.

The total amount of Western aid (almost entirely from the United States) to Tito has amounted in the past ten years to more than one and a half billion dollars. The precise figures are secret, since much of this amount has consisted of military aid.

This country has been forced to spend 30 to 40 billion dollars on defense every year, primarily to protect the free world against the continued threat of Communist aggression and Soviet expansion. By insuring Tito's continued existence, the internal "contradictions" of Soviet-style communism have been kept in the consciousness of the captive peoples. The captive countries can no longer be depended upon as a source of military strength to the Soviet Union in case of war, and their economies can no longer be so flagrantly milked for Soviet benefit. The simple demand of the Yugoslav Communists—not to be made the virtual slaves of Moscow—has resulted in much soul searching and discontent among the captive Communist leaders who survived Stalin's death. On the other hand, the successful existence of an independent Communist state has shaken the prestige and authority of the Kremlin outside the Soviet bloc and has even led to an "agonizing" re-evaluation of Communist ideology as promulgated by the U.S.S.R. within the Kremlin leadership.

The Yugoslav Communists have contributed more than anyone to the fall of the Communist theory of Kremlin infallibility. Perhaps more important has been their contribution to Communist ideology. First of all, they proclaimed that they themselves were the only true Communists, and that Stalin had created a state capitalism which was not only "deviationist" but actually "reactionary." They denounced the bureaucratization and police tactics of the U.S.S.R. as being attributable to the wrong and bloody road upon which Stalin had embarked Russia as soon as he had attained complete control.

The Yugoslavs have attempted to modify the Communist system to reflect "true Marxism-Leninism." Workers' councils, or soviets, have been established in all state enterprises. These workers' councils are elected by secret ballot and in turn choose management boards for the factory or enterprise. The various government ministries which controlled the individual industries were abolished and replaced by co-ordinating councils, with representatives from the different Yugoslav republics. Thus, although the government continues to control all industries at the very top, at the lower level the workers of Yugoslavia, alone among all Communist countries now that the councils have been crushed or emasculated in Hungary and Poland, have some say in their direction and control.

Party leaders were deprived of many of the special privileges they had enjoyed in imitation of Soviet practice. The Communist Parties of the individual republics making up Yugoslavia were given authority to influence political and economic life in their own territories, in marked contrast to the U.S.S.R., where the various component republics and their Communist Parties have only the authority to carry out Moscow's orders.

The Yugoslav courts were "reformed" and the police apparatus was curtailed. In agriculture, forced collectivization was abandoned. This was a policy of crucial importance in a country where two thirds of the population consists of peasants. Stalin's forced collectivization in the early 1930s killed millions of peasants and lowered Russian agricultural production to a point where it had not recovered to the 1916 level as late as 1953. In the captive countries of Communist eastern Europe, where forced collectivization had been pursued against sullen peasant resentment, Tito's new agricultural policy has had repercussions equal to his introduction of the workers' councils. Forced collectivization with different amounts of pressure is the basic Soviet agrarian policy to which all the satellite governments must make their people conform against their wishes. The abandonment of this policy in Yugoslavia not only resulted in a lessening of peasant resentment of the Communist government but soon increased agricultural production.

How did the small group of Yugoslav Marxists start from nothing before World War II and emerge at its end with the power and control to defy both the capitalist West and the entire Soviet bloc? Moscow is not the only answer, since the Kremlin harried as much as helped Tito's group.

Communism never had more than a very tiny following in Yugoslavia. In the interwar (1918–39) period, a small and dedicated underground group barely survived mass indifference and government persecution. With all the economic and social factors favoring communism, it is actually surprising that they never received more support. Poverty and lack of opportunity were chronic problems of the Yugoslav peoples, who were generally apathetic or hostile toward the royal regime, depending on their national origin and economic standing. Perhaps the one aspect in which the monarchy showed zeal was its anti-Communist campaign.

If, then, the essence of Titoism is Tito himself, a brief biography is in order. The man known as Tito was born Josip Broz in a Croatian village in 1892. He had no formal education beyond elementary school. He entered a locksmith's shop as an apprentice and emerged as an excellently trained journeyman mechanic. He left Croatia in the early years of the century and wandered throughout the Austro-Hungarian Empire and Germany in search of work and adventure. In 1913, at the age of twenty-one, he returned to report for military service in the Austro-Hungarian Army, with which he served bravely in World War I.

Young Tito was a good soldier and rose to the rank of sergeant major. He seems to have absorbed the idealistic democratic brand of socialism during his travels, but when he was badly wounded and captured by the Russians he was easily converted to the Bolshevik cause. Still in Russia, he was such an ardent supporter of the October Revolution of 1917 that he volunteered for the Red Army, in which he also fought bravely.

In 1920, as an agent of the Revolution, he returned to Croatia and resumed his work as a locksmith. But he was a locksmith more dedicated to the cause of the Revolution than to his trade. He was a pioneer member of his country's Communist Party, for which he worked cleverly and hard for the next few years, at the same time rising to be secretary of a metal workers' trade-union.

He was arrested in 1927 as an agitator but was shortly released. The police authorities had had an eye on him for some time, and in 1928 he was again arrested. This time, he was sentenced to five years' imprisonment as a Communist agent. Tito spent the five years in study and discussion with his fellow Communist prisoners. The prison regime was not terribly strict. Ironically, together with his fellow graduates, he was later to emerge from prison to eventual control of the country and then to fill this same prison with his own political enemies.

Released in 1933, Tito returned to Moscow, where he rose in the Balkan section of the Comintern apparatus to a position of importance and authority. In 1936, he returned to Yugoslavia illegally under a false name. After reorganizing the tiny and battered Communist underground, he moved throughout central Europe and France as a recruiting agent for the International Brigade in the Spanish Civil War. Whether he himself actually served in Spain is doubtful, although there is a recurrent story to that effect.

Comrade Tito became a hard-bitten and experienced Comintern agent. He shared with other Moscow-trained Comintern agents dedication to the Communist cause and complete loyalty to Moscow. He differed in that he was cleverer and more prepossessing than most, had a ready wit, a pleasant personality, and a sense of humor, something almost unique in that dour tribe.

Tito had married a young Russian girl during his sojourn in Russia, and he brought her back with him to Yugoslavia when he returned in 1920 after the Revolution. She died in 1938, leaving a son, Zarko, whose own two children now make Tito a grandfather. In 1940, Tito married again, this time a Slovenian girl, by whom he also had a son. After the war he divorced his second wife and married for the third time in 1952. His current wife is the darkly handsome Jovanka, whose photograph is familiar to Western newspaper readers, as she has accompanied him on all his trips since their marriage. She is a Serb, who fought with the Partisans during the darkest days of the war. They appear to be happy. They have no children of their own, and she is reportedly very fond of and on the best of terms with her husband's children and grandchildren.

The anti-Soviet revolt by the Hungarian freedom fighters in 1956 was a supreme test for Tito's Marxist-Leninist orthodoxy. There is no doubt that although the Hungarian revolution was finally crushed by the Soviet Army, it was more than an internal Communist revolt. Historically, it was the symbol and portent of the total rejection of Soviet domination and the imposed pattern of communism by the peoples of eastern Europe. What was Tito's attitude toward the Hungarian revolution? Basically he supported it as a manifestation of his own brand of Communist "revisionism." But here again the fundamental differences between democratic freedom and communism, whatever the brand, became evident.

The Hungarian leader Imre Nagy and his colleagues had been promised by the Kremlin a safe-conduct and even an amnesty if they left the Yugoslav embassy in Budapest, where they found asylum after their revolt had been suppressed by the Soviet troops. Yet in one of the most disgusting episodes in the history of Communist deceit, Nagy and his friends were arrested and spirited away by the Soviet secret police immediately after they left the embassy. This incredible act of treachery aroused world-wide indignation, and Communist Yogoslavia was equally bitter at Nikita Khrushchev's betrayal.

What, then, are the lessons posed by Yugoslavia? First of all, Yugoslavia has proved again that nationalism, in the sense of love of country, remains a major human element which is as strong under communism as under any other form of government. Men will always want independence, whether as individuals or as collective members of a nation. And courage, and pride in that courage, are human factors which cannot be legislated or brainwashed out of existence.

Titoist communism, as opposed to Soviet communism, shows differences and similarities. The differences may seem small by Western standards, but by Communist standards they are basic. Ideologically, Titoism stands for the right of a Communist country to work out its destiny independent of Moscow, while retaining the basic tenets of Marx and Lenin.

In internal political policy the difference is in degree rather than in kind. True political democracy is as unknown in Yugoslavia as it is in the U.S.S.R.; in both countries only the ruling

political party is allowed to exist, and the voters are given no
other choice. In Russia there is not even any choice permitted the
voters among the approved Communist candidates, who are simply selected from the top. In Yugoslavia, while all candidates
must be approved by the Communist Party, there is at least some
choice allowed in their nomination at the lower levels.

So, too, with the Constitution, and the legal and political systems. In all these respects, Yugoslavia is more "liberal" than the
U.S.S.R. or its captive countries, but the basic Communist principle under which the needs and aspirations of the individual are
subordinated to those of the state remain the same.

In economic life, both communisms subscribe fully to a totally
planned economy and the rejection in principle of private enterprise and initiative, and to state ownership of "the means of production." It is in the actual working measures that the differences
lie. The workers, while their rights are greatly circumscribed, enjoy much more freedom and independence in Yugoslavia, even
though they do not have any of the basic freedoms enjoyed in
the Western countries. But the Yugoslav workers' councils and
artisans' co-operatives are an enormous advance in democratic
industrial procedure over the virtual enslavement of Soviet-con-
trolled workers. The paradox is that the organization of the
worker's life in Yugoslavia remains serfdom by Western standards, but is considered the rankest radicalism and Western-
type democratic socialism by the Kremlin.

In agriculture, the difference is more basic. The collectivized
Russian peasant does not "own" anything. In Yugoslavia, however,
the peasant producer does not have to join an agricultural collective against his will, and to all practical purposes "owns" his
land, and receives a greater percentage of the benefits of his labor
and production.

In the field of national minorities, Tito's Yugoslavia has accom-
plished a great deal more than the U.S.S.R., which declares it
solved the "nationalities problem" shortly after the Bolshevik revolution. The six component republics making up Yugoslavia enjoy
a limited amount of independence in policy making. In the
U.S.S.R., however, the republics and their legislatures are nothing

but rubber stamps, with no authority even to discuss measures ordained for them from Moscow.

Yugoslavia consists of a collection of minorities, the largest of which is the Serbian, whose political control of interwar Yugoslavia was responsible for much resentment and political instability. Tito's Yugoslavia, perhaps because Tito himself is a Croat, has attempted to show fairness as between its minorities and has allowed them a proportionate share in the government apparatus. Russia is also a collection of minorities, the "Great Russians" representing only about half the population. In the U.S.S.R., however, there is no question of the fact of Great Russian domination. Despite the few Asian members of the Supreme Soviet and of the governments of the Soviet republics, the best jobs and the positions of power and authority in these areas are almost invariably held by Russians appointed from and by Moscow. Nor is there the anti-Semitism in Yugoslavia which has been a hotly denied but incontrovertible fact of Soviet policy for more than a quarter of a century.

Also, in the field of intellectual freedom, Western culture and ideas are far more readily available in Yugoslavia.

The older generation of the men around Tito are old-line Communists who spiritually belong to the East and want to make peace with Moscow. But the younger generation of Yugoslavs, especially students, writers, and painters, is greatly impressed by the economic and cultural achievements of the West, especially the United States, and is eager to learn from it.

At the cafés frequented by writers, artists, and actors, bearded young men and pale-faced peroxide-blond girls discuss earnestly Zen Buddhism, Beatniks, modern painting, and even the novels of Kerouac. As one listens to these young writers and painters, whose work is certainly remote from the stilted and barren Soviet-type socialist realism, an impression emerges of a developing intellectual life. The sickening propaganda and police interference in the individual's private life (provided, of course, he is not a political opponent of the regime) has been largely discarded by Titoism. Unlike the people in Russia or in Moscow's eastern European satellites, the men and women who do not challenge Tito's

Communist dictatorship or remain at least neutral toward it are
by and large free to arrange their lives as they see fit.

Thus, though Tito's secret police is ever present as a potential
threat, it would be wrong to describe Yugoslavia as a terroristic
dictatorship. To be sure, in Yugoslavia, too, the artist's freedom
to create is still strictly limited by the state's economic strangle-
hold. And just as Russia had its Boris Pasternak, Yugoslavia has
Milovan Djilas as eternal evidence that intellectual freedom will
always be precious to men of integrity.

The Yugoslavs have achieved their industrialization without
the years of the workers' grinding effort at the bare subsistence
level which has formed the basis for Soviet industrial might. The
Yugoslavs have not literally starved to death by the hundreds
of thousands due to the stupidity of their Communist masters—as
was the case in the U.S.S.R. in 1932–33, when probably close to
two million blameless Russian peasants needlessly died of hunger
because of Stalin's "anti-kulak" policies. And even though thousands of political prisoners, particularly in the immediate postwar
years, have languished in Titoist camps, forced labor has never
been the economic or socio-political factor it was in Stalin's Russia,
where literally millions of Russian men and women died in the
death camps of Soviet Siberia and the Arctic Circle.

Who will inherit Tito's "throne"? This question is as important for Yugoslav communism as was the succession to Stalin in the
Soviet Union. Tito is said to have already chosen his successors
in a Solomonic solution—two of them, Alexander Ranković to head
the Party and Edward Kardelj the government.

"Collective leadership" didn't work in Communist Russia after
Stalin and there is no reason to believe that it will fare better in
Communist Yugoslavia. The Party and the state have always been
one, and the monolithic state demands monolithic leadership.

Besides, the two "appointees" differ widely in character and
methods, one (Ranković) representing the tough, unrelenting
school of "no compromise with capitalism and the bourgeoisie,"
and the other (Kardelj) typifying the flexible, somewhat liberal
"live and let live" philosophy of pragmatic communism.

These two points of view have been nicely balanced by Tito
up to now, sometimes playing one against the other in palace poli-

tics. In fact, Tito holds the secret of equilibrium in internal politics as the great compromiser not only on the political level but as far as minorities and nationalities are concerned as well. Ranković is a Serbian, Kardelj a Slovenian. The former is dedicated to centralization of power, the latter to decentralization.

With Tito gone, the fusion of Yugoslavia as a nation out of many peoples might slow down, even halt altogether, if the leadership becomes fragmented and old sores and scores allowed to erupt again. The latest conflict within the Party can draw on Marxist political dissension as an added irritant to the basic conflict involving the diverse nationalities, religions, way of life, standards of living that have plagued the lands of the Serbs, Croats, Slovenes for centuries.

Above all, such a conflict after Tito's death would weaken Yugoslavia's present strength as a small independent Communist nation vis-à-vis the Soviet giant. There could well be a realignment on the part of one faction or another toward the Kremlin. This would be a major victory for the Soviet Union, a victory that would help seal the permanent doom of all the "captive nations" who have become reluctant satellites of Moscow over the last fourteen years.

It was mentioned at the beginning of this survey that the two most important dates in Yugoslavia's history occurred in 1914 and 1948—both of which established Yugoslavia's independence from outside domination.

In view of the fierce passion with which the peoples of Yugoslavia fight for what they believe in, there may still come a third important date in a not too distant future. This would be the day of *Sloboda* (freedom) being won inside the nation itself. It was best expressed by a ragged but strong-looking peasant from the Montenegro mountains who was gaping in wonder at the neon-lit stores stocked with plastic plates, cups, and forks in Belgrade's Terazje Boulevard.

"Yes, we need bread, my friend," he said to the American standing beside him. "And we are grateful to you for helping us. But remember this—we need *Sloboda* even more. Man cannot live without *Sloboda*."

GREECE

Charles Hurd

Charles Hurd spent the major portion of his newspaper career with the New York Times, *on assignments ranging from White House correspondent in Washington to European correspondent on a wide range of diplomatic assignments, from 1929 to 1949.*

His experience began with the Associated Press while he was attending Northwestern University and included three years as associate editor of Liberty *magazine, prior to joining the* Times. *Throughout the 1950s Hurd devoted himself to more specialized writing and the establishment of Charles Hurd Associates, an industrial advisory service, serving clients in Europe and British East Africa.*

Hurd has contributed articles to magazines, including Reader's Digest, Life, *and* Redbook *among others. He is the author of* The White House, The Veterans Program, Washington Cavalcade, The Compact History of the Red Cross, *and, with the collaboration of Postmaster General Arthur E. Summerfield,* The Story of the United States Post Office. *He edited the recent* Treasury of Great American Speeches *and is co-editor of this work.*

GREECE

Of all the countries of the Western world, Greece, located at the southern bridge between Asia and Europe, is the greatest enigma and the most ancient. Statistically, this is a small and almost insignificant country among world powers, but a proud nation united under a constitutional monarchy after heartbreaking wars, revolutions, and civil wars that have marked the 130 years of its modern independence. Yet Greece to the outsider is the very foundation of the entire European cavalcade, harking back to an era that ended twenty-three centuries ago, and which, in the course of its being, emanated from a nation that never was.

So today, as the Athenian emerges from his siesta in late afternoon to begin perhaps the busiest part of his working day, or the visitor stands amid the ruins on the Acropolis and views them against a craggy background illuminated by almost blinding sunlight, he stands in the center of a mystical mental fairyland that would all seem as unreal as Homer's legends if the evidences in stone, language, and smilingly inscrutable faces were not all around him.

The laughter and song, the love of dancing, that mark today's Greek are the patina that Mediterranean temperaments develop to overlay an existence which on the average is so meager and hazardous that it probably would destroy the morale of more northern peoples. Yet the proud Greek insists on living joyfully, works prodigiously, and has come to accept the necessity of outside economic assistance, primarily from the United States, as a necessary evil.

Contrasts that verge on the ridiculous in his life and country are accepted, perhaps because the further he reaches back into the misty pages of his history he finds that *contrast* is almost a synonym for his long existence. It is necessary, therefore, to note and brush aside some of these contrasts in order to clarify the picture of Greece today as a living, vital, and determined little country tucked in between the Ionian and the Aegean seas and with land borders abutting three varied but nonetheless firmly rooted Communist countries—reading from west to east, Albania, Yugoslavia, and Bulgaria.

First to be eliminated from the picture of Greece as a modern nation is the loose aggregation known as the "Greek Syndicate," a powerful combination of generally related families who control the gambling privileges of Monte Carlo, collect art and beautiful wives, and own an estimated one third of the world's ocean shipping, but register it mostly under other flags and hence contribute little to the support of their native land. Second to be eliminated is the picturesque ballet-skirted royal guard of soldiers whose medieval costume and play acting belie the ruggedness of the Greek soldiery, who for more than a century have fought outsiders, and often each other, with vicious courage. And third to go from the picture is the pastoral shepherd with his cloak and crook wandering the mountain ranges with his flocks in the security of age-old freedom from the cares of the outside world; the shepherd is there with his crook and his cloak, but the world of confusion, economics, and world politics comes right to his mountain cottage. He is poor, but he is neither illiterate nor less well informed than his peasant counterpart in other Western lands, and he is determinedly individualistic and thoughtful about today and tomorrow.

Under the blue-and-white flag of Greece live slightly more than 8 million individuals, brunet and blond, tall and short—the distillation of countless invasions from East and West—governed by a modern parliament and ruled by a royal family of exclusively British and Germanic blood. The royal family, there by invitation, is headed by King Paul and his beautiful wife, Queen Frederika Louise. Among their cousins is a man who in youth was a prince of Greece, but who forswore his Greek citizenship and titles to become Prince Philip, Duke of Edinburgh and consort to Queen Elizabeth II of Britain. There, as always in the past, Greece remains threaded inevitably into European dynasties as well as world power politics.

The people of Greece live on slightly more than 51,000 square miles of land divided into two main sections. The larger, continental area is dominated by Athens at its southern tip; the peninsula of Peloponnesos to the south is the site of famous Sparta, and Greek land flows on through scores of islands, among which Crete is the largest, and including the Cyclades, Corfu, Chios, Lesbos, Samos, and the Dodecanese.

Wrapped all together, this is a confusing admixture of broken coast lines, tall mountain ranges, and innumerable rivers, mostly underlaid by hard rock that makes agriculture difficult and relatively unproductive. Only one fourth of the land is arable and by no stretch of energy can it feed all the people of Greece. Even the forests have been denuded. So the Greeks face the constantly insuperable task of exporting agricultural products—principally tobacco, currants, olives and olive oil, wine and brandy, citrus fruits, leather, figs, and cotton yarn—in return for imports of coal and supplementary supplies of food and necessary manufactured goods.

Despite this poor economy and political contentions that have torn the political life of Greece right down to the present time, this is an enlightened and modern country, which has little time to dream about the Age of Pericles but is outwardly and actually living for today.

The dominant political force is the Radical Union party. The Communist Party is outlawed. Women have enjoyed equal suffrage and the right to hold any public office since 1952, and women have sat in the Chamber of Deputies in the Capitol at Salonika since 1953. Education is compulsory for all youth, and higher education is served through six universities located in Athens and a seventh at Thessalonica. The state church is Greek Orthodox.

This is the present view of a small country which since 1940 has endured German occupation, a bloody fratricidal revolution after World War II, and terrific tensions over the island of Cyprus, in which Greece found itself caught between the powers of Great Britain and Turkey. An important stone in the foundation that led back to relative security and stability was the Truman Doctrine, under which Greece attained present international security and, equally important, a grant of $300,000,000 with which to restore war's ravages and build for the future.

The medieval and present road to this modern state epitomizes the history of the Balkans, but it lies closer to the heart of Westerners than those other ill-fated Balkan countries because so much that we are rests on the foundations laid by the aggregation of city-states loosely known as ancient Greece. And while the other Balkan countries may be reported as individual entities, the story of Greece runs as a thread through all of this book.

Ruined by internecine warfare between its independent cities and invasions from the East three centuries before Christ, Greece became formalized and relatively "unified" as a Roman province in 43 B.C. From that date until 1829, it never knew a year or a day as a free country or had a national government.

Roman rule, hard and tough, which bled Greece of its physical resources and absorbed the culture whereon was built the golden age of Rome, continued unbroken until after 330 A.D., when Constantine the Great moved his government (and the now officially established eastern Christian Church) to Constantinople in Byzantium, now Turkey. Gradually the culture of Greece, after four centuries of Western orientation, pivoted toward the East and assumed more of the Asiatic flavor of the environment that stemmed from Byzantium. In fact, the Byzantine culture became a Greek model.

When the last of the eastern Roman forces fell to the Ottomans in 1453, the oriental influence engulfed Grecian life, while various Italian states and France continued to hold outposts in its islands. But it was the Ottoman conquest that eventually gave the native Greeks more of a slight hope for rebirth as a people than the formerly "Christian" overlordship.

The Turk was a tough and hard master, but under him the

Greeks as individuals found new opportunities to sharpen their talents as traders, to amass wealth, and to enjoy a degree of self-government that developed a new political pride and experience. Furthermore, as the wars between growing European powers and the entrenched Ottoman Empire became more important to both sides, there grew up a European feeling of desire for a buffer state in the eastern end of the Mediterranean. The buffer state was Greece.

Out of these forces came a revolution by the Greeks in 1821 against their Eastern overlords that resulted in independence in 1829, with guarantees against future invasions, to which Great Britain, France, and Russia subscribed. In 1830 Greece became an independent kingdom.

In 1925 Greece tried forming its government as a republic, but in 1935 reverted to the monarchy.

Italian treachery, this time in Fascist guise, embroiled Greece in 1940. After a brief victory over Fascist forces, it was invaded and occupied by combined armies of Italians, Germans, and Bulgarians, and night settled over the country until 1944, when the Germans, because of defeats elsewhere in Europe, withdrew.

Greek Communists, aided by Yugoslavia, tried to seize the government and thereby precipitated renewed warfare, marked by atrocities on both sides and paralyzing the little country for another half dozen years, until Yugoslavia broke with Moscow and, as a side gesture, ceased to support the Greek Communists.

The tensions over Cyprus finally subsided in 1957, when British policy veered toward negotiation and away from force.

This summary, while it recognizes the modern life of a smaller country in this modern world, must turn back to those long-ago achievements of the Greeks without which there would be great gaps in the cavalcade of Europe.

In briefly reviewing the origins of modern Greece, we come up against two equally clear facts: (1) here developed a state of mind and ideas that are the common heritage of all the Western world, and (2) as modern technologies delve deeper into Greece's past, the fictions of legend progressively achieve more tangible evidence as fact. Who knows? Perhaps there will yet be discovered a skeleton identifiable as the Minotaur of Crete.

Modern culture was hammered out of the Greek mountains, not in the closely organized and protected atmosphere of an Egypt whose Nile development was "civilized" long before the period for which there are decipherable records of ancient Greece, but amidst wars, superstitions that deified the most lustful human passions, and amoral practices that made the blood feud honorable and infanticide a common practice or, as when Agamemnon sacrificed his daughter to the gods of battle, a holy rite.

Yet before the extinction of Athens' light more than twenty centuries ago, the Greek mind had probed into and discovered the fundamentals of virtually every science and art, leaving for successors little more than the development of phases. It is true that Christian thought has changed much of our Western culture, but the practice of brotherly love as an ideal was preached by Greek philosophers long before the time of Jesus, and while Greek architects never discovered the use of the arch or the dome, these contributions were small additions indeed to what Greece gave in form, design, and lasting strength in building.

Long before Western man had emerged even into barbarism there was a civilization in Greece, of which many evidences have come to light only in the last century. On the island of Crete have been found remains of an organized and even luxurious form of life dating at least from 3500 B.C., a thousand years earlier than the dates ascribed to the ruins of Troy, whose own existence was proved only eighty years ago.

Younger by far, but representing the flowering of those beginnings, were Sparta, which became "spartan" only in its latter, warlike centuries, and Athens, the flower of Hellas, whose crowning Acropolis and the newly excavated portions of its Agora stand today as mute testimonials to the farthest-reaching explorations of the mind that man ever knew until the advent of the Machine Age and more recently the Atomic Age.

Through these centuries, spanning the time between the prehistoric—in the sense of the written word decipherable to us today —and the time of detailed scholarly effort crowned by Plato, the

Greeks did the pioneering of the mind on which the structure of Western civilization has been built. And from time to time, as at Marathon, it was Greek soldiers, occasionally united in defense of their own "Western world," who threw back the Asiatic hordes that otherwise would have moved westward and created quite a different history for Italy, France, Germany, Britain, and America.

Behind its mountain fastnesses, in its tiny city-states, supporting physical needs always by their own efforts expended on the rocky fields and in the seas, the Greeks experimented with every common form of government and gave them names—democracy, monarchy, aristocracy, oligarchy, and tyranny (dictatorship).

Here developed the discipline of organized family life marked both by patriarchy and matriarchy (both Greek words), the organization of the clan and of the state, and the idea of constitutional monarchy, with hereditary kings in families serving either on good behavior or by forceful domination of communities, but, in the case of Sparta, subject to removal at any time by the vote of a popular assembly.

Schools and gymnasiums come to us as Greek heritages, and the sciences of mathematics, physics, biology, anatomy, and medicine—however crude were their origins. History, rhetoric, poetry, music, tragedy, and comedy were taught and practiced in such forms as we know them now. There were, too, highly developed schools of religion, philosophy, and government, not much changed in their variations in succeeding centuries. And the art form of the column and, almost as pagan worship, the most beautiful carvings of the human form ever done by man.

When Rome conquered Greece, and in turn was conquered by the Greek arts and sciences, there came into western Europe a ready-made culture on which little was left to develop except the embroidery and the refinement in color and adaptation born in the Renaissance.

To the modern student, there are no present names more familiar from actual acquaintance with their works than those of Aeschylus, Sophocles, Euripides, Aristophanes, Phidias, Socrates, Plato, and Aristotle.

To enhance their contribution further by keeping the records straight, when histories could be set down on papyrus (from which we derive our word "paper") and collected in *bibloi* (we call it bible, meaning "book"), the Greeks developed their own recorders, who delved into the past, from Homeric legend to their own fund of established facts. What would be lost in the story of the European cavalcade but for Hecataeus, in 500 B.C., setting down the history of events and persons who even then were ancient; or Herodotus, Polybius, Callisthenes, Aristotle, Theophrastus, or Thucydides, carefully collecting the knowledge and history then aggregated in the Greek mind? By the sixth century B.C. there were the beginnings of libraries in such a collection as that credited to Polycrates.

Had all this been the flowering of an area as small as Greece, it would have been only an incident, soon forgotten. But the Greeks—hardened by their sparse resources, ever itching for new markets, and reaching out for opportunities—were settling around the Mediterranean from the earliest times, reaching out to colonize ports in northern Africa and along the shores of Italy, Sicily, France, and Spain. By the time that Alexander the Great, pupil of Aristotle and greatest of generals up to his time, conquered most of the then known world of Europe and Asia Minor, his own troops in the fourth century B.C. often were fighting "foreign armies" of men whose descent could be partially traced back to Greek ancestors. In his later tyrannical years he executed his own nephew, the historian Callisthenes named above, but by way of fateful reparation he established Alexandria in Egypt as a cultural center that developed the world's most renowned library of any age.

In the rapidly approaching political eclipse of Greece, it was only the body of the little suicidal country that fell to foreigners; in many respects its soul—the heritage of Europe—grew greater as Roman vied with Roman to use and enhance the Greek heritage.

It was Greek language, Greek philosophy, and Greek concepts of military and political development upon which Rome built and by which the Caesars molded the foundations of Europe. Greek learning was transplanted farther west, and Greek architecture marked the palaces and temples of Rome.

In the midst of the Roman spread of Greek culture, Greek was the language of state and of scholarship, and this was the enduring language in which Luke wrote his histories of the beginning of Christianity and the language used by St. Paul, the Jew who was a Roman citizen of the Greek city of Tarsus, to dictate his rousing Epistles to congregations in Athens, Corinth, Philippi, Galatia, Ephesus, and finally Rome itself. There is significance in the calvacade likewise in the fact that when Paul, as the rousing spirit spreading Christian teaching to the Gentiles, brought young men to share the work in which Luke the Greek physician was helping him, he picked Timotheus and Titus, both Greeks.

Of the tangible monuments left from the Greek past, it may be said more truly than of any other country that these are dispersed literally throughout the world. True, the ruins of beautiful buildings remain at Athens, there are decipherable remnants of great construction at Sparta, the multiple cities that through ages of ancient times occupied the site of Troy have been brought to light, and the palace of Cnossus on Crete, a true labyrinth of walls and rooms, has been uncovered. But to see the physical evidences of art in painting and sculpture is a world-wide quest.

Ironically, the great sculpture of ancient Rome, itself primarily an imitation of the Greek masters, came to light in the Middle Ages, but the originals of Greece in fragmentary form lay hidden under rubble, for the most part, until only the past century.

In 1806 excavation work conducted by Lord Elgin at Athens uncovered the Parthenon frieze credited to Phidias and a column from the Erechtheum. The "Elgin Marbles" are now in the British Museum in London. The heroic Nike of Samothrace dominates the grand staircase of the Louvre in Paris. In the Metropolitan Museum in New York is the world's greatest collection of vase paintings and miniature sculptures dating from Etruscan times, centuries before Rome's founding and done presumably by Greeks who had emigrated from their own islands to the Italian peninsula. The "gold of Troy," exquisitely wrought necklaces and other jewels excavated on the site of that fated city by Heinrich

Schliemann in the 1870s and 1880s, were in the possession of a Berlin museum and at this writing are held somewhere in the Soviet system.

Of the writings of Greek scholars, most were collected in the great library in Alexandria established twenty-three centuries ago and which contained, by Caesar's time, more than 700,000 rolls of manuscripts, including the works done in their lifetimes by such scholars as Aristarchus of Samothrace, specialist in collating Homer's works, Euclid the mathematician, and Herophilus, the anatomist and founder of Alexandria's medical school. In later years—during the earlier centuries of the Christian Era—Alexandria became a notable center for Christian scholars. But ancient man's capacity for destruction—just as modern man's—eliminated much of the evidence of his finer nature.

Some of the most ancient works in the Alexandria library were destroyed by careless, marauding soldiers in the invasion by Julius Caesar in 47 B.C.; others were destroyed by Aurelius. The Christian emperor Theodosius I destroyed in 391 A.D. what remained of the finest of ancient works in a puritanical frenzy to wipe out "pagan" literature. So who can blame the Arabs, who, invading Alexandria in 640 A.D., retaliated by burning the great Christian libraries which were said to include many original texts upon which the Bible was constructed in later years?

Today the great repository of ancient thought evolved in Greece or written in the classical language, when it was contemporary throughout the civilized world, remains principally in the form of manuscript copies collected in the Vatican Library at Rome.

Now, to return to modern Greece, whether the visitor lands by airplane at the great modern airport of Athens, or lands from a ship at the nearby port of Piraeus, here is a country whose modern promise falls short of return to the fabled greatness of its past, but one that, given peace, has a brighter future than in any other modern period.

By American standards, the average citizen of Greece is poor, very poor. But compared with many other countries he enjoys a considerable state of well-being and, more importantly, the rise from the bottom is marked. By the end of 1958 the average per capita income of Greece was $258, but it had risen to that level from only $215 in 1955. Furthermore, the Greek was beginning to enjoy more income and to be able to save more money. In the middle of 1959, the Commercial Bank of Greece, which held more than one third of private savings in Greek banks, reported deposits of $102,000,000, contrasted with only $8,083,000 in 1951. What would have been a sorry story of the plight of Greek economics in 1955 had become by the time of this writing a new story of hope and development.

In 1959 it could be reported that economic development in Greece was surging forward both in agriculture and a growing industry. The currency was strong and trade was growing in volume and variety, under the cloak of a political stability that inevitably would see changes in political administrations but was unlikely to see any overturn of relatively conservative and democratic institutions.

In the face of desperate struggles against nature to develop agriculture, Greece is using irrigation and intensive fertilization to increase production of crops such as grains, tobacco, cotton, fruits, and vegetables. Land not cultivated for 3000 years has been added to the acreage producing wheat and there is newly developed rice cultivation.

Always poor in fuels, Greece has surged ahead in developing water-power resources, which in turn enhance production of mineral resources such as bauxite-aluminum, iron and steels, and fertilizers.

Tourist facilities, which, until recently, ranged from less than average to poor, have been brought to a high standard in many centers of interest.

In sum, modern Greece appears to have recaptured a national stature comparable in some respects with the memories of her past, and it is notable that this small country—until recently a center from which its emigrants moved to all parts of the earth—has now found a pride that, given reasonable stability in the world, will assure its dignity in this present time.

TURKEY

Sam Pope Brewer

Sam Pope Brewer's reporting on Turkey began early in 1940. Since then, he has made many visits as a correspondent and lived there continuously for two years, 1942 to 1944. A foreign correspondent since 1935, he has had wide experience in the Balkan and Middle Eastern countries, important to an understanding of the Turkish story. In December 1958, he completed a three-year stretch as Chief Correspondent for the New York Times *in the Middle East, with headquarters in Beirut and including Turkey in his beat. At present he is on the local staff of the* Times. *He is a New Yorker by birth, now fifty years old. He was educated at Phillips Exeter Academy and Yale, where he took his B.A. in 1931 and his M.A. in 1933, with a year at the Sorbonne in between. He began newspaper work as a reporter for the New York* Herald Tribune *and worked for its European edition in Paris and for the Chicago* Tribune *foreign news service before joining the* Times *at the beginning of 1945. Besides the Balkans and the Middle East, he has covered Spain and Portugal, Italy, England, and South America, with brief assignments in other countries.*

TURKEY

The people of Turkey are of special interest because though they represent a great mixture of strains, the end product is at least as homogeneous as any people in Europe, perhaps more so than any other.

The basic Turkish strain came from central Asia, and it shows in the faces of the majority, above all among the peasants. A group of Turkish soldiers marching down the road, especially in the days before their uniforms were smartened up (with American aid), might easily be taken for a Chinese force from the heart of Asia.

There is a marked difference, for all that homogeneity, between most city dwellers and the Anatolian farmer. Many generations of intermarriage with other nationalities have produced among cityfolk a type that is generally much less Asiatic in appearance, though not for all that very European in facial traits.

Like all generalities, those remarks are full of holes but are basically true. The villager living in the Anatolian plateau, having little real contact even today with the outside world, has remained much like his ancestors. He is likely to have a flatter face, higher cheekbones, and more oriental eyes than the city dweller. His complexion is likely to be like smooth old copper.

The city dweller's ancestors have rubbed against many races, married with them, and passed on traces of their characteristics. Some of these more cosmopolitan types may be found in remote areas, and there are many of the more oriental type to be seen in every city. The division between the two sorts falls largely on social lines.

Until Atatürk's revolution, there was no particular concept of "Turkism." The division was not between Turk and non-Turk, on racial lines, but between the believer and the infidel. The largest racial group in the old empire was made up of Arabs; but Arab blood is a minor element in the area that makes up present-day Turkey.

In geographic Turkey, at the heart of the Empire, Turks, Kurds, Armenians, Greeks, Circassians, and other groups mingled. Even the non-Moslems were not really outcasts. The highest administrative posts under the Sultans were often held by them because they were considered less able than true Turks to intrigue against their masters.

Even before the arrival of the Turks, people of many distinct stocks had swept back and forth over the area. As early as the twelfth century B.C., Greeks fought the Trojan War on the shores of the Dardanelles and in 1184 B.C. destroyed Troy.

In the fourth century B.C., Alexander the Great of Macedonia moved into Anatolia; and at Gordium, about sixty miles west of Ankara, in 333 B.C., he cut the Gordian knot.

For another thousand years before any Turks are known to have come on the scene, armies of many nations and tribes warred back and forth across what is Turkey today. They stayed for varying periods, but the area never was empty, and it is reasonable to suppose that all left behind traces of their blood.

When the Turks did appear, they did not supplant all other inhabitants as neatly as one peg might push another out of a hole. As they moved on to the shores of the Bosporus and the Dardanelles they mingled and married with other peoples.

As early as 1345, Orkhan, son of the Osman whose name was given to the Empire, married a daughter of John VI Cantacuzene, a pretender to the throne of Byzantium, who had taken Orkhan as an ally against the emperor John V Palaeologus.

All through the years of the Ottoman Empire's rise and fall, Turks bred with women of other countries. Sometimes, like Orkhan's wife, they were given to seal an alliance. Sometimes it was as evidence of submission. Sometimes they were simply taken by force. When men taken in battle were put to the sword, the women

generally were simply absorbed into the community as slaves or
concubines.

During most of that time, also, the corps of Janizaries provided
foreign strains. They were Christians captured young and brought
up as a privileged corps of crack troops who were not free in a
legal sense but who for long periods ran the Empire to their taste.

Out of all the extraordinary mixture, there has come a people
that is as homogeneous as any group of 25 million can be. What
is more remarkable is that a good four fifths of them show the
basic Turkish racial origin in their appearance, though put beside
present denizens of central Asia, the modification would be clear.

In looks, the Turk is likely to be stocky and solid, rather than
tall, with dark hair and eyes, rather dark skin, rather high cheekbones, and often a hawk's-beak type of nose.

Their biggest minority, the Kurds, includes many blonds with
blue eyes. Their presence, and marriages with Circassians and
others, has produced many Turks who would not fit that "typical"
description.

To go on with dangerous generalizations, however, the Turk
is remarkably strong and tough physically. He is likely to be of
medium height, stockily built, and much stronger than he looks.
He is inclined to be undemonstrative and almost surly, rough in
his manners but hospitable to strangers, and a good friend if he
accepts you as such.

Many Turks, of course, have as polished manners as any European.

The Turkish villager, like any primitive countryman, is likely
to be suspicious of strangers and possibly hostile until he is sure
they are harmless. He is remarkably honest in his dealings with
them and usually generous if he is satisfied of their good inten-
tions. The city Turk often has been corrupted by commerce, like
city slickers elsewhere.

The strength of Turks is proverbial. The usual French simile
for great strength is not "strong as a bull" but "strong as a Turk."
Their wrestlers are world-famous. Their porters carry loads that
make foreigners stare in awe. It is not unusual to see two men
carrying a piano up a steep street.

Their brigade in Korea won the admiration of everybody who came in contact with it. The British had learned earlier, at the Dardanelles and in Mesopotamia, to respect their fighting ability. "Johnny Turk" was accepted in World War I as one of the toughest of adversaries but a hard, clean fighter.

Turks have not been notable for their contributions to culture. They were warriors who let others handle that aspect of their life. Their architecture came from the Greek past or from their Arab subjects. Their literature derived chiefly from Arabic or Persian backgrounds. For generations their best poets cultivated Persian verse.

There was no distinctively Turkish painting or sculpture. In the days of strict Moslem observance, they were forbidden to represent living creatures. Existing works that offended them were destroyed or plastered over. The decoration that was permitted was not of Turkish origin but typical of Arab or Persian geometric and floral design.

One outcome of Atatürk's revolution has been an earnest effort to produce native Turkish art and literature. Many have followed Western trends, whether in painting or writing. Today there is an increasing movement toward turning out something purely Turkish.

Young writers face a dearth of readers. It is hard to win world recognition when writing in a language that few of the world's literati can read or hope to learn. Many of the young Turks are pressing ahead, nevertheless, with the feeling that it is worth while to create something for their own people, not merely the 25 million people of Turkey but some 50 million Turkish-speakers spreading into Russia and Asia.

It is said by authorities that a native Turkish-speaker can travel east practically to Chunking among people who will understand him. Overzealous nationalists who talked of a "Pan-Turanian" movement on this basis were discouraged when Russians pointed out that there were more Turkish-speakers under Soviet sway than there were in Turkey.

Within Turkey, there is no serious minority problem. Like her neighbors—Iran, Iraq, and Syria—Turkey has to think about the

Kurds; but they insist that the problem is not serious today. There were 1,504,000 Kurds in Turkey at the last census in 1955. Some sources believe the true figure is closer to 2,000,000. The census identification was based on "mother tongue," and under the program of "Turkification," many persons of Kurdish origin might not now be so classified.

Other minorities were: Arabs, 346,000; Circassians, 91,000; Greeks, 82,000; Georgians, 54,000; Armenians, 47,000; Bulgarians, 32,000; Jews, 29,000; and Lazes, 27,000.

Teaching of Turkish is compulsory in all schools now, making identification of minorities more difficult. Even in the 1955 census, for example, only 29,000 were classed in the Jewish minority, though 77,000 persons gave their religion as Jewish.

The Kurds are the only minority to have given trouble. The Turks maintain that they are completely absorbed now; but Russian propaganda has made intensive efforts in recent years to keep the Kurdish spirit of revolt alive.

Most of Turkey's Armenians who were not massacred before then left Turkey when the occupation troops withdrew in 1922. They settled chiefly in Syria and Lebanon. The Greek problem was solved by the exchange of populations in 1923.

The Kurds, though Moslem, have given trouble because they never have really mixed with the Turks but aspire to independence; with their brother Kurds of Iran, Iraq, and Syria, they constitute a total of some 8 million people. They were to have had at least local autonomy under the Treaty of Sèvres after World War I, but it was never ratified. When the Treaty of Lausanne was signed in 1923 with the new republican government, it did not confirm the earlier promise to the Kurds. Minorities, however, are not a problem in Turkey. As long as they are let alone, they are content to be Turks.

If Turkey is very much a part of the European picture politically, and increasingly so culturally, the country still lies geographically mostly in Asia. Ninety-seven per cent of the total area is in Anatolia, or Asia Minor. The remaining 3 per cent, an area of 9256 square miles, about equivalent to the state of Vermont, is in Europe (Eastern Thrace).

The major part of Turkey is a great rough rectangle, about 900 miles from east to west and about 300 from north to south. Most of it is a plateau, some 3000 feet above sea level, bordered with mountains. Toward the eastern end it crumples into a region of wild mountains facing Russia and Iran. Among them is Mount Ararat (16,916 feet), where Noah's ark stranded as the flood subsided. It is a great snow-capped cone on the Russian frontier, visible from many miles away to passing aircraft passengers.

The climate in the central plateau is something like that of New York but with greater extremes. Ankara is blistering hot in summer and bitter cold in winter, with winds sweeping down from Russia and frequent snowstorms.

That ruggedness for which the Turk is famed is necessary for survival in Anatolia. There has been little communication until the last few years. A Turk from an Anatolian village who wanted to travel had to be prepared to cover great distances over rough country on foot; or if he was lucky, on a donkey; or if he was rich, on a horse.

If he was sick, he was not likely to have a doctor. The nearest hospital was probably days away. As recently as fifteen years ago, there were villages within 100 miles of Ankara that were not on a road, had no telephone, no telegraph, no post office, no shop, and no apparent means of subsistence except a few sheep and goats that managed to get along on the sparse vegetation. The villagers managed to raise a little grain when the season was right; they sold their sheep and goats to get other necessities. But they managed to get along.

There are still outlying villages no better off, though the status of the peasants has improved enormously. Electric light and the telephone are reaching to outlying regions. No other country has developed its highways at such a rate as Turkey since World War II. All of this is opening up the country, freeing the Anatolian peasant from the prison of rough territory where he has lived and bringing in influences that will ease his life and make him more a part of the world picture.

With all of this, the average Turk has lived a remarkably simple and isolated life until the last few years. There are still many villages in Turkey that live almost like separate worlds, though communications are improving at a phenomenal rate.

The rugged nature of the terrain and the rigorous climate meant, for the Turkish peasant, a simple life with little variation.

To the tribesmen who came down from the central Asian plateau, it must have seemed a pleasant, gentle land. They brought with them their tradition of living on herds of sheep and goats, sleeping in skin tents or any shelter they could get. They learned the pleasures of the fine fruits that grew in Turkey, but only when they reached the coastal areas. (Upland Turkey now grows fine apples and other fruits of the temperate zone, but those have been imported.) Under this influence they ceased to be nomadic tribesmen and developed into a great imperial power.

The successors of the invaders went on through the centuries living on their flocks and their grain. They lived in mud huts made of a sort of adobe, and they had to balance smoke against cold in winter to keep from either freezing or suffocating.

They changed little through the generations because it was difficult to move about, to exchange goods and ideas and gain material comfort.

One of the most striking points to the foreigner reading ancient history in Turkey a few years ago was the constant movement of whole armies back and forth across that great rough territory as much as four thousand years ago. It sounded simple enough when stated simply that Alexander advanced to Gordium and cut the Gordian knot and then proceeded eastward.

To make the same sort of journey twenty years ago involved considerable effort unless one wanted to stick to the main railroad lines.

As recently as 1940, a trip from Ankara to Konya, 200 miles to the south, involved twelve to fourteen hours in an improvised bus built locally on a truck chassis. The alternative was an overnight train trip to Istanbul and another eighteen hours from there back to Konya, on the days when the train was running.

The bus passengers huddled patiently in cramped wooden benches while the bus wallowed over hills and across salt flats and through deep mudholes. Frequently the passengers had to get out and help to push the bus out of the mud. When the weather was bad, the bus could not pass at all. The salt flats turned into quagmires.

There was no road, nor even a track, between two of Turkey's historic cities. On each high point along the route, a cairn of stones served as a landmark for the driver, and he simply made his way from one cairn to the next.

Today there is a well-paved highway, built with American aid, and the drive can be made in comfort in four hours.

As late as 1944, a trip from the capital to Istanbul, 200 miles as the crow flies, was an adventure. Even in good weather, it took about twenty-four hours, if the authorities would give permission for it to be undertaken. Today there is a good highway, though even now bad weather involves trouble and delays.

Flying over Turkey today, the traveler still sees large areas apparently uninhabited. Where there is a village, or even an extensive town, there often will be no evidence of connection with the outside world except a forlorn track winding off through the rugged hills. If there is any sign of traffic, it is a lone truck or bus marked by the little cloud of dust it trails behind it.

Turkey is generally pretty fertile and it is underpopulated. Famine is not a Turkish problem. In normal years there is not only enough grain and meat to feed the country but some left over for export.

The lowlands around the coast are particularly fertile. There are no better fruits or vegetables anywhere than those that grow in Turkey. They have never had much sale abroad, except for the figs and nuts, because the Turks will not bother about their appearance. They are only beginning to learn about sorting and grading them and presenting them attractively.

Nobody knows how good a fresh apricot or strawberry or raspberry can be until he has tasted them along the Bosporus when they are in season. Smyrna figs have always been the standard for the highest quality. Hazelnuts are shipped all over the world from Turkey, and Turkish pistachio nuts, though they are not as handsome as the ones from Iran, have the finest flavor of any.

Turkish tobacco has always been esteemed, and although the United States is the world's greatest producer of tobacco, popular American cigarettes contain about 4 to 8 per cent of Turkish tobacco for its fragrance.

While life was simple and hard for the peasant, Turkey has always been a land that attracted settlers instead of forcing emigration. Other countries to the east had far harder conditions of life. Wave after wave has moved westward from the inhospitable steppes of central Asia. Turkey was so much more promising that they stayed. When the Turks moved out to conquest, it was not a famished people seeking food but a strong people asserting itself.

There were earlier invasions from Europe based on ambition and later ones on religious feeling, but those who left Turkey left because they were pushed out by stronger forces.

The Turks expanded as an imperial power, but Turks did not tend to emigrate permanently. In fact, the lands they conquered were generally ruled under their suzerainty by local governors from the conquered peoples. When their empire finally fell, the Turks remained on their home ground.

The natural wealth of the land and the subsoil still is not being fully exploited, but development in recent years has been phenomenal. Land under cultivation increased from 9,880,000 acres in 1920 to 22,580,000 in 1945. In the next ten years it nearly doubled, to 43,460,000 acres.

Development naturally cannot continue at that rate forever, but the country is still not being exploited fully.

Turkey's mineral wealth, likewise, is being opened up. Turkey is the world's greatest source of chrome and an important producer of manganese. There is a good supply of coal and iron; and oil is being produced in significant amounts after years of hunting for it. Known oil reserves are estimated at 65,000,000 barrels, but it may well be that there is much more still to be found.

Tourist trade has really begun to develop only since the war, but it has great potentialities. Even in 1939 Americans and most Europeans looked on a visit to Turkey as something of an adventure. Today American tourists pour through in a constant stream, and if the Turks develop the possibilities of the beautiful wooded shores of the Bosporus, the Sea of Marmara, with its Isles of the Princes, and adjacent areas, there are attractions to draw unlimited tourist trade.

Turkey today is a more or less democratic republic. It has a democratic constitution, but the administration runs the country in a way that its opponents call dictatorial.

In the past seven centuries the country has gone through the stages of loose tribal organization, warring principalities, and great empire. When the Empire crumbled, Mustafa Kemal built the republic on its ruins.

Many rulers of many races had come and gone in Anatolia before the Turks appeared on the scene. During the past fifty years much has been learned of the Hittites, who ruled an empire nearly five thousand years ago that was probably the most civilized of its time. The Turks are proud of the Hittite past and like to think of themselves as descendants of the Hittites. There is no historical connection, however, with modern Turkey.

The history even of the Seljuk Turks is sketchy, and the beginning of modern Turkey may fairly be dated to the arrival of bands from central Asia who became the Ottoman Turks.

The Seljuks had come from Asia sometime early in the ninth century. About 1250 a new wave followed them, pressed out of central Asia probably by the Mongols. Their leader, Ertughrul, allied himself with the Seljuks, aided the Sultan of Konya, and was given some land.

By 1310 the Seljuk dynasty ended, and the dominant power was Ertughrul's people, under his son Osman, from whom the new dynasty took the name Osmanli, corrupted by Europeans into "Ottoman."

Anatolia was by no means united at that period. Struggles for power among various local rulers continued, and it was not until about 1480, a quarter century after they had conquered Constantinople, that the Ottomans, then under Mohammed II the Conqueror, finally subjugated all the princes of Asia Minor.

That early period was not a simple, clear-cut struggle between the Turks, pushing westward, and the Christians resisting them. Turks and Christians were frequently allied for their mutual benefit against other Christians, or against Asiatic foes, as the case might be.

The Turks got their first foothold in Europe in 1345, when John VI Cantacuzene, a pretender to the Byzantine throne, called in Orkhan, son of Osman, to aid him against Emperor John V Palaeologus. He gave his daughter in marriage to Orkhan and made the mistake of allowing the Turks in 1352 to establish a garrison at Chimpe, on the Gallipoli Peninsula. They soon occupied the whole of the peninsula and were never again driven completely out of Europe.

During all this era the Ottoman Turks fought a constant succession of wars. As they made conquests in Europe, revolts and invasions would call attention back to Anatolia, but their power and their territory continued to increase.

By 1391, Manuel II Palaeologus, son of John V, allowed them to build a mosque in Constantinople and to establish a Moslem court in the city to try cases between Moslems. At the end of 1394, the caliph in Egypt recognized Sultan Bajazet as "Sultan of Rum (Europe)."

In 1453 Constantinople itself capitulated to Mohammed II.

The Turks rolled on to the very gates of Vienna. Through the sixteenth and much of the seventeenth centuries they continued to be the terror of Europe.

From a group of roving warrior bands, they had come to be an organized empire with a central government and powerful, disciplined armies. In 1554 a Flemish diplomat, Augier Ghislain de Busbecq, wrote of them that he shuddered to think what would be the outcome of a war and that "on their side is the vast wealth of their empire, unimpaired resources, experience and practice in arms, a veteran soldiery, an uninterrupted series of victories, readiness to endure hardships, union, order, discipline, thrift, and watchfulness."

From this period of their might, it became traditional for Europeans to think of the "terrible Turk," cruel and warlike and an enemy of Christianity. Contemporary accounts do not support that picture. Travelers and diplomats were greatly impressed by the orderliness of the country, for those times, and the organization and discipline.

As the Turks subjugated countries, they did not move in with a massive occupation. In most cases they installed governors or merely forced the submission of the local rulers. Contemporary writers testify that in many cases the mass of the people preferred Turkish rule to that of their own aristocratic overlords.

The Sultan, normally, was all-powerful, though at times the corps of Janizaries, technically slaves but the best soldiers of their time and privileged in many ways, imposed their will upon the ruler.

They had no hereditary nobility to contend with. Observers frequently commented on the speed with which a man might rise to high rank and then be removed if the Sultan saw fit.

De Busbecq, for instance, said: "No distinction is attached to birth among the Turks. The deference to be paid to a man is measured by the position he holds in the public service. There is no fighting for precedence: A man's place is marked out by the duties he discharges. . . . Each man in Turkey carries in his own hands his ancestry and his position in life, which he may make or mar as he will. Those who receive the highest offices from the Sultan are for the most part the sons of shepherds or herdsmen, and so far from being ashamed of their parentage they actually glory in it, and consider it a matter of boasting that they owe nothing to the accident of birth."

Mohammed the Conqueror laid the administrative foundations of the Empire. Suleiman I the Magnificent, who won the admiration of Europe expressed in that title, did much to develop them further. Known to Turks as the Lawgiver, he is one of the ten great lawmakers whose portraits hang in the gallery of the United States Senate.

During his long reign (1520–66), the Ottoman Empire reached the peak of its power, but he was more than a mere conqueror. Executive power in Turkey centered in the Army, but the laws were governed by religious leaders.

The power of Turkey continued through the eighteenth century though there were internal quarrels and struggles for power. It was the great libertarian movement exemplified by the French Revolution that brought the real beginning of its decline. Subject peoples grew restive and wanted independence. Revolts broke out, and the Turks were less able to cope with them. In 1770 the British had wiped out the Turkish Mediterranean fleet in a battle off Cheshme, on the southwest coast. In 1821 the Greeks revolted and by 1830 had won their independence. In 1831 there was a revolt in Egypt.

During this period Sultan Mahmud II the Reformer (reigned 1808–39), making concessions to the spirit of the age, began a program of reforms. He dissolved the corps of Janizaries, which had degenerated into a lawless and dangerous military clique. As a symbol of the new spirit, he forbade the wearing of the turban by all but religious leaders and introduced the fez, an Austrian invention. So, a hundred years later, Atatürk in turn abolished the fez and forced the wearing of European headgear.

Turkey acquired her first steam vessel, sanitary laws were passed and hospitals built, and public education was pushed intensively. Unfortunately, Mahmud's reforms were not enough to halt the decline of the Empire. One of the problems was a cumbersome and inefficient bureaucracy.

Abdul-Hamid II gave Turkey her first constitution in 1876, though many of his Moslem subjects were more shocked than pleased at a charter that promised equality to infidels in the country. The first parliament met March 19, 1877. A disastrous defeat by Russia upset the country's development, and in the last years of his reign he made an unenviable name as a despot. His parliament had lasted only a matter of weeks, since in the stress of war he dismissed it in May 1877 and did not call a new session until 1908, when revolution was already at work in the country.

By this time Turkey, shorn of much of her empire, racked by internal troubles, and with her finances in confusion, had earned the famous nickname of "the sick man of Europe." Abdul-Hamid had come to depend on secret police and rigorous suppression of criticism to hold his place. Elements of the Army joined with the liberal-minded youth of the country in the movement known as the Young Turks. When they attempted to set up a political party they were repressed so violently that a revolution broke out in Salonika. The Young Turks captured Istanbul and the Sultan in April 1908. He remained a prisoner until his death in 1918.

The new Sultan, Mohammed V, was dominated by the Young Turks, but the country still was ridden with debt. Turkey had gained her liberal reforms but, through her alliance with Germany and Austria in World War I, was plunged into the final wreck of the Ottoman Empire.

After tribal rule, despotism, and gradually liberalized empire, Turkey emerged through the revolution of Mustafa Kemal as a republic.

By the Treaty of Sèvres at the end of the war, Turkey would have remained in a state of permanent defeat. Her finances were to be under foreign control and her territory occupied. The Turks feared that this was meant to be a permanent partition of their country.

The government was helpless, but Mustafa Kemal, then a young general and a hero of the Gallipoli campaign, refused to accept the situation. When Greek troops landed in Smyrna (now Izmir) in May 1919, Kemal set out to raise the Turks against all the occupiers and the Sultan's government.

Though it lies on the extreme eastern fringe of the Western world, Turkey is still very much a part of it, and any Turk today would resent the suggestion that it was not. They are equally conscious of the fact that they have special ties with Asia. It is an accepted fact that Turkey is a bridge between East and West and firmly rooted at both ends.

Today this is a vigorous country developing rapidly and with great hopes for the future. From being "the sick man of Europe" at the beginning of this century, Turkey has passed through a disastrous defeat and then a national revolution to emerge shorn of all her former empire but soundly organized within.

The new Turkey was created by the phenomenal energy and vision of Mustafa Kemal Pasha, now known as Atatürk, from the wreckage of the Ottoman Empire. It is a nation of almost 25 million people, with one of the world's highest rates of population

increase and, unlike most fast-growing peoples, with room to spare
for its increase. It is a republic and nominally democratic, with a
constitution based on Western models. Some of the methods the
government uses to keep things in order cause Westerners to raise
their eyebrows and the opposition to shout "dictatorship!" But the
democratic forms are there, and the majority of the nation has
continued to vote for the regime.

In the world political situation, Turkey is a stanch ally of the
West, a member of the North Atlantic Treaty Organization, a
zealous member of the United Nations, and a strong foe of communism.

When the United Nations called for troops to defend South
Korea against Communist invasion, Turkey sent a brigade that
won the respect and admiration of all the troops that served beside
them. The Turks say proudly that out of 229 men captured not one
succumbed to Communist brainwashing. Unlike some of the other
prisoners, they maintained strict discipline even in the prison
camps. They looked after each other so well that the death rate
among Turkish prisoners was far lower than among Americans.

Standing at the historic crossroads between Europe and Asia,
and between Russia and the Middle East, Turkey is a rugged
young power determined to keep her independence or be destroyed defending it.

The Turks have had thirteen wars with Russia, beginning in
1663. As recently as 1946 there was fear of a new Russian attack
to enforce demands for the eastern provinces of Kars and
Ardahan. So, apart from communism, the Turks see Russia as a
permanent threat, and they form the strongest single obstacle to
Russian invasion of the Middle East.

They are determined to continue as a part of the Western
world, and for all their strong nationalist spirit, they are open
to outside ideas. Mustafa Kemal made radical and almost incredible changes in the life of the people to adapt them to co-
operation with the Western world and speed their development.
He would have none of the sterile type of nationalism that looks
inward and shuns whatever is foreign. He made changes from
one day to the next that most experienced observers of Turkey

would have said were impossible without long and bloody struggle.

He started by removing religion from the machinery of government. After sealing his victory over the Greeks with the Treaty of Mudania, on October 13, 1922, Atatürk proclaimed the republic on October 29, 1923, at Ankara. The following March 3, he liquidated the caliphate, under which the rulers of Turkey had also been spiritual chiefs of Islam.

In 1925 he took a step that seemed inconsequential if not comic to many Westerners in forbidding Turks to wear their traditional headdress, the brimless red-felt fez. The turban was still allowed for use in religious rites in the mosques. Everywhere else, Turks must wear a Western hat or cap, with brim or peak. Even berets were barred. This was no whim. It had a calculated and important moral effect in marking the break with old traditions and looking to the West. In 1926, a new legal code was adopted, modeled on the Swiss code. Under the Empire, legal matters had been ruled by religious dignitaries. In 1928, a new alphabet was introduced, using Latin characters in place of the decorative but difficult Arab script in which Turkish had been written before.

In 1936 came the introduction of family names, important for questions of identification, of law enforcement, and for general simplification of administration and business life. Until then, the Turks, like the Saudi Arabians today, had depended on simple patronymics. It has been said that at one time there were five generals known simply as Kazim Pasha. To separate them, it was necessary to go into ancestry, official posts, or descriptions.

Kemal Pasha led the way in the name reform by bestowing on his principal general, Ismet Pasha, the name of Inönü, for the town where he won the decisive battle over the Greeks. Kemal himself became Atatürk, Father of the Turks, or the Father-Turk.

Westerners who did not understand the picture frowned on Atatürk as a dictator. Today, even Turks who complained bitterly at that time grant that, in the circumstances, a strong hand was necessary for the good of the country. An effort to work by the methods of Western democracy in a country that had never been trained to self-discipline in public life would have ended in chaos.

There were already some signs of softening in administrative ways when Atatürk died, almost on the eve of World War II, November 10, 1938. After the war, under pressure from the Western Allies, the regime was so liberalized that in national elections the new Democratic party threw out the Republican People's party, the only one that had been allowed under Atatürk.

It has remained in power ever since, with elections in 1954 and 1957 to confirm it. The R.P.P. accuses it of having set the clock back politically. Newspapermen are jailed for mild criticism of government officials. Opposition political activity is almost entirely suppressed. The R.P.P. says: "We used dictatorial methods while they were necessary, but we evolved constantly toward more freedom. Adnan Menderes has restored repressive measures to keep in power."

Whatever its position on liberties, the Democratic administration under Menderes has continued to press economic development of the country as envisioned by Atatürk. Western critics think he is overambitious and that his program for dams, highways, factories, and other developments is overloading the economy. Turks have suffered because all available foreign exchange was taken up in this program. It became difficult, if not impossible, to get such staple items as writing paper, toilet paper, tires for cars, and even their beloved coffee.

The United States has borne most of the burden of keeping Turkey afloat financially during this period, though the Menderes government has refused to make more than minor concessions to American demands that he revise his spending program. Instead of "guns before butter," the Turks have been living under the slogan "dams and seaports before coffee." There has been growing discontent in Turkey, but the government has stood firm. The basic American view has been that Turkey is a loyal and valuable ally and that, if necessary, we must stretch a point to keep her going.

Waves of migration and invasion that have passed over Turkey through nearly six thousand years have left behind a wealth of traces of their passage. Only a beginning has been made even now in unearthing them. Every year brings new discoveries. Monuments built by the Byzantines and their successors are plentiful and well known—churches, palaces, forts, tombs, and waterworks. There are also substantial and well-known architectural evidences of earlier Greek and Roman occupations, such as the great theater at Pergamos (now Bergama) and the theater market place, library, and other ruins at Ephesus (now Selçuk).

Within the past sixty years massive evidence has been found that the Hittites were not an insignificant tribe, as had been supposed, but rulers of an empire, one of the strongest of its era, with its seat in Anatolia. At Alaca Hüyük, remains of a citadel and tombs have been uncovered, with gold, silver, and copper relics, and other material that has made it possible to reconstruct much of the life of the Hittites. Another Hittite site is at Bogazköy, further south.

On the site of ancient Troy, near the Dardanelles, archaeologists have found eleven successive layers of ruins that show successive phases in Turkey's history from about 2750 B.C. Above the earliest traces is a Bronze Age citadel, believed to have been destroyed by the Hittites about 2000 years before Christ.

It was only at the sixth level that there stood the classic Troy, destroyed in the Trojan War about 1200 B.C. After that came the Phrygians, Aeolian Greeks, Persians, and the Macedonians of Alexander the Great. Portions of the wall from the Homeric period are believed to have been identified.

There is ample evidence that Turkey has many more traces of her various cultures to be explored. Turkish sensitivity on national security is one factor that has impeded the exploration. Anatolia is part of an area, with Mesopotamia and Syria (including Jordan, Lebanon, and Palestine), that saw the very germs of our civilization. Since the early Stone Age, this region seems always to have kept up with its times. In spite of gaps in the record, there is material evidence that, from the Stone Age on, Anatolia has been an important area in geopolitics.

Best known of the remaining monuments, to the world at large, are those of Christian Constantinople and of the Ottoman Turks who conquered it in 1453 and made it into Moslem Istanbul.

The most famous of these, undoubtedly, is the great basilica of St. Sophia, one of the world's most famous churches, used as a mosque from 1453 to 1935 and since then a national museum.

Istanbul, with a continuous history since more than six centuries before the birth of Christ, shows much of the country's history in its stones. Around St. Sophia, famous mosques show Greek influence in their general outlines, with Arab decoration and their towering minarets to commemorate the rule of the Ottoman Turks. On Serail Point, in old Istanbul, the Palace of the Sultans holds the memory of Turkey's greatest days in its gardens, halls, and the treasures that are kept there. That, too, has become a museum.

Large portions of the ancient walls that surrounded the city still testify to the defenses that kept Constantinople so long for the decaying Eastern Empire. All travelers passing to or from the city's airport at Yesilköy today pass through gates in that massive masonry.

A little above the city, the fortress known as Rumeli Hisar (the Castle of Europe) marks the Ottoman Turks' first bridgehead on the European shore of the Bosporus. Built by Mohammed the Conqueror in 1452, it marked the beginning of his final drive for Constantinople, which ended in victory the following year. Facing it across the Bosporus is Anadolu Hisar (the Castle of Anatolia), built some sixty years earlier by the Sultan Bajazet and reinforced by Mohammed as he built its brother across the water.

Visiting Americans in this country have often been shocked by the shabby air of Istanbul. The main street of one of the world's most famous cities was a narrow, irregular thoroughfare more like the Bowery than like Fifth Avenue. Its buildings were often more than shabby, and its shops were poorly stocked. None of the city's hotels were really first-class by Western standards.

Those who took the trouble to go behind that first impression were richly rewarded. The mosques and palaces and museums provide enough to keep the most inveterate sight-seer busy for weeks.

Today the city is having a thorough face lifting. Old buildings are being swept away; broad streets are being opened up, not at the cost of ancient monuments, but so as to make those monuments more visible and more accessible.

The Ottomans' predecessors, the Seljuk Turks, never held Istanbul, and so left no traces there, but there are rich remains of their era elsewhere. Konya, the Seljuk capital, has outstanding examples of Seljuk art and architecture. Their great theological school is now an archaeological museum. Mosques and tombs also remain from their time, characterized by fine tilework and strongly influenced by Arab art. The whirling dervishes had their principal mosque there, and it still remains.

Only a few miles from Ankara, at Gordium, recent excavations have brought to light relics of settlement going back to the Bronze Age, some 4000 years ago. Above them are traces of the Hittites, the Phrygians, the Persians, and of the palace of King Midas. It was true that Alexander the Great of Macedonia cut the Gordian knot, which has come to be symbolic of forthright resolution of difficulties.

For Christians, Turkey has other significant sites besides those of Istanbul. Tarsus, in the South, was the birthplace of St. Paul. Antioch (now Antakya) was an important Christian center that saw St. Paul, St. Peter, and St. Barnabas. The little town of Iznik, southeast of Istanbul, was Nicaea, where the great ecumenical council of 325 A.D. condemned the Arian heresy.

The Turks take great pride in their Hittite predecessors. In the Hittite Museum in Ankara they display a collection of implements, ornaments, carvings, and inscriptions that has gone far to re-create Hittite culture.

Ankara itself is a monument to the country's long history. It had sunk to little more than a big town at the crossing of trade routes when Atatürk chose it as his capital in 1923, partly for strategic reasons and partly because he wanted a thoroughly Turkish capital in the heart of Anatolia, in place of cosmopolitan Istanbul.

It is known, however, to have been settled somewhere about 1000 B.C., though little really is known of its early history. Roman baths and temples show that it was a place of importance in their time. St. Peter and St. Paul visited it, and the latter is said to have built a church there.

It was important enough to be the scene of battles at many times in the ages that followed. Its towering citadel, studded with fragments taken from earlier structures, bits of pillars and blocks of stone from the temples, is a slice of the city's history and covers most of the successive phases of Anatolian Turkey. It is topped off with a fast-growing city based chiefly on German ideas of functional architecture.

Until near the end of World War II, Turkey balanced precariously on the fence between the Allies and the Axis. On August 2, 1944, she broke off diplomatic relations with Germany and on February 23, 1945, at the request of the United States and Great Britain, declared war on both Germany and Japan, though she was never involved in hostilities.

On a long-range basis, Turkey's prospects seem better than those of most countries, provided always that she is left in peace and spared internal upheavals.

At present she is passing through difficult times. The ambitious policy of development pursued by Premier Adnan Menderes has outrun the country's financial capacities. There has been serious deficiency in the balance of payments. Menderes has had to impose austerity measures that are unpopular, and the United States, the International Monetary Fund, and the Organization for European Economic Cooperation have had to bail the country out of its money troubles.

Menderes made only minor concessions to the advice of Americans and others that he retrench a little. His line was that if the people would grit their teeth and persevere, the result would be worth the cost.

What he has done is to carry to extremes the policy set in motion by Atatürk, of putting Turkey through an industrial revolution of her own.

A large proportion of the country's intellectuals have been bitter at Menderes, not simply for the personal hardships his economic policies brought but for the general suppression of all criticism.

Numerous newspapermen have been imprisoned, including some of the country's most reputable and distinguished editors.

A newsboy has been jailed as an alarmist for shouting the news of a minister's resignation.

University professors were forced out because they disagreed with some aspects of government activities.

A leader of the once omnipotent Republican People's party was arrested for holding an illegal political rally because he shook hands with admirers who crowded around him when he was making a trip.

Licenses for rallies were restricted to a brief period before elections, which the opposition said was too brief for an effective campaign.

Matters came to a crisis in April 1960. Menderes had become increasingly oppressive in his efforts to muzzle all opposition or criticism. He sent troops to halt a speaking tour by the highly respected former President, Ismet Inönü, in the provinces. On April 27, the Grand National Assembly (Parliament) at his behest passed a bill barring all party political activities for three months. The next day student riots broke out and an undetermined number of persons were killed.

The Army resented the Prime Minister's use of troops as police against political demonstrations. On May 21, a thousand cadets and some young officers staged an anti-Menderes demonstration in Ankara in defiance of martial-law decrees. Troops on duty refused to interfere.

Menderes ordered all universities closed until further notice, and on May 27, the Army suddenly moved in. The Prime Minister, President Celal Bayar, and their associates were arrested. The retiring commander of the Army, General Cemal Gursel, took charge of the country and announced that the Army would supervise free elections and support any President the people chose.

In spite of those domestic troubles, Turkey is in a good position internationally except for the constant and familiar menace of Russia.

Her relations with Iran are good. Her relations with Greece have become relaxed, at least temporarily, with a settlement of the Cyprus dispute that had been straining them. Her relations with her Arab neighbors, Syria and Iraq, are good although Russian influence there has produced alarm.

With other Arab countries, Turkey has cordial relations. Her Foreign Minister, Fatin Rüstü Zorlu, has said that the Turks were happy at the union of Egypt with Syria as the United Arab Republic, but that Syria "has caused us a great deal of worry" by "her policy of drawing close to the Soviet Union and of giving bases to Russia."

The extent of Russian influence in Syria and Egypt has seemed to fluctuate and cannot be accurately measured. Since Mr. Zorlu made his statement to the Turkish Grand National Assembly in 1958, the U.A.R. has appeared to draw away from Moscow's influence.

Turkey's future, therefore, as far as it is possible to guess at anything in this period, would appear to depend, like every other country's, on whether Russia keeps the peace. Within those limits, it is one of the few countries with a vigorous and fast-growing population that can still support more people than it has, and it is just getting into the stride of industrial development.

Barring war, Turkey has fewer problems than most countries of the world.

INDEX

SWEDEN

NORWAY

...as A. Reedy

Drew Middleton

DENMARK

IRELAND

Arthur Settel

GREAT
BRITAIN

NETH.

David M. Nichol

BELGIUM   GERMANY

LUX.

CZECHOSLOVAKIA

POLA...

Fernand Auberjonois

FRANCE   SWITZ.

AUSTRIA   HU...

David Schoenbrun

YUGOSLA...

Leon Den...

ITALY

Emmet Crozier

PORTUGAL

SPAIN

Frank Gervasi